RISK-TAKER
FOR
GOD

Lars B. Dunberg

Cover design: Matt DeCoste

Cover picture: Sheeba R. Subhan

Interior design: Paul Dunberg

ISBN: 978-1-60725-631-1 (Hard cover)
        978-1-60725-632-8 (Soft cover)

Dunberg, Lars B., 1944
Risk-taker for God/by Lars B. Dunberg

To Doreen, Carin, Maria and Paul, who often had to be without husband and father, and who made the risk-taking possible.

TABLE OF CONTENTS

Foreword		vii
Introduction		ix
Chapter 1	"I quit!"	1
Chapter 2	Roots	10
Chapter 3	Molded for the Future	36
Chapter 4	In God's Army	49
Chapter 5	New Ministry	76
Chapter 6	Doreen and Family	89
Chapter 7	"…and some to be Evangelists"	108
Chapter 8	Mentors	119
Chapter 9	Books, Books & More Books	125
Chapter 10	Becoming a Bible Translator	132
Chapter 11	The Word Around the World	141
Chapter 12	Not What It Seems	182
Chapter 13	Marriage Made in Heaven?	196

Chapter 14   Global Action: It's All About Risk   222

Chapter 15   Evangelism and Outreach   230

Chapter 16   Training and Motivation   241

Chapter 17   A Compassionate Response   258

Chapter 18   Children and Youth   285

Chapter 19   Women of Global Action   306

Chapter 20   The Multiplication Factor   318

Chapter 21   A Funny Thing Happened on the Way Around the World   337

Chapter 22   Becoming a Risk-Taker and a Life-Changer   354

Bibliography   376

Foreword

Autobiography or adventure story? Fact or fiction? Perusing these pages, the reader could be forgiven for asking such questions. But, having shared with the author much of what he describes, I can vouch for its authenticity. John Grisham's novels are gripping, but fictional. The Dunberg life story is compelling, but factual.

Few Christian leaders can match the extent of his world travels. This gives him a more balanced and authentic grasp of global mission. And I know of no one with a greater commitment to evangelism, leadership training and demonstrating Christ's love in practical and constructive ways.

When in the earliest days of his ministry he was National Director of British *Youth for Christ* (YFC), I was Associate Director of Europe YFC, based in Geneva, Switzerland, so we were acquainted even before he was married. Our paths crossed again in *Living Bibles International (LBI)* when he began working on a contemporary translation of the Swedish New Testament and I was coordinating similar translations in other languages of East and West Europe.

Even his move to the United States didn't separate us for long as I joined the Board of *LBI* during his presidency. Later on I served on the Board at *International Bible Society (IBS)*, and then as a founder member (later chairman) of the *Global Action* Board. I know the transition involved one of the toughest decisions of his entire ministry. Moving from a presidential office with a worldwide full-time and part-time staff of almost 1,000 people to a trestle table in the basement of his home with a single laptop computer and one volunteer helper called for courage, determination, total dependence on God and the clearest possible sense of Divine direction.

The growth of *Global Action* from modest newcomer on the crowded scene of mission organizations to massive contributor to the cause of Christ worldwide is impressive to say the least. Its excellence and integrity is confirmed by Christian nationals with whom it works in some 70 countries around the world.

Having served on three international Boards where I've been required to check his budgets and accounts, I firmly believe Lars can stretch donation dollars further than anyone I know. For example, he describes where 50 cents provides refugees with two nourishing meals daily. That may sound far-fetched, but it's true. And when he claims that every dollar raised for humanitarian projects provides $20-worth of medical equipment, it's a significant endorsement of his ability to negotiate amazing deals for surplus, but superb, materials.

When chairing his *Global Action* Board, one of my regular responsibilities was to check and sign off his personal expense sheets, and I can confirm that here too he specializes in making a little go a long way. As the title indicates, the author is a risk-taker. I've seen numerous occasions where he's been willing to move far outside his comfort zone when he feels it is God's direction. Someone said that if God sends you on a rough road, He will provide you with strong shoes. At times, Lars Dunberg's road has been very rough but he can always testify to the provision of strong shoes!

David Foster, OBE

Introduction

This book has been in the making for many years. Originally I wrote it for my children, so they could have a context for the ministries in which I served, and understand how a rich heritage shapes a person's life, thought patterns and worldview.

But now I am humbled and thankful that I have an opportunity to share it with you as well. This is a story in the making. Someone mentioned to me the other day, "Lars, the best is yet to come!"

I would like to say a special thank you to Emily Voorhies and Judy Faast who read the manuscript and gave helpful suggestions. An overwhelming thank you to David Foster, who in typical style "nit picked" through many chapters and suggested absolutely needed changes.

I also need to mention my editor, Steve Parolini who spent many hours turning my Swenglish into readable text.

My wife Doreen, as well as my daughters Carin and Maria helped with proofreading and many valuable suggestions, while my son Paul worked on the layout and changed endless corrections.

Most of all, thanks be to God, who encouraged me to be a risk-taker for Him, sometimes willingly and other times reluctantly. Without His mercy and grace, little of the material in this book would ever have taken place.

Colorado Springs July 15, 2008

Lars B. Dunberg

CHAPTER 1
"I Quit!"

"That's it! I'm done. I'm going to resign."

"But what will you do for work? Where will we go? And what will this do to us?"

The conversation was intense as my wife Doreen and I talked over dinner one Monday night in June 1998. Earlier that day I had met with a work-study consultant who had coordinated an anonymous study among board members and staff members of *International Bible Society*, where I had served as president for more than six years. The underlying question among the 60 to 70 questions in the questionnaire was, "Will the president be able to take the organization to the next level, into the 21st century?"

But for me the real issue was totally different!

I had just turned 54 and as my screen-saver reminded me every day - "Step down at 60!" - I had begun to imagine a different future for myself than one defined by the administrative pressures of corporate leadership. I was all for the idea of inviting younger leadership to step in and was looking forward to the possibility of enjoying my last five years at *International Bible Society* as a minister-at-large, concentrating on doing the things that best captured and compelled my heart.

Over the past year I had felt snared in an administrative mire. Sure, I had the corner office with a conference room, a company car and a great retirement plan. However, the gifts God had given me of teaching, preaching and encouraging, were being starved daily. Increasingly, the majority of my time was spent in the internal affairs of an institution that was almost 200 years old.

Several times during the previous months the Lord had gently nudged me to change direction. He was telling me, "Lars, it is time to go and dirty your hands for me again!" As he nudged, I pushed those thoughts away. "Leave me alone, Lord! I am happy with where I am!" Surely I could coast along for the next eleven years until retirement. But God knew me well. I am not the coasting type!

In January 1998 one of my best friends, Rev. Robert Schmidgall at Calvary Church in Naperville, had coffee with some of his church leaders at the local International House of Pancakes. Suddenly he clutched his chest and keeled over the table. He passed away before he reached the hospital. Bob was only a year older than I, and someone who had had a terrific mentoring influence in my life for more than 20 years. We had attended Bob's church for fourteen years when we lived in the Chicago area and I was often invited to preach there. For years I also served as the third organist, which meant I played certain Sunday nights and Wednesday nights. These were the nights when Pastor Bob often led worship sitting on a stool or in a chair on the platform. He would just sit there and start singing, which was great...except that he always sang in the keys of F sharp or C sharp, definitely not my best keys! Thank God for the button on the organ that could transpose half a pitch in either direction, saving me from utter embarrassment!

At Robert Schmidgall's funeral four days later, I sat in the overcrowded church, among some 3,500 people, thinking. A few minutes earlier, I had looked down at my friend Bob, who looked more dead than I could ever imagine anyone could look. As the service proceeded, I heard a quiet whisper in my heart. "Lars, what are you going to do with the rest of your life?" My life was full! "Good question, Lord" was all I could muster and tucked that experience deep into my sub-conscious.

Three months later, it was time for the *International Bible Society* to present its annual award, the Golden Word Award, which was handed out to someone who had accomplished something outstanding for the Word of God and its influence around the world. Through the years I had the privilege to present this award to Joni Erickson Tada, Kenneth N.

Taylor, Charles Swindoll and John Stott. This year the recipients were Dr. Billy Graham and his daughter Anne Graham Lotz. Billy Graham was ill and could not attend, so his daughter came to accept it for both of them.

It was a long ceremony with a carefully choreographed program and we had instructed Anne that she had no more than ten minutes for her award acceptance speech. After she had been handed the award, she slowly and deliberately set it down and then turned to the podium. She didn't launch into a typical acceptance speech. Instead, she stood there in silence for a moment, then began, "This is a word from the Word of God just for you." And then she preached for an hour. Some of the leadership staff snickered at that and said, "Well, that's not what we wanted." But that ceremony – and her message – captured me in such a way that I didn't even notice the time passing.

My assistant Anne Craft, who knew my struggles in this area, said to me afterward, "Lars, did you hear the Word of God tonight?" I sure did. What did Anne Graham Lotz say? She spoke on the passage of Scripture from Revelation 2:1-5.

> *"To the angel of the church in Ephesus write:*
>
> *These are the words of him who holds the seven stars in his right hand and walks among the seven golden lampstands: I know your deeds, your hard work and your perseverance. I know that you cannot tolerate wicked men, that you have tested those who claim to be apostles but are not, and have found them false. You have persevered and have endured hardships for my name, and have not grown weary.*
>
> *Yet I hold this against you: You have forsaken your first love. Remember the height from which you have fallen! Repent and do the things you did at first. If you do not repent, I will come to you and remove your lampstand from its place."*

Anne Graham Lotz explained "most of the Christians in Ephesus were second generation Christians. Paul had been their pastor, John had also been their pastor and Timothy was probably the district superintendent. They knew good teaching. We can all identify with the Ephesians, having worked hard... done a lot for God."

Risk-Taker for God

As I listened to her that night, it was like God was speaking to me through those verses, "You have persevered. You have not grown weary." Presidents—they usually just hand out awards. But God seemed to be giving one to me. "I know what you have done for me," He said. "Good work, Dunberg!" It was like hearing heaven's applause. I had worked hard; the last twenty years had been extremely intense. But God wasn't finished. "I know your deeds...so much work behind the scenes — so many airports and so many hotel rooms, filled with horrible bugs. There are so many lonely times, so many problems that only you and I know about — difficulties you cannot share with anybody else." Yes, this was true. It has not always been easy. And I am thankful for God's closeness in those times. And then God spoke a difficult-to-hear truth, "You have done well...but you have forsaken your first love."

Sitting there, listening to Anne Graham Lotz, listening to God's message to me, my thoughts wandered to those romantic teenage days. I had dated a lot of girls in Sweden. I think I had six not-that-serious girlfriends before I met my wife. I started early —when I was twelve and already 6 feet and 3 inches tall! But I truly fell in love when I moved to Britain as a 19-year-old. We dated for three years and we only saw each other two weeks every year, but it was a passionate romance. Long before the days of e-mail, we wrote letters to one another. I wrote a letter a day for three years — except on the days when I wrote two — and now and then she would write back to me. As often as we could afford it we would visit each other for a few weeks at a time.

On the first few visits I was so nervous, staying in the spare bedroom upstairs. Her mother would fix bacon and eggs like British mothers do. The smell would rise up to my bedroom and that, combined with the sudden realization that I was going to get to spend the whole day with the love of my life, made me completely nauseated. There was no bathroom on the second floor, actually, none in the house, only the toilet outside, off the veranda! In desperation I would open the window and vomit because I felt so nervous.

I was in love. Passionately!

Do you remember that first love for Jesus? You couldn't hear enough about Him. You couldn't read enough about Him. You couldn't talk or listen to Him enough. Through Anne Graham Lotz's words, God reminded me of those days when I was so on fire for Him and couldn't wait to talk to others about Him.

"In your busyness you've lost your first love for Me," He said.

As I examined my heart that night while sitting at the head table — and it's hard to hear this kind of stuff no matter where you're sitting — I said to God, "I'm so sorry. I thought I was just busy and tired. But I've really lost it, haven't I?"

While Anne Graham Lotz continued talking about returning to your first love, I realized a principle that God wants our love for Him more than He wants our service. He wants our love for Him more than He wants all this stuff we do for Him. "Return to your first love!"

That night, I told my wife, "Perhaps God has something really new for us! I have been the president of *Living Bibles International* and *International Bible Society* combined for 21 years. How can I renew myself for another 11 years before we retire?"

I lay in bed that night crying to God to do a fresh work in my life, whatever the price. But in the morning I tucked this desire away in my brain, as far away from the action area as possible.

Three months later the work-study consultant unknowingly brought all these pieces to life. Suddenly those nudges from the Lord became more like a gentle shove in the right direction. There was such a desire to dirty my hands for God, to do something fresh, to take risks for God, but unless I took a step of faith, I would be faced with more months and years of internal meetings, administrative procedures and preparation for the nine boards and six committees I served on. The only way to know what God had in mind was to quit and see what He had for us.

But that is not something you do when you're fifty-four! Still, God's voice was clear. I knew I had to step out of the boat if God would ever show me how to walk on the water.

A few days later I met with the chairman of the Board and then with the executive committee of *International Bible Society.* While my resignation letter to the chairman only contained four sentences, it felt like the longest letter I ever had written. It effectively closed the door to the 26-year long Bible work chapter of my life, and the majority of my time in ministry.

It is with personal regret that I offer you my resignation as of July 31, 1998. It has been my pleasure to serve with you, first at Living Bibles International for so many years, and during the past 6 years at International Bible Society.

I wish IBS, the Board, staff and you especially, God's guidance as you look to the future and the tremendous work that lies before you.

May the Lord richly bless you.

That letter began the most intriguing weeks of my life. What was the Lord trying to tell us? Before He had nudged me so clearly, but where was His direction now?

We began to make lists and charts of ways to minister, laying out options that we all could review as a family. At one family council in our living room, with our two daughters Carin and Maria and their husbands Ron and Andrew and our son Paul present, we let them review the possibilities:

- Should we explore pastoring a church... in Sweden, England or the USA?

- Should we ask if the Salvation Army needs us?

- Could we serve with *Youth with a Mission*?

- Should we move back to Sweden to serve in some kind of ministry?

- Would there be a ministry option in Britain?

- Was there another organization that needed me?

- Should I take a secular job and do ministry on the side?

While the children helped us rule out some of the more unusual options - and we had drawn up some 20 variations - nothing seemed to stand out. My daughter Maria looked at the list and blurted out, "None of this is you, Dad!" And still, I felt within me that the Lord was clearly calling us to ministry, I just could not verbalize the details!

A few weeks later Doreen and I flew to Seattle. We had been invited to spend a week on a motor yacht owned by a couple we had befriended, Ray and Jackie Schenk, from Bainbridge Island. We flew to Seattle, only to find out when we arrived that the boat was misbehaving with an engine problem. Instead we would spend vacation on shore and drive to Canada.

During the trip to Vancouver and back, Doreen and I poured our hearts out to the Schenks, asking them over and over again, "What do you think the Lord has in mind for our lives? It has been absolute silence from God since we left *International Bible Society!*"

As we returned to stay with the Schenks for a few days on Bainbridge Island, Ray had had enough of my constant, go-nowhere questioning. His words practically exploded from his mouth:

"Lars, I'm so tired listening to you harping on the fact you don't know what God wants you to do! Why don't you go into my study, and don't come out until the Lord has told you clearly what to do!"

I immediately took a pad, a pen and headed for the study. After ten minutes I opened the door, peeked out, and said, "Can I come out, I am ready!"

Never could I have imagined what those ten minutes would mean for me and for literally millions of people throughout the world. In those ten minutes the Lord clearly helped me put on paper some guiding principles that were hidden in my heart, and those principles became the very platform that the organization which we eventually launched, *Global Action*, is operating from today.

On the piece of paper I had written:

Evangelistic Ministry and Outreach

Evangelistic events, mainly in India, Philippines, Latin America, Africa, Eastern Europe and Scandinavia.

Citywide impact events and other evangelistic impact events that mobilize the church in a city in the above countries for evangelism and follow up.

Training

Training of pastors and lay people in evangelism, discipleship, leadership and usage of the Word of God in the same parts of the world.

Discipleship training of young people

Strategic Ministry Projects

Involvement in specific strategic projects for maximal impact in areas where above takes place like:

> a) Scripture distribution projects
> b) Assisting with church planting
> c) Specific humanitarian projects in the above
>   mentioned areas

Personal preaching/teaching role

"You need an umbrella organization to do all that," Ray blurted out. I cringed.

"I have just gotten out of running organizations. Never again!" But after talking it through that evening, and after Doreen and I had suffered yet another sleepless night, I could see how it might just work.

"How do we do this?" I asked Ray. "It's not as if I have the names of thousands of people in some database who can support a new cause."

"Write to twenty of your closest friends and advisors," Ray encouraged, "and see what they think. If they are willing to support you, others may follow in their footsteps."

Together we created a simple, straightforward letter and I mailed it to twenty close friends. Nineteen people responded. One did not think it was a very good idea, but eighteen encouraged me to go for it and promised to pray and be financially supportive.

Global Action was born that day. A few weeks later I asked Ray and a few other long time friends, Dave Foster and John Vanderveld, if they would join Doreen and me and serve on the founding board. They agreed.

Global Action was official! Focusing on these specific categories from my piece of paper, we were ready to begin. Later those phrases were developed into six distinctive ministry areas:

Evangelism and Outreach
Training
Compassion Ministries
Children and Youth

Women of Global Action (later changed to Women and Men)
Multiplication

Sitting at our dining room table, in a simple phone conference, the small board constituted itself and incorporation papers were filed August 17, 1998. The next day I set up a folding table and *Global Action* had its first day of operation in our basement office!

CHAPTER 2
Roots

Originally, the family on my father's side came from a Walloon background. At the end of the 16th century a highly developed iron industry blossomed in Walloonia, an area in what is now south Belgium and north France, with the city of Liege as the center. Natural resources of iron ore and forests that could be turned into coal for the blasting furnaces kept the industry expanding. The smithing methods from Walloonia became famous all over Europe.

In the beginning of the 17th century the natural raw materials began to run dry for the Wallonians. At the same time Belgium was forced into war and unemployment became sky-high. A country far in the north of Europe, Sweden, possessed iron ore, forests and power through its many waterfalls, but the iron production was in desperate need of new methods and ideas. At the same time Sweden was also fighting wars with Poland and Denmark and needed more weapons for the war industry. Sweden needed better blasting furnaces and new forges but there simply was not enough capital to reconstruct the industry.

A rich industrialist from Holland, Louis de Geer, came to Sweden and won the confidence of Swedish king Gustavus II Adolphus, by providing a loan for the battles. Having gained the favor of the king, he established himself as a leader within the iron ore industry in Sweden. De Geer realized he needed to import skilled labor for the new furnaces and therefore established recruiting offices in Walloonia.

Although Sweden was looked upon as a dismal country in the far north, where cold and snow made life harsh and unbearable, thousands signed up. It was not just craftsmen in the iron ore industry who were willing to emigrate, but other craftsmen were also eager to seek their fortune in the north. Although most of them signed a two-year contract, many of them brought their families and never returned to their countries of origin.

Several of these immigrants to their newfound homeland had family names that ended in "berg", which means "mountain." Traces of the Walloonian area languages can still be found in the Swedish language, some Flemish, some Dutch. Jokingly we often say that Dutch looks like Swedish, but is badly spelled. The earliest trace of the "Dunberg" family name is in 1672, from a family living in the Dunatorp cottage in Åseda, Sweden, who were named Dunberg. From there the family branched out all across southern Sweden.

Roots on my Father's Side

My paternal great-grandfather, Karl Johan Reinhold Dunberg was born in 1856 and he was the official driver of the horse and carriage for the owner of one of the glass factories in the Småland area, not far from where the better known Orrefors and Kosta glass factories are situated today. In midlife he was invited to become the driver cum coachman for Count Bonde at Hässelby Castle, just outside Stockholm.

My grandfather, Axel Adrian Dunberg, was born January 25, 1885, as number seven in a family of 10 boys and 4 girls. He was 18 years old when he moved with his father to Hässelby Castle, which would prove to be of great value to him and eventually for the entire Dunberg family. There he helped his father in the stables, as well as taking care of typical duties at a huge mansion, such as using the horses and carts to drive the washing to the river as well as collect the water containers needed for such a large household. It did not take long before he ran into a young, attractive dark-haired maid with immense brown eyes, Signe Lundberg, and fell desperately in love. After they married, my grandfather landed a position with the Dairy association of Stockholm as a horse coachman, delivering the heavy metal milk containers from place to place throughout the city.

Risk-Taker for God

My paternal grandmother, Signe Karolina Lundberg hailed from an island called Aspö, right at the southern end of Utö, in the Eastern archipelago towards Finland, where she was born January 16, 1889.

A few years later my paternal grandmother's family moved to Utö Mines, where my great-grandfather leased a small farm, and he also kept cows and a horse. My grandmother used to tell me stories of her rather vague memory of the stable and its eating troughs. Every time she heard the Christmas story, her mind flashed back to that memory.

In the harsh winters the family traveled to the church services by a horse-drawn sleigh. My grandmother used to be frightened by the minister in his ornate "priestly" outfit, but those fears were put to rest when she accompanied her mother to the vicarage, selling milk to the vicar and his family. Occasionally the vicar would pick up little Signe on his lap and talk to her. Since he was also a teacher, he inquired whether Signe would be allowed to attend school, and after much thought her parents granted her the right to get an education of sorts from the local vicar-schoolmaster.

She could not attend school every day because her father needed frequent help with the fishing nets. To increase their meager income, most farmers would take their long rowing boats out to sea to lay their nets and then return in the early hours of the morning to pull them up. It was hard work for such a tiny girl.

The years before Signe became a teenager held her happiest memories. Her mother would take her along to prayer meetings, held in various cottages on the island. Those cottages belonged to people whose hearts had been touched by the Christian revival that swept the islands a few years earlier. She also attended religious services and Sunday school in the chapel. It was during these meetings my grandmother came to personal faith in Christ. Her faith developed through the years and in turn, she influenced my father to commit his life to Christ at a young age. Many weekends she had to look after the cows in the meadows, which hindered her ability to attend chapel. But when the bells began tolling for the church services, she sang her hymns and held her own chapel, surrounded by a congregation of attentive cows.

When Signe turned fifteen, she began serving as a maid at a nearby farm. Every morning at 5.00 a.m. and every afternoon, 16 cows had to be milked by hand. In the winter, one of her responsibilities was to take the ice picks to the lake to cut up ice and carry it back to the cellar where it was placed to keep the milk and other food products cool. The rats were a nuisance and on a daily basis she had to chase them away from the food. Sometimes they fell into the milk containers and spoiled the milk she had toiled so hard with her hands to extract from the cows.

In the summers, she focused mainly on the harvest, working the fields and ensuring that all the workmen had enough food for their breaks. Any time anything was needed from the store, she had to row the huge boat across the bay to the mainland, carry all the groceries down to the boat, and then row back. All that hard work for a monthly pay of less than a dollar.

After a few years she was asked to come and serve at Hässelby Castle, in the outskirts of Stockholm. Hässelby Castle was originally built by Gustaf Bonde who first moved into the castle in 1657. When my grandmother and grandfather served there it was owned by count Carl Trolle-Bonde, who lived there from 1884 to 1912.

The first few months her main duty was to take care of the pigs and the chickens as well as wash and scrub each room's wooden floors. The hard-working girl was noticed by her superiors, and she was promoted to become a chamber maid. The Castle arranged many parties with guests who often stayed overnight. The guest rooms needed to be heated up and warm water carried up to the rooms. At meal times, Signe had to look proper enough to be able to serve the food in the ornate dining room. Many nights she stayed up late to do the washing and iron the guests' clothes.

Roots on My Mother's Side

My maternal great-great-great-grandfather, Reverend Johannes Hardin, (born in 1783) arrived in the tiny village Fröskog, in the province of Dalsland in 1822 to serve as a clergyman in the Swedish Lutheran church. The Hardins already had five children and a further five were born to them there. Their third child, Olof (born 1815) fell desperately in love with one of their maids, Britta Maria Olsdotter (born 1812) and took every opportunity to spend time with her. It did not take long before their passionate love resulted in my great-grandfather, Gustaf Ols Bydén. I am not sure where the family name came from – it's possible his mother made it up. The first part of the family name "by" means village. The official church documents verify the tragic circumstances surrounding his birth: "Gustaf, illegitimate child, born in the village Mo, Dalsland March 16 1835, baptized March 17. Mother: Britta Maria Olsdotter, 23 years old."

There is no mention of the father, who later moved away, joined the military and after serving in the Army for seven years became a surveyor. We never knew if he ever saw his son again. He died 1891 and is buried in Alingsås, 25 miles from where Doreen and I lived for many years and also the very city where our daughter Maria was born.

The young boy Gustaf grew up in various foster homes, until he learned a trade as a sword-smith and married young Eva Lovisa Nilsson (born 1836). Together they had seven children, the oldest being my grandfather Martin Bydén, born September 6, 1859. He died a few months before my parents were married in 1937. My only memories of my maternal grandfather are pictures and paintings of an old gentleman with tiny circular glasses, grey hair and matching mustache. Even my mother's view of her father was of an old man as he was over fifty when she was born. He died tragically of a urinary infection at a time when no medical treatments were available for his ailment.

When Martin was twelve, the family moved to Stockholm. As soon as school was over, he and his brother began working for their father as iron smith assistants. He learned to build ovens for metal products, as well as working the lathes for different metal art forms. Until his death he worked as a foreman in this industry. During his early working days in Stockholm he met a young attractive lady named Emma Charlotta Jansdotter, who was serving as a maid in the city. Emma was born in Svartå, not far from the city of Örebro, March 26, 1863. It did not take long before they were married and began having children. My mother, Gerda Margareta was born as the youngest of nine on January 10, 1910, when my grandmother was 47 and my grandfather was 51. My mother's older sisters were 18 and 22 years old when she was born and her oldest brother was 24! Her closest sibling was 8 years older than her.

My Father's Story

My paternal grandparents Axel and Signe were passionately in love and realized that they'd better get married before their child was born. A few months after the wedding, Signe went to live with her mother and sister on the island of Muskö in the Stockholm archipelago where my father

Axel Bertil Maurits, called Maurits, was born on September 22, 1911 in my great grandmother's tiny weather-beaten cottage. One month later the mother and child returned to Stockholm, before the waters froze and while boats could still make the journey into the capital.

For years my grandparents and my father lived in a one-room apartment with a huge kitchen. My father had to share a bed with his own father until he was fourteen years old. He was often attacked by all kinds of viruses, and later the doctors determined that the reason was that he spent every night in bed with a grown man who frequently carried the germs from the city with him.

My grandmother took my father to the local Covenant Church every Sunday, not only to Sunday school, but to every other service as well. She had made a pact with the Lord that her firstborn would be used in His service. Whether this was a promise made when she realized she was pregnant and unmarried - a commitment out of terrible guilt, or a promise out of her deep piety, she wanted to ensure that she held up her end of the bargain.

Recently my father told me, "I would go along to church and listen intently. The minister, Rev. August Rosén, was a very stern looking man with tiny spectacles and a piercing stare. Though he frightened me, I tried to memorize the sermon points. When I returned home I would stand on a chair and preach the sermon to my Dad, who had chosen not to attend church with my mother and me."

When my father was seven years old, his mother was expecting again. A few weeks before the birth of the baby, my father fell ill in a high fever. The Spanish flu was raging across Sweden and in December 1918, his mother came down with it. It is estimated that between 1918 and 1920 close to 100 million people were killed in this pandemic worldwide, equaling one third of the population of Europe in those days. Her sister came to help and was also stricken by the Spanish flu. People were dying in Stockholm by the thousands. My grandfather would get up 3.00 in the morning, do his rounds delivering milk and then hurry home to act as the nurse for all three.

Just after Christmas it was time for the baby's delivery. That night a heavy snowfall had made the streets impassable. My grandmother and grandfather walked more than 2 miles through the raging snowstorm to the hospital. A few hours later my aunt Gunborg was born.

A few months later my father fell sick again and was sent to the hospital. This time they could not determine the cause of his illness. Because of his weakened condition, the doctors gave him no hope to live. But my grandfather, whose stubbornness I inherited, simply told the doctors, "If there is life there is hope." Of course there were no antibiotics in those days. The best working medicine was "China capsules" and patients were frequently directed to wear wet sweats, which would help them sweat properly. These wet sweats were changed several times a day. My father's fever was so high that he would hallucinate and run wild in the corridors. Finally the hospital had to place boards round his bed and tie him to it.

When my father was finally released from hospital he had lost a lot of time in school. But there was little time to catch up, because little Maurits had to begin earning money to help the family out financially. As soon as school was over, his fourteen-year old legs would run as fast as they could carry him to another part of Stockholm where he worked for three hours each day as an errand boy in a framing store.

The following year school was over for him and he began working full-time at a "gilder store" in the more fashionable area of Stockholm. Maurits had never been to this part of Stockholm, where people had huge apartments, often with a maid and sometimes even a butler. For the first year he did nothing but deliver framed, gilded artwork to these households, all on foot.

At the same time, the idea of full-time service for the Lord lay dormant deep within him. Some of his friends went through short Bible courses, and then were sent out as trainee evangelists to "mission" chapels in the countryside. Others enrolled at the Covenant Seminary in Stockholm to train for the ministry in the Covenant Church. My father wanted so much to fulfill his mother's dream, but for some reason, when he applied to the Bible course, he was not accepted. Often my Dad would say to me after my conversion, "I was not allowed to fulfill the promise, but perhaps you will fulfill my mother's promise and serve the Lord." Talk about feeling pressure! Not only were my father's desires for his own life placed upon my shoulders, but through him the expectations of my grandmother as well.

Instead of going to Bible school, Maurits was asked to learn the trade of a "gilder" at the company where he worked and he learned it from scratch, guided by the "master gilder," who himself had been trained in

Germany. For years he worked as an apprentice until he finally could describe himself as a "master gilder." There were not many master gilders. My Dad used to say with a laugh, "When our national trade union meets, there are only nine of us!"

The ornamental pendulum wall clock became popular in the emerging middle class households, and my father worked on these for many of his working years.

Then came the Second World War. Sweden remained neutral but neighboring Norway and Denmark were occupied by the Nazis on April 9, 1940, while Finland on the other border was fighting their own war with Russia. Sweden mobilized its troops as well as any man that could be drafted. My father was a conscientious objector, and as such was sent to work at local fire stations, or to distant areas to work in the forests or to coastal areas to complete various practical jobs that the military needed to be done.

He was away from home for months with no pay. The company where he had worked for many years folded just before he was drafted, and my Dad had not received his salary for several months. My sister was still a baby, and there simply was no money. The government paid compensation if you used your own bicycle: 14 cents a day. Every ten days he would send home this meager sum of money. Some of the preachers who served with my Dad went out and preached every weekend. One of them often said to my father, "I know you have a difficult time financially and I want to give you what I earned preaching last Sunday." This kept the small family going.

During the next five years of World War II, my Dad was gone on and off for duty to his country. When the war was finally over, May 8 1945, he had a growing family of two children, and no work. He frantically applied for different positions but was turned down everywhere because he was viewed as being too old. He tried the police force, the fire brigade and the Stockholm transportation system without success. And he was only 34!

Through a friend he finally landed a job as gilder for a distributor of pendulum clocks. This time he could work from home, and during my formative years, my father worked from a tiny room next to the kitchen, a room where we ate, my parents slept, and my father worked. Hooks on one wall held a great number of the wooden clock bodies, all in different stages of being gilded by his skilled craftsman hands. It was not a well-paying job, so my mother eked out a meager second income by having piano students come most afternoons, and sometimes in the evenings for lessons.

Dad continued gilding until he retired in 1976. The skill with his hands is something I definitely did not inherit. Several times he wallpapered and painted our small 520 square foot apartment, where I grew up. The last few years he spent in a nursing home before he died in July 2008.

In the Spring of 2008 I opened the door slowly to his room at the nursing home. His heart seemed to be strong despite the heart attack he suffered in 1994. But age was breaking down many of the physical functions and his mind was beginning to wander. But still, it was always important to look proper, so most times I came to see him, he was propped up in a chair, in a full suit and tie.

"Is it Lars?"

"Yes I am here from the USA for a few days...how are you?"

"I have no money for the streetcar!" Street cars have not existed in Stockholm since 1967, so I knew this would be a different kind of conversation.

"Where are you going, Dad?"

"We cannot stay here any more. We all have to leave and I have to take the street car to the new place! But I have no money, they have taken all my money!"

His fingers were moving, his thumb rubbing the next finger, a sign of tension I had seen in my grandmother's hands and something I also do when I get stressed!

"Dad here is 10 kronor for the street car," I said and stuck it in his suit pocket. A smile of satisfaction spread over his old face as he patted the pocket with one of his hands.

The next day I visited him again. He did not mention anything about the street car. We talked about Doreen and the children. His hearing was so decimated that I practically had to yell each sentence into his ear. Sometimes I would get a reaction and other times he would stare into space. Slowly I moved my hand to his suit pocket to see if the money was still there, but it was gone!

Suddenly he broke out in a grin, as his hand went to the shirt pocket: "I still have your money! Now I can go on the streetcar!"

On the next trip I was rushed because of other commitments, but I wanted to ensure I saw him several times. I visited both morning and evening the first days.

"Who is this?"

"It is Lars, Dad...just up from Norrköping to see you." We had a very good, normal conversation. Later that night, I peeked into his room again.

"Who is this?"

"It is Lars, Dad!"

"No, no, Lars was here this morning!" Nothing in the world could change his mind that it was me, so we just chatted and I patted his hand and gave him a hug. The following morning I returned just after he had eaten his breakfast.

"Who is it?"

"It is Lars, Dad!"

"Oh, so good to see you. There was a man here last night, and he really knew you!"

Every time Doreen or I, or my sister and brother-in-law mentioned that we were soon retiring or had retired, he chuckled in a way that I know meant, "Children, you are not telling me the truth!"

Two days after I finished this manuscript, I received the phone call that Dad had gone to be with Jesus! The final week he was able at times to talk to those who visited him. Finally he fell into a sleep and passed on to glory surrounded by my sister and brother-in-law. He was just shy of 97 years old.

My Mother's Story

My mother's upbringing was rather shielded, shaped as it was by senior parents and older siblings. Somehow, this made it appear as if my mother came from a completely different generation than my father, as her sisters and her future mother-in-law were born just a year apart.

Values, behavior and inter-personal relationships were being practiced in the Bydén household in the early 1900s in the same way as when the first siblings came along in the late 1800s. My mother, in turn, passed along to me and my sister these values and behavior that seemed ancient to us, and made us stand out against the family life of our close friends.

Mother was a good student, and also learned to play the piano. Recently I uncovered a receipt for the ebony piano we had at home. My grandfather bought it for his daughter in 1927, when she was seventeen! Her dream was to create a future for herself in the music world, and she was very disappointed when she was turned down at her entry exam to the Royal Academy of Music. Applying that same day was Jussi Björling, Sweden's most beloved opera singer, and he wanted to take my mother out for coffee! Many times we teased her how our lives would have been different if she had sipped coffee with him that day.

My maternal grandmother was an active member in the Covenant church as was my mother's oldest sister and my mother went with them to Sunday school, church services and youth groups. It was there she met Maurits, 1 ½ years younger than she, and they fell in love. They were engaged when she was 20, but their engagement lasted for seven years!

Both before and after she was married, my mother was a piano teacher, and through this she built up a steady income for herself and later for the family.

Mother never worked outside of the home, apart from her piano lessons. After my father retired she quit teaching as her fingers slowly became stiff and soon after, finally gave up playing all together. During her last few years, her mind would wander, and at times all recent memory was gone. On April 13, 1993 a heart attack claimed her life. She died surrounded by my Dad, as well as my sister and her husband and children. I had just left on a trip for Africa and was told upon my arrival to the hotel in Nairobi that Mom had gone to be with the Lord.

My Childhood

I was born in Stockholm, Sweden May 8, 1944 and was given the names Lars Bertil. My sister Margareta Eva Charlotte was five years older than me and enjoyed the idea of having a new brother.

Just before I was born, the Soviets dropped a bomb by mistake a few hundred yards from our home. It shattered the windows of the nearby houses, but more than that, it shattered people's lives and put an increasing fear in their lives about "the Soviet bear" that was less than 200 miles away. I grew up with an ever increasing fear of the Russians, and more than once my older sister would scare me with the statement, "Watch it Lars, the Russians are coming!" Our small apartment was right under the flight path for Stockholm's airport and lying in bed at night, trying to sleep, I could hear the droning of engines as the planes flew over. I often crawled under the blankets, scared out of my wits, thinking, "Is this it? Are they coming now? Is our freedom gone?" It was a fear that stayed with me for many, many years.

During the first few years my sister often took charge of me. She would take my stroller, with me in it, out with her friends, and since our street had a slight slope, they liked to race the "sibling strollers" down the street, letting them roll down on their own. It is a miracle no one ever was hurt or run over by a passing car. Other times she would hook me up to a chain and imagine that I was her dog. Since it would be impossible to have a pet in our crowded apartment, the next best thing – the brother - would have to do.

One of my first memories is my third birthday. My parents had saved a lot of money to buy a tricycle for their little son and proudly wheeled it into my room and woke me up. Instead of being happy and smiling, I broke out into hysterical sobs, "No bell, no bell, no bell!" I was most attracted to the bells on the handlebars…and this model didn't have one!

On one of my sister's birthdays, she received a pair of knitted gloves made by one of our seemingly "old" aunts. My sister tried them on and hated them with a passion because they itched. She took them with her into the small room we shared, and handed them to me along with a pair of scissors. "Cut them," she demanded, "cut them or I will hurt you." I knew what it was like to be hurt by my sister, so I obediently cut big holes in the new gloves. When my mother saw the cut-up gloves and found out I had done it, I was sent to bed early, while my sister went on to enjoy her party. My mother never found out what really happened until we were adults and had left home.

My Early School Years

School in Sweden begins at seven years of age and in those days there was no pre-school or kindergarten. The first year of school was a positive experience for me. At our first end-of-term assembly I was asked to conduct the class choir, which was an honor - and extremely scary.

At the end of my first school year, I experienced the first real trauma in my life, over someone else's misery, a sensation that has followed me through my life.

21

Risk-Taker for God

It was custom, especially for the girls, to bring a wrapped gift for the teacher at the end of the school year. I can still see this nice looking seven-year-old girl, who I admired, arrive in her best dress with her gift-wrapped, satin-ribboned package under her arm. Out of nowhere, a couple of second grader "bully boys" appeared and began to harass the girl, while one of them snatched the package out of her hand. When the girl began crying, the boys simply ripped the gift wrap to pieces, revealing a couple of padded, colorful coat hangers. I began to sob too, realizing that nothing could put that package together again. I so sensed the girl's hurt and can still feel the frustration of not being able to change her sorrow into joy.

After my second school year I applied to a music school, and managed to get in. I could carry a tune, but did not play an instrument seriously. When I turned five my parents rented a violin and started violin lessons for me, which I hated with a passion. Rehearsals at home were a nightmare and I found every excuse not to practice, shedding ample tears. By the time I reached second grade my parents finally gave up on me in despair. The music school was more about music theory and singing and created a real passion within me for music.

I ran into a major problem every day when I returned from school. My mother had piano students every weekday. My room and the bathroom were on the opposite side from the entrance to our apartment, with the piano room between. I was absolutely forbidden to go through the room when Mom had students, so I would sneak into the kitchen, heat a cup of coffee and make myself some cheese sandwiches. Trying to concentrate on my homework I listened to students make the same mistakes with Fur Elise, or Czerny's Etudes or some simplified Chopin piece. There and then I made up my mind that I would never touch the piano!

I hardly ever remember my parents quarreling. My Dad would become quiet when things were not quite right and give all of us "the silent treatment." My mother would rarely tell us when we had offended her, apart from saying, "You know what hurt me…". Most of the time no one would have a clue what had upset her. She would purse her lips in a certain way and her head would shake a little, and you knew at that moment you were in great trouble, without knowing the cause of her upset.

My Greatest Challenges

My parents were believers and heavily involved in the local Evangelical Covenant church – the Andreas Church. My mother played piano for the typical Swedish "string band" and my father took an active part in that singing group, and acted as its president. The group rehearsed every Monday night, when some 30-40 people would come together with violins, guitars, mandolins, trombones, as well as the odd trumpet and accordion, learning Christian songs that were popular in the 40's and 50's. The rehearsals either started or ended with a half-hour prayer meeting. As a child I would copy the adults, dropping to my knees for prayer time, but inside I was secretly hoping that the same people, who prayed every time, would not go on praying for so long. Some Mondays I was excused and was sent to my paternal grandparents' to stay overnight. Those nights were always special.

Other times I was left alone at home. This started when I was nine or ten and these were some of the scariest moments I remember. I would sit in my Dad's workroom and play, often with the Swedish forerunner to Lego, listening to every sound. People walking up and down the stairs outside the apartment made a noise, you could even hear the front door to the apartment complex open and close if you listened carefully. The darkness in other rooms created a frightening atmosphere and some of the paintings in our small apartment took on a life on their own, which created absolute fear for such a small boy.

A few times a year, my Dad arranged singing outreach trips to churches in the countryside. This was a special thrill for me, as we would travel by a rented bus. Sitting in the front, I never tired of watching the bus driver. The services were also extremely special. Usually, my Dad asked the Covenant seminary to send us their most fiery young student-preachers for these trips. I was amazed to hear these young men preach and I observed every move they made.

At the same time I was somewhat embarrassed by the faith of my parents. To be a Christian in post-war Sweden, where secularism and politics had created a welfare state with no room left for God, was no small feat. The worst name you could be called on our street was "religious." When friends came to visit me at home, I made sure that all the hymnals and the Bibles were neatly put away. I was always concerned that my Mom or Dad would make references to church or Christianity while we played indoors.

A favorite topic among my friends at school was a discussion about the latest movie shown at the local theater. Every time I wanted to go with my friends to see a movie, or was invited by their parents to do so, my mother asked, "Is that where you want to be if Jesus comes back today?" That question settled it and I was over 20 before I ever entered a cinema. When I could not take part in the discussion about what Roy Rogers, Alan Ladd or John Wayne had done the day before on the big screen, the rest of the children tended to shout at me with ever greater intensity, "Religious, religious, religious!" Those are some of the most embarrassing moments from my childhood.

I had another major problem in those years. I preferred to play with the girls rather than with the boys. I was therefore looked upon as the sissy of the block. When I first started school, the bullies would grab me as I walked to school, knock me down on the sidewalk, and then run over me with their bicycles. That was not a painless experience! Many times I ran home, sobbing hysterically, to my Dad who worked at home, grabbed him by the hand and asked him to take me to school. As soon as we walked out of the apartment block, hand in hand, there was not one bully in sight. He would walk me to and from school every day for a week, and then I would say, "I can manage on my own now!" As soon as I walked outside alone, the bullies came out of nowhere and cycled over me again. For my first school years, I was very frightened to walk to school and frightened of what the bigger boys would do to me.

But I found other ways to compensate for my inferiority complex. I learned to take charge of others. In the back yard of our apartment building I gathered the kids who were younger than me, called them my army and drilled the 4-7 year olds in precision marching, with sticks as guns and sables, matching what I had seen at the changing of the guard at the Royal palace. I had memorized the commando calls from the royal guards and trained the younger children to march in the same formations. I was their undisputable general, the leader. The bullies would be conquered and the world was at our feet!

Somehow my mother thought I was a terror and I must have affected her nerves, because the year I turned five, I was suddenly sent away, without warning, to live with a childless couple for several months.

The husband was a stern gardener who operated a set of flower and plant nurseries outside Stockholm and his wife was immensely strict. Having had no children of their own, they had little understanding of a five year old's needs nor did they understand the utter fear I experienced having been removed from my parents without explanation, other than the phrase repeated every time I asked, "You have absolutely worn your mother out." I loved my mother and what I could not understand was why my mother had stopped loving me and abandoned me to these horrendous people.

Closing my eyes, I can still see us sitting round the breakfast table. Every morning, the husband read the Bible and prayed and the wife lectured me about proper behavior. It made me always connect daily devotions with admonition for not being well behaved!

There were many tears those nights as I cried myself to sleep. Perhaps this was the time I came to realize I would never live up to my mother's expectations. Even now, I struggle with an inferiority complex of not being good enough, not living up to anyone's expectations. Although my mother has been dead for more than fifteen years, I am somewhat haunted by the memories of not being good enough, however hard I try.

During these formative years I was often taken ill. The doctors believed I was anemic and cod-liver oil, capsules and all kinds of tonics became part of my daily routine. Every day I was supposed to swallow huge speckled green-and-orange colored iron pills. But I couldn't swallow the big pills and so my grandmother would crush them and hide them in the butter on my roll, nicely covered with a slice of cheese. This made the ordeal even worse.

The real fear in those days was polio. It was not until I was in my teens that we could be vaccinated against this illness, which seemed to spread like an epidemic. Every time I had to stay home from school in bed with a fever I feared the worst.

By the age of twelve, when I had grown to 6 foot 3 inches, I began having migraine attacks. As the years went by they became more intense with several attacks a week, until I was almost 50 years old. Through these attacks I grew accustomed to pain and learned to function with a rather high pain tolerance.

While there was a deep and warm Christ-consciousness in my mother and father, there was also a strict behavioral code. Whenever I asked questions that stepped outside the allowed boundaries, I always heard the same response, "Those things you don't talk about!" There were so many things I wanted to know to which there were no answers and because my mother had been raised by much older sisters and brothers and aging parents, it was like we were separated by a double generational gap. Wrestling with questions regarding things outside of church life - the issues my friends at school talked freely about, such as questions about puberty - I was on my own.

My mother also had a built-in aversion to men. Often she would stop doing what she was doing and turn to us children and say, "I think all men should be shot!" It scared me silly when I was small, as I knew I would soon become a man. Would my own mother shoot me? As I grew into adulthood I often wondered what triggered this expression. It bothered me that my father never reacted. What did he feel when his wife expressed those emotional outbursts? He usually just slipped away in silence. She had grown up with five brothers and no doubt they always teased their little sister, but what was the underlying pain? I never found out, and even if I had ever asked, I knew the immediate answer, "Lars, those things we don't talk about!"

My Extended Family

My mother's brothers and sisters were something else. Her oldest brother Axel was born in 1886 and was 24 when his little sister was born. There were some real complications in the family. He married a charming lady, Olga, who later divorced him and married Axel's brother Martin. This caused no end of family strife, and it took years until I understood what was really going on in this matter, because these things we simply never talked about.

Axel was short, but energetic. I suspect I inherited much of my business acumen from him. After some years he was hired by the Swedish Export Council. One of his jobs was to go into Russia and salvage an order that had been placed by Tsar Nicholas II for 1,000 train engines. Then the revolution happened and in the middle of this uncertain time, probably around 1917, my uncle was in Leningrad and Moscow attempting to ensure Sweden was paid for their trains. I think at least 500 were eventually paid for. In latter years my uncle became the Consul General for Dominican Republic, went to the royal palace for state dinners with the king and queen and generally lived in completely different circles than my parents.

He was very brusque and as a young child I was frightened of him. The year I turned 8 he called my mother just before Christmas. "Send Lars over here immediately!" I walked to his very nice apartment (it was almost a half-hour's walk away), with a view over the Lake Mälaren and the Town

Hall. The balconies at his home were so long that in the winter he poured water on them and turned them into skating rinks.

As I entered his apartment, he addressed me in no uncertain manner. "The Christmas tree is outside the main entrance. Hurry down, carry it up and then set it up!" I had never set up a Christmas tree, not even at home! But I dragged the tree upstairs and somehow placed it in the stand. He asked me to climb the ladder to hold it up top while he tightened the screws in the stand. I am so scared of heights that I cannot even stand on a chair! These were nervous moments. When I finished he placed a Swedish krona in my hand and told me to hurry home.

Mom's brother Knut died when she was 20. He had become too friendly with the Swedish aquavit and Tuberculosis took his life while he still had small children at home. His widow estranged herself completely from the family, so I never met these cousins, who were so much older than I was.

My uncle Martin was a cartographer. He was also a very skilled artist. It was not until after his wife Olga died that he took some real interest in me. Often he would call me up and ask if I wanted to visit museums. We would go to art galleries together and then to his apartment, where he explained why he was creating whatever art piece he was working on. He was absent-minded, and once when we had coffee together in his apartment, he emptied the entire ashtray in a pot filled with freshly brewed coffee! When I later became interested in the Salvation Army, he created seven pencil sketches of the first seven world leaders of the Salvation Army, which still hang in my home office.

Daniel was my mother's youngest brother, just eight years older than her. He was a typographer, but had one dream in his life: to run a typical Swedish pension (guest house) in one of the skiing areas in North Sweden. Daniel was a bachelor and gave himself fully to fulfill his dream and in 1954 he opened his center called the Daniel House. That first summer he was short of staff, so he asked my Mom and Dad to come and help. Many summers, and some winters I was up there and these were some of the best times in my life. There I learned both to ski downhill and cross-country, and would often take off on my own, skiing for miles and hours across the mountain slopes. I never realized how dangerous that was and that no one would ever have found me if I had met with an accident or a wild animal.

Risk-Taker for God

My mother's sisters Ruth and Judith were 22 and 18 when my Mom was born, and they became an extra pair of mothers for their younger sister. While Judith married (Uncle Oscar), neither of them ever had any children, and they found it hard to understand their young sister. Every birthday and holiday we would either go to our grandmother's with all these uncles and aunts on my mother's side, or they would come to our small apartment.

My grandparents also had another daughter who they called Gerda. In 1902, at 12 years of age she died of scarlet fever, so when my mother came along they also called her Gerda. It took me many years to figure this out, because these were things we did not talk about.

My cousin Alf, whose mother was Olga and whose father could have been Martin or Axel, was very friendly but 25 years older than me. He was a well-known architect who had designed one of the skyscrapers in Stockholm, the Wenner-Gren center, and was responsible for how to move temples in Upper Egypt to make room for the Aswan Dam.

My father's sister married another cousin, and moved away. My father's brother was ten years younger and after marriage moved to the north of Sweden. Because of the distance we barely met the cousins on my father's side except a few times during our growing up years.

The World Around Me

There was never a TV in our home. TV was not introduced officially in Sweden until 1955, when I was 11 years old. However, as my father worked at home, the radio was on all day, and often my Mom and Dad discussed world events they heard on the news. Though Adolf Hitler had died when I was only a year old, post-war Germany and Europe was a daily discussion topic. I vaguely remember something about the Berlin airlift, and names such as Joseph Stalin, Bulganin, Malenkov and later Khrushchev were often mentioned around the dinner table.

When I was six years old, Sweden's King Gustaf, who had reigned since 1905 and gone through the separation of the union between Sweden and Norway, died of old age. Three years earlier, his grandson, father of four princesses and a small prince had died in a fiery air crash at Copenhagen's airport. I have vivid memories of the magazine and newspaper pictures with the 60-year old son of King Gustaf, now having become King Gustaf

VI Adolf, standing on the balcony of the palace with his four-year old grandson on his arms, the new crown prince of Sweden.

In 1952 I listened with eagerness as Emil Zátopek from Czechoslovakia ran his races at the Helsinki Olympics, and every day poured over the newspaper with the reports of his victories. Zátopek was one of the greatest runners in the 20th century and won the 5,000, the 10,000 and the marathon that year!

He was called the "locomotive." Despite a doctor's warning that he shouldn't compete due to a gland infection two months before, he won these major races and set a new Olympic record in all three events, and he had never run a marathon before!

I remember well the final lap: Chataway sailed past Zátopek with Schade in his shadow. Zátopek was two meters behind them, his speed unequal to theirs, his massive strength drained. Schade asserted his right to the lead. Chataway disputed it, taking command heading into the final turn. The crowd went frantic, howling wildly.

Then the chanting! Zá-to-PEK! Zá-to-PEK! From deep within, the Czech Locomotive summoned the courage of the angels! Zátopek ran, his driving leg pummeling the dirt track. Zátopek was all over them and away, his upper and lower bodies almost going in different directions as he powered through the turn far wider than any of the others. Chataway, passed by three different men in the space of four footsteps, brushed against the turn's pole and crashed to the track.

"Zá-to-PEK! Zá-to-PEK! Zá-to-PEK!" I can hear it now, sitting with my palms all sweaty next to the radio. My Dad took a break from his work, and the atmosphere in his work place could be cut with a knife!

We heard how the Russians entered Budapest in 1956 and how people were shot in the streets. That same year the Italian ship Andrea Doria was rammed by the Swedish-American liner Stockholm outside New York and sank after a few hours. While the information by radio was sketchy, newspapers and weekly news magazines filled the gaps of the tragedies of the world.

I have never been very politically active, perhaps because I have lived in countries where I could not vote! However, my parents were politically involved and I heard a lot about the characteristics of the various political parties without knowing what they really meant. To the far right were the Rightist party (later called the Moderates). This was the party of the rich, and we were certainly not in that group. In the middle was the Farmer's party, focusing on the rural parts of the country. The Liberal party was…well just liberal! On the far left there was the Communist party and they were fighting hard to get into Parliament and did not get far when I was a child. Today they have a role in the parliament. The ruling party was the Social Democratic party. This party came to power in the beginning of the 20th century and ruled during all my childhood years. As my father was a craftsman, and all craftsmen were in trade unions, which all were part of the Party, my father and mother were social democrats. In those days the Social Democratic party were fighting for such basic things as retirement for all and health insurance for all, and they laid the foundation for what became known as the Swedish welfare state, a system with many pluses and equally many minuses.

Until I was in my adolescent years, my father and I walked under the red flags in the Worker's demonstration every first of May. The event had no meaning to me, except the march was good exercise, the bands played well, and the *Internationale* was the catchiest tune I had ever heard.

I had no idea what the clenched fist stood for, but later found out that when this song was sung, that is what one did. The *Internationale*, which was first written in French in the 19th century became the anthem of social democrats, but also socialists and communists. The Chinese version was the rallying song for workers and students at the Tiananmen Square protests in 1989. Today, I look back with horror that I was actually doing this, without any knowledge of its ramifications.

Childhood Memories

As a child I never realized how poor we were, especially during the years my father was out of work. To buy clothes for me and my sister, she in her upper teens and me growing like a beanstalk every year, must have been a horrendous challenge. We always went right to the sales rack and the special offers. I remember my mother's embarrassment, when one of my teenage friends came with us to buy pants and a jacket. "Don't get those," he exclaimed to my mother, "they are ugly. Lars, come here and see the stuff your mother should buy you!" We ended up not buying anything that day, because she simply could not afford any of it.

Somehow, my parents made ends meet beyond anything we understood. We always had people over for dinner. One of the highlights was to bring people home for tea and sandwiches after church services. Hardly a week went by without some couple being asked to come. Often the church had visiting musicians or speakers and they were invited home for dinner. These were highlights for me. I listened to evangelists first hand! I heard missionaries tell their gruesome stories of wild animals, the jungle and weird diseases! The Covenant Church had a strong mission work, which was then known as Belgian and French Congo, and as a young boy I learned all the names of the different mission stations: Kimpese, Mansimou, Pointe Noire, Sundi Luthete just to mention a few.

In my childhood years we did not take any major vacations. Before I was ten we spent several weeks almost every summer with my father's uncle Valle and aunt Gurli who were farmers on the island of Muskö, where my Dad had been born. My father and mother helped at the farm and we children had fun just hanging around. I spent most of my time in the barn, learning how to clean up after the cows, helping feed the pigs, or enjoying time in the dairy, where the eggs were checked and the separator made sure the cream went in one direction and the milk in another. My great aunt made the best tasting butter in the world.

Many hours were spent riding the tractor with my Dad's cousin Olle. Riding high, shaking my insides like I have never been shaken before, I made one of the biggest decisions in life: I was going to be a farmer! Every time I shared this declaration with my parents, I noticed a shadow over my Dad's face. As I went into adolescence I understood why: he and my grandmother had promised me for full-time service for the Lord! The farming plans had to be set aside for sowing into other kinds of fields.

At least once a week we were wakened at 3 a.m. and all the men - and as an 8 to 10-year-old I was counted as one of them - went down to the Baltic Sea and jumped into the long boats. These were rowing boats with two sets of oars. They were indeed long and used to set out and take up fishing nets. The strongest men, sometimes just one man per oar would sit down and five to six of us would be in each boat. In the dark the boats steered out into the open sea, where the nets had been placed the day before. At times it was stormy and the long boats were tossed around like toys in a frothy bathtub. Life vests for private use were certainly not heard of, and it is a miracle that I never fell in the sea. It was always cold and wet and I used to hate these early mornings. By seven or eight o'clock we would be back with the filled nets, in those days mostly cod, whitefish and the ugliest fish I have ever seen, called *simpa* or in English, the cottidae, a fish with a humongous round head full of what looked like warts and a small tail, the whole body and head covered with sharp pointed fins.

As soon as the fish were untangled from the nets and the nets were hung up to dry, the big fish were put on ice to be sold to the fish brokers in Stockholm, while the cottidae were carried up to the house and into the kitchen which was always hot and full of flies. All around the kitchen there were sticky strips of fly paper hanging down from the ceiling, each covered in dead flies. Aunt Gurli would be waiting with a hot frying pan, where the cottidae went in, completely whole. There were always boiled and fried eggs, pickled herring, and lots of bread. We ate the ugly fish for breakfast - nothing could have tasted better!

During my childhood years, I was a very picky eater. The boiled beef often served on a Sunday turned into long strings in my mouth, which no one could swallow! I couldn't even fathom the idea of eating the macaroni cooked in milk. The only thing I would eat were my mother's thin Swedish crepe-like pancakes, served with lingonberry. We ate them so often that our neighbors asked my mother, "Do you eat pancakes every day? We can smell them from here!"

Christmas was a very special time. It was years before I understood why my Dad made such a fuss of Christmas. I was over 50 years old before I was aware that my grandfather had a severe drinking problem while my father was growing up. His own childhood memories of Christmas Eve were of protecting his mother and little sister from his father who had come home drunk. Christmas was the unhappiest of times for my father because of my grandfather's alcohol problems. Knowing my Granddad as I did, I could never ever imagine him drunk or antagonistic, but as you mature you learn all these things.

My Mom and Dad did not have much spending money but somehow they managed to save up for those special gifts that we had wanted all along. While the gifts were placed under the tree the day before Christmas Eve, my parents used to hide the most special gift in a closet. As soon as the presents were placed under the tree, my sister and I would sit there and gently squeeze the beautifully wrapped gifts. Softer packages were usually clothes, or even worse socks and underwear. But the hard ones were definitely worth further examination. Perhaps a book! I loved to read books, including Enid Blyton's translations from Britain of the *Famous Five* mysteries or some of the local books about the twin detectives or Astrid Lindgren's *The Master detective Blomqvist!*

Many of the Christian youth novels were about young boys getting into trouble for smoking or lying and then either being found out or confessing because of their conscience. They had such a strong Christian message and there was always a point in these stories when I would feel so for the hero in the book, that I would burst out crying and sob uncontrollably for hours. Some of my sensitivities as an evangelist to people's guilt were founded in these juvenile novels.

Festive celebrations began several nights before Christmas, when my Dad would melt all the half-burned candles from the past year. He often gathered candles from relatives and friends as well. When the candles were melted, he added more wax and water to a tall, narrow pot. Across our small room he placed two 1 x 1 poles between two chairs, about 3 feet from the floor. Across those 1 x 1 inch poles were narrow pieces of wood, each having four twisted yarns, each a foot long. We would take the sticks and dip them in the high container with the mixture of water and candle wax. We repeated this action until the wax was a half-inch thick. We were making our own candles! Every year some 100-120 candles were made in our kitchen that way.

About that time my mother boiled the Christmas ham, which is a real Swedish tradition. The broth from the boiled ham was turned into cabbage soup and later in the day she would place the boiled ham in the oven, the ham covered with mustard and bread crumbs, and as its aroma filled the apartment, it began to smell like Christmas.

On Christmas Eve morning my sister and I jumped in bed with our parents long before six o'clock. At six o'clock the Swedish radio started its Christmas programs with musicians playing carols on their brass instruments from the top of one of the old town churches, and then the children's programs would follow. That morning we always opened a few small presents that Mom and Dad had prepared for us to keep our suspense at bay.

In the afternoon it was time for the traditional Swedish Christmas table, a variety of the Swedish *smörgåsbord*. I never figured out how my mother and father could prepare so much food for so many in their little 4 x 8 feet kitchen!

Risk-Taker for God

My paternal grandparents would come, my aunt Ruth, aunt Judith and her husband Oscar and sometimes we had other guests as well. The festive dishes were placed in their traditional order: first pickled herring, sardines in tomato sauce, liver pate, pickled cucumber, Swedish ham, head cheese and jellied veal. This was always followed by omelets with asparagus, small meat balls, sausages, and Jansson's temptation, a dish made up with oven baked potatoes, interspersed with anchovies, onion and cream! And these were just the starters! They were followed by the dreaded lutefisk, a cod fish that had been dried months before until it was stiff as a board, then treated in saltpeter and when finally ready, turned into a white mass which is boiled, served with a white sauce and no end of salt and pepper. Lutefisk was always filled with bones and smelled awful. I feared it every Christmas. Fortunately it was soon followed by that wonderful Christmas dessert, rice porridge, served with milk and topped with cinnamon mixed with sugar. It was traditional for every family to hide an almond in the porridge, and the art was to get the almond and keep it in your mouth, so no one knows, while everyone continued to eat more than they could handle in search of the almond! Whoever got the almond was supposed to get married the following year.

After this culinary massacre, all the dishes had to be cleared and washed. We had no dishwasher so it took a while. Then it was time for singing Christmas carols around the piano and listening to the Christmas story from the gospel of Luke. My aunts had a tendency to choose Christmas carols that were so old, and so long-winded that no one could sing them. My sister and I would cringe when they suggested the longest carols they could find.

Finally we came to that moment when we gathered around the big table, everyone with a pair of scissors in their hand. My grandfather would bend down, pick up one package at a time, read the label and pass it to the person. Then we all waited until the person had opened the gift and we listened to everyone's oohs and ahs. During this event – which could take hours - we ate Christmas candy and enjoyed soft drinks especially bought for Christmas. As we came to the last gift, my grandfather would straighten up and with his stoic voice, declare, "Now Christmas is over!"

One of the greatest Christmas gifts I can remember I received when I was eight. In the window in the local toy store, they had advertised this gift for months. It was basically a collection of cars that you could wind up with a key and underneath was a plastic wheel that would follow narrow spiral wires you placed on the floor. There were crossings and tunnels and it was just the most impressive gift any eight-year-old could wish for. When all the gifts had been opened that Christmas Eve, there were no spiral cars in front of me, and my heart sank. At that point my Dad said to my Mom, "Oh, have we forgotten something?" She stood up and said, "Perhaps I left it in the closet..." and sure enough there was another gift, just for me! I can still feel the exhilaration of those cars!

It was hard to go to bed that night, with so many books to read and toys to play with, but we had to be in bed early because seven the following morning we all had to sit in church for *julottan*, the Christmas Day candlelight service. My father and mother would often sing in the church choir, so they needed to be there early. At least it was a service filled with music, so it was easy to stay awake.

CHAPTER 3
Molded for the Future

My upbringing was strict but loving. Though my sister sometimes told me I was adopted, which created fear in me, I knew I was very much like my uncle Daniel, so I had to be part of the family. And while there were a lot of things "banned" by our form of Christianity, I never felt limited, and I always felt loved. When my mother wrapped her arms around me I knew she cared. Many nights I stood at the foot of my father's bed in the middle of the night, with a pillow under my arm, waiting for him to wake up and whisper, "Come." When he did, I made my way between the sheets and he put his arm around me and I knew that he cared.

Early Church Memories

Sunday was a day without play. We went to church in the morning and evening. In the early years, we also went to Sunday school. I could never quite understand Sunday school. In my earliest memories, I enjoyed the sandbox where we placed cutouts to illustrate the Bible stories, then graduated to flannelgraphs, which I also liked, but after that I lost it.

The structure was predictable and boring. We gathered to sing a hymn, the text of which I still don't quite understand, and then prayed, took the offering, which I often had the privilege of collecting.

(My experience with fundraising started early!) The offering box was the ultimate in ethnic diversity. There was a slot where you put the money in and on top of it a black African in a white robe, and for every coin that went in, the figure's head nodded a thank you. That was my first introduction to another culture, as I did not meet any flesh-and-blood black people throughout my entire childhood. Sweden was a very white society, with a few Gypsies and Finns from other cultures, but that was about it.

After the offering we all read the motto of the Sunday school from the Swedish Bible found in 1 Peter 2:17: *"Fear God, Love the brethren, Honor the king."* This sentence never made sense to me, because the word *honor* was so old-fashioned that in my vocabulary it meant *is* a king. This may have been one of my first inclinations to want to make God's Word available so everyone, even children could understand it.

Splitting into different age groups, and by gender, we had question and answer sessions on different Bible passages, which always made me nervous. I was afraid I would answer wrong. My inferiority complex led me to sit as far away from the teacher as possible.

In church I became an expert in counting the window panes in the church during the long, traditional Sunday morning services. The choir, dressed in black, would often sing, and the pastor, who was elderly, would preach a good 45 minutes. Up in front was a massive organ and shielding the pipes was a very intricate woodwork with small wooden squares. It would take me almost half a sermon to count all the squares, because it was easy to lose count, and I would have to start over. The rest of the sermon I spent watching the hand on the clock over the pulpit move slowly a minute at a time. To me, who found it impossible to sit still, church was a rather boring experience.

Good Friday and the entire Easter weekend was a very solemn time. Many Good Fridays I would sit in our living room on an upright chair, dressed in my Sunday best, as hymns like...

> *"O sacred head sore wounded*
> *Defiled and put to scorn*
> *O Kingly head, surrounded*
> *With mocking crown of thorn*
> *What sorrow mass Thy grandeur*
> *Can death Thy bloom deflower?*

Risk-Taker for God

O countenance whose splendor
The hosts of heaven share."

(1607-1676, Paul Gerhardt, Latin hymn)

...floated from the radio, followed by endless hours of dreary organ music. My mother would continually sigh, and then pray. She always cried when she prayed and on Good Friday she walked around in our small apartment, weeping and praying. Those Easter memories are heavy. One time my friends from church wanted to go for a walk on Good Friday, but it was unthinkable for me to join them. How could you walk, talk and have fun, when the Lamb of God was hanging on the cross, suffering for the entire world?

Do's and Don'ts

It was definitely sinful to go to the cinema and the theatre and any form of dance was nothing but an African pre-sexual rite. Playing cards were obviously tools in the devil's hand. When the school held dances, I had to take a note from home to my teacher informing her that I did not dance. When it was time to go and see a movie with the school I was excused.

Earrings and makeup were not introduced into evangelical church circles until the 1950s, but when they were, suddenly my small ears pricked up as my mother described what some of the ladies in church were wearing. When one of my parents' best friends came to visit and I opened the door, I simply left her standing there, and ran to my mother, crying, "Mummy, auntie Karin will not go to heaven! She has earrings!"

Because my mother taught classical music throughout her piano lessons, and played a lot of it on the piano herself, I was rather taken back by her reaction when I had saved enough money to buy my first LP record. I was fourteen, and bought Haydn's trumpet Concerto. My mother went out in the kitchen, crying, and then turned to me with tears streaming down her face, "So, will this music lead you into other interests than the Lord?"

This worry and concern never left her. Many years later, when Doreen and I had been married some 20 years and lived in Chicago, my staff gave us theatre tickets for The Nutcracker Suite at Christmas. As we called my parents to wish them a Merry Christmas I shared this news with her, and she went quiet, and then responded, "How can you as a Christian leader go to the theatre...as well as taking your entire family!"

The Lord had to continually work to free me from these lists of "don'ts." Deeply rooted emotions still surface over some of these issues, as memories emerged from those formative years. Today I am more than troubled over the legalism in these behavioral patterns. At the same time, there are some aspects of pietistic behavior that I miss in church life today. It did set Christians apart from the world in a very visible way and invited a modesty that would not hurt today's modern society. Some of the taboos for which there was no rhyme or reason, and which I am freed from today, still tend to create emotional tugs within me. Even now, I feel uncomfortable when I see a deck of cards, and although my children have had decks of cards, and make fun of their father, they know that I won't take part in any kind of card game.

My Best Friend

I had no close friend among the kids on the street. When I turned seven, a couple moved to our church from the south of Sweden to be caretakers at the church, and they brought along their only son, two years older than me. It did not take long before Conny Björkvall and I became close friends. There was a huge room in the basement of their apartment building, which was owned by the church. His father gave us access to that room as our club room. Conny and I spent hours every week in that room in our pre-teen years. We kept stacks of comics, which we devoured there. In our imaginary world we even became the comic figures Batman and Robin, and made costumes trying to look like them. There were times we played scientists and tried a few chemical experiments, but thankfully, we didn't blow up the building. Ours was a close relationship. Never could I have imagined in those days that Conny was going to marry my sister!

How grateful I am today for having my best friend as my brother-in-law. With a true servant's heart, Conny has helped care for my parents when their health broke down. In these last years he has been my rock to lean on, shouldering most of the responsibilities that would have been mine, had I lived closer to my father.

A Prophetic Blessing

When I was ten years old, my grandmother, who by then was over ninety years old, came close to leaving her earthly life. One day I was over at her house with my mother. My grandmother, who was bedridden, asked me to come to her side. Suddenly she asked me to kneel down by her bed and as I did she put her bony, old, wrinkly hands on my head and in her shaky voice muttered, "I am going to bless you," and then she prayed a prayer that I did not at all understand at that point in my life, but which is etched into my memory. "Lars, I bless you! You are going to preach to thousands of people across the world."

I reasoned with my ten-year-old mind that she did not know what she was talking about. My parents had never traveled anywhere outside Sweden with me, let alone gone to the other side of the world. Our vacations usually consisted of taking a bus and a boat to my Dad's uncle's farm on one of the islands in the Stockholm archipelago. We did not have a car and the only way my parents had traveled any distance was by an old tandem bicycle, which had a flat tire halfway to where they were heading! And I didn't yet know the Lord. In fact, in those pre-puberty years I somewhat detested anything that had to do with publicly displaying Christian faith.

Of course, long before that incident we often played church services at home. My sister and her dolls were forced to be the congregation. Sometimes my mother and father attended Lars' church as well. In one greatly inspired, tongue-twisted prayer, the young child-preacher wished that the Lord "would make all well people sick!" However, this was far from the reality I sensed in my grandmother's prayer.

I had joined a music school, and while I had given up on the violin, it became obvious that I needed to learn another instrument to be able to continue. Being tall, they equipped me with the string bass, the largest instrument in the violin family, and my teacher became one of the leading bass players from the Stockholm Philharmonic Orchestra. Week after week, he came to my school and patiently taught me and a few others, until I could master the instrument. After a year of training I was asked to play in the music school's symphony orchestra.

The school gave quite a few concerts and being the youngest bass player, I was given the added responsibility to move three string basses every time we had a concert. It took three taxies to transport the instruments. Once we had a concert in an old church in Stockholm, and before the concert we stored all the instrument cases in the basement, where people's remains were stored in urns after their cremation. After the concert, everyone left and I went down to place the three string basses in their cases. Suddenly I heard the lock turn and realized that the caretaker had locked me in with the hundreds of urns in the basement. Desperately I cried for help and was let out!

Steps to Conversion

One year a young flamboyant American preacher came to visit Sweden for a few days, and my father and mother took me along to hear him. My mother had seen some newspaper articles about the preacher and was rather upset that his wife seemed to have earrings and lipstick. Surely, no one could go to heaven with such worldly adornments! The concert stage at the nature park of Skansen, Stockholm, was the location for the evening service and some 30,000 people gathered to hear the 35-year-old Billy Graham. People were jammed so tight that there was standing room only. Quite a few fainted in the heat.

Suddenly the music started and the song leader, Cliff Barrows, came to the microphone, playing his trombone, dressed in a light suit and rather gaudy tie and leading some favorite gospel songs with great gusto. I was flabbergasted at the way this man seemed to show his Christianity - he really enjoyed telling people about Jesus! Billy Graham then strolled to the podium and preached a message that I cannot remember, apart from the extremely dynamic way it was presented. That evening had a profound impact on my ten-year-old heart, and laid the foundation for my understanding of the evangelistic message and sharing Christ outside of church.

A few years later, in 1957, a citywide crusade was held in Stockholm. The Christian Business Men's Association of Sweden had responded to the challenge to establish an interdenominational crusade team, representing the best preachers from the Baptists, Covenant church, Pentecostals and The Salvation Army. The Swedish crusade team had been inspired by Billy Graham's team, and had taken on many of its attributes and mannerisms, except for the length of the crusades. For several years this team had held month-long crusades all over Sweden before they attempted to "conquer" the capital.

The Stockholm crusade was held from the beginning of January to the beginning of March, with meetings almost every night. The churches of Stockholm joined together for these meetings and thousands of people thronged into an old church building in central Stockholm, which seated some 3,000 people. My parents and my sister sang in the choir most nights, and since I did not want to sit at home alone, I came with them. Sitting in one of the two balconies I would study my school homework while the choir practiced their warm-up routines.

I had a love-hate relationship with this crusade. I was fascinated by the dramatic preaching, the atmosphere as people walked forward to commit their lives to Christ and by the lively, inspiring music. But I also hated the public awareness this crusade was creating in my neighborhood. It made headline news in the secular press and most of the time the coverage was not very positive. People were talking about it, friends at school asked about it and the kids on the street knew that somehow the "religious Dunbergs" had to be associated with it in one form or another.

I fought against the message preached every night. It was personal and radical and it cut deep into the bones of my 12-year old self. As we traveled home by streetcar every night, my parents would hint to me, "Lars, don't you think that this is the right time for you to commit your life to Christ?" My mother's eyes would well up with tears and her voice would tremble a bit, and I felt extremely awkward. The more they hinted, the more uncomfortable I became. I just wanted to be left alone to sort out my faith on my own.

Finally, the next to last night of the crusade came. The old church had several levels of balconies, and I preferred to sit at the front row on the top one, peering down on the crowds below. Rev. Berthil Paulsson, Sweden's Billy Graham, was preaching that night and I felt that his message was only for me. "He who comes to me I will certainly not throw out," echoed through the massive church. That was not Reverend Paulsson speaking to me, it was Jesus!

The past few months, without my parents knowing, I had been going out almost every night with a gang of boys who liked to run around, knocking out the lights in the street lamps with sling shots. At times we also enjoyed scaring old ladies by sneaking up behind them, surprising them with sudden loud noises or screaming in their ears, and watching the results when they would drop their handbags out of fright. We never stole anything, we just liked to scare them.

Other times, we would go down to a lake that was just a few minutes from my home. In the winter we jumped out on the thin ice, leaping from one ice block to the other, finding our balance while the water seeped between the ice blocks. There were times when I lost my balance and slipped down between the ice blocks. It was a miracle I did not drown in the ice-cold water. I would go to a friend's house, try to dry my wet clothes on the radiators, then sneak home, lying about what had happened. Jumping on the ice at the lake was absolutely forbidden. But suddenly, as I heard Jesus speaking to me I realized I was the biggest sinner in the world. Was it true that Jesus would receive - even me?

When the invitation to receive Christ was given directly after the message I could hardly wait to rush down to the front of the church.

Unfortunately, in my eagerness to get down from the balcony, I took the wrong staircase. When I opened the door in front of me, which I believed led to the main sanctuary of the church, I found myself out on the street! At that point it would have been easier to just go home, but I turned around, hurried through the right door and walked forward with many others. As Rev. Paulsson prayed the prayer for us to commit our lives to Jesus, I prayed with all the sincerity of a twelve-year-old's heart. In the counseling room I struggled through the first sheet of the correspondence Bible course, designed by the Navigators. It was not very user friendly for my age group, and I was embarrassed that I did not understand all the questions. I was already six foot three and people thought I was much older. However, that night, my grandmother's earlier prayer made sense for the first time in my life.

A Rich History

I could hardly wait to share my faith. I simply had to become an evangelist. Although difficult at first, I began sharing my faith at school with my friends and found to my surprise that quite a few of the people in my class at school also had parents who went to church, and that they went with them. Somehow, they had never let anyone know that they were in the same boat as I was.

About a year after my conversion, the church that my parents belonged to decided it was time to renovate their facilities. One of their decisions was to close a little library, which had been maintained for many years. Seeing a pile of hundreds of books lying outside of what had been the library, I went to the pastor and asked if I could buy these books. We set a price of $15 and the 300 titles changed hands. Many of them were very old, but among them were several books that in time would shape my entire life.

As I carried the books home over a couple of days I began to realize what I had purchased. There were biographies of Dwight L. Moody and Ira Sankey, William Carey, Charles Spurgeon, Billy Sunday and Hudson Taylor. There were books describing the revivals sweeping across Europe in the 19th century, Swedish revival history and the stories of Charles Finney and Jonathan Edwards.

I was especially fascinated by Dwight L. Moody, Charles Spurgeon and Billy Sunday. Moody had filled the largest auditoriums across the US and Britain, yet he was an unlearned man. I could identify with him. Among the collection was a book of Sankey's hymns, and I sang them to myself in my room. I also studied the pictures in the books and then practiced "the preacher gestures" in front of the mirror. Who would become a Dwight Moody or a Billy Sunday or even a Billy Graham in my generation?

Charles Spurgeon was special too, because he never went to seminary but he loved to read, just like me. Often he had to use other buildings than his church, as so many people flocked to hear him. London's Crystal Palace was a massive glass structure seating 30,000 people, and his voice was so loud that it could carry across the entire audience. He had a sermon for every situation.

And then there was Billy Sunday. I carefully copied many of his sayings down in a book and memorized them. Here was a man that called sin "sin," who could speak with his whole body, catch the crowds and hold them. I read, prayed and cried, "Lord, raise up new people like Moody, Spurgeon, Sunday and Graham!"

Sweden had been swept up by the Reformation in Europe in the early 16th century, followed by years of focused orthodoxy. The country had a united church to which everyone who was born in Sweden, belonged. Its focus was on right doctrine, liturgy and correct church order. This often resulted in sound doctrine without meaningful spiritual life and people went to church out of duty, more focused on following the letter of the law than learning what it meant to live a daily life of faith.

During the beginning of the 18th century two revival movements landed in Sweden: the Pietistic movement from Germany and the Herrnhut movement from Bohemia (now in the Czech Republic). These movements were transported to Sweden by Swedish prisoners of war, the one-time great warriors from king Carolus XII's war in Russia and the East. After the king's death in 1718 the prisoners of war began to return to Sweden in droves. Many of them had come in contact with the Herrnhut revival and the Pietists, who helped them realize their own sinful nature which resulted in their conversions and deeper spiritual life.

The pietistic teaching started with a German Lutheran clergyman in Frankfurt am Main, Philip Jakob Spener. Through his writings he shaped the teaching of the Pietists, making sure every age group was taught pietist values. It was important to have a personal, living faith, which was received through repentance and conversion. Simply being baptized into the church as an infant was not enough to guarantee a place in heaven.

Through small gatherings in homes, similar to today's cell groups, the teachings of the Pietists spread across northern Europe. Often lay people led these groups. The universal priesthood of believers was an important tenet of the Pietists: every Christian should become a missionary wherever he or she lived.

The other great leader for the Pietists was August Herman Francke. He made the city of Halle in Germany the center for Pietism. Here, students came from different countries to study. Through his own studies of Scripture, Francke realized that the world needed to be evangelized and so he stressed the importance of worldwide mission. Francke started an institution to spread Bibles across the world, which became a forerunner to the Bible society movement around the globe. Francke was also a pioneer in encouraging the church to take social responsibility for the needy.

The founder of the Herrnhut movement was Count Nicolaus Ludvig von Zinzendorf. In Herrnhut he founded a Brethren church for the refugees who were fleeing the surrounding areas because of persecution of their faith. In his core teachings Zinzendorf stressed three things. First of all, the atonement. There was a strong emphasis on "the blood and the wounds of Christ." Secondly, he had a concern for worldwide mission. The world had to be reached with the message of Christ. Thirdly he stressed that the Christian faith needed to be joyful and compassionate. Zinzendorf used to say, "I have only one passion: It's Him, only Him!"

The people from Herrnhut had many intriguing characteristics. They sure could pray. One of their prayer meetings was so intense it lasted unbroken for 100 years! Their mission efforts were endless. They did not just go to a country and lead people through conversion, they also ensured the people were discipled and taught a trade so they could provide for their families.

As the soldiers and officers of the defeated Swedish Army returned, they shared the need for their families and neighbors to get right with God and find the Savior. This did not sit well with the Swedish clergy in the state controlled Lutheran church. Many clergy members were heavy drinkers, and carried out their ministerial duties under less than Christian conditions. This new spiritual awakening became a real threat to their status quo. When the "new" believers insisted that they could no longer take communion in the church together with people who did not really know the Lord, they began meeting in homes and rented school halls for communion services for believers only. The government, spurred on by the bishops, halted that kind of behavior.

A new law was quickly voted in, which forbade religious gatherings in homes unless an ordained Lutheran priest was present. From 1726 until 1858, the local sheriffs or the city police would visit many a home and school hall and drag believers from an ongoing service, handcuff them, place them in a horse-drawn cart and take them to the county jail.

During this time a preacher from Great Britain named George Scott began visiting Sweden and introduced the Methodist church. Meanwhile a Swede who had been to the USA, F. O. Nilsson, returned with a new "sectarian" doctrine and began to secretly baptize the first Baptist believers in the sea in southern Sweden.

This was a time to stand up for your faith and be counted. Despite all these difficulties, thousands of people sought the Lord and found life in Jesus Christ. In homes and in private gatherings, people met to read sermons and religious pamphlets, but most of all, studied the Word. "Where is it written?" was the battle cry, which finally gave the new believers a nickname *läsare* which means readers. I can still remember the scorn I felt, when some young people at school threw that phrase in my face.

In the 19th century two giants emerged in the development of a Swedish version of the Pietist movement. Both were clergymen in the Swedish Lutheran Church and had been affected by the exploding growth of believers within and without the church, since the law against gatherings of believers in other places than the church, or with a clergy present had been repealed in 1858.

C. O. Rosenius published the magazine *The Pietist*, featuring sermons and devotionals by itinerant preachers as well as some more educated academics. One of those was P. P. Waldenström.

"To be made righteous through faith by grace" was the ongoing theme of the sermons and publications. In cottages, school halls and newly-renovated chapels, farmers and teachers, maids and matrons knelt down side by side to confess their sin and accept the work on the cross by Jesus on their behalf.

The word pictures of the Pietists in those days would be a bit too much for us today. Expressions like "Let's plunge in the fountain of blood" and being "bathed in the blood" and resting "in the wounds of the crucified" were among the more vivid descriptions of their excitement about their faith.

An intense theological battle arose over the right interpretation of the atonement. While Rosenius clearly proclaimed that Christ died as a substitute for our sins, to please a God of wrath that could not be satisfied in any other way, Waldenström pointed out that God sent Christ to atone our sins because of God's love and concern for the world. After many years of battles in magazines and in public, the two parted ways and one person's truth became another person's heresy.

Rosenius went on and joined a "low church movement" within the Swedish Lutheran Church. Waldenström joined another group, who in opposition to the Swedish Lutheran Church wanted to conduct communion services only for those who had a personal faith in Jesus Christ. This group, with Waldenström as one of its leaders, founded the Covenant Church of Sweden, the church from which both the Evangelical Covenant Church of North America and the Evangelical Free Church in the USA later originated from.

The library I had purchased also contained books describing more recent Church movements in Sweden, such as the explosion of the Pentecostal Church, which in my youth had grown to be the largest denomination in Sweden.

Responding to the Call

As I read through these old, dusty books filled with stories of conversions, church growth, victories and setbacks, led by original personalities who dared to stand up, take risks and be counted whatever the cost, I was deeply moved. God was speaking to me through the pages and the characters. "Lars, I will do it again, I will do it again." And again, my grandmother's prayer rang in my ears, "You will preach to thousands." My first challenge to become a risk-taker for God was beginning to take shape. I can clearly say that, apart from the Word of God, nothing impacted me more in my youth, than God's Work through people's lives in the rich history of the Church.

During these formative years my parents brought me along to many different services in various denominational churches. Churches in Sweden in those days seemed to cooperate much more, and many churches seemed to be on fire.

Since our own church never held services on Saturdays and Sunday night services had became scarce, we often would visit the huge Filadelfia Church, which had 7,000 members and hear visiting preachers from England or the USA. I was fascinated how the interpreters could be so quick to translate the meaning of what just had been said. I never dreamed that I would preach there myself someday.

At an early age I realized that while we may have some theological idiosyncrasies and see some issues from different angles, we Christians are really a large family that will live together in eternity. This understanding was an immense help as I became active in inter-denominational activities through most of my ministry years.

Whenever there was a crusade, I would go night after night, listen and be moved to tears as the invitation for people to come forward to receive Christ was given. During the summers, such crusade meetings were held in huge circus-like tents. The tents had sawdust on the floor and were heated by kerosene heaters or generators pumping in heated air. There is no smell like the smell of a Swedish tent crusade. Later in life I would conduct many crusade meetings in that kind of atmosphere.

Another one of the great Swedish evangelists came to Stockholm for a tent crusade that lasted just over a month. Every night I played clarinet in the orchestra and studied Rev. John Hedlund up close. I memorized many of his phrases, practiced his gestures and finally plucked up courage to go and see him in his circus-like wagon behind the huge tent.

"So you want to be an evangelist," he said with his sharp, deep voice. "Then I have but one bit of advice to give you. Study all you can, get an undergraduate degree, and then a master's degree, and perhaps even a doctor's degree! Then you may be fit to be an evangelist."

That was not the answer I expected or wanted. Suddenly, I saw another 10-12 years of studies ahead of me and walked away, disappointed at his answer but more determined than ever to become an evangelist as soon as possible.

CHAPTER 4
In God's Army

As part of one of my high school extra-curricular projects, I decided to prepare a major paper on the revival movements in Sweden. Among all church denominations mentioned in my paper, one was missing - The Salvation Army.

I had heard many stories about The Army from my mother, because her father's sister Matilda had met The Salvation Army in Stockholm as a revival movement about 1886, committed her life to Christ and after a short training, began serving as a pioneer officer in Sweden. In 1892 she volunteered to go to America as a missionary. On the way to the new mission field, the group of hopeful missionaries stopped in London. As they met with General William Booth in his office, the world leader for The Salvation Army asked Matilda, "Instead of going to North America, would you consider going to South America as one of our pioneer officers?" Matilda thought for a minute. "North America or South America, it is all the same to me!" and so she set sail for Buenos Aires.

A young man named Alfred Benwell lived in Shoeburyness in Essex and worked at The Salvation Army headquarters in London. One day, when he was 17, he was asked if he was ready to go to South America and help some missionary officers. He asked, "When does the ship sail?" and was told in typical Army ways, "On Tuesday!"

After serving in Buenos Aires for a while, a young Swedish officer, Matilda Bydén, arrived. She sang like a nightingale and won the hearts of the Argentineans as well as Alfred's heart and they soon married.

After a few years the young family returned to Britain where they served for a few more years, and then they were sent to Denmark and on to France, where Matilda died and was buried in 1929, only 63 years old. Uncle Alfred went on to remarry and lead The Salvation Army work in China until World War II broke out, at which time he was sent to lead the work in the Netherlands. After the German occupation of the Netherlands he and his wife were placed under house arrest. Toward the end of the war they were part of a prisoner exchange and settled in California.

My mother was very close to Matilda's and Alfred's daughter Flora, who had also become a Salvation Army officer and served with her husband Sture Larsson in Sweden for many years. Flora's son John (my second cousin) also became an officer and eventually was the national leader first in Great Britain and then in New Zealand and Sweden. He finally served as the General, the world leader of The Salvation Army, while his sister Miriam served as an officer in Denmark, UK and Norway.

We also had a neighbor couple, Mary and Gustaf Kolm, who were soldiers (members) in the local Salvation Army church. He let me borrow a few books about The Salvation Army. Once again, I had little idea then what an impact the content of these books would have on my life.

Among those books were biographies of William and Catherine Booth, the founders of The Salvation Army, and a book chronicling history of the first 50 years of The Salvation Army in Sweden. As I read those early encounters of the pioneers of The Salvation Army, my heart was thrilled. This was evangelism I could relate to. It was radical, it was fresh, it reached the down-and-out people, and it was filled with "passion for souls and for the worst!"

Stirred by Pioneers

William Booth was a young Methodist preacher who had been called by God to be an evangelist. His wife Catherine was just as much on fire as her husband. In 1865, due to internal resistance to his work in the Methodist church, William and Catherine resigned and launched the Christian Mission, an organization that soon employed hundreds of evangelists, sharing the gospel with the poorest of the poor. It did not take long before William, as the general superintendent, was simply called "the general." In 1878 his son Bramwell worked with his father on the headline to a magazine editorial called, "We will be a voluntary army." When Bramwell simply changed the word "voluntary" to "Salvation," The Salvation Army was born. The young evangelists became captains who "opened fire," establishing new centers for worship and evangelism across England and later the world.

One of those pioneers was Elijah Cadman. He was a dwarf-like man who had once been a chimney sweeper. God saved him and turned the former drunkard to a trophy of grace. When Elijah Cadman was sent to a new town to open fire he would turn the entire city upside-down. Loud music, as well as bass drums, placards and posters with incredible slogans would bring people to the services by the hundreds.

Frederick de Latour Tucker was a British aristocrat who had been born and raised in colonial India. Returning to Britain he came into contact with The Salvation Army and sensed God's call to ministry. Marrying Booth's daughter, Emma, and hyphenating his name to Booth-Tucker, the couple set sail with a handful of others to introduce The Army to India.

As the ship arrived in Bombay, dignitaries on the Quay side welcomed them with surprising voices, "Where is the Army? We heard an Army was coming!" They looked on suspiciously as the nine salvationists came off the ship. However, within a few years that small army had exploded to a mighty force, reaching out to help with India's enormous physical and spiritual problems. Booth-Tucker and his followers laid aside any hint of British aristocracy. They wore Indian dress, ate poverty-level food and walked barefoot everywhere until their feet blistered and bled. Through these stories from India I saw Christian workers who identified with the people they had gone to serve. Today The Salvation Army church has more than a quarter million members in India alone.

Another pioneer was Scott Railton, William Booth's friend and advisor. Booth sent Railton with some Salvation Amy lassies to open fire in North America. At the farewell meeting Booth prayed, "Lord, make them succeed - and if they won't succeed, let the ship sink on its way there!"

Saintly Commissioner David Rees used to spend hours on his knees everyday with one single prayer on his lips, "Lord, give me a clean heart." For some years he led The Salvation Army in Sweden as well as Canada, before he had an untimely death in 1914. Together with salvationists from Canada he boarded a ship bound for the international congress in London, *Empress of Ireland*, which sank in a storm at the mouth of the St. Lawrence River. As there were not enough life vests for everyone, many of the salvationists handed theirs to others. These people knew they were on their way to heaven, so why worry about death? Kneeling on deck, surrounded by praying salvationists, Rees and his companions drowned.

Samuel Logan Brengle was a congregational minister in Boston when he came across The Salvation Army. Moved by its fervor he traveled to London to meet William Booth, who sent him to the training college for future officers.

There, the dynamic, eloquent speaker was placed to clean the shoes of his fellow students! What could have caused bitterness and grief became a further stepping stone for Brengle to a holier life. His prayer was, "If you want me to stutter, I will still serve you."

Brengle became the leading teacher of The Salvation Army doctrine of holiness and wrote scores of books on the subject as he traveled the world leading people, both within and outside the Army, into a deeper walk with the Lord.

General Booth's own daughter Catherine Booth was barely out of her teens when she was sent to France to open fire for The Salvation Army's pioneer work in this rather pagan nation. Nicknamed *Le Maréchal* by her father, she and a few other young Salvation Army ladies started a work in the worst slums of Paris which is still going on today. Their youth knew no fear and that boldness brought the gospel to thousands of French people.

Single-mindedness and focus was well portrayed in the lives of two Salvation Army officers, George Pollard and Edward Wright, who were sent from England in 1883 to "take New Zealand for Christ." After a short stop in Australia, where they found three helpers, they sailed for Dunedin, New Zealand. On the way Pollard told Wright, "You go to Auckland in the North and I'll go to Dunedin in the south. We'll work towards Wellington in the middle and shake hands when we get there."

They arrived in April 1883. Nine months later the Army had its first congress in Wellington with thirty officers (full-time pastors, mainly New Zealanders) and 500 soldiers (church members) who had further signed up to work full-time. In nine months The Salvation Army had seen over 5,000 converts. It was the greatest revival in the history of New Zealand. They literally took New Zealand for Christ.

A young Swede, Karl Larsson, heard the gospel in the province of Småland, and became an avid follower of Jesus Christ. Entering into full-time service he was willing to become a risk-taker, and pioneered the work of The Salvation Army into Russia. He lived through the Russian revolution, pioneered the work into Czechoslovakia as well as served the Army in Europe, which was cut off from its heart-center London during World War II. As a young boy I had heard Karl Larsson speak, and was mesmerized by this white-haired giant in Christ. It was his son Sture, who married my mother's cousin Flora.

Joining the Army

As I read the pages of Army history, many stories like these came to the forefront and impregnated me with the idea that risk-taking, boldness, holiness and being a fool for Christ would bring others into the Kingdom. The question growing within me was simply, "How do I enroll in such an Army?"

I could hardly wait for the next weekend. I knew where I was going to worship that following Sunday night. As I sat in the last row in the local Salvation Army church, listening to very much the same passion, the same fervor I had read about in these books, and seeing the same kind of people finding the Lord Jesus Christ, I knew I was in the right place.

That night, the local Salvation Army hall had a visit from the Salvation Army training college for officers, and these young students were fired up! Their testimonies, music accompanied by accordions and guitars, and radical preaching about salvation confirmed that I had found the place where I wanted to serve God.

In the late 1950s, The Salvation Army still used the traditional revival meeting format. As the fiery message came to an end, the singers began to sing softly while the speaker urged people to come forward to kneel at the altar which in Army terms is called the mercy seat or the penitent-form. Other young people slowly came down from the platform, walked through the hall, and found someone they felt led to talk to. They simply sat down to speak to that person. Later I learned that this was called "pew fishing" and I was amazed at their boldness. One of the students became so exited that he jumped over a couple of pews to get from one person to the next. This was probably confrontational evangelism at its worst, but in those days it was acceptable and fascinated a fourteen-year old young man, who that very day was dreaming about becoming an evangelist!

Sunday after Sunday I went to The Salvation Army, reading more and more of the books and magazines, learning about their work and structure around the world. I even wrote letters to their international headquarters trying to find out as much information as possible.

After visiting the local Salvation Army church for more than a year I was ready to take a major step and join their forces. On November 22, 1959 I was sworn in as a soldier of The Salvation Army by Major Arne Weibull, the commanding officer of the Stockholm III corps (church). On a Sunday night, not long after that, the bandmaster of the brass band, a rather gruff man, named Stig Bengtsson, placed an old beaten cornet in my hand and muttered, "Learn the basics and make sure you are here at band practice on Wednesday." I knew how to play the string bass, but this was a brass instrument. I had never attempted any brass instruments, because my father played a wind instrument, the clarinet, and therefore I had tried to be obedient by having clarinet lessons since I was twelve. I was not sure that playing a brass instrument suited my lips!

But my interests were not just in music. I wanted to see people come into the Kingdom, and I wanted to see the worst! Many nights I would go and visit the pubs and restaurants of Stockholm, distributing The Salvation Army paper the "War Cry" as well as sharing the gospel to the down-and-outs, telling them that Jesus loved them. For a fifteen-year-old this was rather frightening and it took all my courage every time as I walked through the pub doors, fully prepared to be sneered at and certainly laughed at.

During this time I had moved from the Swedish middle school to the senior high school. I was not a very good student. Languages were particularly difficult for me. In those days children began learning English in 5th grade, German in 7th grade and French in 9th grade. I struggled with math, physics, chemistry and biology, while history, geography and religious instruction were my favorites. The school I attended was a special music school, so apart from orchestra rehearsals every day we also had music theory, conducting, music history and choir.

"Follow Me"

When I was in High School, the Lord clearly started to speak to me. I knew that the Lord wanted me to serve Him full-time, but I was only sixteen years old. They didn't have sixteen-year old preachers even in The Salvation Army! To enter their training college for full-time service I needed to be at least 18. Over and over the words from Luke 9:23-5 came to me:

"Then he (Jesus) said to them all: 'If anyone would come after me, he must deny himself and take up his cross daily and follow me. For whoever wants to save his life for me will love it, but whoever loses his life for me will save it. What good is it for a man to gain the whole world, and yet lose or forfeit his very self?'"

I knew I had heard Jesus say, "Follow me." I knew He was calling me. But how could that happen? Long discussions with my parents soon followed. I worked hard at convincing them that Algebra and English had nothing to do with following Jesus and were not needed to become a preacher and would certainly not bring anyone into the Kingdom of God!

The message of Luke 9 became so crystal clear that as I left for school every morning, I would leave all the Bibles I could find at home opened to Luke 9:62, so my mother could come to the same understanding, *"No one who puts his hand to the plow and looks back is fit for service in the kingdom of God."* The words were etched into my teenage heart. The world was going to hell and I was stuck in school! The emotions within me were so strong that I could not sleep at night, I daydreamed at school - and continued to struggle with English, German, French and Math! All my final exams that year in those four subjects came back marked "failed" and more than one parent-teacher conference was held on my behalf.

My mother realized that there had to be a solution to release this tension within me. She and I went for a long walk and talked it through. While I was in my second year toward the *studentexamen* (the foundational exam to enter university) there was at that time another lower type exam available, the *realexamen*, which you could take at age 17. After some discussion with the school principal, I was allowed to step down into this lower form of schooling and suddenly found myself with only four months of schooling left. It became a golden opportunity for fast education! Suddenly my English improved and so did my German. I had already studied the math and therefore I could graduate with honors in the spring of 1961.

After applying for a job with the Swedish Internal Revenue service, I was hired as a tax assistant in the department dealing with delinquent alimony payments from divorced fathers. In the system in those days, these payments were collected right out of the fathers' paychecks, even before the income tax was paid. At seventeen I was placed in charge of a small department with four ladies working with me, and learned from scratch what it means to manage.

I also learned perseverance! Many of these fathers were avoiding the law by changing jobs and addresses frequently, living on the streets, at times with no known forwarding address. It was often just like detective work. We followed leads, made phone calls all over the country as well as abroad and tracked these people down. But inside, I was feeling a great conflict of interest. I wanted to lead these men to Jesus, not rob them of the little money they still possessed!

The Preaching Begins

During this time I had my first preaching opportunity and it almost turned out to be my last. One Monday morning, an officer in The Salvation Army, Captain Gunvor Bodin in Nynäshamn, called me to inform me that she would be gone the following Sunday. "Lars, can you come and take the service?" Nynäshamn is a town not more than 25 miles away from Stockholm and I immediately said yes, sensing that this was an invitation from God to "try my wings."

That whole week I couldn't eat, not because of a deeply rooted spirituality leading me to a weeklong fast, but because of nervousness. I borrowed my father's Bible, which was big and looked impressive. It contained maps and had soft leather binding with yaps (covers that overhung) and it was well worn, which would add to my public image of spiritual maturity. I found a book of sermons by Commissioner Karl Larsson, the old Army veteran, and carefully chose the one that I felt was the hottest subject. "Flee for your life" was the Lord's message to Lot in Genesis 19, as he attempted his escape from the condemned city of Sodom.

Although I had memorized the entire sermon, I felt the delivery was a disaster. If this was what it was like to preach, I would never again stand up in front of a crowd. I returned home feeling utterly spent and a complete failure.

A few days later the phone rang again. It was another Salvation Army officer, Captain Vincent Wiberg from Hallstavik and he called to tell me that he had heard that I had spoken in Nynäshamn. "Can you come and bring a group of musicians with you to Hallstavik for a long weekend?" And so it started. Sunday after Sunday I would travel to different places, sharing Christ, learning to put messages together, eager to share the burden God had given me from the Word. It did not take me long to understand the preacher's creed, "Borrowing from one is plagiarism; borrowing from many is research."

After working for a year I had scraped together enough money to pay for the tuition at The Salvation Army School for Officers Training as well as being ready to leave home.

As I prepared myself for the School for Officers Training, I was still struggling for assurance regarding my calling. When the time came closer to begin my studies, I prayed, "God, please show me clearly that this is your will. Let me know beyond a shadow of a doubt that you want me to serve you in full-time ministry." Soon after that prayer, I was asked to conduct a Saturday night meeting at my own Salvation Army church. The young people of the church would share in song and music and I would lead the service and preach. People rarely wanted to leave their TVs to go to church on Saturday nights, but I decided to take on the challenge. When young people gathered for several weeks beforehand in prayer, I told them, "We are going to hold this meeting for the Lord Jesus Christ." Handbills and posters were made, pasted on walls and circulated and as we continued to pray, our prayer was, "Lord, perform a miracle among us."

I also made a personal pledge, almost a fleece, with the Lord. "I want to see this hall filled. As I ask for people to seek God, let me see the mercy seat surrounded by people seeking your face. By this I will know that you have called me." This prayer was not prayed out of a desire to be great or famous, but because I desperately needed the confirmation that the Lord could use a young and fairly uneducated person.

To my amazement the hall was filled when we marched in from the prayer meeting and we shared our testimonies and songs with gusto. My sermon was taken from Acts 3:12-21, which was Peter's sermon to the onlookers in Solomon's Colonnade in the Jerusalem temple. As I invited people to come forward to dedicate their lives to the Lord, row after row after row of pews filled with people kneeling, seeking the Lord with tears, and many gave their lives to Christ that night. With amazement I watched the Lord answer prayer and confirm stronger than ever His purposes in my life.

Training College

Throughout 1961 and part of 1962 I went through the selection process, complete with interviews and written exams, to be accepted at the Training College for officers in Stockholm. A few years earlier the educational program had been expanded from a one-year school to a two-year school. While the training program had been ongoing since 1883, the actual building used in the 70's had been built in 1915 and was a Salvation Army landmark. The building was eventually sold and turned into a hotel.

The curriculum was fairly basic for any Bible college: New Testament, Old Testament, Homiletics, Doctrine, Church History as well as Salvation Army history. Because the officers also had to oversee much of the administration, there were also basic courses in accounting and statistics. Basic English and learning how to lead church services in English was also part of the weekly studies.

The training that most shaped my life was the spiritual and practical dimension. I truly enjoyed the prayer meetings and the spiritual emphasis days, when leaders who in my eyes were spiritual giants shared their own hearts and the Word of God. And, of course, we were out almost every weekend holding services at various Salvation Army churches in Stockholm. A huge leather box that had been used by other students for more than 50 years was filled with sandwiches and every late Sunday afternoon we would march away to some corps (church), flag in front and the leather box between us. Now and then we took the streetcar, especially in bad weather.

As I observed some of the teachers, I began to get a glimpse of what it means to be a role model. The officer in charge of the male students, Erik Gustafsson and his wife Rut, had served with the Army for 30 years before coming to the Training College. Erik was a serious student of the Word of God and could exposit it in a way that I had never heard before. By sharing examples from his time in ministry he influenced us one by one to discover our potential and be obedient to the will of God in our lives, whatever may come in our way.

Anders Wigholm was the educational officer. He had one great hobby and that was to study prophecy. Today he would probably be categorized as an extremely conservative fundamentalist, but he taught me to trust the Word of God beyond any shadow of a doubt. He was a firm believer in the biblical record of creation, and was always quoting new books coming from Britain and the USA. Often he would stray from the subject at hand as he stood in front of the class, and develop some theme he had read that morning. He was well versed in Hebrew and Greek, and would write the characters on the black board while his squeaky voice became more and more excited. It was Anders Wigholm who introduced me to the English Christian publishing world and to such exotic sounding publishing names as Zondervan, Baker, Eerdmans and Paternoster Press. He would lend me their book catalogues, and encourage me to order books to study these topics further.

The officer's school in Sweden was a time of learning discipline. I decided that the best learning time was not during school hours but before they started. So I turned the temperature down in my room to make sure I would wake up at 4.00 a.m. every morning, not by my alarm clock, but by it being so cold that I had to get up. With a blanket wrapped around me I would study all kinds of books, not just theological books and books on Army history, but other subjects as well. My sister was just then graduating as a registered nurse and I borrowed all her books on psychiatry, psychology and nursing and I read them cover to cover. From the library I found books on the history of revivals, sermons by famous preachers and I devoured them. All the time I was driven by an inner force to study, learn, apply and then apply again.

One of my major problems in school had been English. I could never grasp language, and time and time again I failed the tests because I simply did not understand how to put this strange language together. One day the principal of the School for Officers, Lieutenant-Colonel George Perry, called me into his office and said, "We have decided to send you to our school in London for the second year. There you will be able to learn English better and this will be an excellent help for you and useful to you and for The Salvation Army in the future."

Risk-Taker for God

The First Trip

In August 1963, I set out for my first major overseas trip to attend the William Booth memorial Training College in London, England.

It was a post-war Britain I arrived in. While the Second World War had ended some 18 years earlier, the reconstruction of war-torn London was still ongoing. Bombed-out buildings, with brick heaps overgrown by grass could still be seen in many parts of London. It wasn't uncommon to hear someone say, "Well, it has been like this since the War, you know." I often wondered why people didn't just make an effort to fix what was broken!

My first assignment with a group of students to the suburb of Deptford shocked me. The area around The Salvation Army church had been severely bombed, and one of the walls of The Salvation Army building as well as the roof still had gaping holes. The dampness in the building, offset by gas heaters giving their smelly heat, did not alleviate the chills that everyone experienced throughout the services.

The William Booth Memorial Training College for Officer's Training at Denmark Hill, London was opened in 1929 and was designed by the same architect who designed the University library in Cambridge. The school is dominated by a tall tower and when the school was built The Salvation Army had hoped to install a major beacon, which would spread its light over the south of London. But because airplanes and zeppelins began to fly over the city around the same time, the permission was never granted.

The Salvation Army headquarters at 101, Queen Victoria Street had been completely destroyed by bombs during the Second World War and since then the headquarters had shared space with students at the International Training College. This created closeness to the worldwide movement and the students at the college bumped into the worldwide leaders of the Army on a daily basis. A few months after I arrived at the college, the Queen Mother opened the new headquarters building and I was chosen to be in the honor guard. It was a great experience to be addressed by the Queen Mother as she walked through the hall where we stood in line.

The college in London was completely different from the tiny school in Stockholm. In Stockholm, there were 33 in my class the first year and 30 in the second year. In London there were 300 students in the school and many of them came from other parts of the world. For the first time I was exposed to cultural behavior from other nations, and what it meant to live out your cultural heritage with a group of people from different nations.

Five of us from five different nations created a brotherhood: Dirk Verpoorte from Holland, who had met the Army in Kinshasa and come to the Lord there, Francois Thöni from Switzerland, Erling Maeland from Norway, Keith Banks from Britain and myself. We met almost every night in one of our rooms for coffee and fellowship. We called ourselves "The Fivians." Sometimes Dirk would receive a whole Edam cheese wheel from home and we split it five ways and ate the whole thing! Other times either Erling or I had care packages from Scandinavia and we shared freely. These bonds became so strong that we still have contact with one another.

Learning English

The educational system was obviously different from what I'd known and with my limited English it was extremely difficult to understand the basic instructions, let alone any of the finer points. Throughout every lecture I attempted to memorize a new word or a new phrase, then hurried back to my room and looked that phrase or word up in my English/Swedish dictionary. During the first exams, I was allowed to bring my dictionary, and desperately tried to figure out the essence of the questions.

After a few months they felt that my English had improved enough that I could start to speak publicly. My first sermon was held at Speakers Corner in Hyde Park. That was a real challenge. For each sentence you spoke you would get three back from hecklers. This really helped to improve your self-confidence!

My second sermon in English, given in a small Salvation Army church hall in north London, was an absolute disaster. I could not understand why the people looked so horrified at the young Swede, as he was preaching his heart out about the atonement through Christ's death on the cross. What the Swede did not know is that one of the worst swear words in Anglicized English is the word "bloody" and I was using it frequently, preaching about the "bloody way to the cross."

Although the college was great for theoretical, biblical training, the practical training was what helped shape the evangelistic fervor in my life. Several Saturday afternoons we would march single-file, led by my piano-accordion, down one of the high streets of London's busy shopping areas, where market stalls crowded the entire area and people mingled along the entire street and sidewalks to purchase fruits, vegetables, second-hand clothes and books, instruments and knick-knacks. In the middle of this British Saturday afternoon bazaar we would march in, then stand about a hundred and fifty to two hundred yards apart, each of us starting our own open air meeting. We would sing, preach and share the Word single-handedly, while people threw old tomatoes and at times rotten eggs at us. This was another important experience in gaining confidence! We were indeed fools for Christ and at times perhaps a bit too foolish.

Other times we would go to any length to grab the attention of the British, who usually never stopped to listen to anybody. One of us would pull an old bathtub into the middle of the street and start washing clothes in detergent, while other students would stand next to us and preach about the blood of Jesus which could wash whiter than snow, whiter than any detergent. In this way, the scriptural truths were applied to people.

There were many opportunities to share the gospel, not just with down-and-outs, as we did through juvenile detention centers and The Salvation Army social services programs, but also to the people "of the world." Some nights we were sent to the nightclub district Soho, where there were endless striptease clubs, nightclubs and variety shows. Prostitution was openly rampant in those days. We were sent into the clubs when they had a break to share the gospel with people and we did our best to find ways to get them out of there. Some of these people, who were far from home, testing the "sinful" life in the big city, would walk out with us under conviction and kneel in the gutter as we prayed with them for their salvation.

A New Spiritual Dimension

It was during this year in Britain I had a fresh encounter with the Word of God and the Spirit's presence in my life. Although we were Bible students and busy with the Word of God, I had moved away from the Word, and felt at times that my life was so mixed up and full of lies, temptation, hate, envy and emptiness that there was no way that the Lord could use me. As we traveled out for a special week of meetings in the northern part of England, I felt the lowest I could imagine. Packed like sardines in a mini-van, with me closest to the back doors, I thought to myself, "If these doors fling open and I fall out on the road and die, I am not sure where I am headed." But through a series of events I started to read the Scriptures with new interest: First the book of Acts, then Romans, followed by the life of the Church in the epistles and through these studies the Lord started to speak afresh to me.

One day, after intensive Bible study and prayer, it was like the Lord, through His Spirit, just overwhelmed me in my little cubicle room, and I knelt down by my bed. When I read the pages of my Bible, God's Word spoke to me in a fresh, meaningful way and I knew without a shadow of a doubt that God's Word and His Spirit worked hand in hand to convict people of sin and righteousness. That moment was nothing short of a baptism in love and fire and power from God. In an instant I understood what D. L. Moody, Charles Finney and A. Simpson had talked about when they mentioned "another blessing" in their lives. In that moment I was ready to hug the entire world! Suddenly I had but one desire and that was to live my life for Him and live out that life in a holy way. I sat down and penned letters, which needed to be written to people I had offended and to those I knew that I had harbored resentment to, asking for forgiveness.

On Fridays we had to set aside a few hours for cleaning. Every door in the building had brass kick plates and brass handle knobs, and each window had brass handles. All these had to be polished. The floors were made of reddish slabs that had to be swept, washed and then polished with a sticky red polish. All communal bathrooms and restrooms had to be cleaned. After the public areas had been cleaned, our own rooms had to be dusted and the tiny rugs taken out, shaken and beaten. Around the small walls of each tiny room was a picture rail where we could hang our pictures, and no end of dust gathered on those rails.

Before we could have our own private time off, the officer in charge of our building would come around for inspection. After checking that the brass was properly polished, his fingers would sweep over the picture rails and the bookshelves to ensure that everything was dusted.

One day the "inspector" happened to be my second cousin, John Larsson, who was one of the teachers at the school and later became the world leader of the Salvation Army! Everything was going great, and I was looking forward to a nice break. Suddenly John pointed to the small rug on the floor and inquired, "Have you cleaned this one?" "Yes, of course!" I responded, then added silently to myself, "…but not today!" The evening came and it was time for my devotional prayer, but I could not pray. All I saw before my closed eyes was that tiny rug. Days went by and I still couldn't pray. Then days became weeks. My prayer life had come to an end, all because of a rug!

As the Lord dealt with me on a November day and so thoroughly filled me with His Spirit, I immediately walked down to John Larsson's office and knocked on the door, "Captain Larsson," I said (we were that formal in those days), "I have a confession to make. I lied to you a few weeks ago!" What a relief! 35 years later I reminded him of the incident, which he had totally forgotten.

Graduation

The months went by quickly as I grappled with theological issues, spiritual longings and practical ministry expressions. My vocabulary improved, preaching in a strange language came more natural and working through a different culture became easier. In the beginning I made the typical mistakes of someone entering a new culture for the first time: I criticized everything as being bad. "Why can't the British insulate their houses?" "Why do the Brits let their pipes freeze in the winter by placing them outside their houses instead of inside?" "Why do they separate food into savory and sweet?" And then the language! So many strange spellings! And the use of the word "please" after every request. Swedish does not have a word for "please." At a dinner table we simply ask for the salt or the butter, and people hand it to you. At that point we add "thank you." Many times I was brusquely told off for simply forgetting to add the word "please."

One day one of the students looked me straight in the eyes, while I was complaining and telling a group how things were so much better in Sweden. "Why don't you return there immediately, if it is so much better!" he exclaimed in disgust. My face quickly reddened and I suddenly understood how inappropriate I had been. From that moment forward, I began learning step by step that other cultures are not worse than your own, just different. Toward the end of my year in Britain, I had assimilated a lot of the cultural behavior and felt very much at home and part of daily British life.

My parents and sister made the long journey to London to attend the graduation in The Royal Albert Hall. The ordination service was held in the morning and as the graduates sat on the ground floor of the Hall, I sensed the seriousness in this holy moment. While the voice of the training principal's wife echoed through the building my thoughts wandered to my call to be an evangelist, and I wondered if this was the ultimate fulfillment of God's promises to me. In the background I heard her read from the Scriptures: A charge to Timothy from Paul....preach at all times...

The festive commissioning service was held in the afternoon. During this service, we found out to what Salvation Army church, or other responsibility, we would be sent to. My name was called and I stepped forward to receive the orders from the hand of the second-in-command of The Salvation Army, the chief-of-staff, Commissioner Erik Wickberg. As I came up to him, someone whispered to him, "It is Lars' birthday today!" So on my 20th birthday, May 8, over 7,000 people spontaneously broke out into "Happy birthday to you!" The appointment for me was an immediate special appointment to the music group the *Joystrings*, followed by being second-in-command (associate pastor) at The Salvation Army church in Malmö, Sweden.

Joystrings

During the time I was at the Training College a new world leader was elected for The Salvation Army. At his first press conference, General Frederick Coutts fielded many questions from the secular press regarding the Army's ability to reach out to the youth in the "Swinging Sixties." Beatle-mania was rampant in these days and the press eagerly asked the new leader how The Salvation Army would meet those musical needs among modern young people? Surely the new General would realize that while brass bands may have been at the top of the list of the musical communication tools in the last century, it would not meet the needs of today's youth pop culture. General Coutts confirmed that The Salvation Army would be able to use all the modern methods to communicate the gospel, even through a group similar to the Beatles.

The following day the secular press had a heyday with cartoons and headlines featuring the "with it" Salvation Army. The day after that, the press called for evidential photos. In desperation the new General called the Training College and asked their music department to bail him out.

Risk-Taker for God

One of the music teachers, Captain Joy Webb, had written many popular songs and experimented a bit with guitar music and even formed a Dixieland band. But a pop group like the Beatles? That was an enormous challenge in 1963. Joy Webb took a group of female students and promised to pose for pictures. Those pictures were taken in front of the Houses of Parliament and The Salvation Army lassies were photographed from all angles with Big Ben in the background.

Then came the real challenge. On a Friday, the "Tonight" TV program called and wanted a music feature in their Tuesday evening program. No such music group existed yet! The Army's publicity department also called and pressed for some men to be included as well.

Quickly, Joy thought of Peter Dalziel, a young student who had recently arrived from Australia. Peter brought along his friend Bill Davidson, who was a great singer but could not play a guitar. Overnight he was taught how! Another teacher at the school, Handel Everett, borrowed an old string bass from a school, a drummer was "imported" and a group was formed.

One of Joy Webb's songs was rearranged for pop sound and overnight the *Joystrings* became a hit with her popular, "It's an Open Secret." That song had been born right at the Training College. At a New Year's party for the teachers a year before, Joy in a relaxed atmosphere with a cup of coffee in her hand waas listening to the wife of the Training Principal read the Scriptures. She was reading the words of Paul from the Living Letters, which had just been published. *"Our love for Christ is an open secret."* The word "secret" stuck in Joy's mind. In no time she had penned the words that would be sung on streets, buses and the London "underground" by literally millions of Brits:

> *It's an open secret that Jesus is mine*
> *It's an open secret, this gladness divine*
> *It's an open secret, I want you to know,*
> *It's an open secret, I love my Savior so.*

After the *Joystrings* cut their first single, the group began to sing on TV-shows, at night clubs, for radio programs and concerts, and within weeks the group made it onto the secular charts, the top of the pops, together with groups like the Beatles.

One day I was called into the principal's office and was surprised to see Captain Joy Webb in there. "We know that you play the string bass…" she began, because I had played bass in her Dixieland band from time to time. "Well, the bass player in the *Joystrings* will be transferred from the college, and we need to replace him," added the principal. "We want you to go on tour with the *Joystrings*, as soon as you graduate."

The day after graduation, we began a hectic tour. We rode in a rented minibus that barely could hold the eight group members. The string bass was strapped onto the roof, but as soon as it began to rain, the bus screeched to a halt and we all ran out to get the bass down. We sat for hours with it on our knees, packed together with our luggage in the back of the van. Driving the bus was a young officer from the Training College, Alex Hughes, who became one of my closest friends. Before he retired he was the leader for the work of The Salvation Army in Great Britain.

We would leave the school on a Saturday morning and travel around Britain until the following Thursday night. After the concert that night, we would drive home to the Training College to have a day of laundry, personal business and rest. Being "on the road" was tough. There were interviews, people wanting to talk to you everywhere, autographs, setting up and packing it all down. Day after day.

Every night we played for full concert halls or theaters, seating 3,000-5,000 people. The daytime was filled with performances on the local radio, national TV, or at open-air concerts, such as on the steps of St. Paul's Cathedral in London, where we caused traffic to come to a halt for two hours at lunchtime.

Many people were horrified that Christian people could sing Christian lyrics to this kind of musical accompaniment, but some of the critics changed their minds after sitting through one of the concerts, seeing secular young people filling the concert halls, hearing the gospel through our songs and then listening to the clear, simple message being preached and observing people coming forward to receive Christ night after night. During those intensive weeks, hundreds of young men and women found Christ, through a gospel presentation that in those days was revolutionary. Some were shocked by our methods, but I learned that the Lord can use all kinds of methods to convincingly bring His message to the hearts of people who otherwise never would have been touched by the gospel.

The day before my departure to Sweden, one of the largest Swedish daily newspapers turned up for an interview. The result was an article informing the Swedish public that a young Swede was returning to Sweden after being "trained to save people through Beatle rhythms!"

Working for The Salvation Army in Sweden

When the major tour with the *Joystrings* came to an end, I headed to The Salvation Army church in Malmö in the south of Sweden. The church had a membership of approximately 400 people in those days, a band and a choir. I lived in a small room behind the office with my windows at street level facing a back street. Almost every night, drunks would knock on the window, wanting the young lieutenant to come out and give them money.

The church was situated in the downtown area. Many of the street drunks came to the services. At one service, one of them slowly walked up the middle aisle at the end of the service, as I invited people to find Christ and to come forward and kneel at the mercy seat. When I knelt beside the man, he turned to me and through his beer-smelling breath said as loud as he could, "Come on, give me five *kronor* (a dollar) for a beer, Jesus would have given it to me!"

Another time, a man came to me and insisted that he had been hired for a job in a nearby town, but he had no money for his train fare. Wanting to believe him I marched him down to the train station, bought a non-refundable ticket, put him on the train and waved him off, while he held up his fist against me. He did not want to go anywhere. He just wanted some money for the next beer.

After five months in Malmö, I was given farewell orders and sent out on my own to a small community, Skutskär, some 100 miles north of Stockholm. Skutskär had begun as a lumber town and now it housed one of the largest sulphite and sulphate factories in Sweden, which spilled its sweet and sour aroma all over the town. There were approximately 50 members in the little Army church, but most of them had not attended for several years. Infighting and other problems had kept the people away. No Sunday morning services had been held for years, only a Sunday night meeting apart from the normal youth activities and women's meetings. There were no leaders for any of the groups. I had barely celebrated my 20th birthday and this was my first major challenge in ministry.

The first service I held on my own was attended by one man, and I conducted the service for him, sang, played the piano, preached and even took the offering. After the service I realized that the man was somewhat mentally retarded, and as I sat in my room above the meeting hall, contemplating what had happened. That evening there was a knock on the door. Outside stood five scouts who had been part of a uniformed program. They informed me they were sorry that I had come, because they enjoyed the previous leader! As they handed me a package they snickered, "Take our uniforms, we have decided never to come back."

The following day, the old grandfather living in the house across the road died. According to old tradition in this part of the country, a minister had to come and "read out the dead." This meant that as soon as the person had been placed in an open casket, a church service was held in the home. It was the responsibility of the minister to sing, share Scripture and pray for the family. I had no handbook for these kinds of rites and had to create a service on the spur of the moment, without knowing if I was doing the right thing. This was the first time I had seen a dead person, and the imagery stayed with me for months, every time I attempted to fall asleep in my tiny apartment.

The residence for the officer was in the former balcony of The Salvation Army church, which had been turned into two small rooms and a kitchen. The bathroom was shared with the church hall downstairs and consisted of a small closet with a toilet and hand basin. There was no bath or shower, so every Friday I walked to one of the members' homes and borrowed their bathroom for a proper bath. The small kitchen had no fridge but a pantry with an outside vent. The first weekend I was there, a strange smell filled the kitchen. My immediate reaction was that I had left something in the pantry and that it had "turned bad." However, when I opened the window to clear the air, the sweet, sickly aroma from the factory welled in through the window and I was "baptized" in the Skutskär foul-smelling air from the factories.

Despite these setbacks, I was determined to make this place work. I began advertising in the newspapers, made sure the press wrote articles about the Army, hand-painted posters that were 10 feet high and 5 feet wide, painted rectangular posters with large footprints, all pointing in the direction of the Army hall, and then tied them to the picket fences close to the hall. If you followed the footsteps you would end up at the Army church.

Risk-Taker for God

After announcing that a Sunday morning service would be held every week, three Baptist ladies began to attend. They were my only faithful attendees for the next six months. Others began to drift in from time to time. Offerings were meager. I learned the principle that if I wanted to get paid that week, I needed to give more in the offering myself. With such a small crowd, I seldom received my full pay and some weeks I went without salary. One Sunday morning I prayed that God would bring some new people to the service. To my surprise the audience was double the normal. A Mercedes stopped outside the church just as the service began and a middle-aged gentleman stepped out, walked in and sat through the service. When the offering was being taken, I peeked over the hymnal on the piano bench, from where I was leading the singing. The man stuffed a wad of notes in the collection box. Before the service was over he stood up and walked out. When we counted the offering, there was more than six week's salary in the offering, and I felt as if we had had a visit from an angel. Perhaps we had. I never saw the man again.

Some weeks I could buy food, other weeks I was invited out to dinner, even being offered five dinners in one day. To my amazement I ate them all! One week I lived on a can of sardines and water. Another week, I had food perhaps three out of seven days and when Sunday came, I was extremely hungry. After the service was over one Sunday, I returned to my apartment only to realize that the pantry was empty. I went downstairs, out into the front yard and sat down near the picket fence and prayed, "Lord, send someone to invite me for dinner today, because I am so hungry!" It was a silly prayer, because by this time most people would already be sitting down at their dinner tables. Suddenly, a tiny, white haired lady, a retired Salvation Army officer, Elsa Andersson, came racing up on a bicycle, far too fast for her age. "Oh, there you are," she called out over the handle bars, "we were just sitting down for dinner, saying grace, when the Lord spoke to me and said, 'Go and get Lars.' Have you eaten already?"

One way the Army kept the income going for a small place like this was to visit the farms in the area, and ask them for a sack or two of wheat after the harvest. Later in the year, I would then go around and collect the grain and sell it to the mill. An older gentleman, who was not a Salvationist but owned a small car of the 'Mr. Bean mini' model, offered to help me. With both of us in the car, there was not much more room than for two additional sacks, so we made many trips between farms and the mill.

Through blizzards and rain we gathered the sacks of wheat and it brought a good income, but I am sure the Army ruined this old gentleman's car in the process.

I had no transportation except my old bicycle, which was a present for my twelfth birthday. Soon I realized that it was too far to the outposts, where services should be held regularly, and I needed something better. For $15 I bought a second-hand moped that became an absolute luxury. It was 12 miles into the nearest big city, and I was often asked to come in and help them with special services on the weekdays. One time in the winter I went there on the moped, with my accordion strapped on my back, not realizing how cold it was! When I arrived at The Salvation Army in that city, they had to lift me off the bike, as my arms and legs were absolutely frozen stiff.

Lessons Learned and the Spirit's Leading

During my year at Skutskär I learned basic lessons about planning and leadership. At first I was the leader for every group: the music, the youth program, the ladies' ministry and I even did all the bookkeeping and the cleaning. But as people began to return to the church, and new people also turned up, I took advantage of opportunities to train them and place them in leadership positions. At the end of my time there, the hall was often full and a string band of 15-20 lead the singing and the music. To make it look crowded, I would take out several rows of seats, so that more seats had to be brought in when people attended the services. This creative "marketing" led people to go and tell their friends that the Army hall was full, which brought even more people. Even the local papers carried the headline stating, "Extra chairs at The Salvation Army. Standing room only!"

One day I was at the barber shop having a haircut. Suddenly the barber turned to me and said, "A British registered ship docked at the harbor this morning." I gave it no further thought until I was reading my Bible that afternoon. That still voice of the Holy Spirit kept nudging me, "Go down to the harbor...a sailor needs you right now!" I thought the entire idea silly, but decided to take my moped down to the harbor. As I was stopped by the guard at the harbor gate, I said, "I have a message for a man on the British ship." Seeing my Salvation Army uniform he let me through.

When I rode up to the side of the ship and the gangway, several sailors leaning over the ship's side smoking, began to shout to each other, "He is here! He is here!"

I walked on board and they explained to me that one of the sailors was sitting in his cabin crying, absolutely beside himself and his mates did not know why. Several times he had sobbed, "Send for The Salvation Army, send for The Salvation Army." But his friends told him that no one spoke English in Sweden, so what good would that do?

Entering the cabin, a rough but heart-broken British sailor grabbed my hands and attempted to tell his sad story. He had wandered far from his mother's prayers and somehow the Holy Spirit had convicted him during this particular journey. We prayed together and as far as I could see he understood what we were doing. Fortunately, I had brought an English New Testament with me and gave it to him.

As it was Sunday the following day, I drew him a map and invited him to the morning service, not having much hope that he would turn up. Sunday came, I started the service and no sailor was present. But then the door swung open and there he was. This turned out to be one of the few times I interpreted myself as I preached. After taking him to lunch where I further explained the gospel and the first steps of discipleship, I gave him some contact addresses to The Salvation Army in England. As I waved farewell to him, I marveled once again over the guidance and clarity of the Holy Spirit's instructions!

Of course there were also many difficult spiritual battles. Many times, I sensed darker powers at work while I tried to prepare my messages for the growing congregation. Rumors circulated in the town about occult practices having taken place in the Army building long ago. Trying to understand such issues with spiritual discernment, you tended to extend all the internal antennas, looking for real and imagined signals.

One week, when my mother was visiting me, she came out in the kitchen from the room where she had slept and said to me, "What went on in the hall last night? All through the night I heard people singing and moving furniture." "Mom, you heard it too?" Many nights I would wake up from loud singing, as if the hall was packed with people, and I would look at my watch and notice it was the middle of the night! This happened several times throughout the year. A couple of days later, my mother and I sat at the kitchen table and heard the front door downstairs open, listened to shuffling steps up the creaky stairs to the second floor, and saw the door handle turn but the door did not open. I rushed up from the table and went to the door, but there was no one there! Many nights I would be on my knees all night, pleading the blood of Jesus over my life, when all these strange things went on. I have never liked the dark, and from that time on, I took a great dislike to going into dark rooms, without knowing where the light switch was!

Enlarging the Field of Service

As I struggled through this year, I also wrestled with my long term future. What did God have in mind for me? While I was caught up in the Army as a vehicle for ministry, I questioned many of the procedures and processes.

One month I read through Nobel Prize winner Selma Lagerlöf's trilogy: *The ring of the Löwenskölds - The General's ring, Charlotte Löwensköld* and *Anna Svärd*. These books had a great impact on me. One of the main characters is a young clergyman in the Swedish Lutheran church. Through a set of circumstances he leaves his pastorate and becomes a roving street preacher, visiting burlesque carnivals, speaking for an audience that heckles him at every sentence.

One Wednesday I took the bus to the next town of Tierp. The officers at that church had asked me for help. "Would you come and bring your accordion and help us sing at the market?" While we were standing there, singing away in a noisy carnival atmosphere, I could see an inward, mental picture of this fictional wayward clergyman and as I daydreamed, the images rolled into one. I was the clergyman, and the question echoed within me, "What on earth am I doing here? Is this what I will be doing for the rest of my life?" My decision to resign from The Salvation Army was decided there and then.

Doctrinal questions had also surfaced as I kept reading and re-reading my Bible. The Salvation Army holds a position against using the sacraments, due to the fact that in the early days many of the converts were alcoholics and serving communion wine would be an enormous temptation. William Booth also saw the Army more as a revival movement than a church, and did not want to confuse the power of salvation with sacred rituals. If people wanted to take communion and be baptized, they simply could attend another church to do so. I could defend this position and understood the reason behind it, but as I studied Scripture and read other books and talked with many respected Christian leaders outside the Army, my position crumbled before me. My initial calling as an evangelist also burned within me. I loved the Army and its people, and under no circumstances wanted to leave that fellowship, but at the same time I felt like I was being held in a tight vice.

After a year in Skutskär I was called up for obligatory military service. Many young men within church circles in Sweden are conscientious objectors. My father had been one, all my friends were, and with Sweden not having been to war for 150 years, I did not see any reason to learn to kill. However, conscientious objectors had to serve longer time in alternative services, like at civil firefighting stations or in community service. Initially, I was sent to Arlanda airport (Stockholm) to train as a fireman and after the six-week training course my assignment for the next 380 days was Torslanda airport in Gothenburg, the second largest city in Sweden. Every weekend I continued preaching at Army churches, but I was still wrestling with the sacrament issues. Finally, I came to the conclusion: I would take the risk and resign, whatever the cost and see if the Lord would open other doors.

Training as a fireman did not go well for me. I have always been afraid of heights and climbing straight up the 90-foot free standing ladder, hooking yourself on the top with my belt hook, climbing over the top and then down on the other side, was not my forte.

When I see blood I tend to faint, something that started when I was still in school. I passed out while we were being taught the theory of blood circulation in high school. Now I had to sit and watch movies of road accidents, air crashes, fires and view the most horrendous wounds, as well as identify bodies that were more or less reduced to charred skeletons. I passed out every time, and the rest of the gang practiced mouth to mouth resuscitation on me, and how to take care of an unconscious person, put him on a stretcher and place him into the ambulance. They used a very real me for training instead of the usual fake dummy.

When I arrived at Torslanda airport I realized that some of my mishaps must have been recorded, because I was appointed as personal assistant to the Fire Captain, which meant that I cooked breakfast for him, shopped for him and wrote the daily report, as well as a catastrophe report every time the fire brigade had to go into action.

A Difficult Ending

One day I sat down and penned the dreaded resignation letter to The Salvation Army headquarters, citing the sacraments as one reason for leaving. Soon after the Army leadership received my resignation letter, I was called before them. In retrospect this whole issue was handled poorly from both sides, I was a "green" young man, who viewed issues more black and white than they really were. The Army leadership in those days was not as wise as I know them to be now, and the confrontation became ugly. They wanted me to rescind my resignation, and it was acceptable to them if I believed in being baptized, as long as I did not talk to anyone about it. I had no intention to talk to anyone about it, but felt it was wrong to remain in the Army's service if I could not speak what was on my heart. After our meeting, the leader for the Salvation Army in Sweden wrote me a letter, accepting my resignation but also stating, "If I believed this was God's will for your life, I would wish you God's blessing, but now I simply cannot do that." I wept for hours with my head face down in my pillow and the letter in my hand!

At the same time, a circular went out to all Salvation Army places of worship in Sweden, stating that Lars Dunberg was not allowed to minister in their halls, a decision that placed deep scars in my young soul. Suddenly my best friends were supposed to be the enemy! How I wished the former leader was alive today so we could talk this over now.

On another occasion, long before I had decided to resign, one of the Army leaders had told me, "Lars, if you ever leave the Army, don't bad-mouth it, because you never spit on your own mother." Those words have followed me for more than 40 years, and I am grateful for every opportunity I have had to work together with The Salvation Army or take part in any of their functions. I still owe a debt to The Salvation Army, in teaching me compassion, conviction, boldness and perseverance, a debt that I can never repay.

In the late 90s I was invited to conduct the Officers Councils (pastors meetings) for several groups of Salvation Army officers in Sweden, as well as act as a trainer/consultant for the leadership group of the Army in Sweden over a period of three years. I had come full circle. I had returned in some way, where I fully accepted them and they fully accepted me, and a 35-year old scar could be removed.

CHAPTER 5
New Ministry

Arriving in Torslanda, outside Gothenburg on the west coast of Sweden, was a completely new experience for me. With so much free time on my hands, I began intensive self-studies and took every opportunity to preach. Invitations came from some of the churches represented by the young men who spent time in the fire brigade with me. Because many of the young men going through this training were believers, we talked about putting together a group to visit different churches. We formed a music group and went on tours. There was hardly a weekend when I wasn't preaching somewhere in southern Sweden. Since I didn't have a car, I traveled by train or bus, asked people to give me rides or even hitchhiked. Many weekends I didn't return until 3 or 4 in the morning. One time the fire alarm went off soon after I had returned late. I had just fallen asleep and never heard the alarm, or the stomping of boots as all the boys jumped into their clothes and ran for the trucks, with their sirens blaring.

Usually the music group would leave on Friday afternoon, drive for a few hours, and then have meetings that night, Saturday and all day Sunday before returning home. Accompanied by my piano accordion and a few guitars, we would sing the gospel songs popular in those days. The fellows would share their testimonies and I preached my heart out. We saw many people come to Christ, while others rededicated their lives to Him.

A Sacramental Decision

As I have mentioned, I had been struggling for years with the Army's position on the sacraments. Though I had not been baptized, I was convinced that adult baptism was important – that it was needed to show the world you were willing to obey the Lord. Over Pentecost weekend in 1966 I was invited to come up to an area in Sweden by a new friend who was the pastor of the Covenant Church there. Previously, I had invited him to come to the Army church where I had been a pastor, and he and I had daily discussion during those days about the sacraments, evangelism and serving Christ. Now he invited me to visit him and speak in some of the services. Casually he mentioned, "We will have a baptismal service on Pentecost Sunday in the old Baptist chapel. Do you want to be baptized?" Of course I did! As I stepped down into the baptistery that day with my friend Habil Bolin, it felt as if the heavens were opened.

Doors Open Locally

In Gothenburg many of the leading evangelical businessmen had formed an association to motivate and encourage Christian young people. This association purchased a plot of land in the middle of a city park and built a Youth Center, which had meeting rooms, a restaurant and activity rooms. Prior to my arrival in Gothenburg, a full-time youth leader had been hired and he was running several exciting programs.

Every Sunday night at 9 p.m. he led a program (which later became a TV special) called *Ungdomsträngsel*, "Youth Crush." As services finished in the churches across town, the young people, together with their non-churched friends, would flock to these relaxed youth services. Music groups and well-known speakers would come to be part of the two-hour "variety show"-cum-evangelistic program.

When the leader, George Svensson, noticed that I had a lot of free time on my hands, he asked me to get involved. It was at this center I learned what networking really means. After a few months I moved from the fire station and spent afternoons, evenings and nights at the center returning to the airport at 6 a.m. every morning.

People from other parts of Sweden and Europe often came to visit. Every time someone's message needed interpretation, I was elected to be the interpreter. Many deep bonds were formed with some of these visiting preachers from all over Europe and North America.

Risk-Taker for God

One day a pastor in his late 30's, Vilme Eriksson, moved to town. He had been invited to work among drug addicts in Gothenburg. This was just after David Wilkerson published *The Cross and the Switchblade*. Drug addiction was rampant and few Christians in Sweden were working among them. The Swedish Drug Addiction Mission was incorporated and young people from the youth center became the core volunteers to help with the mission.

Night after night we went out on the streets of Gothenburg to find young people high on drugs. It wasn't long before one of the girls came to know the Lord and introduced us to many of her friends who were all addicts. The youth center became a place where drug addicts could come to stay for the night, going "cold turkey" through immediate withdrawal, while we sat at their bedside during the night, helping them through the delirious moments and praying for power for both them and us to hold out for a breakthrough. In retrospect we probably had more zeal than wisdom, and certainly no experience.

Often these addicts would hand over their needles, "cooking" utensils, and sometimes, even their drugs. As it was a criminal offense to possess these drugs, this made our work a bit difficult. One night I was at the main city square talking to addicts, having just been handed a box of needles and drugs from one addict, when the police turned up for a raid. Here I was, a 22-year-old pastor, arrested for possession of drugs. At the police station I managed to explain the situation and I was immediately released.

As the months went by at the fire station, I continued wrestling with my future. Where did the Lord want me? In those days, every leading denomination in Sweden employed a number of evangelists, who held month-long interdenominational crusades in different parts of the country. Some were my heroes. I would travel miles just to sit under their ministry. These were men, who in contrast with many of their American counterparts, were not working independently using Elmer Gantry-style fundraising tactics, but, like the Billy Graham team, were invited to area after area, in well-planned, interdenominational crusades, their entire funding handled by a denominational office.

These positions were well sought after and although many young men felt called, few were chosen. Adding to the problem, Doreen and I had just become engaged, and since she didn't speak a word of Swedish, she felt I needed to come to Britain to serve rather than her moving out of a familiar, safe environment. I knew no one in Britain, except one of my mentors, Denis Clark, who I had met several times during his frequent preaching tours of Sweden. I had already talked to him, wondering if he would take me under his wing, but as he had not "heard from the Lord" in this matter, that door remained shut.

Doors Open Globally

In early June of 1966 I was getting frantic. I prayed and prayed but did not find any open door. One day, as I traveled by train back from a visit to my parents in Stockholm, I went on my knees in the empty train compartment. I had just read Gideon's story that morning and I was ready to put out a fleece, crying out in desperation to the Lord.

"Lord," I prayed, "I have heard so much about the *Youth for Christ* movement around the world. It seems to be a place where people are being used in evangelism! Please, Lord, open a door to YFC! Please, Lord, put me in contact with someone in Britain today who knows about YFC!" A rather far-fetched prayer, as I had neither met anyone from the evangelical churches in Britain before, nor met anyone actively involved with YFC.

As soon as the train arrived in Gothenburg I took the street car to the youth center Björngårdsvillan and went to my little room to continue praying. I had barely arrived when the phone rang and I answered. It was the woman at the reception desk. "Lars, you have to come down and help me! There is a man here and he doesn't speak Swedish, and I don't know what to say!"

I hurried down to the reception area where a gentleman patiently waited. "Good to see you," he said with an American twang, "my name is Bill Yoder. I am on my way to Finland but my plane had engine trouble and they landed here in Gothenburg. I can't leave until tomorrow. I have heard so much about this youth center and just wanted to check it out. Can you show me around and tell me more of what you do here?"

Delighted, I showed him the center and explained the programs. Then I gathered my courage and asked him, "Bill, do you know anyone in *Youth For Christ* in Britain?" He laughed out loud and I wondered what kind of stupid question I had asked.

"Do I know anyone? Of course I do! I am the Europe director of YFC. I am in contact with YFC in Britain every week. Why do you ask? Give me your name and I'll write to them."

That night I praised God. A mechanical fault on an airplane! A man's impulse to come and see the center! My return happening just in time for his visit! Coincidence? Hardly, but a real answer to prayer.

Bill Yoder did indeed write to YFC in Britain, but nothing happened immediately. At least I knew who to speak to. Late that summer I went to Britain for a week's visit for Doreen's 25th birthday. Together we decided to drive to London and visit the YFC office. Not one of the leaders was there, because of summer vacation, but I spoke with the staff members. I arranged with the secretary to come back and meet the director in January of the following year, when I would have completed my military service.

I was released from military service in December and left for England just after Christmas. The first week of January, the national YFC director Rev. Owen Gregory met me in London. He discouraged me from joining YFC in Britain. "The organization has no money," he told me, "and they have not hired anyone new for several years."

"Let alone someone from abroad who does not even speak English properly," I thought out loud. However, he promised to put me on the agenda for the board meeting in February, and if the Board was interested, they would ask me to appear before them.

I was called before the YFC Board and for over two hours they grilled me on everything from theology and evangelism to my publishing experience and working with drug addicts in Sweden. After these grueling hours I was told to return within four hours and later that afternoon I was informed that I had been hired as their full-time evangelist, starting September 1967 with a generous salary of 15 pounds sterling a week (approximately $30). But that was seven months away!

While I was happy, it was also frightening. I was living in the spare bedroom at my future in-laws' home. Fortunately I had some previously-arranged speaking engagements to fill my time. In February that year I preached in a small campaign in a West Indian house church in a basement in Brixton, London, where I was invited back again for the month of June. For three months I was back in Sweden, holding my first full-fledged evangelistic campaign: one with all churches in a town called Kinna and then one with the Alliance church in the city of Forserum.

Questions of Calling

During these months before my new employment with YFC and my upcoming wedding, I continued wrestling with questions of my calling. Did God really want me in Britain? What if the Lord would not supply enough to meet our needs? What if people couldn't understand my English? Lying on a fold-up-bed in a makeshift bedroom in the pastor's study in the West Indian church, I urged the Lord for yet another confirmation. Knowing how little I had been paid the time before I had visited this church, I made a bold claim, "Lord, when the love offering is taken for me tomorrow night, let it be double what it was last time I was here! Make it be 22 pounds and 10 shillings. Nothing more, nothing less!"

When the time for the offering came, Rev McCarthy spoke warmly about the volunteer services of the young Swedish evangelist, and suggested that everyone should give what they could. After the service, he handed me an envelope and thanked me for the week. I hurried to the study and tore open the envelope. It contained two crisp 10 pound notes. That was the biggest gift I had ever received, but not quite what I had prayed for. I went to bed that night, not sure what to make of it all, when there suddenly was a knock on the door. Outside was a man from the church, who sheepishly said, "Did I wake you? The Lord told me to put this in an envelope and give it to you tonight. I am just being obedient to the Lord. Good night!" I tore yet another envelope open to find two wrinkled pound notes... and a ten shilling note.

Youth for Christ

Britain's *Youth for Christ* program had begun after Billy Graham's first visit in 1946. The program consisted of monthly youth rallies, Bible quizzes, and conferences to train young people in the Bible as well as the publishing of a youth magazine, *Vista*. Contrary to YFC in the USA, there were no school programs. Most were handled by local committees with voluntary staff. Only one of the 103 locations in Great Britain had any full-time staff. Including me, there were five of us in the office. British YFC was also the distributor and rental agency of Gospel Films and International Films from the United States. Every Tuesday, hundreds of 16-millimeter films came back in special boxes from showings in churches. Broken sprockets were mended and replaced by hand and the films were repacked to be mailed out by Thursday for the following weekend showings! When the staff members who normally serviced the films were sick, I had to hand-crank through these films and fix them myself.

While the movement had been strong in Britain during the 1950s, it was losing some of the wind in its sails. The theme, "Geared to the times, anchored to the rock" showed an organization that perhaps was more stuck on the rock than geared to the swinging 60s.

Britain was very different from Sweden. I had expected to speak in campaigns lasting for at least three weeks. I ended up speaking at no end of one-night youth rallies, church services and the odd youth barbeque, which was a completely new communication tool for me.

In the beginning I still had enormous problems in finding the right words. You had to be "on the ball" to speak to teens and other young people. I brought down the house in Kensington Temple (one of London's largest churches) when I spoke at the youth service, quoting Jesus instructing His disciples not to look back if they had put their hand to the pluff! The British spelling of the word "*plow*" is "*plough*." After all, I knew how to pronounce *tough*, so why should not plough be pronounced the same way?

Most Sundays I traveled to churches of every possible denomination. Before we had children, Doreen would accompany me. At times it was a challenge to ensure we fit into the denominational behavior. One time we arrived at the Brethren assembly church, only to learn that Doreen had to wear a hat to be accepted into the worship service. Hats were provided, but to Doreen's amazement they were taken off when the ladies went into another room to teach Sunday school. On another occasion, we visited a different Brethren assembly, where I spoke and a young man with a high-pitched voice sang. The three of us sat together on the front row. As I preached, the young man from the West Indies expressed himself in an appropriate way for his cultural background, with a "praise the Lord" and "hallelujah" here and there. During the prayer time after the message, he became louder. Suddenly the lady behind Doreen, thinking it was her speaking in tongues, which would be unthinkable in a Brethren assembly, tapped her on the shoulder and whispered sternly, "Will you stop that! We don't do this in our church!"

I learned several leadership lessons during those formative years at YFC. One day I found a leadership guide from YFC in USA in one of the drawers, and realized what a potential such a guide could be in a British setting. For weeks I spent my spare time working and reworking such a guide for the UK. The national director, who only worked part-time and spent the rest of his time pastoring a Baptist church hours away in Wales, showed no interest when I presented the American version to him. However, I was sure he would love to see a British edition. To my amazement, he became furious when the new British copy landed on his desk. "Who authorized this?" he demanded. To make matters worse I had simultaneously sent a copy to our new chairman, Cyril Evans, who called me and explained how well he liked it. I learnt quickly never to work around "the boss" and not to place surprises before people in leadership!

Reading books was my favorite pastime, and spending two to three hours on the underground every day going to and from the office, made it possible for me to read some 15-20 books a week. But books were expensive. I began to wonder, what would happen if YFC could offer Christian books cheaper to its constituencies? This was before the days of Christian book clubs, and the principle appealed to me. After making the rounds to several publishing houses and finding out what discounts YFC could receive as a book distributor, we made a simple catalog and sent it out to our contacts across Britain. Within a few days angry phone calls came from Christian bookshops, "What is this? Don't you know that booksellers in Britain work on a set price per book called the Net Agreement? Are you trying to ruin the business for us?" Another lesson learned! It is always better to research something thoroughly before launching a program!

Moving Into leadership

After serving as an evangelist for the first seven months, I was suddenly called before a committee of the Board. The national director was moving to Australia, and they wanted to know if I would consider becoming the national coordinator for YFC in Britain. This was not what I had anticipated. Against my wishes, I was encouraged to downplay my role as an evangelist and spend more time administering a program. The need was there, and although I felt uncomfortable about it, I accepted.

One of my greatest challenges was how to involve young people in direct ministry. A friend was running a program for drug addicts in London, and I attempted to involve young people in this kind of ministry. But how could I get young people to get a vision for the world? In those days YFC in the USA often sent out youth teams to other parts of the world. Perhaps we could do the same for Britain? In 1968 the first British youth team left for a six-week tour of Sweden. A record was made of their songs and we had meetings lined up every night. The board was suspicious. They were concerned about the cost. It was with great pleasure I returned with the team, having ministered in some 45 different places. We'd sold all the records and received offerings to cover all of our costs and give YFC a surplus that was enough to pay my salary and other expenses for six months!

The following year I faced a greater cultural challenge when I took a folk singing team, *Folk Five*, first to the south coast and then to the center of France. I went through culture shock as I tried to lead this team, who had no previous overseas experience. I spoke no French and most French people we met did not communicate in English. The French lived out their evangelical Christianity in a completely different mode. Our team was made up of great musicians though and their folk singing went down extremely well.

The team had the opportunity to minister in many situations where few if any evangelistic meetings had ever been held, including musical concerts in the city of Cluny, a city filled with monasteries, vineyards and an ancient culture. The team would introduce their songs, weave testimony into them, and I would attempt to present the gospel, through an interpreter, in a way that would include its power without coming across as something too offensive. Many people wanted to talk afterwards and for the first time, I experienced trying to share biblical truths in a society that had no biblical frame of reference.

Impacting a City for Jesus

The summer of 1969, *Youth for Christ* in Britain hosted the annual Europe outreach program. It was decided that we would bring in some 250 European young Christians, train them in evangelism, send them door to door to share their faith and sell a special evangelistic edition of YFC's youth magazine *Vista* as well as hold evangelistic youth rallies every night for two weeks.

Under the title *Outreach 69*, I learned what it takes to organize a citywide event, involving some 10-15 different cultures. Two years earlier I had taken part in a similar project in Helsinki, Finland where I was responsible for a plane-load of 35 British young people. I had seen first-hand what worked and what didn't and this time I wanted to make sure we got it right.

For over a year I spent a week each a month in Newcastle, meeting with a committee representing all the denominations and independent churches in Newcastle. I visited meeting sites, searched for places to house 250 young people and checked out places where food could be provided for so many people. At times the "northerners" in Newcastle could not quite grasp what we had in mind, and weekly we fought against evangelical traditionalism, leaders who wanted to impose activities that just didn't fit, and some who would not work with anyone else than people from their own denomination. Somehow we moved forward step by step.

Eventually we held the youth rallies in Newcastle Town hall, with Rev. David Burnham from the Chapel on Fir Hill, Akron, Ohio as the main speaker. Visiting music groups from all over Europe and America sang and played every night, and night after night Newcastle's young people came, listened and responded. A team of us was invited to visit several of the night clubs in town to put on a brief music program. A friendly Chinese restaurant served us lunch and dinner every day for 2 weeks. Well, there is just so much Chinese food one can eat in a lifetime. My daughter Carin was one year old and had to learn to eat Chinese food twice a day! Thousands of magazines were distributed by young Christian people from all around Europe.

It was in one of the churches in Newcastle where one of the most intriguing conversion stories in my life took place. One Sunday night I had been invited to speak in this rather large church, and even for a Sunday night, the church was packed. That night I preached on the power in the word "salvation" and the fact that the blood of Jesus can cleanse us from all sin. As I gave the invitation for people to come forward to receive Christ, one man stood up at the back of the church. But instead of moving to the area in front of me, where others were gathering to commit their lives to Christ, he walked straight past me, opened the door and stepped into the pastor's vestry that was situated behind the pulpit. I handed over the service to the pastor, and followed the man into the vestry. Immediately the man grabbed hold of my jacket lapels and put his angry face up close to mine. "Who told you about me," he hissed through his clenched teeth, "how do you know everything about me?"

I knew nothing of this man, but afterward people told me that every Sunday night he would come to the service, not to be blessed, but to observe everything so he could make fun of the church, the pastor, Christians and the Christian faith on Monday as he worked together with several people from the church. "He used to be like a devil on Mondays," they exclaimed. Now he stood here before me.

"Is it true what you told me? That there is forgiveness for me?" Then he began to tell me his story, as later confirmed by his workmates. I told him that he could be forgiven. "But you haven't heard it all," he continued, and spewed out a life of moral decay, incestuous living and behavior that was more than I had faced from anyone else. "Is there really forgiveness for me?" he cried out as he fell to the floor.

"The blood of Jesus Christ cleanses from all sin," I quickly replied.

Then followed a wrestling match in prayer that I have never experienced since. Darkness so completely surrounded this man as he tried to confess and ask for forgiveness and cleansing. And then in a flash, the atmosphere changed. It was like lights had been turned on everywhere in the pastor's study as the man rose, with his face shining. "What has happened to me?" he asked, tears streaming down his face, "I have not cried like this since I was a little boy!" God's forgiveness and transformation set in with a power seldom observed, and I realized again the enormous power in the cleansing blood of Jesus.

God Works Through Young People

One day I received a call from YFC in the south of Cornwall. Would I come down and visit? The local YFC program had experienced an explosive growth in a local Baptist church. It turned out that a group of ladies in the church had been praying for revival, and the Lord heard their prayers through a group of young people. They came to the Lord in droves and engaged themselves in the local church that had been without a pastor. When I arrived to Redruth I was asked to come to a house meeting with the local youth leaders. That night hundreds of kids gathered in a huge living room. They sat, stood and squeezed in everywhere. I sat on top of the piano (the only seat left in the house) to speak to them. They shared with me how the ladies' prayers were answered as one by one, they came to know Christ. As soon as they came to Christ they wanted to be baptized and join the little church. The ladies did not know what had happened to them. After a year the church was packed with young people – they had 16-year-old ushers, a 19-year-old chairman of the deacon board and the expanding congregation was ready to call a full-time pastor!

Some experiences were not that positive. One day in 1969 I spoke at a YFC rally in the city of Loughton, just a few miles from where we lived. It was one of those horrible nights that you want to forget. The stage was too high, distancing me too far from the audience. The hall was narrow and rectangular. It was barely half filled this night and people tended to sit at the back. I needed binoculars to see them! A lady sang before I gave my message and let's just say that singing was not her forte. When I spoke, it was like every word formed a huge crystal bubble that floated a few seconds in the air and then crashed to the floor right in front of the stage. I was not communicating with anybody. That night I went home and told my wife that I should probably give up preaching, because I did not seem to be able to convincingly share the gospel.

Fifteen years later, long after I left *Youth For Christ*, I attended a worldwide YFC convocation in Hong Kong. Stepping into the elevator in the high-rise hotel to go down for breakfast, the elevator's only other occupant, a Western man, eyed me up and down until I felt uncomfortable. Suddenly he addressed me, "You are Lars Dunberg, aren't you?" I nodded. "I can't believe how fat you are…" he said with a smile. I beckoned to him to sit down with me in the lobby and he told his story. "Last time I met you, you were as thin as a rake. It was at a YFC rally in Loughton… do you remember that night?" Yes I did remember the failed night, but I had no memory of the young man sitting in front of me. He continued, "That night I sat in that audience and you preached the gospel, and when I returned home I invited Jesus to come into my life." Then Bob Moffat continued to share with me how he had become involved in youth work through YFC, literally ministering to thousands of kids in Europe. Even a failed presentation can lead people to Christ!

God Has Other Plans

After almost three years of intense administration and ministry, with little funds for the ministry and a meager salary, I hit the wall. How could I continue to support my family? Where was the ministry the Lord had called me to personally? During a time when I was fighting a virus infection I went into a deep depression, wondering what the future would hold. I had several letter exchanges with one of my mentors, Rev. Berthil Paulsson, who contacted the leadership of the Covenant Church of Sweden. One day I received a request: Would I be willing to spend four years at their seminary in Stockholm and become a pastor in the Covenant Church?

This was not at all what I had in mind. It was now more than five years since I had graduated from The Salvation Army College and I could not imagine being in seminary for another four years! The request came back asking for at least a year, but again I refused.

Then out of the blue I received a letter of invitation to become an evangelist for the Covenant Church in Southwest Sweden. I would not need to attend seminary, but would be required to study, at my own speed, from home, the entire four year seminary course, except I would be released from Greek.

My wife Doreen and I prayed. I was excited and she was apprehensive. I would return to my real calling and my homeland and a manageable salary. She would have to move to a strange country, where she did not know the culture and the language. In retrospect I am full of admiration for her decision to accept.

CHAPTER 6
Doreen and Family

During one of the concert trips with the *Joystrings*, the music group was scheduled to visit the city of Cambridge. We arrived very late at night before the day of our performance. I was twenty years old and I had been praying for some time that God would lead me to a woman who I could love unconditionally, who would be at my side for the rest of my life, who would have the same wish to see the gospel go forward around the world, and who could show me love, despite how awkward and strange I could be at times.

The next morning I was having my devotion in the house of the family where I was staying, when something odd happened. Either it was a vision or a dream, but in The Salvation Army we were not accustomed to visions, so I was not sure what it was. As I prayed, it was like I saw a huge concert hall before my eyes, which was completely empty, apart from the fact that on the seventh row, in a certain seat, sat a young lady. I immediately recognized her.

About six months earlier, five of us students had been sent to a small village, Histon, north of Cambridge, to conduct a weekend of services. During that weekend I stayed in the home of The Salvation Army church's sergeant-major, the equivalent of chairman of the elder board.

The daughter of the house didn't happen to be home the day we arrived as she was visiting in the nearby city of Bedford, where her boyfriend lived. I found that out while walking to the Army church for the 7 a.m. prayer meeting with the sergeant-major. He had the strongest accent I had ever come across, swallowing his "h's," and most of the time I nodded, and responded with, "aha" and "uhm," while he talked non-stop. I had no idea what he was talking about most of that time. As the Sunday morning service progressed, I noted a beautiful young lady leading the children's choir. To my surprise she turned to me after the service and said, "Come with me in the car so we can go home for dinner!" Later that night as we were ready to return to the Training College, I boldly asked her, "So, when are you going into training to become a Salvation Army officer?" Most young people in the Army at least toyed with the idea of full-time service sometime in their young lives. To my astonishment, she looked me straight in the face and responded, "I'm not!" After the evening service we waved goodbye to them all and I completely forgot her.

Four months later, together with another group of students, we were sent to Bedford Salvation Army Congress Hall for the Easter celebrations. I ended up staying with a couple whose son conducted the band. As I was having breakfast the first day, his mother brought out a photograph of a young lady, explaining how sad she was that this lady had suddenly broken off the courtship with her son. I stared at the picture: It was the same young lady whose home I had visited in Histon a few months earlier!

And now she was the young lady in my dream. There she was, sitting alone in row seven. In my vision I heard the Lord whispering to me in that still, small voice, "That lady is your wife."

I put the vision aside. That night we were ready to give yet another performance, this time in the City Guild Hall of Cambridge. It was jam-packed with people, and there were long lines outside.

As we walked onto the stage to pick up our instruments I was apprehensive. We started playing and when the curtains parted, I quickly looked out over the audience. It was the same hall I had seen in my dream that morning. But it was packed to capacity. There in the seventh row in that particular seat sat the young lady I had seen in my vision.

After the concert I went down from the stage to find her. We chatted briefly before her parents called her, telling her it was time to leave. And so she did. At that point, one of her friends, who had lingered started to chat. Very discreetly I asked her for the name and address of her friend and she gave it to me with a chuckle. When I returned to the college for our weekly day off later that same week, I composed and carefully typed a note to the young lady, asking her to come hear us in concert at a place not far from where she lived, where we would be playing the following week.

Sure enough, she turned up and we had yet another little talk. When I asked her whether she would write to me when I moved back to Sweden the following week she agreed. After that we did not meet for another 13 months, when she came over to Sweden to visit me.

Doreen's Childhood

Doreen grew up in a typical English village, with a village green, pond, ducks and pubs. Her great-grandfather, Mr. Charlie Love, had been the village butcher, while her paternal grandfather, Fredrick Willson owned a nursery as well as served as a cobbler. In his young years he had served in the Boer War. Her maternal grandfather, Albert Vale took care of the horses for the nearby Chivers farm and jam factory. He died a premature and mysterious death. Her maternal grandmother, Ethel Vale, who soon after her husband's death also lost a daughter, took the remaining three children and moved to The Green in Histon. Ethel had been a Baptist, but when she and her children began to attend the Baptist church in Histon, they simply did not feel welcome. However, The Salvation Army was holding its open air meetings, inviting people to their church, and Ethel followed along, and within weeks donned the uniform of a Salvation Army lass, as did her children.

The youngest daughter Joyce Sybil, rather shy and introverted, learned to play the cornet and within a few weeks she joined the band in the open-air meetings in the village square. Passing by was a young Methodist lad, who had cut his teeth as a carpenter by making coffins for an undertaker. Recently he had been hired by the Chivers jam factory to be their in-house carpenter, building benches, tables, gates or whatever else needed to be tailor-made for the factory. As he stopped to listen to the band he noticed a beautiful dark-haired girl playing the cornet, and George Victor Willson rather suddenly lost his heart. That put an end to his attendance at the Methodist church and within weeks he joined the Army and also began marching in the band, first playing the cornet and then the huge bass tuba.

Victor and Joyce were married in 1939. Victor was 27 and Joyce 21. Nine months later David John was born. Doreen Mary followed some

17 months later, August 17, 1941. Within a year of Doreen's birth, Victor was called up to join the Royal Navy to help with the war effort in North Africa, and was stationed in Alexandria, Egypt for a few years. When he finally returned home, Doreen hid and cried. Who was this strange man invading the home?

During the final war years, the air raid sirens sounded with frightening regularity. Cambridge is surrounded by Air Force fields and the German attacks came frequently. An air raid shelter had been dug out at the end of the garden, but Doreen's most vivid memories are all about hiding in the closet under the stairs while the bombs fell around them.

As the children grew up there was much sibling rivalry. Doreen often was hurt when there was any quarreling, because David was so much stronger. And every "battle" always ended in tears, making the neighbor's son repeat his famous phrase, "There she goes again."

At one of her birthday parties her mother became tired of the noise, and since it was August and nice outside she ordered the birthday girl and her friends to play outside. Doreen wanted to be inside where the new presents were, and banged her fist so hard on the window that she broke the glass. That party ended quickly. The children were sent home and Doreen was sent off to bed.

In school David became a leader and this made Doreen feel like the underdog. She was as sweet and reserved as David was outgoing and at times a bit wild. People who know them today often burst out, "They cannot be brother and sister! They are so completely different from each other!"

David became Prefect and Head boy of the school, which meant that he had a lot of special privileges his sister could not even imagine. She did not seem to be getting anywhere. In those days the grade and middle school followed a system with an A, B and C stream. If you ended up in the B or C stream you were rarely encouraged to do further studies. If you were not among the top of the class there was little interest in you. So, when the B stream came to an end, Doreen left school. She was 15 years old.

She wanted to work with animals and applied for a post at the Physiological Laboratory at Cambridge University, serving the academic institutions in Cambridge that trained physicians and veterinarians.

For ten years she was responsible for preparing experiments for incoming medical and veterinary students as well as those that were further along in their four year studies. She wore a white lab coat as she prepared for the experiments, mostly experiments that utilized rabbits and frogs. After the students had done their part, Doreen and her colleagues ensured the lab was all cleaned up and the room tidied and ready for the next day.

Because she was in The Salvation Army the other staff often joked around with her. She was looked upon as being perfect, because of what she represented. But it was friendly joking and she handled it well. Generally she was respected for taking a positive stand for her faith in Jesus Christ.

David and Doreen grew up in a very protected environment, because almost all their free time was spent at The Salvation Army church. It was simply unheard of to do anything outside Army circles. Doreen was seven when she accepted Jesus as her Savior in Sunday school, which at that young age really meant she was accepted into the children's choir and could sing and perform with them! Soon she learned to play a cornet like her mother, and was invited to play in the band. When I met her she had transferred to a much larger instrument, the euphonium.

It was not until her teenage years that her faith really became meaningful and she realized what being a Christian was all about. One Sunday when she was in her mid-teens, this became so obvious to her that she went forward at the end of the service and dedicated her life to God.

The Salvation Army held their meetings in a building that was more like a hut made out of corrugated tin. Early every Sunday her father went down to the hall, as it was referred to, to stoke up the potbelly stove, attempting to chase away the chilling cold. Several times on Sunday the tin hut would be jam packed with 80-100 people. Many of the families were related to each other and Doreen's aunts and uncles and cousins were a major stabilizing factor in the small church. It was exciting when the time came to move into a proper building, but there were many good experiences and memories in the tin hut.

The preaching was convicting and close to the heart. Young people and down-and-outs alike were challenged to come to the mercy seat at the front of the Army hall to commit their lives to Christ. When the atmosphere of God's presence became so rich, the entire congregation would break out in a "hallelujah march." While the band played a rousing hymn, the congregation would take the army flags, and march single file around the hall singing, waving their flags and clapping their hands to the beat. Those moments impressed young hearts yearning for God.

Every week was full of activities with band practice on Tuesday, children's choir on Wednesday, choir practice on Thursday and a fellowship-type gathering, called the "popular meeting" on Saturday. As soon as the popular meeting was over, Doreen, wearing the Salvation Army uniform and bonnet, would take a package of The Salvation Army evangelistic newspaper *The War Cry* and a collection box down to the pubs, where she would go from person to person and sell the paper and collect money for the Army. She was always apprehensive before going, but once there, she relaxed. The Army lassies were often asked to sing in the pubs, and the most popular request was "The Old Rugged Cross!"

And then there was Sunday - hardly a day of rest for the Salvationists. At 10 in the morning Doreen taught Sunday school, followed by the morning service at 11 or holiness meeting as it is still called. The band and the choir always took part. After rushing home to eat Sunday dinner there was yet another Sunday school class at 2 p.m. followed by the praise meeting at 3 p.m., where all musical groups, including the children's choir and often the children's band participated. Running home for a quick cup of tea and warm up by the coal fire in the winter, it was then time for the march to the open-air meeting outside the Co-op at 6 p.m, which was followed by a march with the band playing and the flags swirling in the wind back to the hall. At 6:45 p.m. the final service of the day was held, the salvation meeting, which could last two hours. A few years before we married, Doreen took leadership for the children's choir in addition to all the other tasks she had.

There were several boys showing interest in the beautiful young lady in her Salvation Army uniform. Most of them did not amount to more than a few dates, but one became more serious. She befriended the young man who led the band in a Salvation Army church in Bedford some 30 miles away. It was at that point I stepped into her life!

The Beginning of Something Beautiful

I can still see us walking outside the home where I stayed after the concert in Stowmarket, where she had come with her friend to hear the *Joystrings*. We quickly drank a cup of cocoa and then went for a walk. "I am going back to Sweden at the end of next week," I said, "but we have a few concerts left in this part of the country. Will you come to Chingford next week and attend my last concert?" She hesitated, and uttered the phrase that I would learn to live with for more than forty years. "I don't know," she said, "I cannot make up my mind!"

"If you don't come, will you write to me?" I queried and she promised. There was no question of love, or of intimacy of any kind, not even holding hands. We just walked and talked.

The following week we held our final concert at Chingford. I stood for an hour outside the concert hall, checking the people streaming in, but Doreen never showed up.

In Stowmarket one of the *Joystrings* members had noticed her talking to me. We were always on our watch for what we called "followers," young ladies and young men who were after us to form any kind of relationship. As she went to her car, I told her that one of them said to me, "So she is a *Joystrings* follower, eh?" She hated that stigma and decided not to show up!

As the ship steamed out of Tilbury harbor the following day, I sat on deck and wrote my first letter to her, apart from my first introduction a few weeks earlier. That letter would be followed by a letter every day for three years, except the days I wrote two.

As the year went by, the tone in the letters went from formal to personal as a bond was created. After writing for a few months, I began asking Doreen to come visit me in Sweden. In those days The Salvation Army had a national congress in Stockholm every year and that would be a great time for her to visit. Having checked out the possibilities and because she had some vacation time, Doreen booked the first flight of her life, the night flight, which was so much cheaper, on British European Airways, flying the prone-to-accident and later outlawed Comet jet, arriving just before midnight the first night of the congress.

On the way to the bus terminal in central London where you could check in for flights in those days, she turned to her father and burst out, "Whatever made me say I would go?" Even now, after knowing her more than forty years, I am amazed that she actually went on her own.

Arriving at Arlanda airport outside Stockholm I met her with a bouquet of flowers. I can still see her coming down the stairs from customs dressed in a blue coat. While a friend of mine drove us to my parents' house, we sat in the dark in the back seat and held hands.

For months I had told my parents that a friend was coming to see me from England during the congress and could this friend stay with us in our small apartment? My mother thought that was a good idea, but it was just the week before that I realized my mom was going to let us sleep in the same room. It dawned on me that I had never told my parents about the English girl! So I finally blurted out, "Mom, my friend is a lady!" There have always been places for people to sleep in our apartment, so my mother slept on the little sofa in the living room, while my Dad had a fold up bed in the hallway, and Doreen got my parents' bedroom which also doubled up as our place to eat meals, just outside the little kitchen!

When we entered the apartment that night about 1 a.m., my mom and Dad were there as well as my sister and her fiancé. Tea and sandwiches were neatly arranged on plates in the living room. Doreen was so nervous she could hardly eat a bite and my mother was practicing her school English from 1920-1930 on Doreen! My father only knew one phrase in English, and he repeated it often with people who didn't speak Swedish. Looking at them he used to say, "I have a fine little garden," referring to the three trays of geraniums he used to have hanging on the tiny apartment's balcony railing. Doreen looked bewildered as he tried the phrase out on her.

After the congress, where I introduced Doreen to many of my friends, we took the train up to Skutskär where I was pastoring the small Salvation Army church. Within minutes of arrival, the whole little town knew that Doreen was there! "Is she sleeping in there?" whispered one neighbor to the nice Salvation Army lady of my church that was hosting Doreen in her home. Everyone wondered what had happened to the young pastor.

During that week we really wrestled with the issues. There was no question we were in love! But how could we work this out? I was a Salvation Army officer and in those days officers could not marry ordinary members – both had to be in full-time ministry to be able to marry, or you would have to resign as an officer and leave. Secondly, because of the commitment of one of my former girlfriends to be a missionary in South America, I had on the spur of the moment offered to do the same, and was preparing myself for such a change, learning Spanish as fast as I could, without making much headway.

I began to wonder if I was pushed in that direction, or if I really was called to Latin America. The more I read my Bible and my books, the more I sensed a call to the world, and hoped I could fulfill that through a global organization like The Salvation Army. And then there was my call to be an evangelist! While I enjoyed pastoring the church, I knew that this was not really what God wanted me to do.

As Doreen's time in Sweden was coming to an end, we went out for a meal in Stockholm and talked. "This won't work," Doreen whispered. "I am not called to be an officer, and am not going to do that just to marry you. I also have to listen to what God is saying to me. I am not a public person; I cannot preach and have not been told by God to move in that direction."

Being such a Salvationist through and through, "army barmy" as we used to call any people who knew no Christian world outside the Army, I did not even dare share with her my concerns and growing convictions about the Army's view on the sacraments, and how I sensed a need to be baptized as an adult.

On the forty-five minute bus-ride to the airport, I suddenly took her hand and in the most un-dramatic roundabout way asked her if she would marry me, and to my utter surprise she did not hesitate! Now it was up to the Lord to work out the details!

Three months later I entered my military service. That fall I managed to buy a cheap plane ticket and went on the first flight in my life to London for Christmas. Due to a snowstorm in Sweden, the plane was delayed and it was a nightmare trying to travel the two-hour journey from Gothenburg to London. After an eleven-hour try via Copenhagen and Amsterdam, I finally arrived, with Doreen still waiting at terminal 2. There had been no way to communicate with one another during the day, and her faithfulness proved solid even there!

Soon after I returned from Christmas and New Year in Histon I wrote my letter of resignation to the Army and when Doreen turned up in Stockholm for two weeks that summer, we were engaged. Selfishly I was most concerned whether she would be able to handle a husband who traveled as an evangelist! What lessons I had to learn!

Facing the Challenges

The next few months were the hardest. While I came over by ship for a few days for her 25th birthday in August that year, we did not see each other until after Christmas. Letters were okay, but I wanted to talk to her every day. Phone calls were very expensive. I would save up Swedish *kronor* (today about 15 cents each), and for 20 of those I could talk for 10 minutes. The only way to reach her by phone was to call her at work because her parents had no phone at home. Half of my phone time would disappear while the switchboard operator tried to locate her, and then I would hear her distinct voice say, "hello." After that often followed nothing but silence. I would talk, knowing I would soon run out of coins, but she would be speechless. Not being used to speaking on a phone, she simply could not communicate. This became very frustrating for both of us.

Just after the New Year I came by boat to England and moved into the guest room in her parents' home. I had been invited to speak at a few meetings in February in the West Indian church in Brixton. Doreen's brother David, who I had never met before, had come back from Germany and taken a Salvation Army church in nearby Bishop's Stortford, and he invited me for meetings as well. And then I also needed to go for the interviews with *Youth for Christ*.

Having communicated only almost exclusively by letters, now suddenly communicating across the dinner table every day was difficult. Many days I would walk three miles into Cambridge to have lunch with Doreen, and then she would drive me half the distance back, and I would walk another mile. No wonder I was slim! Almost every night Doreen was at the Army. She came home, we ate, and she was off again! I sat at home, watching British movies on television. When she finally returned we would all sit in the tiny living room, waiting for her parents to go to bed so we could have a few minutes to ourselves. My English was not that great, and many times I offended her parents by saying the wrong things without knowing it.

We had tentatively set the date for our wedding in July of 1967, to make it possible for my parents to come from Sweden during their summer vacation. But this was a tentative date. Soon after I arrived in the United Kingdom, I was invited by the director of *Youth for Christ*, Rev. Owen Gregory, to come to his church in Wales, where he pastored part-time. No doubt he wanted to check me out before the interview at YFC the following month.

Doreen was invited as well and after we had changed trains in Cardiff, and settled down in the compartment in the tiny train heading to the mining village of Tredegar, Doreen whispered, "I want to postpone the wedding. I am not ready!" My world collapsed! Here we were on our way to my first job interview, and suddenly we didn't know when we were getting married. My mother and father, sister and future brother-in-law had already booked the ship for July! What would I tell them?

We arrived in Tredegar and I felt like I had been flattened to the pavement. Ten deacons stared up at me from the deacon bench in the Baptist Chapel and lambs stood on the slag heaps outside the window at the same level as the elevated pulpit, "bahhing." While this Swedish preacher tried to preach, I was not exactly at my best.

Finally, after several weeks of waiting until Doreen felt she would be ready, we settled on September 9, just two months later than the original date. It all worked out. My parents changed their tickets. I got the job at YFC, but some of the "not ready" tension lingered.

Meeting Doreen after work just three weeks before the wedding, we got into her father's car, which she used much more than he did. With tears flowing down her face, she turned to me, "This isn't working," she cried as she slid behind the steering wheel. "I cannot go through with it." She burst out, "You are too demanding. You use the word "must" all the time. You must do this, you must do that...I can't take it anymore." It dawned on me that I was transliterating Swedish where the word "must" is much weaker, like "we need to consider." This was a major linguistic blunder. But when we drove home that night there was no reconciliation. I went directly to my room, pulled out my cases and began to pack. Doreen went to her room sobbing.

Suddenly her father burst into my room, asking what was going on. I explained that Doreen had called off the wedding and I was packing and would he help me order a taxi or drive me to the train station. I was not quite sure where to go, except I already had a key to the small apartment where we were planning to live. It was furnished, so I could move right in.

He left and went to talk to Doreen, giving her one of the most challenging talks of his life. "You cannot sit on the fence," he told her. "Either you are determined it will never work, and you need to let him go or you decide that he is the man for you in your life and you go and reconcile with him. But you cannot sit on the fence."

Doreen gave the fatherly advice a lot of thought, because suddenly the door opened and she came in, taking me in her arms as we cried together and forgave each other, went to our knees and prayed that God would anchor our marriage on Him. There was no pre-marital counseling in those days, so we simply learned to sort these things out for ourselves.

A Wedding!

Three weeks later the wedding took place in The Salvation Army hall. A thick fog lingered that morning, making us nervous that people coming from London would not make it, but an hour before the service the fog lifted.

The Army hall was packed with Doreen's relatives and friends plus my parents, sister and brother-in-law. When it was time for the service, I stepped forward with my best man, Captain Keith Banks, who had been my best friend in The Salvation Army Training College, and waited for the bride. After ten minutes, I wondered if her uncle's car had broken down. After twenty minutes I was sure she had turned into a run-away bride. But suddenly the wedding march began to pour out of the portable, peddle organ on the stage, and there she was! A friend of both Doreen's parents and my parents, Lieutenant-Colonel Wesley Evans (with a Swedish wife who was sister-in-law to my mother's cousin Flora), conducted the ceremony, and Joy Webb, the leader of the *Joystrings* sang.

After an enjoyable wedding lunch that cost 67 pounds (approximately $130 for the 110 guests), Doreen and I were ready to leave for our new apartment in Buckhurst Hill in the outskirts of London. The couple who had conducted our wedding kindly drove us there...we had no other means of transportation!

We rented this small apartment from one of the YFC board members. It was furnished, so the only piece of furniture we actually owned was a bedside table and some bookshelves I had purchased as well as some that I had made myself. Sitting in our little living room drinking tea that night, tears began trickling down Doreen's cheeks. She was 26 and this was the first time she had lived away from her parents. She was jobless, and suddenly felt that her whole life had changed that day. It had!

The following day we had our honeymoon: We took the underground to central London, went to an inexpensive restaurant for lunch and saw *The Sound of Music!*

I had officially started my role as an evangelist with *Youth for Christ* on September first, and on the Monday after our wedding the chairman called and wondered why I wasn't in the office. By Tuesday I was in there and a string of meetings, outreaches and programs began.

Living on $30 a week became quite a challenge. After $ 3-4 dollars were given to the church, the rent was $15 dollars; groceries cost at least $10 dollars, just leaving $3 for electricity, heat and telephone. There was no money left for vacation or incidentals. About every three months we splurged by going to a restaurant.

Doreen had hoped to find work in London, but as she was pregnant a month after our wedding, that did not materialize. After our first daughter Carin came along, finances became even tighter! When I became director of YFC I also needed a car. We purchased an old Ford Cortina and paid most of it on a long-term payment plan. The Cortina was a joke! Every time I put it in reverse, the gearstick came loose in my hand. Sometimes I could fix it, but most of the time we had to call out a mechanic!

While I was zealous to hand in every gift given to me for speaking, I also did extra work for Christian newspapers in Sweden to make up the gaps in our income. I wrote about current Christian affairs in Britain, or in the USA for that matter. About every 8 to 10 weeks a check would arrive for the articles. On those days we celebrated, going down to the pastry shop and buying two-day old Danish pastries and other goodies for half price!

As our daughter Carin grew out of her baby crib, we needed to buy blankets and sheets. There was only one gas element in the living room, the rest of the apartment was freezing cold. At night, we would have to wrap her up so well that only the tip of her nose could be seen. My nylon shirts almost stood by themselves in a corner of the room in the morning and the condensation could be scraped off the inside of the windows, where it had frozen to ice.

We didn't have money for sheets for Carin. I was beside myself for not being able to provide enough income. We prayed and prayed. One morning I was desperate! I prayed, asking God to provide immediately. As I walked out of the door to go to the YFC office, I kicked the door mat. Under it was an envelope…no name…just two crisp 10 pound bills inside - the equivalent of $ 40! What a celebration!

The first few weeks of our married life, Doreen attended the local Salvation Army in Woodford while I was gone. However, soon she traveled with me and the Sundays when we were at home, we walked down to the local Baptist church, more out of convenience than anything else. The Baptist crowd were great people, but it was a traditional service, and we both missed the inspirational singing and sharing of testimonies we were used to from the Army.

After two years in Buckhurst Hill I was invited to join the staff of the Evangelical Covenant Church denomination in Sweden. This prompted many discussions with Doreen. What would it be like? Where would we live? What would we do with the language issues?

A Growing Family

When it was time for us to really consider moving, I called the pastors in three different towns and cities in southwest Sweden where I would serve. I told them that we would move to the town or city of the person who found an apartment for us first. The pastor in Herrljunga, a small town of 4,000 people, called me back within 15 minutes! So, in January 1970 we sold our car, took the ship from UK to Sweden and settled into Swedish life.

Doreen was pregnant with our daughter Maria, it was winter and cold and I was gone every Wednesday to Sunday for crusades. We lived a 20-minute walk from shops and the church and every Sunday Doreen would walk down to the church and sit in the services, not understanding a word. Few people spoke English in those days, so no one talked to her except one old lady who spoke no English but took a great interest in her. When it was time for visits to midwives, doctors or dentists I came along and served as the interpreter.

Having not been a bookworm or particularly studious, going to school to learn Swedish was not really an option for Doreen. Instead, we watched US/UK films with sub-titles on our old black and white TV and within a year she had learned enough Swedish to handle conversations. By the time we left eight years later she was fluent in Swedish, which she has kept up these past 30 years.

By the time our two daughters started school, we had become quite the typical Swedish family. We lived in a closed-knit community where we could walk to everything. Our life centered around my work, the church and the family. Doreen sang in the choir, and for a while played in the church brass band. During the first two years in Sweden, Doreen became convinced that she needed to be baptized and followed my theological shift from the Army position without any pressure from me whatsoever.

We had great times with the kids. Carin was introverted and shy while Maria was extroverted and forward. One year Maria demonstrated that vividly in the traditional Christmas morning service. The church was packed. Doreen sang in the choir while I sat in the audience with four-year old Carin beside me and 2 1/2-year old Maria on my lap. The reader had just read the story about Mary (Maria in Swedish) giving birth to Jesus and there was a hushed silence in the church. Maria suddenly burst out so loud that the entire church could hear it, "Maria, that is me! Did I have the baby Jesus?"

Carin had moved from an English speaking culture to Sweden, and although she was only 1½ years old at the time of the move, it seems to have influenced her psyche. She was afraid to be left alone. She tended to throw such temper tantrums that we did not know what to do with her. Often I would sigh, "She will never be able to live a normal adult life, not with those tantrums!" The move to Chicago did her a lot of good. She loved *Awana*, the children's program in the church, and the tantrums went away. I smile as I look back to those days. Today, Carin is a trusted advisor and confidant in my life! During the first eight years of *Global Action's* existence she worked with the accounts, until it became too much to handle for one person.

Maria had her other things to deal with. It took her almost 30 years to confess to me that she had a deeply rooted resentment for me because I was gone on an international trip on her 8th birthday. I know something forced that particular trip, but when I look back I see the many times when I needed to reschedule trips to give more time to my wife and my children. Her most embarrassing moment was when we visited the United States in 1976. Maria was six years old. We were staying with Kenneth and Margaret Taylor in Wheaton, and Doreen and the children went over to the home of Mark Taylor, the president of Tyndale House, to visit. When it was time to go to bed, we realized Maria had a small toy in her pocket, which she had pocketed during the visit to Mark's home. We walked back to his home, where Maria had to confess her theft and hand back the toy! She never stole again. It taught her a great principle for life.

Maria developed from a little rascal into a woman who wanted to serve God. In 1986 I took my family to Billy Graham's conference for itinerant evangelists called *Amsterdam 1986*. Carin and Maria served on the steward staff, helping with myriad details behind the scenes while

Doreen and our son Paul, only 9 years old, served in the *Living Bibles International* booth.

One day Maria had an afternoon off, and I decided to take her out to show her Amsterdam. "Where do you want to go?" I inquired. To my utter surprise the 15-year old blond answered, "Dad, I want you to walk me through the Red Light district!" A few months earlier Floyd McClung, leader of *Youth with a Mission,* had visited our church. He and his family had ministered in the Red Light district, and Maria sensed a call in her life at that point. So, we walked through the Red Light district where Dutch women exhibit their bodies in skimpy clothing in huge shop windows. As we finished the embarrassing walk, Maria turned to me and said, "I will work here one day!" Her dream came true. She went through the Discipleship Training School with *Youth with a Mission* in Sweden, stayed on their staff for many years, and for a while ministered in that very place.

In 1976 I was visiting England for staff meetings with the coordinators for *Living Bibles International.* Standing in the phone booth in the lobby of the Queen's hotel in Eastbourne, I called home and heard a most fascinating story from my wife. "Your parents have been here for a few days, and the other day I had such pain in my stomach, that your dad gave me some medicine to ease the pain. But it would not go away, so I finally went to the doctor. Lars, I'm pregnant!" Jokingly I exclaimed, "You can't be - I haven't been home long enough!"

In the early summer of 1977, Carin then 9 and Maria then 7, were blessed with a baby brother Paul Kenneth, and we entered into the diaper-period of family life again. I had just accepted the new position as international director of *Living Bibles International,* and I was very concerned what all my required travel would do to Doreen and the three kids. How would she cope when I traveled so much?

We had hoped that when the girls were a bit older, Doreen would be able to travel more, but those plans had to be placed on the back burner. After all, we added a son to the family! Doreen never liked traveling much, although we crossed the North Sea some 30 times back and forth without and with kids over the years. That could be a horrendous journey as there often was a storm on the sea and most journeys included two nights in one of the cheap cabins down below or just above car deck.

Twice she was able to go with me to the USA, first in 1974 to attend the Christian Booksellers convention while my in-laws looked after the girls, and the second time in 1976 when we took the girls with us to attend several meetings for *LBI* as well as the Christian Booksellers convention in Atlantic City. We flew from Chicago to Denver, bought a used Dodge Dart and traveled to the West Coast and then all the way back to Atlantic City, finally shipping the car to Sweden from Newark!

Several times during these two trips, Doreen would turn to me and say, "Pretty nice country. Good place to visit but I would never like to live here or raise my kids here!" Little did we know! Every time we were ready to go on a trip, Doreen would mutter to herself, and sometimes aloud to the kids and me, "I wish I'd said I'd never go!" However, when she went on a trip she usually enjoyed it. Later, when I became involved in fundraising, it was invaluable when she came with me. People donated more – and still do - with Doreen along!

Then came the bombshell. The Board of *LBI* demanded that I move with my family to Chicago within a year. When Doreen heard the news, she said, "You can go. I will stay here." Having moved to Sweden and learned the language and the culture, she was comfortable with the small town atmosphere, where everyone knew each other and you could walk to the stores, church or school. The kids played freely in the streets without fear of kidnapping. When shopping for the kids, the store owner told her to bring home as many clothes as she wanted to let the kids try on, then simply return the ones she didn't want. The store owner trusted her completely. She could not imagine leaving all this behind for the gangster city of Chicago!

It got to be so bad that we could not even bring up the word United States. It became like a swear word. At the same time, the pressure mounted on me to inform the board when we would be ready to come and where we would settle.

Finally, after several months, one of our mutual friends, Dr. Börje Axelsson, came to the rescue. We had met several years earlier when I stayed with the Axelsson family during a crusade in their town. We became best friends, spent vacations together and Börje also served on the Board of *LBI* in Europe. He sat down and had a long talk with Doreen about what this would mean for me if we did not move and how she would have to live with that the rest of her life. Placing a spiritual emphasis on the whole matter, Doreen finally "caved in" and said yes. We agreed to limit our time commitment in the US to four years.

A Time to Move

In the winter of 1978 I flew to Chicago and trudged through the heavy snow with a realtor to find a house. It is scary, if not impossible, to buy a house on your own. Doreen insisted it had to be close to a church, the school and to the stores, because we could only afford one car and she preferred to walk to those places.

Finally I settled for a home in Villa Park. In July I went over alone again, meeting the container with our household goods, and within 24 hours I had placed all the furniture in the house with the help of my staff, washed all the dishes, making the home look lived in. I rushed back to England where Doreen was waiting with the children at her parents' house.

Arriving back a week later was a relief. She loved the house! But the first night brought many tears since everything was so different. The humidity and the heat were intense. The thunderstorms were the biggest we had ever seen or heard. Doreen walked to the store – once! It was too muggy, too far and every package was so much bigger. For $ 800 I bought her an old Ford which lasted for a few years.

After a few years we moved to Naperville to be closer to work and church. Doreen began to like her surroundings, her church and choir and her new friends. Eventually she became a US citizen, something I still have left to do!

Our home became a haven for staff visiting from around the world. Friends from Sweden came. Both sets of parents came to visit. And sometimes people who just knew us through other friends came and stayed for long stretches of time. Doreen developed a gift she does not even acknowledge much – a tremendous gift of hospitality.

Carin graduated from Taylor University with a degree in accounting. At the university she met Ron Symonette from the Bahamas and they married in August 1991. Today they have two children, Amanda and Joshua, and live in Colorado Springs.

Maria went to serve with *Youth with a Mission* for many years, mainly based in Sweden, leading teams to various parts of the world. At

YWAM she met Andrew Sturt from Great Britain and they married in 1994. Today they have three children, Ryan, Eleanor and Katelyn and they also live in Colorado Springs.

The move from Naperville to Colorado Springs was good for Paul. He found many friends in high school who also attended our church, Woodmen Valley Chapel. He enrolled with his saxophone in marching band, and during his final year in High School they won the state championships! Since 2000, after a few years of college, Paul has worked with *Global Action* and is involved with team ministry, photography and videography.

With me gone more than half the time in any given year, *Living Bibles International* and later *International Bible Society* and *Global Action* would never have been able to use me as they did, if it had not been for Doreen's servant heart. She raised the children, mostly on her own. Re-entry was often difficult for me. She and the children already had their routines, and "Dad" better not step in and upset what was working. I would never have made it without her. She was and is God's choice for my life.

CHAPTER 7
"...and some to be Evangelists"

I have always been fascinated by evangelists. Not the Elmer Gantry types or the Televangelists we are so used to today, but the biblical concept of people using the gift of evangelism. Evangelists are men and women whom God has given a special calling to challenge people to a commitment for Jesus Christ – whether you are a believer and need to be "revived," or an unbeliever who needs to be exposed to the claims of Christ.

The word "evangelist" comes directly from the New Testament. Ephesians 4:11 explains it well:

> *"..these are the gifts Christ gave to the church: the apostles, the prophets, the evangelists and the pastors and teachers."*

In the New Testament it wasn't simply apostle "So and So," or evangelist "So and So" or prophet "He or She." The church recognized that these were god-appointed tasks in the early Church. Christ gave us some to be evangelists. To his young friend and co-worker Timothy, Paul writes, *"...do the work of an evangelist..."*

The evangelist is appointed by God for a specific task. God is into specializing. We learn how the evangelist first functioned in the church from Philip. In Acts 8, Philip not only stood alongside the pastor, he worked on his own. Philip was well-equipped for several ministries in the church in Samaria and later for an evangelistic encounter with the Ethiopian finance minister on the road to Gaza.

From these descriptions we can conclude that the evangelist is a pioneer worker. Philip was sent out as the frontrunner of the Christian Church, and a pioneer in areas where the gospel had yet to be preached.

Second, he preached and accompanied his message with signs and wonders. His preaching was a proclamation of the basic message of salvation.

Third, he had to concentrate on the main points of the gospel. The more detailed teaching was handed over to the other teachers.

Fourth, he was on the move. Led by the Spirit he went here and there to lead people to Christ. Acts 8:40 states, *"Meanwhile, Philip found himself farther north of the town of Azotus. He preached the Good News there and in every town along the way until he came to Caesarea."*

This was the atmosphere in which I grew up. The evangelist was still the pioneer, going to areas where the gospel had not been heard clearly. Where the Church had become stifled within its walls, it was the job of the evangelist to get the believers to move outside the walls, to become salt and light in the world.

The message of the evangelist needed to be a clear proclamation of salvation. While he had to be theologically trained, he should not be a theological expert. The evangelist was called to be someone who clearly defined the borders between the kingdom of God and the kingdoms of this world. His job was to win the lost at any cost.

Inspired by Other Evangelists

When I was 13 I came across a small book published by the Covenant church called *Some to Evangelists*. It described the history of the denomination's evangelists during the past fifty years. What heroes these people were. There was Israel August Åström. In early years he had spent time in Buffalo, New York and returned home to little Sweden with new methods and a strong message. At times the methods he used were quite wild. Eventually he was called in to the denominational headquarters to face stern questions by the leadership.

"Is it true that you, an evangelist in the Covenant Church, stood on your head in front of three ladies? Please explain yourself!"

"Does the chairman of the board of the Covenant Church of Sweden, the distinguished member of parliament, Sven Bengtsson, believe that I, Israel August Åström, ever have had an audience of only three old ladies?"

"I don't know," answered the chairman.

"Does the chairman of the board of the Covenant Church of Sweden, the distinguished member of parliament Sven Bengtsson, believe that I, Israel August Åström, stood on my head in front of only three old ladies?"

"I don't know," was the answer.

Turning to the president of the denomination, Åström continued.

"Does our honorable president, Rev. Nyrén really believe that I, Israel August Åström, stood on my head for three old ladies?"

"Who knows?" was the answer.

The questions were left unanswered. When the evangelists left the meeting, one of them turned to Åström and said, "But dear Israel August, did you really stand on your head for these old women?"

They all burst out laughing as Åström replied, "I never denied it. I just wanted to know if those old guys believed it!"

Åström was the kind of preacher you really had to see in action, something I never had the opportunity to, as he died several years before I was born. However, during my adolescence my parents made friends with his daughter and son-in-law and through them I heard about the more difficult aspects in the life of the evangelist – many days away from the family, difficult re-entries after weeks of separation, somewhat of a distance from the family – things I would experience myself.

Another one of the great evangelists I read about in this book was Josef Roth, a well-educated aristocrat who could communicate the gospel just as well in the pulpit as in the nicest parlors of the wealthy upper-class society of Sweden. Roth read at least three books a week and memorized much of what he read. He could quote the Bible and the classics equally well, and he dared to put his finger on sore spots in people's lives when he talked to them. It was this sort of risk-taking and radicalism that appealed to me.

One day a well-to-do man had invited Roth to his home. During small talk over dinner the host explained, "The happiest time in my life was when I was a poor man." Without sounding superior, Roth immediately responded, "That kind of happiness can return to you today. Give away what you have to the poor, and you will be back in your lost paradise!"

Roth was most influential in the early 20th century. He, too, died before I was born, but I read everything that was written about him or written by him.

And then there was Karl Agathon Essloff. He had been rather wild as a young man, playing music at the village dances, but one day the Lord took hold of him and transformed his life. He was choleric by nature, could preach about hell in such a way that the audience almost smelled the sulfur, but at the same time had a soft heart that yearned to see people come to Christ. I only heard him once, a year before he died, and I was five years old! All I can remember is his enormous hair that almost stood straight up. He moved like a rubber ball across the platform.

In his early days of ministry, Essloff was known as a great swimmer, and he reached out to the young people by organizing swimming competitions. Of course they wanted to come and listen to their swim instructor in the tent after that! However, one afternoon Essloff had a problem. He wanted to take a swim in a nearby lake before the service. Having no swimsuit with him, he just stripped and ran down to the lake. As he tip-toed back to the tent stark-naked he noticed to his astonishment that a few ladies had arrived early for the evening service. His clothes were behind the platform inside! He ran as fast as he could through the tent, with his dark hair flying in every direction. Afterwards the ladies exclaimed, "We saw the devil himself run through the tent! We better pray more for the evangelist and his protection."

Thousands of people heard the gospel wherever his campaigns were heard. He died just having turned fifty, but the memory of him lingered.

While I was in my teens there were three major evangelists at work in Sweden. Berthil Paulsson, under whose ministry I came to Christ, had his own team under the name *New Life*, and his crusades had major impact across the nation. Berthil's bible-centered messages touched people's hearts deeply. The formats of his services, and his focus on the Word became one of my models for ministry.

John Hedlund had a way to stir any city with his advertising and outrageous methods. Every election year he would invite each party leader to his crusade tent, seating several thousand people. He would interview each one of them, and this became a standard procedure every year there was an election. Other nights he would invite the motorcycle gangs to drive their bikes into the tent and listen to a message geared just for them. I studied his marketing methods very closely.

The "king" of them all, Frank Mangs, had already stepped into retirement when I began in ministry. Rev Mangs was born in the Swedish-speaking part of Finland. In the early 20th century he became the evangelist in Scandinavia. Businesses closed their doors when Frank Mangs came to town. There were no lines at the cinemas. The bars were empty. Thousands of people in the Free Church movement could point to their conversion during one of his many campaigns. Many young preachers began speaking with a Finnish-Swedish accent like Mangs, although they had never been to that part of the world. Mangs published a lot of his sermons so his material was easily accessible, and as a young Salvation Army officer, I memorized several of them and preached them with gusto. By being open to all denominations, he became a model for me of working with the larger body of Christ.

So when the invitation letter arrived from the Covenant Church in Sweden, asking me to become their evangelist, I knew a dream had come true. It was not only God's calling on my life, it was all I ever had wanted to see happen. However, the evangelists I had admired had been mature men and women. When my call came I had barely turned 25!

The Work Begins in Earnest

After moving back to Sweden, the diary began filling up as different cities found out that there was a new young evangelist in the country, and within months, my next three years were planned out. As soon as I had held my first campaign it became evident that I needed help with the music. I came across a man, who was a year younger than me, with a wonderful baritone voice, and asked him if he would become the soloist for my campaigns. Rolf Lideberg joined the crusade team and served in most crusades for the next four years. In the beginning I played the piano for him, but soon his younger brother Bert joined the team as our pianist.

When Rolf married and the family came along, it was harder for him to travel, so other people joined my team, like Stig Östlund, who was a Pentecostal pastor and later became a vicar in the Lutheran church.

Another evangelist, Leif Karlsson, who had a unique gift of praying for people, also joined me in many of the bigger campaigns.

Most of the crusades were organized by local evangelical alliances, and churches in their geographical area would come together for a month or six weeks for these meetings. In the summers we rented huge marquees, some of which could seat a thousand people, while in the winter, we rented a sports arena or took turns using the participating churches. Staying in hotels was unheard of, so the evangelist and his team moved in with different families for the entire time of the crusade. Often there was no spare guest room, so your arrival would either displace a child from his or her room, or you simply shared a bedroom with one of the children. Every day we visited different families for lunch and dinner, which was a wonderful way to get to know many of the people in the pew.

Several churches had guest rooms within their facilities and thought it best for the visiting preacher to stay in one of those rooms, preparing breakfast on his own. While this seemed like a great arrangement, I hated it. When told that this was the plan, I would plead to stay with a family. "I am fighting with the enemy all evening in the service. Then you want me to stay behind and fight with him all night as well? I miss my family, let me at least stay with someone else's family." I learned quickly to eliminate all noise within a yard from me. I simply switched off outside noise and concentrated on my reading, studying or typing.

During my first crusade years I studied day and night for my four years of seminary, which I pressed into two years of external studies. After graduation I began working on a New Testament translation in modern Swedish, together with a group of writers and scholars. I had to filter out all disturbances, often sitting at the kitchen table with my portable typewriter in the middle of household activities.

The atmosphere in these crusade meetings varied greatly. In the summers, when we used the marquees, there was always a separate tent at the front, set to the side of the marquee, with another tent aisle leading to it. This was used as a prayer tent. Half an hour before every service, that tent would be filled by prayer partners, praying up a storm. As the service started, the marquee would be packed with people, especially over the weekend. Church members brought their non-Christian friends, the youth of surrounding towns would often turn up with their mopeds and motorbikes or second-hand cars. For most young Christian people in the area, it was a given to turn up at the evangelistic meetings.

We held special services to ensure that Wednesdays through Fridays also filled up the tent. Often a visiting music group from another city would be invited for those weeknights. I was very pragmatic about this. If a choir of 50 singers came from another city, they filled up the front of the tent and made it easy to preach. They would also draw a wider audience.

Other nights, like on a Thursday, we would invite the local newspaper reporters and hold an event called the "The press presses the priest!" The reporters could ask any questions they wanted. Sometimes we took questions from the audience, too. For an under-30 evangelist, this was risk-taking 101. You never knew what they might ask, from biblical issues to morality issues (including questions about marriage versus co-habitation, which was becoming prevalent in those days). With so many denominations involved some of the questions were doctrinal, and difficult.

In one city, baptism was the hot issue. Some people were very sarcastic about baptism by immersion. On one of these evenings, a man tried to make fun of the whole idea, and asked, "Why don't you baptize forward instead of backwards?" That night I spent at least 20 minutes answering the question about baptism in general. I didn't hold back! Three weeks after the crusade was over I received a telegram from the same man who had asked the question. It simply read, "15 of us baptized – backwards - last night – hallelujah!"

Most crusade meetings followed a similar pattern: Rousing congregational hymns, followed by songs from the singers in a typical string band style with a choir made up of people from all churches accompanied by guitars, brass instruments, accordions and any other instruments. The soloist would sing, there would be an offering, and at times brief testimonies. I made sure I was in the pulpit 45 minutes after the service had begun, giving me approximately 30 minutes for the message. While most messages had an evangelistic flavor, they were also focused on a deeper life with Christ, what it really means to live out the Christian life.

No message was given without leading to a point of decision or commitment. As the message concluded, I would ask the singers or the soloist to sing an appropriate song, while I urged people to respond and walk into the prayer tent. We always had prayer partners, who also walked into the tent, encouraging others to follow them. Some nights, very few would go to the tent, while other nights God's presence was so obvious, that I had barely asked the question before people literally ran into the tent.

As one of the local pastors finished the service, or continued to invite people to come, I would move around the prayer tent asking who wanted special prayer. At that point everyone was already on their knees next to simple benches or planks placed over trusses. As individuals raised their hands, prayer partners or other pastors would come alongside these people and counsel them. At times people came for salvation, other times to confirm their faith, or many times to be counseled regarding deep personal issues. Often I would invite people to meet with me for individual counselling the following day.

Saturdays were very special, because every Saturday night there would be two services, the ordinary crusade service starting at 7 or 7:30 p.m. and then the youth service, which often began either at 10:22 p.m. or 22:22, as we called it since we used European 24-hour timing.

The youth services were often a bit wild. The marquees or the halls would be jam-packed. Visiting youth groups or gospel choirs would lead music and the volume was always sky high! Young people shared testimonies and then it was my turn. I really worked hard on my messages for these moments, as I knew I was influencing a whole new generation for the gospel. Many of these young people had grown up in Christian homes, but had never been confronted with the claims of Christ. These nights were "in your face" preaching like never before, challenging young people to become followers of Christ and live whole-heartedly for Him. Thirty-five years later I still bump into middle-age Swedes who found Christ during those youth nights.

Openness to the Gospel

Though Sweden had begun its secularization at least twenty years before we moved back to Sweden, there was still openness to the gospel. The results of the revivals of the 19th century and the beginning of the 20th century had left their influence. There was not one family without at least one relative in the Free Church movement. Religious education at school still included reading the Bible. The difference between the 70s and today is like 20,000 miles apart.

In one town, Hova, where we held a crusade in 1971, a leading pastor of one of the churches was in charge of the advertising. When I turned up in the town and opened the local newspaper the headlines screamed at me in huge black print, "God has promised to show up in church tonight!" Well, that was a tall order. However, this particular crusade was so bathed in prayer by church members, that God did indeed show up night after night.

One of the most memorable things from this crusade happened on one of the Saturday nights. Because of the large crowds none of the churches could hold the audience, so we rented the dining hall in the nearby high school. As I began preaching that night, I was interrupted by a lady who stood up at the back and began walking down the middle aisle, crying. Halfway down to the aisle, she fell to her knees, wailing from the pit of her innermost being. Between her noise and sobs, she cried, "Is there salvation for me?" Of course there was, and that night the entire audience turned into a giant prayer meeting for this lady, and for many others. I didn't even finish the sermon! Just the other year, I spoke in a church in southern Sweden, when someone came up to me and asked me if I remembered this service. How could I forget? It was the wife of the pastor, who had prayed with this woman that night and told me how she joined the church and served for more than 30 years, before she went to be with the Lord.

One of the greatest challenges that often happened was when the local committee decided to extend a crusade another week. People were coming to the Lord, many were rededicating their lives, so how could the evangelist go home and not come back? Sometimes this meant giving up a week of rest at home. In some cases, it meant postponing the first week of the next crusade.

I always tried to pick sermon topics to draw people to the crusade, like "God - old Santa Claus or the creator of the world?" or "Jesus Christ – real superstar" or even "Is there life after sex?" The year Sweden had elections, I often spoke on the subject "Do we need a new government?" obviously referring to the government of our lives.

Most days during the crusade we had day activities such as visiting the local factories for a short service on the factory floor and open-air meetings or morning assemblies at the local public schools. When we visited university cities, we would hold assemblies or debate gatherings with the university's Christian groups. We always invited non-Christians to participate as well.

There was a tendency to treat the morning assemblies as opportunities to present a meek, non-threatening gospel. That didn't fit my style. In one city, Skara, while speaking to the teacher's training college assembly, I was particularly bold. I ran to the pulpit, opened my Bible to Proverbs 28:1 and read, *"The wicked run away when no one is chasing them, but the godly are as bold as lions."* I presented the emptiness of Swedish non-Christian life as running without direction, and then introduced them to the joy of salvation.

Was it all a victorious time? Far from it! Some of the local ministers did not believe in confrontational evangelism and ignored the visiting team, or entered into somewhat rude smearing attacks of the methods and the evangelist.

One night the crusade committee wanted to meet with me. "How come you have your hands in your pockets when you pray?" they demanded. "I'll tell you that if you tell me what you were doing looking at me during prayer!" I retorted.

Other times, we didn't have any breakthrough at all. Perhaps the ground was not prepared or the expectations were too high. During these crusades, I would still preach my heart out night after night, but nothing seemed to happen. Those were days when I wished I was doing something different. I struggled those days to not be depressed or sarcastic, and did not always succeed.

As soon as we finished praying with individuals Sunday night, I would get in the car and drive home, however many hours the journey took. Often I would arrive home at 3 or 4 in the morning and finally just drop into bed. Preaching with an invitation for people to respond is exhausting. Many times there were snowstorms, and the journey home was a real challenge. During those few Mondays and Tuesdays when I was home, I taught English at the local middle school, paid bills, tried to spend some time with the family, and then drove off again Wednesday morning. Now and then Doreen came with me, especially before the children were in school.

A New Opportunity

It was at this time I was approached by *Living Bibles International* to serve as its Europe director, working with Bible translations in Western and Eastern Europe. I did so with the understanding that I could continue to hold several crusades a year. Surprisingly (and thankfully), the invitations came at a rate that was workable. When I was appointed president of *LBI* in 1977, most of the crusade invitations beyond 1978 had stopped. That was the year when *LBI* asked me to move with my family to the United States.

After we moved to the United States we had sporadic invitations from Sweden over the next ten years, and I also conducted a few crusades in India. I had hoped there might be more opportunity for evangelistic preaching in the USA, but those opportunities never materialized, and to some degree my gift as an evangelist was buried under a busy schedule of administering worldwide mission programs and organizational speaking.

Does the church need the gift of the evangelist today? Probably more than ever, especially in a climate where so many people in the pew are not sure about their faith and in a day and time when repentance has disappeared from our vocabulary. Without evangelists we end up with a weakened church desperately in need of Jesus-followers.

CHAPTER 8
Mentors

W hen I look back to my teens and early years of ministry, I wonder where I would have been without my mentors. Hebrews 13: 6 says, *"Remember your leaders who went before you."* There are foremost five people who I consider my closest mentors. Of those, only one is alive today, but their influence still speaks beyond their graves.

Berthil Paulsson

As I write this book, Berthil Paulsson is 97 years old and lives just outside Stockholm, Sweden. In his most energetic ministry days he was called Sweden's Billy Graham, a title that suited him perfectly. Berthil was an evangelist with the Covenant Church of Sweden and during the 50's was the key evangelist in the interdenominational crusade team called the All Christian Evangelistic Team. It was during their three-month-long Stockholm crusade in the spring of 1957 that I came to Christ and asked Him to transform my life. During those three months of rallies, I heard a lot of sermons. I don't remember any of them, except portions of the one Berthil preached the night I was saved. But I vividly remember the way he preached, the tone of his voice, the gestures and the conviction that rubbed off on my twelve-year old soul. I can still envision him and hear his voice more than 50 years later!

Risk-Taker for God

After I went into the ministry, Berthil and I struck up a friendship, often writing each other or calling each other. When you talk with him, it is as if you are the only one who exists. His superlatives explode as you tell him of anything that has happened in your life. He always has had a word of advice, until recently when he moved into a nursing home.

One year after we were married, Doreen and I visited Sweden with one of the YFC Youth teams and then stayed behind for a week. We met with Berthil and his wife in their home. Animatedly he looked at me over a cup of coffee. "I am conducting a huge New Life crusade in the city of Nässjö. Are you going back to England via Gothenburg?" When I mentioned that we were, he interrupted me and said, "Fine! I want you to come Thursday night and preach for me in the crusade."

Traveling halfway down the country toward Gothenburg, I left Doreen, Carin and Doreen's parents with a mutual friend, and drove to the city of Nässjö. The whole city knew about the New Life Crusade. The choir was huge, the soloist one of the gospel singer attractions of Sweden. I thought Berthil would be away that night and secretly hoped he would be, but lo and behold, there he was, sitting on the platform. The huge tent was absolutely jam-packed with people, some standing outside as well. That night he acted as if I was Billy Graham visiting him!

Sitting on the platform, I panicked. What could I preach? Here was my hero, sitting alongside at least another 30 pastors on the podium. My mind froze. Bible texts and sermon outlines whirled through my head and my palms went completely wet while the singers sang. One obscure text came to my mind – one with a rather bold message, but that was not at all what I had prepared. "Lord, help me!" I whispered, "confirm this to me!" As the song ended and it was absolutely silent, one of the Pentecostals broke out in a message of tongues, rather unusual for joint services like this, followed immediately by someone else interpreting. The message given was my outline! When I was introduced, I rushed up into the pulpit and preached my heart out. Literally hundreds filled the prayer tent after the message, seeking God! I knew beyond a shadow of a doubt, that this was what God wanted me to do for the foreseeable future. Berthil's encouragement from that night has often helped me in the darker moments of ministry.

Berthil Paulsson taught me a lesson I have tried to implement in others: Every person, however young or inexperienced, is important and needs to be treated with respect, encouragement and interest.

George Perry

George Perry was the Training Principal at the School for Officers Training in Sweden, where I attended from 1962 to 1963. Perry had spent most of his active ministry life in the USA, pastoring in Chicago, Duluth and Minneapolis. For seven years he pastored an exploding Salvation Army church in Rockford. During those years revival broke out and lasted for the entire time he was there. Some of the conversion stories from that time are still imprinted in my heart and mind.

Lieutenant-Colonel Perry had a heart for evangelism, for the lost and for seeing the fire of the Holy Spirit burn within his students. He modeled a Christian life for me in such a way that I knew that high ideals could be lived out.

George Perry had been involved in many revivals outside of the Army in the USA. He would invite me to his home for coffee and just sit and talk about the times God's Spirit showed up in such a tangible way that people cried out over their sins, pleaded for repentance and were transformed. He walked me through his huge library with books in English from various Christian authors, and as he took out volume after volume and explained its significance, my love for books just kept growing.

After I left the Army he continued to write me notes and stay in touch. He died far too soon in 1969, but his life is still reflected in some of my behavior. George Perry left this mark on my life: Ideals can become reality by living out Christ's values in every day life.

Clarence Wiseman

After a year in Sweden under Perry's leadership I was transferred to London and to William Booth Memorial Training College, where Commissioner Clarence Wiseman was the principal. He was originally from Canada, had served the Lord in Africa, and later went on to be the world leader - the General of The Salvation Army.

He was a man who taught us to merge academic studies with fervent evangelism. We would finish a "finals" exam one afternoon, then immediately march single file down the street to the bus station, accompanied by my accordion. The bus would take us to an evangelistic effort, either at a youth hostel, youth prison or around the night clubs.

Risk-Taker for God

Commissioner Wiseman taught me how to deal with difficult issues in front of a group of students and staff. When there was a severe breach in personal relationships that affected others, his candor in dealing with such student problems showed me how to deal tenderly with complex issues without giving up firm principles. He also taught us that current events can be interpreted from Scripture. His passionate messages in front of the student body were often delivered with *Time* magazine in one hand and the Bible in the other.

All the teachers and the principal were invited to the Christmas party for the men at the college. This particular year, I had been given the challenge of presenting an imitation of the principal! For weeks I listened to every intonation, studied every gesture as he lectured. Finally the night came. Dressed in a commissioner's uniform, which I had borrowed from the college archives, I strutted across the stage holding a *Time* magazine in one hand and the Bible in the other, and in my best Canadian accent, repeated his favorite phrase before every paragraph, "My dear cadets, my dear cadets!"

From Clarence Wiseman I learned that if the gospel is shared in faith, people respond in the most unlikely environments.

Denis Clark

Denis Clark was a businessman from South Africa who received a calling to preach when he was in his thirties. Through his association with *Youth For Christ*, he moved to Europe and later worked as an independent evangelist across the world.

I first met Denis in Sweden where he was holding several crusades. A lot of his preaching was focused on the deeper spiritual life of the believer. No one has ever opened up the Word of God for me as Denis did. He modeled prayer life and heart knowledge of the Scriptures that not just focused on the mind, but was filled with the presence of the Holy Spirit, and applied the Word of God to daily situations.

My friend Habil Bolin, who had baptized me, was his interpreter in Sweden, so he invited me to spend several days with them during their campaigns. One day I had the privilege to interpret for Denis, which was a scary experience because he had a habit of using his interpreters as the object lesson for his sermons! During Denis's crusade in the city of

Linköping in 1967, we even sang a duet which was recorded and made into an EP record.

Later, I invited him to serve on the *Youth For Christ* Board in Britain, and many were the times when he took on a strategic personal mentoring role in my life, dealing with all kinds of issues: from how to get more faith for our meager finances to questions of accountability and integrity. Denis was a man who walked with God, and God took him home in the prime of his life to be with Him.

Denis Clark taught me that power to live for Christ comes through a combination of His living Word, prayer and the indwelling and presence of His Holy Spirit.

Harold Shaw

Harold Shaw, originally from Canada, was almost 30 years my senior when I started to work with him at *Living Bibles International*, where he served on the board. He had worked with Moody Bible Institute, then at Tyndale House Publishers, while also operating his own publishing firm, Harold Shaw Publishers. Everything I know about publishing, accounting, cash flow management, warehousing, turning over inventory, pricing and marketing I learned from Harold.

He often came to Sweden to spend three or four days with me and when he did, we worked 18-hour days. I was a sponge, soaking up everything he could teach me. But in all the business dealings, it was Harold's spiritual insight that impressed me most. Harold had his roots in the Plymouth Brethren, but was open to a deeper walk in the Spirit, uniting the love for the Word with the presence of the Holy Spirit.

We became the best of friends. We traveled the world together several times when I became the president of *Living Bibles International*. When we moved to the USA, Harold was a great listening post. Almost every week I was in his office for an hour or vice versa, and as I poured out my heart, Harold listened intently. Then he would always say, "Lars, I see three things here...," and the solutions would be presented for me to make a choice!

Far too early Harold was hit by cancer. I served on the board of Harold Shaw Publishers, helping his wife Luci during those difficult days when she had to run a business with her husband in bed. The day before

Harold went to be with the Lord I sat at his bed, thanking the Lord and Harold for the tremendous influence he had been in my life.

Harold Shaw taught me that spiritual discernment needs to go hand-in-hand with the way we operate. Listening and encouraging others to find the answers is often more important than telling them what to do.

Through the lives of these men I learned the importance of mentoring others. Our lives reflect into the lives of others. Who we are speaks much louder than our words. Our actions, deliberate or subconscious, are instruments of learning for future generations. What an awesome responsibility we carry!

Many others could be added to my mentor list, people who have taught me invaluable lessons, such as Roy Hession, who had an office next to mine at YFC and helped me through some spiritual issues just a few months before we were married; Bill Yoder, whose leadership at YFC guided me through several personal issues; David Foster, who has been my friend, my employee as well as my employer for more than forty years; Ken and Mark Taylor, who worked with me as soon as I became involved with Bible projects across the world; Victor Oliver who was my chairman all the years I was the president of *LBI*, and also served on the board of *IBS* when I left there; and John Vanderveld, who became the first chairman of the Board of *Global Action*.

Paul was a great mentor. Jesus was the Master mentor for twelve people in the inner circle and some 70 in the extended circle. He had time for them and they knew that they could always come to Him. Mentors can play an enormous role in any person's life. Let us take time to be mentored. Let us take time to mentor others.

CHAPTER 9
Books, Books & More Books

It was Benjamin Franklin who said, "Give me 26 lead soldiers and I will conquer the world." Franklin knew that a printing press loaded with the 26 letters of the alphabet had more power than loaded guns. So did Karl Marx. The world hasn't yet recovered from the changes Marx began with only ink and paper.

The printed word is a powerful medium; a God-given invention designed to fuel a different type of revolution. Centuries after Gutenberg invented moveable type to produce the Bible, the printing press is still one of the most strategic, front-line weapons ever created for dispersing truth in a deep and enduring way. Christian literature still fuels Christian revolutions all over the world.

I have always loved books. Over the years in Britain and Sweden I tried to build a personal library as fast as I could.

During my time in military service, I found that many young people needed tracts to evangelize. I was also very interested in publishing. Using a box of materials under my bed, I launched *Gospel Publications*. The first publication was a small English tract called *The 23rd Channel*, comparing people's interest in TV to that of the Shepherd. We also needed material for the work we were involved in with drug addicts in Gothenburg, so I wrote to *Teen Challenge* in New York and received permission to publish David Wilkerson's pamphlet *A Positive Cure for Drug Addicts* as well as their tracts *Chicken* and *Trapped*. Operation Mobilization became our biggest customer!

While in Britain I had come across a book by David and Susan Foster, called *Mainly for Teenagers*. I loved the book. Not knowing much about publishing I translated the book in my spare time and then sent it to a Swedish publisher. It was turned down, and I learned my first publishing lesson: you really need personal contacts to get anything published!

After I moved to Britain, my mother and a friend from the work with drug addicts, Harriet Jönsson, took on operating *Gospel Publications*, and many more tracts were published and distributed.

Entering the Publishing World

When I returned to Sweden, it was time to take publishing a step further. We formed a limited company named *Gospel Ltd*, and incorporated the tract firm into it. One of my favorite authors in those days was Michael Green, who was an Anglican clergyman in Britain and a sought-after speaker for evangelistic rallies. He had written some books that really communicated to the secular intellectuals and university students. From Inter-Varsity Press in Britain I secured the rights to *Choose Freedom* and *Run-Away World*. The boxes under the bed had to be moved into our basement as the publishing work expanded.

After meeting Kenneth Taylor from Tyndale House, he was willing to ensure that the Swedish *Living New Testament* had a solid backing, so he encouraged me to launch yet another publishing house, owned and operated by Tyndale House. In the spring of 1974 *InterSkrift* was launched, and over the next few years made a name for itself as one of the largest evangelical publishers in Sweden.

As the publisher and editor-in-chief I began reading about 20 books a week. How could we have a cutting-edge over other publishers? I found that the rights to many books being published in the USA often had been signed up for Sweden, but that very few of them were ever published. After some inquiries I realized that many of the Swedish publishers went to CBA (Christian Booksellers Association's annual exhibition) to sign up the rights, so I went on my first visit to CBA in 1974. To my amazement I noticed that the publishers had one purpose at CBA, to sell books. They did not have much time for foreign publishers. So I developed a new strategy. Every year I made a trip to the USA right after the New Year to meet publishers in their offices. I was given much more time and also found out which books they were going to publish by the summer, although most of them were still in manuscript form.

I came home with my briefcase full of options and contracts, many steps ahead of the other publishers. Soon *Interskrift* published some 40-50 titles a year, including authors like Billy Graham, John Sherrill, Pat Boone, David Wilkerson, J. I. Packer and Francis Schaeffer.

At the same time we believed in developing Swedish authors. We found quite a few developing Bible commentaries, biographies and even poetry. I even tried my skills as an author, putting together a book called *Lilies in the Field*, a compilation of some 16 biographies from women in different kinds of ministry.

We also tried to bring back Christian classics to the Swedish scene. One of our greatest customers was *Proclama*, which had come into being out of *Operation Mobilization*. Trying to launch a distribution stand of Christian books into food stores and wherever people sold anything, *Proclama* needed many new titles. This prompted us to publish low cost paperbacks, which at times failed miserably and at other times worked extremely well.

Now and then I acted as translator for books that needed to be produced quickly, like *The Yellow Robe*, the story of the India "saint" Sadhu Sundar Singh. Other times the translations simply were not up to par and had to be re-edited over and over again. Still, mistakes would slip through, turning into classic blunders, like in the book *Born Again*, where the "yellow caterpillar" mentioned for the *metamorphosis* of new life, passed through all editing hands as "a yellow earth remover!"

Two special books stand out during these publishing years. One was *The Hiding Place* by Corrie ten Boom. The Covenant Press in Sweden had printed 2,000 copies in hardcover, featuring a very artistic black and white cover with a drawing of a conservative-looking lady. It simply was not selling. I negotiated the rights from the Covenant Press, reset the book in paperback and negotiated for the full-color cover used in the British paperback edition, which showed a Nazi boot stepping on a Jewish Star of David. We printed 20,000 copies and launched the book in time for Corrie ten Boom's visit to Sweden in conjunction with a Billy Graham Crusade in Gothenburg. The book met with immediate success, and we had to go back to print.

I spent as much time with auntie Corrie as I could. We continued to be the publisher for all her books after that. One night, as we were traveling on the special guests' bus to the Graham Crusade, she looked at Doreen. "You are pregnant?" she enquired, and Doreen nodded. She placed her hand on Doreen's stomach and prayed for the child inside. Paul will probably never imagine what that prayer of blessing from Corrie meant for us as parents!

The other book was *Born Again* by Chuck Colson. Because the title did not have the same connotation in Sweden as it had in the US, we changed it to *New Light,* something I am not sure Chuck Colson ever forgave me for! Chuck and his wife Patty came to Sweden for a book tour during the launch. The day of the press conference in Stockholm, the largest national evening newspaper carried an entire chapter from the book in their middle section. You could not have had better publicity!

One of the greatest publishing adventures I was involved in happened through a visit to an art gallery in Jerusalem! David Foster and I were there to work with the distributor for the Hebrew New Testament. One day we were strolling through an art gallery, admiring paintings by the well-known Jewish artist Jossi Stern. As we were talking to the owner, he said, "Would you like to meet him?" He lifted the phone and called for Mr. Stern who joined us for coffee

That became the beginning of a long friendship which developed into a coffee-table book called *The People of the Book,* featuring Jossi's black and white sketches as well as full-color paintings, accompanied by appropriate Bible text from the Living Bible. David Foster acted as the editor, choosing both pictures and text, and I agreed to publish the book. But publishing only in Swedish would be too limiting, so we engaged Angus Hudson from Britain, one of the best co-edition publishers I have ever met, and who both David and I knew well. Through his work we managed to get Lady Collins of Collins publishers interested in a US and British edition. The project was launched at the Frankfurt Book fair and many other languages were added.

During the Frankfurt Book Fair David and I bumped into the former foreign minister of Israel, Abba Eban, who wondered if it would be possible for *InterSkrift* to publish some of his books!

Facing the Challenges of Publishing

Publishing for a country with no greater population than Chicago wasn't easy. To make the books affordable we tried to keep the print runs around 3,000 copies. However, to sell out any edition even at 3,000 copies took major efforts. In those days there were 48 Christian bookstores in the country; very few secular stores took Christian books. We experimented with a variety of marketing methods, including Book parties, based on the success of the Tupperware parties in the seventies.

Over the years *InterSkrift* kept on growing. We took over another publishing house and three different film companies, marketing Christian films to the public. At the height of its operation, the staff filled the entire two-story office building in Herrljunga.

Having learned every aspect of publishing from acquisition of the manuscript, writing contracts, editing, typesetting, proofing, printing the book, packing the books in cartons and working every angle in distribution, I realized I did not know much about the bookstore side of marketing. Together with my team colleague Stig Östlund, we decided on the spur of the moment to purchase the secular bookstore in town that also functioned as the source of office supplies and toys, much against the advice of our wives.

Being a secular bookstore meant that we had to carry at least one copy of every book published by secular publishers, though we could return it at a discounted rate if it would not sell. We expanded the bookstore to include Christian books, and overnight I had to learn how to run a retail store. The store had six employees, so it needed major net income to survive. We also bought the property where the bookstore was located, so suddenly we were also landlords to a couple of other stores.

The shop needed expensive modernization, new shelving and a whole new way of operating. We changed the shelving, and opened a second floor completely dedicated to toys. To save costs we tried to do a lot of the renovation ourselves. The night before re-opening, we worked through the night, laying carpet and putting shelves in place. At 3 a.m. we finished the vacuuming on the new second floor. Completely exhausted, I opened the window and Stig threw the vacuum cleaner out from the second floor with me almost going with it. I forgot to let go!

It is a miracle that we were not bankrupted. None of us had retail experience! One day I returned home from a trip and realized we had over 3,000 sunglasses in stock. Stig had negotiated such a good unit price on the volume! But with only 4,000 people in the town and surrounding villages, how would we move that many? We sold discounted sun glasses as long as we operated the store.

After two years, I had learned everything I needed to know about book-retailing and through God's grace we found a buyer for both the store and the property and got out of an operation which would have proven disastrous had we continued.

When *Living Bibles International* tried to create a donor base in Sweden, it became very hard to present this organization as needing money for Bible programs around the world. After all, we were known as the publishers of Christian books as well as the Swedish Living Bible, so why would we need money? At the same time, cash flow became increasingly difficult. In 1985 we came to a very hard decision. It would be better to sell the publishing company and concentrate on the not-for-profit work. Finally the publishing house was sold to Dagen Publishing Group. I cried that day. It was like losing a child.

During my time as Europe director, I also helped Tyndale House establish a French publishing house, *Maison Farel*. Not knowing how businesses operated in France, this was a real challenge. Then Tyndale House granted its UK branch *Coverdale*, which later changed to *Kingsway Books*, to *LBI*, and for a while I served on its Board and assisted in oversight there.

When I became president of *LBI*, I found we operated 10 bookstores in India under the name Living Literature Centers as well as bookstores in Kenya and Nigeria. Some of these provided more challenges than I wanted. These shops served the Christian community well, but they were wrought with significant management problems. One store in Nigeria was always short of cash, until we set a trap one night and found that the store manager was stealing! At one point the stores in India seemed to be doing extremely well, until I began charting all their transactions, and found that they were selling material to each other, inflating the sales figures! When *LBI* and *IBS* merged we distanced ourselves from operating bookstores.

At home the books continued to add up, and when we moved to Naperville in the year 2000 I established a small library in my basement.

In 2003 we went to Europe for six weeks, attending meetings and enjoying some vacation. It was a dark day when I received a phone call informing me that a thunderstorm had filled our basement with several feet of water and most of my library was destroyed. When we returned home, we found a huge sign on our garage door, reading, "Please do not open until Christmas!" Inside were thousands of ruined books stacked upon each other still reeking of the waste water that had backed up into our basement. For days I sat on a chair in the basement, looking at each book before tossing them in plastic bags for the garbage, tears streaming down my face. It has taken me 25 years to replace many of these books and I trust we will not have a new flood!

Because of the need for ministry tools since the launch of *Global Action* I have had the privilege of writing several new books, including the booklets *Becoming a Risk-Taker for God*, *101 Ways to be a Risk-Taker*, *Mentoring Risk-Takers and What Bible Should I Read*. For the Global Module Training program, I have completed *God at Work in History* (Church history) and co-authored *Preaching So People Hear from God* with Sid Buzzell and *Leadership that Makes a Difference* with George Carr, as well a book on *Mentoring* for the second year of the pastors' study program.

CHAPTER 10
Becoming a Bible Translator

Have you ever thought about what it takes to be a Bible translator? Why does one do it? Not only are the daily tasks tedious, demanding and long-suffering, but those who commit their lives to that which enables others to know Christ are nothing short of extraordinary. Becoming a Bible translator had never entered my radar screen, and it was a simple incident that moved me into such a noble profession.

During the time I was an itinerant evangelist for the Covenant Church in Sweden I became deeply interested in Bible translation, simply because many young people who were coming to the Lord were struggling with understanding the traditional Swedish Bible. They wanted to know what His Word had to say to them.

In the spring of 1970, I had been invited to speak at a youth camp and was struggling with what to communicate. The book *How to be a Christian Without Being Religious*, authored by Fritz Ridenour had been published by Regal a few years earlier. It contained the entire book of Romans from *The Living Bible*, Ridenour's comments and some humorous drawings to further communicate its message.

I said to Doreen, "What about using this as a basis for the Bible studies?

"Good idea, but you don't have the Bible text or the drawings!"

Never one to give up easily, I found 200 four-feet-by-three-feet poster boards and said, "We'll draw them together!" Doreen reluctantly

My maternal grandparents
Martin and Emma Bydén

My paternal grandparents
Axel and Signe Dunberg
at their wedding in 1911

My maternal grandmother
Emma, as I remember her

Me at a few months old

Me posing, two years old

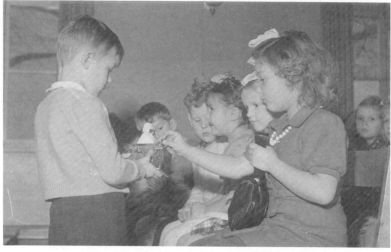

The first offering? I am five years old here, collecting
for missions in Sunday School

I'm standing in the back row,
after responding to the invitation
March 2, 1957

Graduating from
confirmation classes at
Andreaskyrkan (Andrew church)
in 1958

Family picture in 1961: My sister Margareta, Me,
my mother Gerda and my father Maurits

Addressing fellow students at the
welcome meeting for officers in training
at The Salvation Army Temple Church
in Stockholm, September 1962

Singing a solo at my
welcome meeting in
Malmö Church in
August 1964

Stopping the traffic at lunch time,
Joystrings playing on the steps of
St Paul's Cathedral, May 1964

The Joystrings just before they headed out
on tour in the spring of 1964

Doreen and I at a Salvation
Army church, after I joined
Youth for Christ

Doreen's parents,
Victor and Joyce Willson

Doreen and I engaged
June 24, 1966

Doreen and I were married in
Histon, UK on September 9th 1967

Working on the Swedish translation of
the New Testament in 1970

Crusade meeting in one of the many tents
used during the summers of 1970-1976

Me and Per-Ove Lannerö (now chair of
Global Action Sweden board) review Bible
text in a hotel room in London 1976

Open-air meeting in Bodafors during a crusade in 1975

Typical teaching pose
(Leadership seminar in late
80's in India)

Preaching in William Carey Memorial church in Kolkata in 1978

Dr. Jake Bellig and Dr. Holland London
bestowing me with an honorary
doctorate from the *California Graduate
School of Theology* in May 1980

Me and Dr. Ken Taylor at a *Living Bibles International* Conference in the 80's

Dr. Jeremiah Okorie (national director in Nigeria) and Dr. Betta Mengistu (executive director, *LBI/IBS* Africa) look on while I review a New Testament manuscript in Igbo

Raising money at a LBI-kathon in 1982, followed by my daughters Carin and Maria and my assistant Ray Knighton (Founder of MAP) just to the left of me

agreed, and as she is better at freehand drawing than I am, she enlarged the cartoons in pencil, and I filled them in with colored markers.

The Bible text was a bit more difficult. With my old portable typewriter in place, I decided to translate the Bible text and duplicate it for each delegate. I soon realized Romans is a long book and translating literally from one Bible paraphrase into Swedish was not a simple task, nor was it the most accurate way to go about things. But I did not give up. As I worked on this translation, I would read it to friends, we would discuss the words, and I would make corrections. After all, I figured, this book of Romans would only be used in this Bible study and discarded afterwards.

The completed project was an immediate success. "Where can we buy the whole Bible like this?" "We can understand what God means!"

Living Bibles International

Recognizing the need for a contemporary Swedish Bible, I gathered a group of young writers and scholars and began to see if we could create a straightforward translation that would fill this void. The work progressed slowly, because I had no funding, except my enthusiasm for the project.

During my first "preaching tour" to the United States in May 1972, my planned meetings in Wheaton, Illinois fell through. I was staying with an old YFC friend, Ron Wilson, who lived in Glen Ellyn at the time, and so I told him about the Bible project.

"Have you ever met Ken Taylor?" Ron inquired. "Ken who?" I responded. "The man behind the Living Bible!" he exclaimed. I perked up. The book of Romans I had used for my Bible study was based on that Bible. Five years earlier, at a YFC conference in Helsinki, I had read the *Living Gospels* for the first time, and mentioned to a group of Swedes that this was the version we all needed to understand the Word of God more clearly. Jörgen Edelgård, who was with me at that time, pointed out that such a translation would be impossible. Little did we know at that point that we would work together for many years doing just that!

On my 28th birthday (and I later found it was Ken's 55th birthday as well) we met in his office. "I have just started an organization called *Living Bibles International*," Ken began with his quiet, raspy voice, "not to translate the Living Bible like you did with Romans, but to create modern readable translations that people of different language groups can understand. Could you help us coordinate our work in the Nordic countries?"

I immediately inquired how much time was required, and in Ken Taylor's typical fashion, he responded, "Only one to two days a month." I quickly agreed. If I had known what journey I had embarked on at that moment, I would probably never have agreed so quickly.

Serving as the Nordic Director of *Living Bibles International* took much more time than I ever imagined. I began to travel to Norway, Finland, Denmark and Iceland to locate evangelical leaders and possible Bible translators. Selling the concept was more difficult than finding capable people, but finally we were up and running in all these countries. Three years later, I was asked to direct *LBI*'s Europe work full-time, which I did for another two years, while at the same time being the editor-in-chief for the entire Swedish Bible.

I became the Europe director in May of 1975, with the understanding that I could continue my evangelistic crusades in Sweden. I began dividing my time between traveling to the countries in Eastern and Western Europe plus Israel and holding crusades. The time at home quickly disappeared, and when I was home I was busy at the office with both administrative work and ensuring that *InterSkrift* survived.

Then one day in April 1977 there was a phone call from the chairman of *LBI*, Victor Oliver. "The board has decided that it is time for a full-time person to step in as the Executive Director for *LBI*, and the Board has voted for you!" Ken Taylor had been handling this position part-time since the launch of *LBI* in 1968 and it was obviously time for a full-time director. "We don't want you to get involved in much administration and fundraising. We want you to develop the *LBI* program around the world. And you can live wherever you like!" That sounded good, but I had not yet turned 33 and felt very limited in my knowledge about anything around the world apart from Europe. How would I ever even learn the names of languages and projects we were working in?

Victor Oliver demanded an answer within a week, as the international board and staff were scheduled to meet in Dublin, Ireland. Doreen and I prayed. The only thing that made her agree was the fact that we could live anywhere, and we decided to stay where we were. We contacted the chairman of the Europe Board, Rev. Elon Svanell, who so ably had been Billy Graham's interpreter in Sweden, and asked, "Would you be interested in succeeding me as Europe Director?" With his "maybe" and my "yes" in my portfolio, I headed for Dublin!

The Need for Different Translations

Don't the vast populations around the world have the Bible in their own language? Well, yes and no. There are some 6 ½ billion people in this world today, speaking close to 7,000 languages. Of those only 429 have complete Bibles and 1,144 have only the New Testament. Of these languages a further 2,251 still need God's Word in their language. Many of the Bibles and New Testaments that were translated a long time ago desperately need new renderings to be able to communicate to people in the 21st century. In my own country the official Bible translation of 1917 had been in the making for 200 years before it was published. No wonder people found it hard to read.

Why Today's Translations Are So Different

During the past 300 years, earlier, more reliable texts have been found in both Hebrew and Greek, which were not available when older translations were created. Today most Bible translators use two source texts: The Masoretic Text for the Old Testament and the Nestle Text for the New Testament.

Changes in Language

Sometimes we have the misguided notion that the more obscure the text, the holier the book! But the Bible was never written to sound old fashioned! It was written to communicate to ordinary people. Since the days of translating the King James Version, the English language, for example, has changed drastically. Unless you study Shakespearean English, you would not understand such a language. Still we believe somehow that this is how God speaks to us!

Different Ways to Communicate

Each language has its own distinctiveness, its own special character. Each has its own grammatical patterns, peculiar idioms, weaknesses and limitations. To communicate effectively in another language, one must respect these distinctives and work within them. Anything that can be said in one language can be represented adequately in another, though never exactly. To preserve the content of the message, the form must be changed. The further the languages are from each other linguistically and culturally, the more changes need to be made to the form.

The languages of the Bible are subject to the same limitations as any other languages. They have strengths in some areas, and limitations in other areas. It is the message of the Bible that is sacred, not the languages, even if it is within those languages that the sacred message is conveyed. The writers of the Bible books expected to be understood. They were not trying to be obscure.

So we can either translate from the Biblical languages word-for-word, and not make much sense, or we can translate, as any modern interpreter knows, meaning-for-meaning to make the text absolutely clear. The Bible is full of idioms. To translate them accurately, you have to find idioms with the same meaning in the receptor language. In Zimbabwe you do not "hit the nail on the head." Instead you "shoot the baboon in the mouth!" "Whiter than snow" means nothing to people who have no concept of snow. You may have to say, "Whiter than an egret's feathers" to carry the same connotation. In some African countries only the thief knocks on the door. To describe Jesus standing outside your door and knocking will give the exact opposite connotation than intended. In that culture, friends call outside the door, so in translation, Rev 3:20 has to be rendered, *"Behold I stand outside the door and call."*

Literal Versus Thought-for-Thought Translation

In the field of Bible translation, people distinguish between literal translations (word-for-word) which is called formal correspondence translation, and meaning-for-meaning (or thought-for-thought) which is called dynamic equivalence translation. In a literal translation, the translators attempt to render the original language as literally as possible in the new (receptor) language. The translator attempts to render a given word in the source language with the same word in the receptor language. Even the word order of the source language is often followed. The aim of the formal correspondence translation is to be faithful to the original documents. The faithfulness focuses on the form of the language. However, when the forms are retained from culture to culture or language to language, the meanings are inevitably changed, and sometimes lost all together.

The underlying aim for a dynamic equivalence translation is to go beyond the focus on earlier translation theory. While the focus is on absolute faithfulness to the original, it communicates that faithfulness by building a bridge between the ancient author and the contemporary hearer. The guiding principal is to communicate the meaning as clearly as possible. By analyzing both the source text and the receptor language, the translator has to transfer the meaning to the receptor language while at the same time ensuring that the results communicate the same message as the source.

Anyone who knows me knows that I am a robust, get-things-done sort of person. Is my personality type the one best suited for translation work? Or is the best personality type for the job one that is single-focused, meticulous and literary? Or, what about the personality type that seeks interpersonal interaction with others? Can this personality be effective as a translator?

Translation work requires all types of personalities and God uses all kinds of people! Envisioning the larger picture and overall purpose of a project enables the translator to persevere until completion. Obviously, a translator needs to be diligent to the task but the most important quality of a translator is patience. This work takes lots of time and effort. Very few people can sit and translate eight hours a day.

In those early years, *LBI* tried to find one or two translators for each language, and then utilize a group of theological and linguistic reviewers, who checked over the translation. Since the availability of scholars worldwide is limited, many translators only worked part-time while maintaining positions as professors, seminary presidents or senior pastors. Such a network created an excellent caliber of people. In some cases we were also able to find experts in Greek and Hebrew, but in many language groups, those skills were simply not available. So we used an eclectic approach, having the translation team work from all their known translations, whether in their own language or in major languages such as English, French or Spanish, creating a text that would be true to the meaning of the original but communicate clearly in their own language.

When work is translated from Greek and Hebrew texts, translators must be able to translate from one literary form into another that is fully comprehended in the receptor language. Translators, who are well versed and competent scholars of Greek and Hebrew, can at times have difficulty with such a linguistic jump. It was very important to me that we had translators who were literary. They may not have known Greek and Hebrew as well as some, but they could apply a basic knowledge of it. By using the combined skills of a team of scholars, the work was translated into the right form for the receptor language.

When I worked in the translation field I often got upset with academic types who tended to see translation as something in itself. If they had their way, they would translate simply because they enjoyed an academic debate about which word to use. But that is not what motivated me to spend several of my most productive years pouring over translated Bible texts in Swedish and helping translation teams in over 100 languages. My motivation was, and remains, to see the Word of God presented in a meaningful and understandable way so people can have it in their hearts as well as in their hands. Only then can it change their lives.

Naturally, linguistic skills and knowledge are important aspects of translation, but heart is more important. Skill can be acquired, heart cannot. Of course I recruited those who had the skills to do the job, but most of all I tried to find those who possessed a heart for it.

It was essential to me that every translator and reviewer knew Jesus Christ and understood that translating the Bible is holy work. It was not to be taken lightly. A translator must honor the text so that he translates the message Christ intended. I found that in other translation organizations this was not so important. As long as the translator was a good linguist, he could be a Buddhist or an atheist as far as they were concerned.

Beyond personal satisfaction and the sense of accomplishment that comes with translating the meaning of God's Word, I found that the hours spent in God's Word were very helpful to my spiritual life. I was paid to spend as many hours as I liked studying the Bible. But this perk can also have its down side. Sometimes I found it difficult to come home and have devotional time with my wife. I had had enough Bible reading for one day - especially on days when I spent eight to 12 hours reading, proofing and marking text.

But all in all, most translators agree that the work offers great gratification - especially since they appreciate the significance of being able to read the Bible in their mother-tongue. One can never underestimate the significance of communing with God in that special way made possible only through a mother-tongue language. It doesn't matter how proficient you become in another language, a deep level of understanding is never fully acquired in a second language. After considering what *Living Bibles International, International Bible Society*, United Bible Societies or Wycliffe Bible Translators and others involved in translations have done to provide Scripture in mother tongue languages, it becomes clear just how tremendous is the impact. Sometimes I have taken it for granted myself. But when I contemplate the value of providing Scriptures in "the language of the heart," I realize it can never be underestimated.

Translating words, sentences and passages requires a great deal of diligence and commitment. A translator typically begins his or her work with multiple translations from several versions, and reads the same segment from each so composite meaning can be created within a contextual framework. This process can involve taking a sentence and deriving its meaning, then creating a new sentence meaning the same thing in the receptor language.

To ensure that the translations were readable, various linguistic tests were administered to random groups of people for evaluating the readability and cultural applicability. Did the text communicate the meaning accurately? For example, the term, "born again" in a Buddhist culture could imply hell because it is the reincarnated state of *nirvana* that typically equates with eternal life.

Our biggest challenge around the world today is to bring the Bible back into focus as the platform upon which the Church will build for the future. Without God's Word as the foundation, we cannot do anything to promote the cause of Christ.

God's Word Has Impact

For four years, a group of young theologians and writers and I worked through the Swedish New Testament. In those days there were no personal computers, so between 1970 and 1974 I retyped the New Testament manuscript 33 times with carbon copies on my small portable typewriter, using two finger typing, the same way I still type today.

We managed to get different groups together to pre-order thousands of copies of the New Testament. Through a miracle we were also able to place it in kiosks selling newspapers at railway stations and airports.

The day of publication, Swedish national TV turned up in our home cum office.

"Can you sleep at night when you have distorted the Word of God?" asked the journalist. I responded, "I would not be able to sleep at night if I had left it unreadable and unable to be understood by young people!"

The newspapers were extremely critical. The Bible Commission of the Swedish government, the only government committee in the world that is charged with Bible translation, came at us with guns blazing! But people bought it and liked it.

I thought, "I can go to glory now! At least 50,000 young people can read and understand God's Word." Never could I have imagined that 15 years later, the New Testament would be re-edited again, a project I would help with, and presented as *A Living Book* to almost every home and classroom in the country, with a circulation of over 2 million copies!

The New Testatment was published in different formats. One edition was called "The Bible, Part 2." One of the editions had headings all across the cover, like any other teenage book. "Love, see page so and so." "Ten infected men, see page so and so." Soon the letters poured in. One young student wrote to us, "At least Jesus makes sense now. We can see who He is." Another said, "I only knew Jesus as a swear word. Now I have met the author of the book!"

Comments like this, not only from Sweden, but from all over the world, made the endless hours and days hovering over manuscripts, dictionaries and commentaries more than worthwhile, indeed they made ministry of this kind the most fulfilling imaginable.

CHAPTER 11
The Word Around the World

Working with *Living Bibles International* was a great inspiration for me. I was invited to staff, board and translation conferences with *LBI* leaders in Athens, Rio de Janeiro, Geneva, London, Chicago and Tokyo. Suddenly I was traveling around the world, meeting people from many nations. Having never traveled like this, I spent most of the time at the first conference in Athens worried about how I would have to pay for the hotel room. I didn't realize that all my expenses would be taken care of.

Overnight I was working with translators and publishers in Europe, dealing with linguistic and theological issues, and trying to get people from various denominations to agree on a modern Bible translation. This was difficult, especially within Eastern Europe, where they had been used to just one translation. As a group of church leaders told Ken Taylor and me in Sofia, Bulgaria in 1977, "Our Bible is difficult, but the Holy Spirit interprets it for us," to which Ken replied, "If that is so, why don't you read it in Hebrew and Greek?"

The Man With the Vision

During these first years with *Living Bibles International* I had the opportunity to get to know the founder better. Kenneth N. Taylor had worked with Inter-Varsity Fellowship before becoming an editor and publisher at Moody Press. Marrying Margaret West, they had 10 children, growing up in the Chicago suburb of Wheaton. Ken wrote many children's books and also edited and published scores of other authors' books. He was one of the co-founders of the Christian Book Sellers Association and the recipient of numerous doctorates and awards. But his real claim to fame was the *Living Bible* that he began penning for his children.

When reading the Bible to his children at family devotions, he would simply explain what it meant, and one day one of his children asked, "If that is what it means, why didn't it say so in the first place?" That question haunted Ken. He began paraphrasing the epistles in what he called a "living language." When he finished the manuscript, he read it again and edited it once more. After seven edits and seven years, he was ready to publish it, but every publisher he sent it to, turned it down. With a loan from a friend, he printed 2,000 copies of *Living Letters* and launched Tyndale House Publishers in 1962. He rented half a booth at the Christian bookseller's convention…and only sold a few hundred copies. It seemed a project doomed to failure.

One day he received a call from the Billy Graham Association, asking if they could use the book as a premium. The association was granted permission for 60,000 copies. A few weeks later came another call. "We did not print 60,000, we printed 600,000 and used them all."

Because they offered a royalty for the use of the books, Ken set up Tyndale House Foundation to receive all the royalties. He said, "This is God's Word so it is His money." Little did he dream of royalty streams in the millions of dollars that over the next 40 years would fund ministries and Bible translation and distribution all over the world.

In 1968 he founded *Living Letters Overseas*, with the plan to translate the *Living Bible* text from English into other languages. In 1971 the entire *Living Bible* was published, immediately selling millions of copies. In 1972, *Living Letters Overseas* changed its name to *Living Bibles International*. The organization's purpose was not to translate the Living Bible literally, but to create modern translations that would affect other languages in the same way the *Living Bible* had touched audiences in English.

Ken Taylor was a humble man, and at the same time he could be very stubborn. He always carried little blue slips in his pocket and when he took one of those out and started to write, I always knew I was in trouble.

We used to jokingly say about these blue slips, "Ken is writing down that one ship can cross the Atlantic in seven days. If we get seven ships we can cross the Atlantic in one day!"

Ken had a phenomenal way of seeing the impossible as possibile. As Harold Shaw used to say, "The frustrating part is that more than half of his ideas really work!" I saw those blue notes lead to a massive distribution system of books under the name UNILIT; publishing houses established in France and in Latin America as well as Sweden, and Bible products like the *One Year Bible, Life Application Bible* and *The Book* come to fruition.

Ken could be very generous and at the same time a miser. One time I left him at Heathrow airport in London since he was flying to Switzerland to visit L'Abri. "What are you doing this weekend?" he inquired. "I am at a wedding Saturday morning," I answered. "I'll buy you a ticket and you can fly out and be with me for the weekend," he casually said as I waved him goodbye. Sure enough, a ticket was waiting for me when I returned to the airport, so I flew out to the Swiss Alps for the weekend. When I arrived, we went out for dinner. There was still snow on the ground and for two hours we walked through the snow from restaurant to restaurant to find a cheaper menu, as Ken thought the meals cost too much!

Working with him created an enormous loyalty. I often said, "If Ken asked me to open a publishing house on the moon, my first question would be, 'When does the first rocket leave?'"

One time some of the staff met Ken at Heathrow airport. Ken shared how he had sat next to an Indian pastor, and together they had studied God's Word from the *Living Bible*. "Wasn't he surprised when he found out he was sitting next to the man behind *The Living Bible*?" Ken responded, "I never told him."

When I became the president of *LBI*, Ken stayed in constant contact with me. We would meet to pray in his office. And he would send me memos on every idea that he came up with to further the Word of God around the world. Jokingly, Doreen used to say, "Lars, when you are in the retirement center, Ken will write you notes from the nursing center!"

Well, that didn't happen! Ken continued to be a close supporter of *Global Action* as we developed. On my visit to Tyndale House Publisher three months before he died, I spoke in the chapel and Ken was there, bent over, walking with a stick. He asked me to come to his office afterwards, and as usual we prayed together for our families, for our ministries and for the world. Just a few months later, it was an honor to go with the family to the graveside and celebrate Ken going to his heavenly reward, having opened so many people's eyes for the Word of God in his lifetime.

It Takes Money

Right after I became the worldwide leader for the organization, I was faced with a massive dilemma. At one of the first Board meetings, Mark Taylor, who headed up the Tyndale House Foundation that funded us 100%, took me aside and said, "Lars, there is a problem. Over the next years, the income to the foundation will diminish. We will fund the program 66% next year, 33% the following year and probably nothing for a few years after that. We need to find income sources just to keep the *LBI* program!"

My fundraising experience was limited and we were talking about having to raise millions! Through some consultants, I quickly learned about direct mail, and we made some good attempts to build up a mailing list, but it took years before we had more than 10,000 donors.

Ken Taylor had been to several development events with other organizations and believed we needed to launch a major funding campaign. We hired a capital campaign firm in Dallas. We tried desperately to get this campaign off the ground and while Ken Taylor was the great drawing card, he was also a man of firm principle. As we sat in the office of the man the firm had chosen to head up our capital campaign, Ken suddenly spoke up, "I just read your annual reports last night, and realize that although you are a believer, you also operate a night club. It is nice to have met you, but I don't think you are our man!" Ken stood up, said goodbye and walked out, while the fellows from the capital campaign firm panicked!

I was sent to see the next level candidate in another city on the East Coast. What I did not know was that he was no fan of the *Living Bible*. As I walked into his office, he said, "Young man you are wasting your time. Do you remember the two men who came with messages to King David? The first man ran fast, like you, but he had the wrong message!" I looked at him, my heart sinking, having used our last dollars to fly out and see him, and responded, "Sir, just be aware of one thing. The slow runner may never arrive with any message at all!"

Having perused the donor list more than once, I knew there were only three who had given a gift of more than $1,000 at one time, and probably about ten who had given single gifts of $500 at one time. I set out to visit them one by one, with some desperation, as I knew that none of my staff would eat or be able to work if I did not succeed. I learned networking before I even knew this was a good development concept.

Despite the fact that the capital campaign never got off the ground, Ken Taylor was willing to help raise funds. The board encouraged both Ken and me to ask for bigger gifts. They said, "When you get used to the idea, you'll find it as easy to ask for $25,000 as it is to ask for $ 25!"

Ken went to Houston for a breakfast meeting, while I stayed at home. He had a gift card on which people could indicate giving $25, $50 or $100. He asked us to add another line, stating "Here's my gift for $25,000." I thought that was a bit bold for a small breakfast meeting. But after all he was the founder!

As the breakfast ended one man handed him the card having filled in exactly that amount! We were overwhelmed. Later, that man organized a banquet for Ken and me, with over 150 people present. We used the same card, and another man filled in the $25,000! What a joy! I learned that you must dare to ask. "You have not, because you ask not," says the Word. This increased my boldness as a fund raiser.

Eventually we decided to hold ministry weekends, inviting some of our core friends who in turn invited their friends (who we sponsored). We brought our area leaders from around the world to the first weekend in Dallas. It was a success. In the next few years we held over 30 of these weekends around the country, building deep friendships that have lasted until now.

The Green Leader

I had just turned 33 after my appointment as the international leader of *LBI*. I was so green that I had even forgotten to ask if or what they would pay me. As the first payday came around I had to cycle down to an office building that had a telex machine. Eagerly I typed out the message on the telex machine and sent it to the US. I sat and waited for quite some time before the message finally came back. I would be paid!

I knew very little about organization or administration except what I had learned by doing. Having never even taken more than a basic accounting class at the Army training college, I was suddenly responsible for a multimillion-dollar budget operating in some 60 different currencies! It was not just the administration I had to learn, I had to understand the culture of many different countries and language groups. I admire the Board for their risk-taking in hiring this Swedish, immature, greenhorn!

Finding Visionary Leaders

One of the toughest issues facing me when I took office was prompted by the fact that during the first nine years of *LBI*, all the leaders around the world had been missionaries. Without much discussion, the board encouraged me to change all the area leadership around the world to nationals, and also ensure that those under their leadership also were nationals.

While these missionaries were in agreement about the plan for national leadership, it was like pulling teeth to implement the board's desires. It took 8 to 9 years to finally accomplish this task. Being in my early thirties I decided to find leaders around the same age. Here are some of them:

Emily Voorhies

Back in Sweden, I needed help to set up the international office so I asked Victor Oliver to find a candidate who could serve as my administrative assistant. Shortly afterwards he called and mentioned the name of a student who had just graduated from the Wheaton Graduate School with a Master's degree in cross-cultural communication. Emily Defee was working at the Wheaton Bible Church while she was deciding what her next ministry area would be.

Emily and I had several long phone conversations, and I hired her "sight unseen" to come and work for *LBI* in Sweden. She committed to come for at least one year. Neither she nor I realized at that point that this was the beginning of a work relationship that would last more than 31 years.

Growing up in a Christian family, Emily was exposed to global missions at an early age. This exposure to missions gave her an appreciation for what God was doing around the world.

After graduating from college, she became involved in a church whose pastor was a graduate of Wheaton Graduate School. That pastor became a mentor and encouraged her to look at Wheaton, instead of a large state university where she planned to continue her graduate studies in Biology. Through his encouragement, she enrolled in Wheaton and met Christians from around the world who continued to stretch her worldview. Her parents were also supportive of her decision to pursue her graduate degree at a Christian college.

During her graduate studies in intercultural communication, God provided friendships with many international students and several professors who encouraged Emily to learn about global ministry. When she completed her degree, she was encouraged to get some practical experience in cross-cultural ministry. So when Victor Oliver called and encouraged her to work for me, she was open to such a wild idea. Moving to a village of 4,000 people in Sweden was a giant step from Chicago with its almost 10 million people. During her time in Sweden, she helped the organization establish much-needed systems for global work, some of which are still applicable at *Global Action* today.

After a year in Sweden, the office was moved to USA. Emily assisted with the transfer to Wheaton, and helped our family become acquainted with the culture in the United States. Together we built the needed administration and fundraising staff in a small office. While in Sweden, Emily had made contact with a former student colleague, Sam Voorhies. When she returned to Wheaton, their relationship developed into a full-fledged courtship and marriage. In the summer of 1979, it was my privilege to conduct their wedding. Both Emily and Sam felt called to Africa, so when the Africa office was established in Nairobi, Kenya, Emily assumed the position of Associate Director for Africa, working with Africa director, Betta Mengistu. Emily and Sam lived in Kenya for seven years and Zimbabwe for five years, where Sam worked for World Vision. During this time, they became parents to Seth, Sean (who was born in Kenya) and Jessica.

While Sam was completing his doctoral studies or based at World Vision's international headquarters in Los Angeles, Emily worked with me in development, except for the year she served as Executive Director of *Youth for Christ* in Los Angeles.

Less than a year after *Global Action* had started, Emily came to join us. "I cannot afford you," I chuckled to her, "not even your phone bills!" "I'll come anyway," Emily responded and has been working with *Global Action* since, my foremost sounding board and colleague.

Risk-Taker for God

Betta Mengistu

To lead the work in Africa I located a young Ethiopian who was studying for his doctorate in Illinois and served as associate pastor of the church we attended, Calvary Church in Naperville. Betta had a fascinating story to tell when we first met.

Steeped in the tradition of the Ethiopian Orthodox Church, Betta learned to revere God. But the teaching he received included nothing about life after death, so as a youngster he was very fearful. His father's death increased his fear and compelled him to go the extra mile to fulfill church rituals. He read 12 prayer books dedicated to different saints and daily devoted himself to the type of fasting reserved for priests and monks. In doing so, he thought he would gain virtue.

"The closest I came to any spiritual experience was when I bowed reverently to kiss the church door upon entry or the extended cross presented by the priest, and when I was sprinkled by or drank holy water after Mass," he remembers. "The Word of God was never presented in a way I understood because Mass was recited in the ancient church language, *Geez*, the equivalent of Latin. *Geez* was understood only by the priests."

During his primary school days, Betta studied English because this was the language used for most secondary school subjects. Still in his teens, he won a three-year scholarship to a teachers training institute in another region of the country, thus easing some of the family's financial burden. At the institute, he continued his religious fervor, but during his second year he was diagnosed with leukemia. He lived in despair and without hope of regaining his health.

At that desperate hour and in a weakened condition, he went to the school library. Here, for the first time in his life, he discovered a Bible written in his own language, and he began to read it. As he did, hope grew within him. Simply having God's Word in his mother-tongue was an encouragement even though, at this stage, his understanding of it was limited. But when he discovered John 10:10 where Jesus said, *"The thief comes only to steal and kill and destroy. I have come that they may have life, and have it to the full...,"* this promise of life seemed to leap from the page.

"Scales fell from my eyes and God revealed a precious truth to me," Betta told me. "Until that moment, I thought Mohammed had come so people in some areas of the world would become Muslims, and Christ had come so others could become Christians. Now for the first time, I associated Christ with life - my life. That revelation stimulated my child-like faith to believe that, if Christ comes to give life, I would not die of leukemia."

That was 1964. Betta is alive and well today, serving the Lord with much joy, overseeing exploding churches in Kenya and Ethiopia. Following his understanding of the promise in John 10, he committed his life to Christ, and the Word of God became vital to everything he said and did. He joined a group of 15 Christian young people and began to study the Bible. Their desire was to become people of the Word who put into practice whatever they read from Scripture.

When they discovered that the early Christians who believed had been baptized, they wanted to do the same. But when they asked the orthodox bishop in their area to baptize them with water, he refused. He explained that in the orthodox tradition newborn boys were baptized after 40 days and girls after 80 days. To baptize them again would contradict church tradition. Unconvinced by the bishop's argument, the young believers countered that since they had not believed when they were baptized, they needed to be baptized again.

Then they read in Acts about the Ethiopian eunuch who, when he believed, was baptized by Philip. They returned to the bishop and used this Scripture to prove that an Ethiopian, like them, was baptized when he believed. They asked again what would prevent them from doing the same, but the bishop adamantly held to his argument. Disappointed, but in obedience to the Word of God and regardless of the consequences, they found a small farm pond used to water animals. There they baptized each other in the name of the Father, Son and Holy Spirit.

God's revelation to Betta was part of a wider phenomenon happening throughout Ethiopia. A nationwide awakening initiated tremendous evangelistic fervor. It became foundational in strengthening the Church for the time when it was forced underground for 17 years by Marxist oppression. Today the Church there continues to thrive and flourish.

After studying in Singapore, Betta and his wife Sophia came to Gordon-Conwell Seminary where Betta earned a Master's degree. Then he enrolled in Wheaton College Graduate School for his second Master's degree. He completed his doctoral program at Northern Illinois University.

Meeting Dr. Kenneth Taylor, whose name he knew through *The Living Bible*, was a highlight of Betta's time in Wheaton. A class project required interviewing Dr. Taylor and writing an article about him. "I was impressed with his humility, vision and dedication to providing God's Word to the unchurched," Betta remembers. "Understanding the impact and power of the Word, I resonated with him about the value of sharing it in the language people understood."

"During the interview, I didn't learn enough to satisfy my curiosity, so I made another appointment to ask how God had used him to generate worldwide Bible translations. Dr. Taylor told me he was motivated to organize *Living Bibles International* after completing work on *The Living Bible*. Toward the end of our discussion, I asked him if anyone had been assigned to make a contemporary translation of the Bible in my mother tongue, Amharic." He answered, "No, would you like to do it?"

"When I left his office that day in 1974, I had accepted an assignment to create a contemporary translation of the Bible in my own language. It would not be a translation of *The Living Bible*, but a fresh Amharic translation to communicate God's Word to Ethiopians in contemporary and understandable terms. Naively, I thought the work might take two years or so but, after a series of extensive revisions, it was finally published in 1985. Today more than 100,000 copies are in circulation."

In the spring of 1978, Betta met me in my role as newly-appointed president of *Living Bibles International*. Over lunch, I asked him and Sophia to consider returning to Africa to direct *LBI*'s work there. Kneeling at their coffee table in prayer, they realized the decision required them both to seek God's direction. After earning his doctorate in 1979, Betta Mengistu returned to Africa to establish the continental *LBI* office in Nairobi, Kenya, a work he continued until year 2000.

Betta was adamant on one point. "In Africa we can do without many things. We can do without church buildings by simply worshiping under a tree. We can do without hymnals by singing the songs of our hearts. We can do without pews by standing and listening to the Word of God. We can even do without pastors by ministering to one another. But we cannot do without the Word of God if Africa's Christians are going to be discipled."

"More than 6 million people a year are added to the Church in Africa, but where are the 6 million Bibles to nourish their faith?" Betta often asked. "As a recipient of God's blessing when the Word became flesh and dwelt among us, I want to get this gospel to others. It must be made available in understandable forms for our generation and those to come. The world has not experienced the power of Africa. All it sees is the depravity, the fragmentation and the hopelessness. But there is great potential here, and this can be expressed as our people are gripped by the Word of God. The Bible is His gift to us all. It is not a gift from the West to the East, nor a gift from the East to the West. It is our inheritance together. As such, we have equal responsibility for handling and dispensing it."

Today Betta and Sophia oversee several churches in Ethiopia and Kenya as well as partner with *Global Action* in a micro-enterprise program for former prostitutes in Addis Ababa through their Beza International Ministry.

P. L. N. Murthy

Over the years, I worked with many Indian translation teams as well as leaders. During a visit in 1984 I noticed a young energetic man, called P. L. N. Murthy, who worked on one of our translation projects in Hyderabad. He was born in Husnabad, India, a small town with a name meaning "A place of beauty." Having given up hope of ever having a child, P. L. N. Murthy's mother conceived when she was 45 and his father, 50. They were overwhelmed with the idea of having a male heir to continue the family traditions and legacy, as well as perform the Hindu funeral rites at their deaths.

Following his primary school education, Murthy and his family moved to Hyderabad, the capital city of Andhra Pradesh, leaving behind their ancestral home. His father, the eldest of 16 brothers and sisters, and his mother, the eldest in her family, were looked upon as the highly respected elders of their clan. Their word was law and they settled all the family disputes. No one dared defy their authority because they were the custodians of the ancestral properties and legacies.

"Following Brahmin traditions, my parents' marriage was arranged by their families when my father was 10 and my mother only five," Murthy explained. "Prearranged marriages have been practiced among orthodox Hindu families since ancient times because they believe such unions are made in heaven before the birth of every human being. The belief that one is destined to marry a specific person sooner or later encourages parents to arrange their children's marriages before they are exposed to worldly influences and responsibilities."

India is a country of paradoxes. Rich and poor exist and work side by side. People are highly superstitious. Most claim to be religious. Murthy became accustomed to the ritual of waking every morning at 4:30 to recite Hindu scriptures. Regardless of seasonal changes, the family was required to take a cold bath fully dressed and wear the wet clothes while meditating or memorizing scripture verses. Activities for the day did not begin until after this two hour ritual.

Until the 1930s when Mahatma Gandhi called for independence, India was controlled by Muslim and British rulers. Born in the post-independence era, Murthy saw India struggle to rebuild its economy and social life. He became disillusioned by the social hypocrisy. After completing pre-university exams at 17, he returned home for the holidays. To pass time, he wanted to read something other than a textbook so he began looking through books in the home library. There he found a New Testament. This was very strange because a Christian book is rarely found in an orthodox Hindu home. Christianity is associated with the low castes, and such caste distinctions were observed rigorously in Murthy's family. To this day, he has no idea where the New Testament came from, nor how it became part of his father's library.

Out of curiosity, he began reading. The first time, he understood nothing. Strange-sounding names, places, terms and events made the text boring and uninteresting. But he felt an innate yearning to read it again, this time more slowly. As he did, he began to understand a few passages. The teachings of Jesus were intriguing. When he began reading it for the third time, he carefully studied each verse.

As he read Matthew 11:28, *"Come to me, all you who are weary and burdened, and I will give you rest,"* Murthy's mind began to ponder the extent of its meaning in relation to the burden he carried from his Hindu childhood: striving to attain salvation. Instead, Jesus was encouraging him to come to Him for rest.

"The religious exercises I practiced began scrolling through my mind. The meditations, rigorous discipline and rituals were heavy and depressing," Murthy remembers. "My spiritual life was going nowhere. Finally, I said to myself, 'I no longer want to carry this burden that offers no hope, certainty or satisfaction. I will go to this Jesus who tells me He will give me rest.' Then without hesitation I said, 'Lord, here I am; give me that rest.' Immediately, I felt His touch as the mental heaviness lifted and tranquility filled my mind. The release was indescribable. I sensed peace and rest."

Murthy continued reading and analyzing each verse to see how it applied to his life. When he read John 3, the phrase "born again" piqued his interest. Jesus was emphatic about its importance, and Murthy knew it was what he wanted. He wanted to be a new creation. (Hindus believe in rebirth, but not a concept of this kind.)

By the time he had finished his third reading, he was a changed person. The words "repentance" and "cleansing" had shown him the path to victory. With each passing day, his reading offered new insights and experiences. It was a spiritual metamorphosis.

Under the influence of God's Word, he began abstaining from the daily Hindu meditation and rituals, and his father noticed. To see his son neglecting worship of the Hindu gods was offensive and, therefore, sinful. Murthy's abstinence made his father furious. As the only biological child of the family elders, he was expected to provide future leadership for the family's religious practices. Eventually, it became unbearable for Murthy's father to see his only son drifting away from Hinduism.

Pressure from relatives prompted him to deal with his son sternly. When the college holidays were over and Murthy was preparing to return to school, his father issued an ultimatum, "If you want to continue reading this Christian book, I will not send you to college. You must remain at home until you change."

Murthy responded, "I am sorry, but I cannot stop." So he was kept at home. Believing his behavior was the result of inexperience and stubbornness, his father's anger increased until he could no longer bear the humiliation from relatives. Determined to change his son's mind, he stormed, "In spite of the warnings I have given you, I have lost face and am no longer respected. You have no place in my house. From now on, I will consider my son dead." In his anger he grabbed Murthy, opened the door and pushed him out of the house, saying, "When you are hungry, you will come back home. But don't come back as a Christian, only as a Hindu. We'll see how your Christ takes care of you!"

Murthy was stunned. He knew his father was unhappy about his Christian faith, but he never thought he would be driven from his home.

He wondered, what should I do? Where can I go? He had never even met a Christian, nor attended a church. He knew no one who shared his newfound faith. But while his mind raced, his heart felt absolute peace and joy because he knew he had stood for Christ and openly confessed Him.

Murthy walked aimlessly for a long time, not knowing where to go. After a while, he saw a church and paused to wonder what went on inside. Entering the compound, he met a man supervising some people who were cleaning up the yard. Seeing the young stranger, the man said, "You are quite early for church. The worship will not start for another hour." Murthy replied, "I will wait."

When the service began, he realized that the man he had met was the pastor. After the service the pastor invited Murthy to his study. When he heard what had happened he invited Murthy to stay until his father would call him back.

No word came, so his stay at the church compound continued. Murthy studied, meditated and prayed. His needs for food, clothing and shelter were met in ways his father could not have foreseen. He had warned his son, "If you continue as a Christian, you will not inherit any of my properties. Everything will be given to your cousin and you will have to beg in the streets."

Murthy continued trusting God for everything. "In the early days of my Christian life, I made it a point not to ask anyone for money or help," he recalls. "I was determined to depend only on Jesus for every need, though at times that proved difficult."

His father held out hope that he would return to Hinduism, but when Murthy married a Christian woman his hopes were dashed. True to his word, he left all his wealth to Murthy's relatives when he died.

In India, parents or elders arrange most marriages, even among Christians. They study backgrounds of potential couples before any alliance is allowed to form. Such procedures have proven to be quite successful as evidenced from a very low national divorce rate.

In Murthy's case his parents had nothing to do with his marriage. The initiative came from a visitor from Bombay who was attending Murthy's church in Secunderabad. The man was searching for a match for his eldest daughter, Bridget, then 22, and after meeting his potential son-in-law, made the proposal. Later, Bridget was pointed out to Murthy during dinner at a friend's home. Even though only allowed to see her from a distance, he agreed to marry her. The wedding took place two months later.

In 1985 Murthy joined the *LBI* India staff and within a few years headed up all of South Asia. "It is a joy to see people turn to the Lord daily through reading His Word," Murthy told me. "The Church has a great responsibility for reaching the world with His Word. It is alive, powerful and life-changing, and eternity will reveal those lives that have been transformed by it."

"It is my dream and prayer that during my lifetime, the Word of God will be placed in the hands of every Indian. In this way, they will become aware of the cross of Christ and have opportunity to receive the eternal life He offers. To fulfill this dream, we are taking Scripture to schools, prisons, hospitals, villages and places where people are located even in the remotest areas."

P. L. N. Murthy continued to serve and give leadership to the work of *International Bible Society* in Asia, Africa as well as Australia. Since the beginning of *Global Action* in India, he served as the chair of the Board there. Recently he stepped down from these posts and has joined forces with *Global Action* to encourage people around the world to partner with us in every possible way.

Galo Vasquez

For years we searched for a leader for Latin America. Finally, someone told me, "You need to meet Galo. Your heart and his are ticking to the same beat!" When I finally sat down with him, I realized how true that was.

Galo Vasquez was born in Ecuador. Humble Catholics with strong moral values, the Vasquez family was actively involved in the church. From an early age, the Vasquez brothers served as altar boys. Eventually, they would go their separate ways, only to meet again at the foot of the Cross. Galo shared his story with me.

"As Roman Catholics, we were very religious. On the Saturday before Easter, my brothers and I would walk through the streets of my city carrying a huge image of the Virgin Mary on our shoulders and ringing a big bell to wake people in time for morning Mass. At one point, we were invited by the local archbishop to study in Spain for the priesthood, but my father rejected the idea.

Risk-Taker for God

"From a young age, I had a consciousness of God but, over time, I learned to acknowledge His presence and developed a reverence for Him. Later, however, I noticed my behavior was no different from those who did not attend church. I may have been aware of His presence in church but once outside its doors, I was no different from others. While church was a good place to be forgiven, it had little to do with my daily life.

"We were the typical Latin American extended family with uncles, aunts, grandparents and cousins all living in the same house. My father served in the military, first in the army and then in a branch of law enforcement. He was away from home a lot and, as the youngest son, I simply did not know what it was like to have him around. I first remember meeting him when I was seven. I heard he was coming home, so I stood in the middle of the patio waiting for him. When someone said, 'There is your father,' I saw a tall man in uniform coming to greet me. But I did not know how to relate to him.

"It was my mother who kept us going. She worked from home as a seamstress using a hand-operated sewing machine. She cleaned, cooked, taught us manners and made sure we went to school. Whatever the situation, she upheld high standards. Our pants may have had patches, but they were clean and pressed; our shoes may have had holes in the soles, but they were polished and shined.

"We experienced much financial hardship. When we thought things were improving, a new crisis would occur to restart the cycle of need. Sometimes we had to borrow money, sell possessions, or move to another location. Other times, when there was only a cup of sugar, some coffee or a piece of stale bread available, we wondered where the next meal would come from. I would say to myself, I will never live like this when I grow up. I wanted to be like the well-dressed business executives I saw going in and out of office buildings.

"After our family moved to Quito, I enrolled in grammar school and my older brother went to University where his life changed completely. He became an atheist, joined the communist Party and, subsequently, became its General Secretary. His name often appeared in the news and, when he returned home, he brought leftist literature with him. Sometimes he'd attend clandestine meetings with various Indian groups in the mountains, or he'd bring them into the city. Because of his political activities, my family lived in constant fear of the police.

"When a military junta overthrew the government, my brother fled Quito for the mountain jungles because the new regime banned all political parties. One day on a visit to a remote village for food, he met a British missionary from the Plymouth Brethren. They developed an unlikely friendship and after several meetings and discussions, the missionary led my brother, the Communist revolutionary, to Christ. After daily Bible study and two years of discipleship by the missionary, my brother returned home carrying a Bible and was totally transformed.

"The family was shocked. Catholics in Latin America did not own Bibles at the time and, to my parents, becoming a Protestant was worse than being a Communist, especially as he couldn't stop talking about evangelical Christianity. Even though the family rejected his ideas, he continued to share his newfound faith. He invited us to church and encouraged us to read the Bible. One day, I simply ran out of excuses for not going and joined him. The minister, a Canadian missionary, explained how the Creator was a personal God. This was news to me. As a Catholic, I believed in Jesus Christ as ruler of the Universe, but not as someone with whom I could have a personal relationship. Though the minister was not seminary-trained, he knew God's Word and could communicate it to young people. I was impressed. The following Sunday he spoke of Jesus dying for my sins. For the first time in my life, I heard about an alternative to penance.

"After the service we went to the minister's home. Very inquisitive, I spent hours asking questions about Christianity. I appreciated that he never offered his opinions, but always used God's Word to explain things. Until now, the Bible had not been available to the common people of Ecuador because we were told only clergy members were taught to understand it. But as I began to read it, I understood and sensed a need to have my sins forgiven. The minister asked, 'Galo, are you prepared to recognize your sin against God? Are you ready to turn your life over to Him? Are you willing to invite Christ into your life as Savior and Lord?'

"My response was typical of a Latin American Roman Catholic at the time: 'Sir, what do I have to do?' Years of penance, including crawling on my knees on a gravel road, flashed through my memory. When he replied, 'It's been done by Jesus,' it was both a revelation and relief. 'Your part is simply to accept what has already been accomplished and thank Him.' My brother was living testimony to what this meant, so I was prepared, ready and willing to take this step of faith. We prayed, and I poured out my heart to Jesus, putting my trust in Him.

"I was 18 then, had just finished Teacher's Training and was working in a Catholic school. It was a government program to educate street children. I taught history, math, language and other subjects. Although employed by the government, I reported to the Jesuit priest. When I began asking him questions about the Bible, he became aware of my newfound faith.

"'Are you having problems with money?' he asked. At that time, it was thought that if you were poor, it was advantageous to convert to evangelical Protestantism because you could receive food, clothing and, at times, money. 'We can take care of your money problems,' he continued, 'but you must stop studying this Book!'"

Through a miracle, Galo wound up studying abroad. When he returned to Ecuador, doors opened for him. He was invited to speak in many churches. Instead of returning to his job, he continued speaking for the Lord, though seldom receiving any money or support.

While being in Mexico City, another life-changing experience occurred. As he was speaking in a church one day, he noticed among all the Mexicans - mostly men with enormous mustaches - a blue-eyed, blonde young woman. As he did, he almost lost track of where he was in the message. Many years prior, his grandmother had predicted he would marry a *gringo* (anglo) – and here she was!

After the service he wanted to meet her, so he introduced himself. She was with a group of young missionaries involved in literature distribution and church planting activities. She did not know Spanish, and he did not know English except for "good morning" and "one, two, three, four, five." Through a friend who knew some English, they talked and he found out more about her. Her name was Joanne, and she had just arrived from Canada. When she was nine, she heard the story of the Auca Indians killing five missionaries to Ecuador. Since that day, she had made a commitment to become a missionary to Ecuador and later applied to International Teams for training. She was sent to Mexico for a time and this is when she met Galo. Galo offered to teach her Spanish. She offered to teach him English and it was not long before they were married!

One day Galo received a call from Luis Palau with whose crusade he had worked with in El Salvador.

"Where have you been? We need you," he said. "Will you join my team and do other things as well as the children's crusades?" For seven years Joanne and Galo worked with the Palau team. They rarely stayed more than three months in each country before moving on to the next. Fulfilling the role of advance man for the crusade, Galo trained people in personal evangelism, set up pastors' conferences and prepared cities for Palau's arrival. He used to say, "God has given this man a message, and we are willing to give of ourselves so as many as possible can hear him."

When CONELA, an organization for evangelicals in Latin America, was formed in 1982, Galo became its first chief executive. Accepting the position required them to move from Guatemala to the newly established headquarters in Mexico City. He arrived in November and immediately felt challenged by what he saw and experienced in the world's largest city. At the time, the metropolitan population was 18 million. He did not observe any concerted gospel outreach there and it bothered him. Pastors and churches were few and there was little or no coordination, media outreach or out door ministry.

One night Galo went to the top of the Latin American tower in Mexico City and looked out over the city. Standing there, he understood why Jesus wept when He looked on Jerusalem. Here he was with all his background in evangelism, facing a massive city and thinking, how can this place ever be reached with the gospel? But in the back of his mind, he heard the words of Christ, "I will build my church."

Over time, the Lord gave him a vision for Mexico City: to enable every person to attend a Bible study within a short walk from home. He called it "10,000 by Year 2000" and prayed God would help them plant thousands of local Bible studies throughout the city.

It was during these years in Mexico City that I made contact with Galo. First we invited Galo to serve on the board for *LBI*. Later, as Bible distribution blossomed throughout Latin America, more leadership was needed, so we offered him to lead the Bible work for the entire continent.

"God's Word changed the life and political revolutionary outlook of my brother," Galo said. "Seeing the miraculous change in his life led to my own encounter with Christ. The pattern continues as we benefit from Scripture and pass it on to others."

Today Galo leads the work of *Vision for Evangelization in Latin America (VELA)*, while also serving with Franklin Graham in the Latin ministries of the *Billy Graham Evangelistic Association*.

Similar leaders were found in the Far East where Somporn Sirikolkarn from Thailand headed up East Asia, Maged took leadership in the Middle East and Jörgen Edelgård and Hans-Lennart Raask shared responsibilities for Eastern and Western Europe. In Canada, Garth Hunt, a former Christian and Missionary Alliance missionary, having served in Vietnam, launched *Living Bibles International* of Canada.

My office was served by excellent assistants such as Donna Birkey, who had been personal assistant to Kenneth Taylor, and Kerstin Lindqvist, who took over when Donna stepped down. Within a few years my leadership team around the world was comprised of a group of men and women - most of whom were under 40 - ready to give what it took to change the world.

Around the World in 14 Years

Within weeks of my appointment as international leader for *LBI*, I began a hectic travel schedule to visit as many countries as possible, meet with translation teams and set up organizational structures, finding staff and board members to solidify the program.

Traveling the world was very different from traveling in Europe. It was not just long journeys with jetlag, but different cultures and customs and food. I tried to learn as fast as I could, to be able to work alongside people rather than lord it over them. At the same time I was amazed by what God was doing in nation after nation.

Africa

Africa is a continent of many nations, countless tribes and a myriad of languages. It has enormous linguistic challenges when it comes to Bible translations. Many of the "missionary Bible editions" that had been created in past centuries were simply attempts to unite the various tribal languages, taking expressions from multiple tribal dialects. This meant that some Bible translations did not represent any spoken language. Our goal was to concentrate on the major languages, to find a way to communicate clearly, especially to the church of under 25 year olds.

Among the first New Testaments to be released in Africa were the Kiswahili and Luganda in 1984. The political situation in Uganda was still unstable - the country's dictator Idi Amin had been expelled only five years earlier - and civil war was still raging in parts of the country. To be able to get to the release ceremonies in time, Ken and Margaret Taylor, the Africa leadership team and I were flown in a small private plane from Nairobi, Kenya to Dar es Salaam, Tanzania for the Kiswahili release and on to Entebbe, Uganda for the Luganda release. Hundreds of pastors were present in each location and praised the translations that would make church work so much easier for them, and help the young people understand the Word of God.

Dr. Mavumi-sa Kiantandu, nicknamed Kian, wrote to us from Zaire, "My vision is that of having the Word of God translated into every African language, by Africans, in simple, readable, accurate, comprehensive, clear and culturally adapted form. Jesus must speak to them in their own dialect; he must use their idioms, their proverbs, their enigma, their figures of speech."

In his biography, *My Life - A Guided Tour*, Ken Taylor writes this about Kian, "Born in a small village in Zaire, he felt called to full-time ministry at age seventeen. He graduated from an African seminary with honors and earned his doctorate in missiology in the United States. He began translating the Bible into his own language, Kikongo-Fioti, and this work eventually put him in touch with Betta Mengistu, the Africa director of *LBI*."

It wasn't long before Kian was named director of the *LBI* work in French-speaking Africa, a large area encompassing 23 countries and 67 major languages. He wanted to see a Living translation in all of them, but he sensed he would not have a long life.

LBI's African budget permitted him to begin his pioneer work in humble surroundings – an old barn that had been converted to office space. How did he answer the Africans who thought he was wasting his talents and asked, "Can't you find anything better to do?"

Kian replied, "With my qualifications? Of course I can but my job would not be as exciting and challenging as this is. Don't forget my friend, that when we were youngsters our first class room was under a mango tree. If the Swedish missionary who was teaching us under that tree had demanded a better facility before accepting the assignment of teaching us to read and write, you and I would not hold the Ph.D.s we have today. I am in this barn because that is the price you pay when you are a pioneer."

From his death bed in March 1990, Kian wrote, "I have happy news to report to you. We have finished the manuscripts of the Kiyombe, Lingala, Kiswahili, and Kikongo Living New Testaments. We would like to publish these as soon as possible – I have been in such poor health. Meanwhile the work continues...."

Kian died three days later, at the age of forty-five, with a writing pad in his hand. He was in the process of making final corrections to one of the chapters.

In Zimbabwe, bishop N. S. Ndhlovu of the Brethren in Christ Church commented on the release of the Ndebele New Testament, "After reading a few chapters I found I could not put it down. The language used is the language spoken by our people at this time. Other Bibles have Zulu connotation in them, but this translation is pure Ndebele. It speaks to the present generation."

Du Toit van der Merwe was one of the people working on the Afrikaans Bible, which was published in 1982. When we asked him what was the most enjoyable part of the translation work, he answered, "I was struck by the power of God's word, the incomparable personality of Jesus Christ and the moving example of Paul under difficult circumstances. Often I would struggle with an expression for days and the solution would dawn upon me later at the most improbable time – in bed at night or in the course of a conversation about something different. When a solution came, it would sometime seem unbelievably simple. For example I wrestled in my mind with the expression 'after the order of Melchisedek' in Hebrews for months, even after I had completed the draft translation of the book. Nothing I tried seem to fit on the level I wanted it to be, until one day the thought struck me; why not say Christ was the same kind of priest as Melchisedek was?"

When asked how people responded to the New Testament, van der Merwe remarked, "Although the target was teenage language, we hear about people 70 to 80 years and older who read it with pleasure as well as children of seven years old! Although we aimed at the comprehension level of people with little education it is also appreciated by ministers who testify that many portions have come alive for them and strike them as if they had never heard them before, even texts upon which they had previously prepared sermons."

In 1988 we dedicated the Igbo Bible in Nigeria. As Jeremiah Okorie, who had led the translation team and headed up our work in

Nigeria received the first copies, he conducted a victory dance right in front of our eyes. For the first time I saw pastors literally fist fight for the first copies. One stayed up through the night, reading the Bible. "Tonight I have read in my own language about the Jesus I have loved so long," he said as tears streamed down his wrinkly face.

During my tenure at *LBI* we were able to publish many Scriptures for Africa, such as New Testaments in Igbo, Kiswahili, Luganda, Afrikaans, Ewe, Amharic and the Bible in Afrikaans, Igbo and Amharic. In 1987 we were also able to host Luis Palau for his first Africa evangelistic meeting at the Kenyatta Center in Nairobi.

Middle East

One of the first people I met after becoming the international director for *LBI* was the coordinator for the Berber languages in North Africa. We met for a meeting in Ajaccio, Corsica. As we talked about the translation of several New Testament booklets into the languages of Tamazight, Kabyle and Tashelhiyt, she told a horrific story. "One of our translators is on the run. The parents of this young man found out that he had become a Christian and was working on the holy book of the Christians. To stop him they slowly poisoned his food. He became aware of what was going on and fled. He is now in a safe house." Often I have thought back to this young man and wondered what happened to him.

Skinny Luke in North Africa is not a person on a special diet. It was a "slim line" gospel prepared for mailing to North Africa. The cover was "turned inside out" to create neutrality for the envelope. Thousands of these gospels were mailed to people responding to radio programs.

In another Middle Eastern country I arrived with Ken Taylor to meet a Bible translator. His city was completely Muslim. This man was a professor at a national university, where he held a high academic position. We were supposed to meet with him for dinner but he did not show up so we went to the college the next afternoon where we found him in his office.

When Ken asked him how the translation work was going, a shadow went over his face. He got up and locked the door and pulled down the window shades. He leaned toward us and whispered, "I can't do this work, and still I must do it. The Lord has told me to do it, but I can't do it!" He could not continue to work on the translation from home because his Muslim wife had found part of the manuscript and burned it. The only way to continue was to come early to the office and work on it long before anyone else turned up or work.

He pulled out a box full of manuscript pages from a closet. "I have finished this much, but I am so afraid." Tears welled up in his eyes. "My wife has not betrayed me yet," he said "and with God's help I will continue."

We never managed to print the entire New Testament, but key Scripture portions were published in his language and are still in use today reaching out to the Muslim population in his country.

Work on the Arabic Bible began in Beirut and was completed in Cairo. The initial team was a group of young men and women from the Middle East working under the auspices of Operation Mobilization in Beirut. Soon they were more or less working full-time on the Bible project, under the leadership of Georges Houssney, who now is the president of *Horizons International* in Boulder, Colorado.

These were not easy days. A full war was blazing across Lebanon and Beirut was right in the middle of it. One day, as the translators and reviewers were at work in one of the apartments in Beirut, a fire bomb penetrated the walls, landing in a crate of grapes without exploding. The team rushed downstairs for safety, and as tension died down one of them said, "I am going up to make sure the manuscript is safe!" That is when he saw the rocket-like bomb in the crate of grapes cooling down. Amazing grapes, how sweet the sound!

After many years of work involving scholars, writers and theologians from several Arab countries, we were ready to print. We were told not to overstate the print runs. "Five thousand copies of a new translation will last at least ten years," we were warned. The Arabic New Testament was released at the Cairo Book Fair in 1982 and that first week 7,000 copies were sold. To date over three million copies have been distributed and since the entire Bible was released in 1988 some 700,000 copies of it are in circulation.

The Living New Testament in Greece received more publicity than we ever could have counted on. At one time the *Anastasis*, one of the Mercy Ships, which in those days were closely associated with *Youth with a Mission*, came to Greece. One young man received a New Testament and came to faith in Christ. His mother became part of a lawsuit against Don

Stephens, the director of Mercy Ships and our national director Costas Makris, for proselytizing. But not everything was negative! Everyone wanted a copy of this book. One lady in a women's fellowship in Athens exclaimed, "I understand it! I understand it! God has spoken to me."

Translation work also went on in Dari and Kurdish. One translation project I was very involved in was the Farsi in Iran. When the New Testament was printed it became an intriguing evangelical tool for the tiny church. During the time of the American hostage crisis in the fall of 1979, with instability in the city as it fell into the hands of the religious Mullahs, many Iranians eagerly read the New Testament to find out more about Christianity.

East Asia

Our success in Chinese began in Taiwan. When we first published the New Testament we were told that 10,000 would be enough for this small island. But when eager Christian leaders got hold of it, they found it an excellent tool for evangelism and within the next two years almost 2 million copies were distributed.

We completed the entire Bible text in the simplified Script for Mainland China and this Bible is still being used and reprinted every year. *Global Action* is still involved in its distribution.

Are Bibles not printed in People's Republic of China? Of course they are. The Amity Press, in cooperation with the Three-Self Movement and the United Bible Societies are publishing at least two million Bibles for People's Republic of China each year. That's a tremendous step forward and this has been going on now for the past 15-20 years. However, it is certainly not enough to fill the need for the exploding Chinese church. Yet at this rate, if we want to see God's Word in the hands of every Chinese, it would take 600 years!

The very first time I took the train to China, almost everyone walked around in green uniforms and carried the little red book of Mao. On one of my latest visits to Shanghai, young people walked around in shorts and sunglasses, talking on cell phones. The contrast is unbelievable.

During one of these first visits I met with some of the Chinese house church leaders and listened to their story. Most of these brothers had spent 20 years or more in prison for their faith. "It was not easy to worship when they took everything away from us. They have forbidden us to worship together. I told my people not to come, but soon 20 came back and I would sit down and share fellowship with them. Then 40 came and suddenly there were 100 and after a few weeks we were back to more than 1,000 people. At that point I brought the pulpit out of the closet and began preaching again!"

Thanking us for all the Bibles we had sent their way, one of them told me, "We could use thousands of copies if you only could find ways of getting them to us."

One Chinese worker in People's Republic of China wrote, "After reading the Chinese New Testament, I decided to believe in Christ." A student from the same country commented, "I know what the gospel is about after reading the Chinese Living New Testament."

In the beginning we worked with Open Doors in Asia, and later with one of their offshoot organizations Living Water International, through whom we distributed many Chinese Bibles. In one of the northwest provinces where they worked there are 16 villages with a Christian population of over 250,000. In those days there were only three Bibles between these Christians.

One elderly Japanese Christian lady, who was partially blind, sensed God's call to help with the Scripture distribution. But she was so weak that she did not know how she would have the strength to carry many Bibles. She began practicing at home. The first week she carried five copies around the house. The following week she increased it to ten. Finally she could carry 35 copies.

When she finally made her trip with the Bibles, she earnestly prayed for the Lord's help. Fear and anxiety overwhelmed her as she got close to customs, but she prayed again and the Lord answered her prayers, because the suitcase suddenly was as light as a feather. She describes it this way, "The Lord put wings on my suitcase."

In Seoul, South Korea, *Living Bibles International* took part in a special program at the 1988 Summer Olympics. A 32-page, full color booklet was printed in 26 languages for distribution among the athletes and the spectators. The 515,000 booklets entitled *How to Be A Winner* contained color photographs of Olympic Events and testimonies of prominent Christian athletes and were strategically distributed through a network of volunteers from Seoul churches and para-church organizations. Smiling, the *Youth with a Mission* Korean director pronounced the book's title "How to be a wiener" and told incredible stories about its use in and around the Olympic village. Because of their souvenir quality, thousands were taken home and the Christian message shared with friends and relatives in otherwise non-accessed countries. The booklet contained a tear-out response sheet and, for years afterward, we continued to receive completed forms from many countries, including those behind the Iron Curtain in Eastern Europe and Muslim nations of the world.

Japan has been a challenge for anyone working with Bibles or Christian literature. Ken McVethy, who headed up the Word of Life Press in Tokyo, and I dreamed of a variety of ways to communicate to the Japanese audience. Cartoons are an excellent way to communicate to both children and adults. Through a series of events, Ken began negotiating with Christian Broadcasting Network and sharing this vision. The result became the TV-series *The Flying House*, which was originally created for Japan. We produced New Testaments with pictures from the series and placed them in secular bookstores, where over one million Japanese bought them and took them home to read. Only in heaven will we find out what hearts were penetrated by the power of the Spirit and the power of God's word.

Bangkok, the capital of Thailand, is bisected by the slow-moving Chao Phraya River, whose shallow waters form an intricate network of canals that serve as highways and streets for more than half-a-million people who live along the canals or "clongs."

Recognizing the need to proclaim the hope-giving message of Jesus Christ among the canals of Bangkok, a project was inaugurated in 1985 to reach 150,000 canal homes with God's Word. That goal was reached in the fall of 1987. Because of the initial success of the project it was decided to continue with the distribution until even the most inaccessible homes had been reached.

Traveling along the canals in narrow boats, *LBI* staff and volunteer workers gave their personal testimonies and left a special evangelistic copy of the Living Scriptures in Thai at each home they visited. More than 20 Bangkok churches helped incorporate new believers into local congregations.

In the Philippines, *LBI* worked with OMF publishers for the first few years on distribution of the Tagalog New Testament. As translation work spread out, we needed to set up our own office in Manila, which we did in 1989. Arriving in Manila on a January day in 1989, I had a terrible migraine and just wanted to go to bed. I told our coordinator, Leo Alconga, that I hoped there were no meetings that day. "Hurry to change!" he told me, "we are going to a prayer meeting in half an hour." I needed a prayer meeting like a hole in my head! "You will address them," Leo continued, "we are meeting in a park!" I had a vision of a handful of people meeting under a tree, and shook my head. Before I could protest, Leo exclaimed, "There are at least 30,000 people waiting for you in the park!" He was right! What a meeting we had.

Later that year I was back for the Lausanne Convocation. On a Sunday I was invited to speak in the *Jesus is Lord* church pastored by Eddie Villanueva. "Where is the church?" I inquired, as we drove through monsoon rains. "We don't have a building," yelled the pastor, over the noise from the rain hitting the car. "We meet in the grounds of a high school, between the buildings!" More than 30,000 people were jammed into this square with umbrellas held tightly. They stood for several hours of worship and preaching, while the steam rose from all the hot and damp bodies!

With dedication like this, we had enormous distribution of our various Scripture publications in the Philippines.

In Indonesia, where it seems that 1 million more children are born every month, distribution of the New Testament had been a success. While Indonesia is the most populated Islamic nation, it seemed in those days that the religious beliefs were more or less a cultural veneer. People responded gladly to the gospel and eagerly read the New Testament. One of the distribution projects took place in Kalimantan (former Borneo), where a special edition reached out to the tribal people there. Working with Kalam Hidup Publishers in Indonesia, we had a solid distribution base all over this island nation.

When the Bible in Indonesia was ready to be printed in 1990, we had a major, and familiar, problem: we had no money to print it! However, at the same time, the Indonesian government came and asked if they could purchase thousands of our New Testaments, which we had in stock, for religious instruction classes. Funds from an Islamic government paid for the printing of the Indonesian Bible!

For years we worked with a team in Vietnam. Garth Hunt, who headed up *LBI* in Canada, had been a missionary with Christian and

Missionary Alliance in Vietnam for many years. He spoke the language and was well connected. During the latter part of the war he made many dangerous trips into the country, working with the translation team and ensuring that the manuscript was safe. Toward the end he helped the manuscripts and the translators make it safely out of the country.

During my years at *LBI*, the following major Scriptures were published and distributed in East Asia: New Testaments in Korean, Japanese, Chinese for Taiwan, Mainland Chinese, Tagalog, Indonesian, Vietnamese, Thai, and Burmese, as well as complete Bibles in Japanese, Korean, Chinese, Indonesian, and Vietnamese.

South Asia

Calcutta, now Kolkata, has been called the Black Hole of the world. A city darkened by idolatry, poverty and sin needs God's light. In 1986, working with the major churches of the city, we mobilized a group of evangelists from every walk of life to reach the three million homes in Calcutta. This represented at least eleven languages, so we specially prepared a Scripture booklet, Bible study correspondence courses and a New Testament provided by *LBI*. The booklet was called *It's a Great Life* and led to numerous conversions and many new home churches.

When I visited the project in 1987, I was invited to a small home church. There was one bed on one side of the room, lifted off the floor by bricks, and people sitting both on the bed and under the bed. There were at least 30 people jammed into this small room and the heat was unbearable. As I tried to get ready to share my message, one lady on top of the bed raised her hand and asked if she could share her story. "Last year I was a Hindu living in absolute darkness. I had no hope. But the evangelist came with the booklet and later gave me a New Testament. I found Jesus Christ and now I have light inside!"

Another man under the bed asked if he could add his story. "I was an idol maker, that was my livelihood. The evangelists came by with a little booklet and I took it and began to read. It did not take too long before I understood that Jesus was my Savior and I began attending church and continued my livelihood. But one day, when I was ready to put the eyes on the idol and he stared back at me, I knew I had to quit my job and follow Jesus completely!"

Risk-Taker for God

Almost half of the population in India cannot read, but they all have ears needing to hear the gospel. "Living Thoughts" was a five-minute action-filled dramatic radio program broadcasting hope through the gospel to millions of Indians 365 days a year. Several thousand Hindus wrote every month for follow-up or correspondence courses. Further follow-up through *LBI's* Seekers Conferences brought the radio listeners into daily fellowship with Jesus Christ. These daily broadcasts were made in six languages: Kannada, Telugu, Oriya, Hindi, Marathi and Malayalam.

We had 300 responses a month in the Kannada language alone. Over half of the Hindus who attended the Seeker's conferences came to the Lord. In Orissa, our coordinator PK Das conducted one Seekers conference where 75% of the Hindus attending gave their hearts to Jesus.

Sri Sankarsans Panda, from Cuttack told us, "Listening to your program day after day, many questions rose in my mind and I wanted to solve those by a personal encounter. My joy knew no bounds when I got an invitation to attend this conference. Previously I had received a Living New Testament in my language. At this conference I surrendered my life to Christ and repented from my sins. I have found answers to all my questions."

Another listener, SC Rana, said, "My life was full of worldly pleasure and lust. Instead of being happy I was more and more burdened. I started worshipping all the Gods that I know, but nothing could give me happiness. In the meantime I listened to this radio program *Amruta Dhara* that was so different from other programs. I started worshipping Christ in my heart and left all the other gods."

In Kottayam, in Malayalam, we received this note from a listener, "I was born into a Hindu family. I am extremely happy that I could find salvation through Jesus Christ. I cannot express enough gratefulness for hearing the radio program. Please send me the New Testament so I can find out more about Jesus Christ."

"I long to know more about Jesus," wrote another listener. "We are Muslims, but still if I find Jesus to be the Living God, I will live for Him. Kindly send me a Bible and also tell me more about Jesus."

Still another wrote, "I am a Hindu. Even though I hate Christians I listened to your radio program, and it made me restless but I decided to know more about Christ. Will you please send me a copy of that Bible you read from every day?" Someone wrote, "I have accepted Jesus Christ as my personal Savior after hearing that Jesus died on the cross in my place to save me. Your program is very meaningful and easy to understand. I have decided to throw away the idols from my house, but please pray that my relatives may not cause problems for me."

A Hindu scholar in his homeland India, R. R. K. Murthy was well known for his strong Hindu beliefs, which he shared with his wife. One day missionaries asked him to give his reaction to the Gospel of John, which they had just translated into his language. Looking at the way they had mishandled his beautiful language, he exclaimed, "Give me some time and I will help you translate this text into beautiful Telugu."

As he began working on the Gospel, he met the man in the story, Jesus Christ, and his life was immediately transformed. When he told his wife, she would have nothing to do with it. For 15 years they lived in the same house, ate at the same table and slept in the same bed without her uttering a word, while he tried to demonstrate the love of Jesus to her.

One day after all those years he came home and found his wife crying. She exclaimed, "How can you love me after all the horrible things I have done to you?" He again shared Christ's love with her, and she committed her life to Christ. Together they began a ministry to reach out to the Hindus around them.

One day, when disaster had struck the area, all the Hindu priests were out leading a procession of Hindus, who were carrying the idols on their shoulders. R. R. K. Murthy told them, "When you have a crisis, you carry your gods. When I have a crisis my God carries me!" This gave him a great opportunity to share the love of Jesus with his people.

One of the textual reviewers, D Devendrakumar Hakari, reading through the New Testament in Kannada to offer helpful comments, told us, "I am not a Christian, but I am very impressed with the Bible. If *LBI* really can communicate the message of the Bible with its emphasis on love so it can be understood, The Bible will finally be relevant to Christians and non-Chistians alike. The Bible appeals to the poor. As the people in the rural areas learn to read, *LBI* in the next ten years will have tremendous scope."

Apart from publishing hundreds of thousands of New Testaments for groups like Every Home for Christ, OM and other mission agencies, we distributed our own versions as well, in India's many languages. *LBI* laid a foundation for many of the programs *Global Action* is running in

India today. I conducted leadership seminars, management courses for Christian leaders as well as pastors' conferences, in every major city where we worked, including a full-blown crusade in the city of Cuttack in 1986!

For South Asia we published and distributed New Testaments in Hindi, Nepalese, Bengali, Oriya, Tamil, Telugu, Marathi, Kannada, Malayalam, Gujarati, Sinhala and Sri Lankan Tamil, as well as complete Bibles in Marathi and Telugu.

Europe

Of course, Scandinavia was my first stomping ground in Europe, and there we worked on translations in Norwegian, Danish, Finnish, Swedish and Icelandic. Though Iceland only has a population of some 300,000 people they read six books per person per year, the highest average in the world. In the mid-seventies they used to shut off all TV programs once a week, so people could take time to read!

When I became Europe director, translation programs came to fruition in various countries. David Foster coordinated the Italian translation program, but I went with him to interview possible translators. First we drove through the country to see a group of pastors in southern Italy who had been recommended to us. Over lunch they bluntly pointed out that, "You cannot be a Christian and not be a communist!" We realized that our sponsors would not back a translation made by these men, so we headed north!

In the city of Modena, one young communicator, Rosanna Marinelli, had come to Christ several years before through the work of missionaries in that city. After testing her translation skills, it was obvious that she was the right choice and together with a group of evangelical scholars, she completed the draft of the translation into modern Italian.

Dave Foster took the completed manuscript to one of the largest and most respected secular publishers in Italy. They were impressed with it and asked a number of questions about how it had been prepared. When they discovered that there had been no Roman Catholic input, they said it would be imperative to get some kind of endorsement from the Vatican, preferably an official imprimatur. A meeting was arranged with a Vatican official who identified himself as a theological advisor. So along with Jörgen Edelgård, one of my successors as *LBI*'s Europe Director and Dave, I walked into this very impressive office close to Rome's St Peter's Square.

The man we met was interested in the translation and suggested that, instead of reviewing the entire manuscript himself, he would keep just one part and pass other parts to a team of theological advisors. We were told to return in three months for their verdict.

Only Dave was able to make it for the second meeting, and, when he arrived, the man's personal assistant apologized that he was delayed in traffic on the other side of the city. He then took Dave into the inner private office, served him coffee, and left him alone.

Dave remembers, "Glancing around the office I saw bits of our manuscript on a bookcase. Dying to know which part of the New Testament he'd retained for his own reading, I sneaked a look. When I saw it was Paul's Epistle to the Romans, I was not too thrilled at the prospect of discussing and perhaps defending its finer points with such an eminent theologian!"

Then he appeared, breathless and apologetic. What happened next surprised Dave. The man who had welcomed us with the utmost formality three months earlier, now hugged my friend and exclaimed, "It's wonderful!" Somewhat bemused at this enthusiastic greeting, Dave asked, "What's wonderful?"

"This manuscript!" said the theologian excitedly. "It's so easy to read and so simple to understand as a daily newspaper!"

"You must know," he continued, "that for centuries we instructed our people that only a priest was qualified to explain Scripture to them, so they should never try to read it for themselves. Then came the Second Vatican Council when we encouraged lay people to read and study Scripture for themselves. But it didn't work. They found it too difficult and decided we were right to say that only a priest could interpret it. But this version of Scripture is so easy to read, that they will not only understand the Word of God, they will grow to love it!" This resulted in the first edition of our contemporary language Italian New Testament being printed on Vatican presses.

The translation of the Polish New Testament progressed slowly, mainly because of the communist regime in the country. Very few had Bibles. Photocopying the manuscript for reviewers to work on was difficult. One of the people helping us with the translation worked at a Warsaw hospital. One day she took the book of Luke to the photocopying room and began making copies. Someone came by and inquired what she was doing. Immediately she answered, "I am just copying some of Dr Luke's notes!" and the person was satisfied and left!

One of the chief reviewers, Joseph Prower, who also worked on the manuscript, spoke fairly good English. We brought him out to Sweden for a few weeks so he could work on the text without being interrupted. Some time after he returned home, he was taken ill. To my horror, I received a telegram from his wife in July of 1985, "Joseph died yesterday of a heart attack." A few days later I drove to Joseph's hometown Bielsko-Biala, not far from the Auschwitz concentration camp. As I sat in the Prower family's kitchen, Mrs Prower served me coffee and sandwiches. "Take a piece of cheese," Mrs Prower urged me, "that's the cheese Joseph liked the best and ate just before he died!" I swallowed a piece, asked for the manuscript and hurried away, before she could serve me something else, which may have caused his heart attack. By the time the New Testament was ready to be published, restrictions had been eased and it could be distributed freely.

In 1987 evangelist Luis Palau held a series of crusade meetings in Poland, and *LBI* printed some 30,000 copies of the gospel of Luke. One mission leader commented, "The power of God's Word was clearly evident throughout the week of meetings. The preached Word, the spoken Word and especially the written Word enabled Christians to share their faith and demonstrate the relevance of the Gospel to contemporary problems and needs."

The Russian translation had been started before I came to *LBI*, but needed a lot of work. Through the late 80s we worked as hard as we could and by the time the wall came down, it was ready. Working with many different Bible organizations, including *Bibles to All*, we figured out how to bring in as many as possible. Paperback New Testaments were printed in Sweden and brought by the truckloads into the former Soviet Union.

Bibles to All and the *Book of Hope* worked together on a project they called *Book of Life*, which was a synopsis of the life of Christ from the four gospels. Thousands of these were produced in Russian and introduced to the school system. Meeting with the vice-mayor of (then) Leningrad, he told me, "I am not a believer. But I have already seen the influence this book has on the children in the schools in my city. I want you to take them to every school and I will work on placing it in schools in every city of my nation."

Later I visited with the Ministry of Religious Affairs in Moscow, who expressed the need for a copy of the New Testament for every person in the Moscow White House. That's 5,000 copies, one copy for everyone from the president to the person cleaning the floors!

One of the first *LBI* translation projects was in the Czech language. This was during some of the darkest days of Communist oppression. There was intense pressure on Christians. Though publishing Scripture was prohibited, several church leaders wanted to get a contemporary translation underway. A translation team was formed, but they lived in different parts of the country and could not easily communicate. Telephones were tapped. Letters were opened and read by Party officials. One of the team had been given a suspended sentence for previous Christian activity, so, if he had been caught working in this way, he would have been imprisoned immediately. So the translation work continued clandestinely. It was imperative for the team to meet, but this was arranged with maximum security.

Meetings of Christians in many parts of Eastern Europe were hazardous affairs in those days. They had to make sure they weren't followed and meetings were often conducted in whispers, especially in apartments with thin walls! Pillows were placed over telephones because conversations within the room could be monitored even though the phone was firmly on the hook. Every noise outside the apartment, even footsteps, was treated with suspicion.

Meeting with foreigners was forbidden. But if the Secret Police became aware of any such contact, the person concerned was subject to intense interrogation.

Long before personal computers, manuscripts were typed with several carbon copies so that if any were discovered by the authorities, all would not be lost. Photocopiers were unavailable and any kind of reproduction equipment, even typewriters, were required to be registered with the authorities.

On the rare occasions when we could meet with the team, getting together was fraught with tension. Nearing the venue, we would circle the block, then walk back and forth to ensure we were not being followed. All this was worth it simply to spend time with the team and be in the presence of some very special servants of God.

One of us would take copies of the manuscript out of the country, praying that this work in the mother-tongue of the airport officials who might stop and search us would not be discovered. There were some close calls, especially on one occasion when Ken Taylor volunteered to carry the manuscript of the Gospel of Mark in his briefcase!

With all these restrictions, this manuscript took the longest of any language translation, no less than 17 years of painstaking and hazardous work. Linguistic experts who saw the manuscript were enthusiastic about its quality and accuracy. One described it as "a gem of the Czech language." Yet these very factors could discourage authorities from allowing its production and circulation.

An informal survey of denominational leaders indicated the need for an initial print-run of 100,000, but this was beyond the wildest dreams of even the most optimistic. A series of requests to publish through different denominations and then the Ecumenical Council failed.

But during the many months of frustrating refusals, our Czech coordinator Jiri Drejnar devised ways for people to hear rather than read the text. He enlisted the help of leading actors to read the entire Gospel of John in one of Prague's largest churches. Hundreds of people packed the sanctuary to hear God's Word read in a language they could understand. On another occasion, Scriptures related to Christ's first and second advents attracted another packed audience. All this helped increase anticipation of the published New Testament when, just as the situation seemed hopeless, Baptists gained permission for a print run of 10,000 copies!

But official permission for this limited edition was just one hurdle in a long and often frustrating process. Some printers, when they saw the text, were afraid to print it, even when assured that official permission had been given. At the same time, paper was almost impossible to obtain because printers were using all that was available to meet government orders, some with jobs scheduled for years ahead. Technology was outdated and equipment was subject to constant breakdowns.

Yet God enabled the obstacles to be overcome, step by step. A chance meeting on a train put our coordinator in touch with someone who could provide the needed paper. A willing printer was unable to do the job because a vital part had broken on his equipment, and it was impossible for him to replace it. The replacement part was obtained in Western Europe and taken to him. But when printing was complete, he had no folding equipment, so ten metric tons of flat sheets were transported to another facility for folding and binding. Yet when the manager of the plant saw the text, he refused the job.

Finally, Jiri approached an agricultural cooperative and offered workers a way to supplement their income by folding the flat sheets and collating them manually! It was a slow process, but it worked, and our fears that Acts might appear between Mark and Luke, and Revelation might show up in the middle of Paul's epistles were unfounded! The final stage, binding the pages in plastic covers, was completed by a couple who silk-screened the titles on them by hand.

When the translation team met to dedicate the completed New Testament, Jiri Drejnar calculated that he had driven 7,000 miles to troubleshoot the many production problems. As he held the computer diskettes containing almost two decades of work, he smiled and said, "Despite stone-age production procedures, the entire Czech New Testament is contained on these!"

We knew that the first 10,000 copies would fall far short of the demand, but God had another miracle in store. In 1990, with the collapse of Communism, known as the Velvet Revolution in Czechoslovakia, restrictions were lifted and a second edition of 100,000 was printed. God's Word was spread by radio and television. Media interest was considerable. The New Testament was accepted not only in churches, but it fulfilled a vision of communicating God's Word to those who had been denied access to it for so long.

President Vaclav Havel endorsed this translation. Education authorities embraced it and paved the way for its use in schools across the nation. On one occasion when copies were presented to schoolchildren in an entire area of the country, the ceremony took place in a former Communist meeting hall. The main speakers were Jiri Drejnar, a representative of President Havel and our own coordinator of the translation, David Foster. Just before he got up to speak, the President's representative leaned across to Dave and said, "Be sure to tell them how God performed miracles and is enabling them to receive this translation of His Word."

When our Dutch translator completed Mark's Gospel, we decided to do some market research by printing several thousand copies and getting reactions from readers. The booklet, illustrated with color photographs of Holy Land locations, was dedicated at a ceremony attended by various church leaders. One of those present was Lieutenant-Colonel Alida Bosshardt of The Salvation Army. She lived and worked within

Amsterdam's infamous Red Light District and was well-known for her ministry to the many hundreds of prostitutes who operate there.

When she saw this attractive Scripture booklet and realized it was so easy to read and understand, she said she wanted copies for all her Red Light ladies. So the contemporary Dutch translation had an interesting initial readership!

The complete Bible was released in 1988, with the title *Het Boek* (The Book) encouraging comments such as "How clear!" and "How beautiful!"

One person who had attended the release ceremony later met our National Director in the street and said, "My father-in-law had never read the Bible, but when I came home and left a copy of this one on the living room table, he sat up half the night reading! Before this, I was never able to speak to him about the Lord, but today we had a fruitful talk about the Kingdom of God."

A pastor said, "Yesterday, we had family devotions around the dinner table. The children are usually fidgety and can't wait for this to end. But this time we read the entire book of Colossians and they listened intently."

Over the years, *LBI* published and distributed the following major Bible portions in Europe: New Testaments in Danish, Finnish, Norwegian, Swedish, Icelandic, German, Dutch, French, Portuguese, Italian, Croatian, Slovak, Czech, Polish, Russian, and Hebrew as well as Bibles in Dutch and Swedish.

The Americas

As early as 1974 *World Home Bible League's* Chet Schemer had met with the minister of education for Bolivia, who asked for a copy of the New Testament in Spanish for all the teachers of religion in the public school system. Not long afterward, Chet Schemper contacted Ken Taylor and asked for one million copies, so every school child could have a copy, not only to study at school, but also take home to share with his or her family. Eventually the minister of education and the President of Brazil heard about this and became interested in placing the Portuguese New Testament in their schools.

The request was for 25 million Portuguese New Testaments! Cooperation between *LBI*, *Bibles to All* and *World Home Bible League* resulted in distribution of over 18 million copies.

Earthquake victims in Mexico City needed clothes, shelter and comfort. Comfort was provided through a special edition of the Spanish Living New Testament. This version included full-color pictures from the disaster and was called T*he Earth Trembles...Jesus Is Coming.* The edition became so popular that several reprints had to be made.

When the Soccer World Championship took place in Mexico City in 1986, *LBI* was there. A special edition of the Spanish Living New Testament entitled *The Road to Victory*, with pictures of sports stars and additional text, helped visitors and spectators alike to find out more about the ultimate Victor.

There were not many opportunities for distribution in the U.S. as most of that was handled by Tyndale House Publishers. However, in Indianapolis, *LBI* produced more than 80,000 Spanish-English parallel New Testaments for distribution at the PAN AM Games. It was estimated that close to a million Spanish-speaking athletes, coaches and spectators were in Indiana for these games.

For the Goodwill Games in Seattle, *LBI* prepared an evangelistic booklet. David Foster and Frank Arthur, who helped us with the sports booklets for the Olympics in 1988, worked on the project with a couple of key athletes, including Steve Largent, who then played football for the Seattle Seahawks.

At the end of the 80s one of our financial partners was wondering what we were doing to provide Christian values through other media than just giving people a Bible. She said, "If someone can come up with anything that will help even my own daughters, I will fund it." Board member Mark Taylor, Paul van Oss (a member of my development staff) and I gathered some creative people from Los Angeles, met with the donor several times, and slowly but surely a video series was produced that taught biblical and moral values without being preachy, but still included the Word of God. The series was called *McGee and Me*. While *LBI* was the product owner and copyright holder, Tyndale House Publisher became the publishers, and Focus on the Family became a special "backer" of the project. Within months it was a success and eventually resulted in 12 separate episodes produced between 1989 and 1992.

In all of these personal stories the Word of God showed its incredible power to move from just being ink, paper, covers and glue into something that brings people to Christ. Christ, who is the living Word, works through the written Word to create and give life to those that are eager to find it.

If we believe in the Word of God as the foundation for faith and the church, we need to begin to act by sharing it with others around us, perhaps beginning with a portion, like a gospel.

The Lord only gave us two weapons for evangelism, and I'm not referring to Radio and Television! He gave us His Word and His Spirit. The Bible describes the Word as a sword that is able to penetrate the deepest hurts and needs of the human heart. We need to be willing to pull it out of its sheath and turn it loose. If we do, we will see its incredible power function in our lives, church, neighborhood and country.

The Enemy of the Word

Because I sometimes don't understand why things happen, I have many questions I want to ask one day in heaven, even though I know for sure *"that God causes everything to work together for the good of those who love God and are called according to his purpose for them"* (Rom 8:28).

From the very first day God's Word was printed, like on two tablets of stone, the enemy was not happy. The tablets were smashed and had to be "re-printed." Almost every time we worked on a publication of a New Testament or a Bible, we encountered something out of the ordinary.

For years we had worked intensely to get a New Testament ready in one particular language. Because we wanted to use the best specialists, it was printed in Germany. We had no money but went ahead in faith. But to the printer's dismay, every page looked like it had been printed with tar and the pages stuck together. The project had to be started all over.

Another time, a Scripture portion for a different country, one where God's Word had to be distributed in secret, was printed and placed on a truck. Halfway to its destination, the truck caught fire and burned, and all the Scripture portions went up in smoke.

In the 80s we worked for months to get a special edition of the Spanish New Testament ready so we could load 15,000 copies on the Operation Mobilization ship LOGOS. As the ship docked outside Santiago,

Chile, the books were carefully put on board and we rejoiced. Two days later LOGOS sank off the coast of Chile and all the Scriptures were lost.

For some years we worked to launch an office in Mexico, and one day it became reality on the first floor in a skyscraper in downtown Mexico City. We equipped it with the latest in office equipment, but a few months later an earthquake struck and the whole building tumbled down on our office, which was totally destroyed!

CHAPTER 12
Not What It Seems

O ver the years of early leadership I often struggled with being the person ultimately in charge, with the balance between work and family life and with the future. What was God's purpose in everything that had come my way? Often I would write down my frustrations and review them, as well as pray over them. Even in later ministry years, I have my bouts of discouragement as plans, people or promises don't work out the way we expected or hoped.

There were other times when major doubts crossed my mind. One day, sitting in Kolkata, I was completely overwhelmed. How could a loving and kind God send all these people to eternal separation from Him, when they had not heard about Him? How could God forgive a church that had heard about Him but did not seem to care about those who had not? Which sin was the greatest? How would He deal with it?

That morning we had been to the railroad station to consider ways to get the Scriptures to people in the slums and among street people. The station was so crowded you had to press yourself in between people to move forward. Everywhere you turned, there were kids begging, stealing, accosting you for every possible service they could provide. Finally I could not take it anymore and we grabbed a cab and returned to the hotel.

Sitting in my hotel room I argued with God. Was there really any hope? Did it matter one iota what I did or did not do? Why was I killing myself with so much hard work? Why was I away from my family two-thirds of the year - if it did not really matter?

Late that afternoon we had tea with a dear old woman in Kolkata, and I was sharing my frustrations. She took my hand in hers and looked me straight in the eye. "Dr. Lars, don't be frustrated! People are born one at a time, live one at a time and die one at a time - and you share the love of Jesus with them one at a time!" Mother Theresa's words to me that afternoon are still an encouragement when I feel overwhelmed and frustrated.

There were other times when I simply did not feel capable for the task the Lord and other responsible people had placed on my shoulders. How can I, a Swede, with a language complex and very little formal education, make the work be as successful as it should? Has the lack of funds resulted in me not being capable to run an organization like I should have? I have said no to enough projects and people throughout the years. While I at times trust people too much and am slow to let people go, I have turned down more projects than I have accepted. But the sense of not having a Harvard MBA, but being a "simple" evangelist from a small country has always haunted me.

On top of that I still struggle, almost daily, with a major inferiority complex. When I took part in discussions as a juvenile and later as an adult, there always seemed to be one or two who came up with ideas that were brilliant and in conflict with my own thoughts. They sounded so logical and right, and in turn made my feeble contribution look really foolish. Time and again I vowed never to be part of any discussion groups.

When I heard others speak in public, I listened carefully and realized that I had nothing to offer in this arena either. Why would I ever even attempt to speak in public? The underlying question I wrestled with was, "Who am I? Is there any purpose to my life, or am I just driven by the opportunities in front of me?"

In 1982, *Living Bibles International* split into several area organizations around the world, a US organization and the worldwide umbrella organization. While I continued to be the worldwide president, an Executive Director was hired for the U.S.. He seemed to be a brilliant young man with a lot of gifts in fundraising and public relations. Within months his staff grew and he became the rising star.

The more I watched the operation grow, the more uncomfortable I became as the funds available for ministry around the world became more and more limited. Tensions grew, accusations flew from both directions, and because my new leader was so brilliant, my inferiority complex exploded until I finally could not handle it any more. By the time the summer began in 1983, I had resigned. We returned to Sweden for meetings and vacation, as well as to attend the *Billy Graham Conference for Itinerant Evangelists* in Amsterdam.

At the conference I interviewed with people from many different organizations. Luis Palau and I talked about me joining his staff for Europe, while several denominations in Sweden began dialoging with me. I went to a church in Sweden to preach "with a view" to be the senior pastor. But nothing really seemed to fit. Where was the Lord in all this? My heart was still in *Living Bibles International* and the need for God's Word around the world.

A few weeks later I received a call from the Chairman of the Board. After I'd left, he had worked closely with the new executive director and found that there was truth behind many of my statements and concerns. There were major integrity issues at stake. Finally he said on the phone, "We fired him this morning and we are asking: Will you come back, please?" What a confirmation! I thanked God that I had not acted out of eagerness to get another position, before I felt at peace.

In 1984 I attended a conference in Hong Kong arranged by YFC. I had to speak once or twice, but most of the time I was simply an attendee, listening to such speaker "stars" as Torrey Johnson, the founder of YFC, Werner Burklin, Jim Wilson from Canada as well as Jim Gruen from Denver. Ravi Zacharias gave us the Bible study each morning, dazzling us with his rich content and precise delivery.

Spending many hours alone in my hotel room, I read through the New Testament several times and asked myself if I was even close to the place where God could use me. I began penning the thoughts that boomeranged in my head:

> *"I feel like I am two persons: On one hand I am trying to be the business leader of Living Bibles International with a burden for staff and the work and I feel enslaved. The other burning desire is to have no position but serve the Lord in any form, wherever, in a way where ministry comes before money.*

Should we go back to Sweden as a family? Will Örebromissionen (now Global Action's partner InterAct) have me? I don't think I can handle the formality of the Covenant Church and I cannot see myself as any part of the Swedish Pentecostal Movement.

Is it time to forget the dreams of attempting to conquer the world for Christ? Why not settle for something less, like the city of Norrköping? (a provincial Swedish town). How about serving as pastor of a church 75% of the time and be a traveling evangelist 25% of the time, so I can be home with the family more? If the Covenant Church would take me back as an evangelist I would say "yes," but they won't take me, because they probably don't want evangelists anymore.

I must stay outside all things that deal with:

a) Money
b) Fundraising
c) Business
d) Having staff working for me

I cannot continue without a good computer and a good printer. I will never again become:

a) Missions leader
b) Publisher
c) Book store owner
d) Fundraiser

I would love to travel within a country to speak in churches or other meetings. I am no good one on one. I feel imprisoned without any real use of the gifts God has given me. I am trapped.

If we move to Sweden we may still be able to buy a townhouse or a modern big apartment. I will not attempt to do hard physical work again and anything that takes a practical hand I should not even think about. We need to be close to our parents and we need to be in touch with our children."

These inward discussions surfaced time and time again. In 1985 I worked myself beyond what my body could handle. The budget was tight, the fundraising was not going well and there was always more pressure for money from the area directors around the world than we ever could meet. The cultural collisions between how they and I viewed the world, and how the Board, executive committee and US based staff viewed the world, were intense. It was like looking at two different worlds. In those days I would say, "I feel like a man standing on a railroad, with an express train coming from each direction. You hold out your arms as far as you can to soften the impact, but sooner or later you will be squashed in the middle."

The Frustration Builds

By the fall of 1985 I wrote a letter to the board outlining my frustration of leading both the US and the global *LBI* organizations, being the chief fundraiser as well as trying to fulfill a contract that specified that I should be free to do evangelism three months out of the year. When I added up all the days, including vacation I found that I needed over 450 days to handle it! They felt my frustration but some began looking for my replacement rather than finding immediate solutions to my daily dilemma. That time the situation solved itself because one of the board members, Paul van Oss, who at that point was the development director for World Vision, resigned, moved to Chicago and became my chief fundraiser. What a relief! Paul became the best fundraiser I have ever known. He woke up every morning ready and able to connect ministry with people who had resources to make it happen.

But the internal questions kept stirring. Doreen and I found it hard to talk about these things when we were together. As I led the annual *LBI* worldwide leadership team meeting in 1988, this time on the island of Rhodes in Greece, I simply had had enough.

On the plane back from Greece to Europe, to attend some meetings, I began writing a memo to Doreen, which vented my frustrations. Here are a few excerpts from that memo, still in my computer:

My Darling Doreen,

Because I find it so difficult to express myself in words to you (which is stupid after 21 years) I prefer to write some of these thoughts down to share with you in this form because I think it will be easier for you to react to it all if you read it through rather than listen to me trying to explain it all.

During the last year I have been struggling with loads of questions which I don't think I have been able to share adequately with you and I know that I need to do that for us to be able to solve them and move on in such a way that we can be united about it.

There are so many things I wrestle with and one by one they may seem insignificant but when you put them all together they become a mountain which I do not seem to be able to remove.

This trip has clarified quite a few things for me. I arrived in Greece having written my resignation from LBI while in Africa. The resignation was not written out of disagreement with what LBI is doing or stands for or with any bad feelings towards any person, but just out of a feeling of despair. The work has become so complicated and I feel I cannot do anything well although I seem to be involved in every aspect of the work. Here are some of my despair points:

Work

I am still bothered about the circumstances which made me take the leadership of LBI. Eleven years later it is almost impossible for me to get over the thought that I came to: a) Administer the field work b) Develop the work in all the nations c) No fundraising d) No administration e) Live wherever I wanted...and ended up in the situation we are in now.

I know all the rules changed, and I know it was necessary to make these changes for the work to go on, but I am still stuck in a situation of almost bitterness over all this.

I realize that the workload, especially over the last five years, has become inhuman and that I have gotten so used to that level of work that it is almost impossible to slow down to a different level and take it a bit more easy.

I am feeling pressured by the "no cash situation." For years I have heartily believed that the situation would get better and that LBI's stable income source was just around the corner. However, at this point my faith has faltered and perhaps I do not see any hope around the corner.

I am struggling with the notion that LBI rests and falls with me. I know that it stands and falls with the Lord, but somehow I am carrying the burden for Him because it is so hard to let go. What if I let go, and there are no funds for anybody....

I am struggling with the fact that we moved from Sweden to the U.S. I know that your perception is that I was very happy to move and that you were forced to go there. Most times when you get angry with me, this comes up and it hurts me so much. The fact is that although I was excited to go to the U.S, I firmly believed it was for a few years only. Many times in the past 11 years, I have deeply regretted that we ever agreed to such a move. Actually, many lonely nights in hotel rooms, I have cried over the perceived agony I have given you and the children.

I realize now that the decision we made then, will entirely change the lives of our children and I ask myself, "What have I done to my loved ones? What have I done to my parents and your parents?" I feel a terrible burden of guilt over all this, although I try to understand that the Lord can even use mistakes for His glory.

I have to admit that I enjoy the traveling part of my work, apart from the pain of being away from home. It is when I get out and meet with the staff and interact with them that I feel that I am accomplishing something for the Lord, although lately most of my time has been dealing with sorting out interpersonal problems, an area which I am not so good at and where I feel I have most difficulties to be of any use.

The actual physical traveling of course has worn very thin and I have had my fill of airports, planes and hotels. Although I hate that part of it, I feel it would be difficult to change it, and again I feel trapped.

As I look at the next 24 months, there is only a miracle which can save LBI from going under. When I look at the needs in the next three months, a major miracle will have to take place or the whole organization will come to a halt. I know I need to play a great part in this and I feel trapped.

Physical situation

There is no doubt in my mind that most of my aches and pains are psychosomatic. But even so, they are real and the more stress and hopelessness I feel, the worse my physical condition is. This last week I have had 4 out of 7 days with severe migraine. My stomach is aching constantly and I just feel sheer uncomfortable. I know that I need to get off medication, walk more, be better, but I know that if the situation around me does not change it does not matter how hard I try so I feel trapped.

Home situation

I don't know how to say this without being misunderstood but I feel totally trapped at home as well. I suffer terribly during "reentry" to normal family life again. You have learned to cope and manage very well without me, and when I come home and try to feel like I am part of the decision making process, I feel awkward. If I correct the children on any point, you often change it (Not that you shouldn't) but it makes me feel so foolish, and at times I wish I had not said anything.

I realize that you and the children have built up a relationship together that I do not have and at times I feel a bit envious. I suffer because you and I seem to find it so difficult to express our innermost feelings for each other, and when we do we often do it clumsily and misunderstand each other, creating more hurt instead of helping each other open up.

I suffer because we seem to feel so awkward about sharing spiritual victories and defeats, or have an ongoing prayer life together. I think you perceive me as not wanting it, and that makes me feel awkward in starting so I go my way and deal with all this on my own as well as you do. With so many frequent separations it is also difficult to keep any regularity.

The college education of Carin this year has taken all our savings. The college education for Carin next year will require a major loan. The college education the following year will require an even bigger loan. Under normal circumstances I am willing to take those loans, but if something would happen to me, I get sicker, or just cannot keep the pressure up anymore; I don't know where to turn.

Sometimes I feel like I need to do something to make extra money, whether get involved in the stock market, or even take on an extra job, but I am not allowed to take an extra job for LBI so I feel trapped.

I am really struggling with the materialistic life style of the U.S. Should people live as they do? Should we live as we do? What would Jesus do or doesn't it matter?

When I sometimes say I wish I could become an officer in The Salvation Army again, I believe there is a longing to the simple life style, where you are not expected to keep up something because everyone knows your furniture is not your own, and the house is not your own etc. That is why I am drawn to organizations like OM or YWAM, although I see how impractical it would be to join them with family responsibilities as we have. Perhaps the big question I am asking myself and you is this, "What is really important to us? Is it being together, having an open and loving relationship, or stretching and pressing forward so much to maintain what we in the long run will never keep anyway?"

When I see what you have to do to keep the house up while I am away, it makes me feel so guilty. When I hear you say over the phone (from the other part of the world, "I am so tired, I don't know how I can go through this one more day...") I realize that we must make some changes.

I struggle with the question of roots, and I know that you do that too, although you may not express it as strongly as I do. This is linked to the question where we want to retire. Do you and I belong in the US forever? Do we belong in Britain or do we belong in Sweden? Is it the reality of Europe we are longing for? Just being in Greece gave me a feeling of belonging! Walking through the small villages, smelling the hay and seeing village life - I cried. It is so far from the fast pace, elbows, concrete and the automatic society we have become part of. I feel so trapped.

Calling

I still wrestle a lot with the question of my calling and my gifts. I realize time after time (as I did this trip as well) that I feel really fulfilled when I can share publicly with people from the Word and know that this part of me needs to be fulfilled.

I am not sure how I would handle today to pastor a church (which we often have joked about), or if I am ready for the itinerant evangelism which I was involved in before I joined LBI. I just know that my calling needs to be fulfilled, and at this point so many other overshadowing things at LBI makes that difficult.

I will try to pace the program in the U.S. better next year. This year it is already arranged and cannot be changed. The area directors left Greece in the hope that their actions will help me and take off some of the burden. Of course, if LBI had a million dollars today, some of these things would solve themselves. Other things, such as me feeling so uncomfortable in the US while the rest of the family has become rooted, with Paul knowing nothing else, is very difficult to solve.

I hope you take this for what it is: a cry from the depths of my heart, a cry somewhat of despair, frustration, and inability to lead not just the organization but my own family.

It is a cry for a shoulder to lean on, someone who will not just understand but share the burden and find the solution together with me. It is a cry reaching out to you for understanding and a shared solution.

I am not coming to you with any ready solutions to these complex problems. I am coming asking for you to have a totally open heart and mind. I will never again force you in a direction you feel uncomfortable with. You have suffered from that and I am still suffering from that. But I want us to seek the Lord together and hear his clear direction for our lives and our future.

I love you.

God led us through these questions of doubt and self pity step by step. As we continued to read the Word of God we realized over and over again that our trust was not in ourselves, our trust was in the Lord. The power of the Holy Spirit was not just a theological concept. He was and is reality in our lives.

Again I realized that faith is taking the first step out of the boat. That step is risking it all for God, because if the water outside the boat doesn't carry you, you sink forever!

It all became a matter of trust in a God that was bigger than anything we could face, that could make my aversion against fundraising turn into joy as I challenged people to use their resources for the sake of the Kingdom of God.

In Sickness and Health

Since I was 12 years old I have struggled with migraines. Not just ordinary little headaches, but the type where you wake up in the middle of the night and know the next 48 hours will be spent in bed, with an ice pack on your head and severe vomiting for at least 12 of those hours. As stress increased I tended to have one or even two a week - especially on free days. It was hard to plan. Doreen feared those Sundays when she would have to find a phone number to the church where I was supposed to preach and then call them to say that I could not attend.

One Wednesday when we had just been in Colorado Springs a little over a year, it felt like a hand was gripping my neck and the right side of the face. The pain was excruciating and I felt nauseous. My assistant recommended I go to a chiropractor which I did. As he examined me he found that my blood pressure was sky high – he dared not touch me. Instead he placed me in his car and drove me to the emergency room at the hospital, where they immediately did a set of tests. They could not figure out what was wrong, so they told me to go home.

The pain did not subside and I could barely get out of bed for several days. I went back to my physician, who could not find anything wrong, but recommended that I go back to work. "Should I see a neurologist?" I inquired. He said that would be a good idea. Two days later my wife and I walked into the neurologist's office. He looked at me intently and said, "You have had a spontaneous dissection on your carotid artery." At that moment I went unconscious, and didn't wake up until I was in the ambulance on the way to the hospital. An angiogram confirmed the diagnosis, and I was told that the dissection was behind the bone and inoperable. "You will be living on borrowed time," was the word from the neurologist. Many years later, I met the doctor who had treated me before. Looking at my chart, he exclaimed, "Dunberg, are you still alive? You should have died from this a long time ago!"

After launching *Global Action* and sensing God's presence with us, I believed the time of these kinds of illnesses was over. However, Doreen was concerned. Several times she would be awake at night, listening to my breathing – or lack thereof. I would hold my breath, sometimes for 45 seconds between heavy snoring periods. Hearing about a friend with similar problems, which almost cost him his life, Doreen booked me into the "sleep doctor." Sure enough, I was diagnosed with severe sleep apnea. The recommended treatment was to use a B-pap machine that would breathe with me. I looked at the machine, and asked, "And how often will I use this contraption?" I could not believe my ears when the doctor replied, "Every night until you die!" For the last eight years I have traveled around the world with a padded suitcase, dragging this machine with me.

A few months earlier Doreen had noticed a spot on my cheek. "Ask the doctor about it," she said, and he told me it was nothing to worry about. But by the spring of 2000 the spot seemed to have grown and I went back to the doctor who sent me to a specialist, who in turn did a biopsy. While I was in a telephone board meeting, my other phone rang, and it was the specialist. "We will have to take a sixth of your face away," he said cheerfully, "you have a sarcoma cancer. And if we don't operate immediately, it may end your life." When I asked him how many of these operations he had performed, he told me I would be his first patient. As I am depending on my face for my livelihood, I decided I would not let him practice on me. Instead I asked for the records to be submitted to Mayo Clinic and I headed to Rochester, Minnesota.

Risk-Taker for God

When I heard this diagnosis, I was reminded of my Mom's brother Harry who, before I was born, had a facial cancer growth in roughly the same place. In those days, there was none of the plastic surgery that was available to me. Uncle Harry simply wound up with a hole in the side of his face. This, combined with a hoarse voice caused by chain smoking made him look and sound grotesque. I was mildly comforted by the fact that plastic surgery, unavailable to him in his day, might provide some kind of cosmetic coverage for me.

At Mayo Clinic the medical team confirmed the diagnosis. The night before the operation, the chief surgeon informed me that I would probably never be able to speak publicly again, as they most likely would have to cut off the nerves on the right side of my face, leaving me drooling. I looked at the surgeon and said, "If you believe there will be another higher surgeon guiding your hand, I will be a good patient. And by the way, you will need to avoid cutting the nerves, because in two days I have to be back in Colorado Springs to speak in the Saturday evening service at church, where I will dedicate my grandson. And then, next week, when the stitches come out, I have to fly to Sweden and speak 50 times in 19 days!" He chuckled, and said, "Mr. Dunberg, that is not going to be possible!"

While Doreen was in the waiting room during the operation she began talking to a lady she had never met. They struck up a conversation and she found out that the woman was a believer. Her husband was also there for cancer surgery, so they prayed earnestly for each other and for their husbands and their surgeries.

The operation was successful and as I came around Doreen informed me that I had 48 stitches in my face. They had simply lifted the face up, taken out one-sixth of it including the sarcoma cancer underneath, padded it with whatever they put in there and closed it up. Because of some complications, I was not released the following day. Saturday at 5 in the morning, I sat in my hospital bed sending emails to my friends at church and around the world. At 9 a.m. I was released and we headed for the airport. After a flight and a brief stop at home, we headed for the church where I dedicated my grandson without drooling, turning the best cheek to the audience. The following week I flew to Sweden and spoke in all the 50 gatherings, without one drool! When I returned to the clinic, the surgeon looked at me, and exclaimed, "Mr. Dunberg, you are our miracle man!"

We praised God for all the prayers that had uplifted me through this bout with cancer. Eight years later, and after frequent visits to Mayo Clinic, I am still cancer free.

However, in 2006 my body began to ache all over and I found it harder and harder to get out of chairs, cars and airplane seats. The doctor sent me to Denver University Hospital to see a neurologist, this time for my entire body. After an intriguing test where they stuck needles linked with wires connected to a computer into many muscles in my body and then wiggled them around, I was ready for the biopsy! "You have polymyocitus," informed the neurologist, "and there is no cure. We can slow it down with steroids, but you will most likely be in a wheelchair within a year, after that in a horizontal position until the muscles just stop functioning." I looked in horror at the neurologist. I had always admired Joni Earickson Tada flying around the world in a wheel chair, and I knew I could do that if I needed to. But no one ever traveled the world in a hospital bed! Would I be the first? Doreen announced that she would not push me around in a wheelchair, so there!

I tried the steroids with horrible side effects! It was like all barriers in my life had been torn down. If I became angry, there was nothing to stop its expressions. Temptations wanted to turn into reality in every aspect of my life. I could not stay on this medicine and be in Christian ministry, so I quit the medicine all together. The result is incredible pain, toothache–like pain in most muscles 24/7. But I am no closer to a wheelchair in 2008 than I was in 2006!

Through all these medical ailments, I have come to realize that God's grace is enormous and His strength can be counted on. Do I believe in healing? Absolutely! And while I wait for God to do whatever He needs to do to move me forward, I trust Him for His presence in every aspect of my life. I live on borrowed time. Therefore every day is important to me and I want to live as if this day is my last – taking risks for God and doing what I can to further His kingdom around the world.

CHAPTER 13
Marriage Made in Heaven?

During the early 1990s, *Living Bibles International* went through a difficult period. Cash was in short supply and the programs seemed to be growing endlessly. Many translations were coming to fruition and the printing of completed manuscripts was a very expensive proposition. Every one of the 110 or so translation projects would sooner or later come to an end and need to be published to reach their intended audiences.

Tyndale House Publishers had begun working on a monumental task: a new translation. A team of scholars and writers were taking the foundational work completed by Kenneth Taylor in the *Living Bible* and turning that paraphrase into a translation. In practical terms this meant that eventually *The Living Bible* would be phased out and a new translation phased in. This translation became the *New Living Translation* (NLT).

While *LBI* was not translating *The Living Bible*, we were certainly named after it. We began to fear that we would be an organization named after a product that had ceased to exist. Desperately I began looking for name alternatives. What might be a better name to sum up all the entrepreneurial ministry projects we were involved in?

One of the best names available was *Bibles for All* but we found that this name was already used by a Norwegian organization. There was another movement, which had been launched in Sweden under the name *Bibles To All (BTA)* and this organization was already using the *LBI* translations around the world for its Scripture distribution programs. After an initial contact with their CEO, I met with the chairman of their board to discuss possible cooperation or even a merger. BTA was rooted in the Pentecostal movement, and after some meetings they came to the conclusion that we were not Pentecostal but were open to all evangelical denominations, so there was no hope for marriage. The search continued.

One day in February 1991 I attended the Christian Management Association annual conference, which was held in Chicago that year. Jim Powell, who was the president of *International Bible Society* and a good friend, bumped into me and asked if he could have coffee with me the following day. "I have some bad news I want to share with you," he smilingly said, as we set the time for the appointment.

As we met together, he shared some intriguing news. "Our board has decided that we will create modern language translations of the Bible in the major languages of the world," Jim explained, "and I wanted you to be one of the first to know, as we will walk all over you!"

"How are you going to accomplish this?" I inquired.

"Well, we haven't figured all that out yet," Jim responded.

Flippantly I retorted, "Perhaps we should just merge and we will take care of that problem for you. After all, we have contacts with the major evangelical leaders around the world, and many of them are working on our various translation projects!"

Jim laughed with me as we shook our heads and continued our conversation about other matters. The next day Jim came back to me.

"I couldn't sleep last night," he told me, "because of what you said. Let's mention it to our executive committees, and if they are interested, this will take its own course."

A Rich History

Founded in 1809 as the New York Bible Society, *International Bible Society* fostered a vision for transforming the world with the Word from its infancy. No one knows who attended the first founding board meeting of the Society in 1809 as no minutes were kept. But by 1810 the Board kept minutes, issued annual reports and adopted a constitution.

In 1810, it granted missionary translator William Carey $1,000 to help translate the Bible into the Bengali language. That Bible, with some revisions, is still being used in India today. In 1814, the Society was again involved in international translations, publishing a French Bible for distribution in Quebec, Canada and the new American state of Louisiana.

From 1892 to 1954, the Society carried out an extensive ministry to immigrants as they arrived at New York's Ellis Island. An average of 40,000 New Testaments and far more Scripture portions in many languages were distributed annually.

In 1958, the New York Bible Society offered to sponsor a new contemporary translation of Scripture. For ten years, some 100 scholars representing more than 20 different denominations, as well as editors and reviewers, worked on what was to become the New International Version (NIV). The team was created and charged with the mandate to accurately and faithfully translate the original Greek, Hebrew, and Aramaic texts into clearly understandable English. The entire NIV Bible was published in 1978.

Ten years after its publication, New York Bible Society changed its name to *International Bible Society* (*IBS*) and moved to Colorado Springs to better fulfill its role of serving the Church.

Through its history, the board maintained a strong evangelical stance and ensured that the foundational mission of *IBS* would be carried out. In 1961, the Board underwent a crisis when it was very close to losing this foundational distinction. Through God's grace and the wisdom of some Board members, the Society was able to maintain its evangelical flavor.

Merger

During the next few months after my initial meeting with Jim Powell, our executive committees met to see if there was any synergy between the two organizations. The more we met, the more I found a merger with me still in the picture impossible. The leadership was squarely in Jim's hands, and he was such a role model for me anyway, I could not see myself adding anything to his leadership team. I was also concerned about the limited exposure *IBS* seemed to have around the world. One of their committee members told me, "Lars, don't worry, we are international! After all, we send Bibles overseas!"

Six months later the talks had come to a standstill and I was convinced that *LBI* needed to find another way forward. However, just before Thanksgiving I received a phone call from the chairman of my board, Victor Oliver. "Don't overreact now," he warned me, "but you will receive a phone call shortly from the Board of *IBS*. Their president has just left, and they want to see if the merger talks can be revived immediately."

A new merger meeting was planned for six days later in our office in Naperville. Understanding the severity of the situation, I went to work in overdrive and compiled a merger manual, with over 200 pages, including drafted bylaws, operational procedures, merged finance reports as well as worldwide organizational charts. When the *IBS* and *LBI* committee members sat down at the negotiation table, one of the *IBS* members commented, "Well, I presume we have to start from scratch!" With astonishment he opened the merger manual which was placed in front of each committee member.

Within weeks, each executive committee had unanimously agreed to the merger and passed on recommendations to their respective Boards, who in turn voted within weeks. Quickly I had to learn as much as I could about *IBS* and how it operated. As I studied the organization, I realized there was a big difference between operating an office staff of 15 to 20 and 135! *IBS* was rather compartmentalized with four separate divisions working somewhat independently from one another. It appeared that cash was available for any urgent program or capital needs. As I looked over everything, I tried to imagine what needed to be done to make the merger go smoothly.

I also found I had some misconceptions: I believed *IBS* was publishing Scriptures for other translation organizations. But while *IBS* provided the cash, others actually made the publishing decisions. The print runs of these New Testaments were small and the unit prices were extremely high. Furthermore, some of the language groups these were published for had an oral tradition - recorded Scriptures would have been an even better fit to communicate the gospel.

Victor Oliver and I were asked to appear before the *IBS* board members who lived in the New York area (this was 85% of the board members). We met for lunch in the Metropolitan Club, on the top floor of which used to be the Pan Am building in Manhattan. The Board members grilled Victor and me from every possible angle. At the end I gave a speech and quoted an intriguing Scripture verse from Isaiah 61:5-6. *"Aliens will shepherd your flocks; foreigners will work your fields and vineyards. And you will be called priests of the LORD, you will be named ministers of our God. You will feed on the wealth of nations, and in their riches you will boast."*

On February 3, 1992 I was in England to celebrate my father-in-law's 80th birthday when I received a phone call to inform me that I had been appointed the new president of the merged *IBS*, and that the merger would be official by the first week of March. I hurried home, repacked my bags and flew to Colorado Springs to take office, as the lawyers continued to do due diligence and hammer out the finer print in the merger agreement.

LBI closed its office in Wheaton, released the staff, and we took only a handful, 3 to 4 members with us to Colorado Springs. Our assets were the worldwide staff and projects, the "international" part that *IBS* had only in name. There was much pain when we said goodbye to the U.S. staff, who had served us faithfully for many years. I was taken aback when I met a whole group of ladies in the phone sales department of *IBS* the following week. They were wearing huge badges stating, "We survived the merger!" They did indeed, as it had not hurt them in any way. Meanwhile, many in *LBI* lost their jobs.

At the time of the merger, the *IBS* Board was made up of 19 members, most of whom had served more than ten years already. One of them, John Kubach, who at this point was over 90 years old, had served on the Board faithfully since 1947. Apart from three members, the board was made up of representatives from the East Coast, with a huge cluster from the greater New York area.

Among these board members you would find Fred Russ Esty, who could quote massive chunks of Scripture from memory, Brewster Kopp, who had been the assistant secretary of the Army and served on no end of different boards, Ron Youngblood who was a professor at Bethel Seminary in San Diego, to just name a few.

These 19 members joined forces with *LBI*'s fourteen members, including Mark Taylor, the president of Tyndale House Publisher, his father Kenneth, the evangelist Luis Palau, the president of Bofors Guns in Sweden, Egon Linderoth, and a whole cadre of people from Hong Kong,

India, Africa and Canada, as well as my friend for many years David Foster from Britain. Suddenly the Board was made up of 33 members!

By 1994, eight board members retired because of reaching or having reached an age limit of 75, something that had been established in the merger agreement. Some resigned and some transitioned off having served their terms. By the time I left *IBS* in 1998, only seven of the original board members from the merger remained on the Board. During my tenure I worked with the nominating committee to bring 10 new board members to the Board.

One of our board members, Bill Hanson, had Salvation Army background and I suggested to him that we should invite General Eva Burrows to serve on the Board. She had just retired after serving two terms as the worldwide leader for The Salvation Army and moved back to her home country Australia. "Impossible, she will never say yes!" was his immediate response.

I called Eva Burrows and made a lunch appointment. I found a low-fare plane ticket and flew to Melbourne from Colorado Springs, met her for lunch, and then turned immediately back and flew home again, a journey of some 19 hours each way! Her response was, "How can I say no to anyone flying that far to invite me to serve on a board?" She joined the board in 1994 and served for several years after I had stepped down.

I invited her to share in the devotions at her first board meeting. Knowing that several board members were from Brethren background and from denominations where women could not preach, I tried to mitigate potential concerns, introducing her by saying, "Now General Burrows will share her story." Eva Burrows responded in her first opening remarks, "I will not share! I am here to preach!" With her Australian accent and tremendous communication skills, she had the entire audience in her hands within seconds!

Other new board members included the professor of zoology at Nairobi University, George Kinoti, who had served as the chair for *LBI*'s Africa board for many years, Mike Richards, state senator, banker and insurance businessman from Houston, Texas, who became the chairman and later the president for a short while for *IBS*, poet Luci Shaw, who also served as professor in creative writing at Regent University in Vancouver, Don Argue, who was the president of the National Association of Evangelicals and later went on to be the principal of Northwest Bible

College in Kirkland, Washington, as well as businessman and author Stephen Arterburn, the president of Herr Foods in Pennsylvania, J.M. Herr, the investor Randy Samelson, who moved in to Colorado Springs from Detroit, the chairman of our board in the Philippines, a businessman by the name of Lawrence Ty, the chairman of our board in Brazil, Ricardo Glaser and from Britain Gospatric Home, who was in charge of the Christian Resources Exhibition in that country.

At the merger weekend, several board members talked about this merger as a marriage made in heaven.

Greater Muscle, Greater Impact

Overnight we were a strong program organization. The former *LBI* offices reorganized themselves as *IBS* in their respective countries and immediately received positive responses from the evangelical community.

Projects that had slowed suddenly moved forward with great speed. The *NIV* was of course the flagship, and while translation work had begun in French and Spanish it was also launched in Brazil in the Portuguese language.

Strong Commitments

We crafted a positioning statement showing the direction we wanted to go. This is how it read then:

> *"Commitment to the Local Church*
>
> The call to bring God's transforming Word to the world begins with an unchanging commitment to the Church. This *IBS* commitment to equip the Church for service transcends denominational barriers. God's Word provides an umbrella that allows *IBS* to bring together diverse churches and ministries, in unity and faith, to uphold the centrality and use of Scripture.
>
> Recently, for example, *IBS* worked with a number of ministries to provide 1 million copies of the Gospel of Luke throughout North Africa. In the U.S., *IBS* partnered with Promise Keepers by developing a New Testament for their men's movement. In the U.S., *IBS* sponsors an annual Church Planters Forum attended by

denominational and church leaders from throughout the country. And while such evangelistic efforts are consistently at the forefront of the *IBS* ministry, discipleship is also an integral part of the cooperative role of *IBS* with the local church.

Commitment to Quality Translations

The cornerstone of the *IBS* ministry is its commitment to quality translations. To this end, *IBS* sponsored the *New International Version* translation of the Bible, completed in 1978 after 10 years of work by more than 100 evangelical scholars. NIV Scripture translations are now available in French, Spanish and Portuguese. Also, the *New International Readers Version* of the New Testament and Bible were printed and released in the U.S. in 1996 and 1997.

The *IBS* conviction that God's Word can transform the world is based on the belief that the Bible, in its entirety, is God's revelation of Himself and His purpose for humanity. *IBS* believes His message to people of every age and tongue is crucial to their salvation and growth in Christ.

Urgency in translating God's Word into all known languages is critical. It is estimated that there are 6,500 distinct languages spoken in the world. Of these, more than 4,000 have no Scripture translation. At least 350 million people have no Scripture in their mother-tongue. Millions more have Scripture translations that are over a hundred years old, filled with antiquated phraseology irrelevant in today's world.

As a result of the worldwide network of *IBS* translators and partnerships with Wycliffe Bible Translators and other organizations, *IBS* publishes accurate, contemporary Scripture translations for an ever-increasing number of people groups each year. Presently, *IBS* is working in 85 languages involving approximately 100 counties.

Commitment to National Leadership

For *IBS* to achieve its mission, it is essential that it has the ability to touch the pulse of the global community. To this end, *IBS* has qualified nationals in 50 offices strategically placed around the world in Africa, East Asia, Europe, Latin America, the Middle East, South Asia, Canada and the United States of America.

IBS indigenous staff are in day-to-day living and working relationships with their own cultures and are able to quickly identify, evaluate and provide for the immediate and long-term Scripture needs of local churches and communities.

Commitment to Worldwide Publishing and Distribution

Providing low-cost Scriptures for evangelism and discipleship is a fundamental part of the ministry of *IBS*.

From the global office, the *IBS* staff keeps a telescopic view of the need for God's Word worldwide. Through close communication and global networking with area offices, mutual expertise is shared to find the most cost-effective means to print and publish high-quality Scriptures anywhere in the world.

Reaching the world involves reaching individuals. For this purpose, *IBS* publishes customized Scriptures for select people groups, athletes, students and others. *IBS* Scriptures with *Life Application* notes are available in more than 10 major languages and are a valuable tool for the spiritual growth of millions of Christians worldwide."

God's Word Speeds Around the World

In Africa, New Testaments and Bibles were completed at a fast rate. In the Middle East the distribution of Arabic Scriptures multiplied through partnerships and in Eastern Europe, Scripture distribution of New Testaments continued as well as *My First Bible*, translated and adapted from a best-selling children's publication of Bible stories by Ken Taylor. Published in many languages, it was distributed in state-run orphanages of former Soviet bloc countries. In Bulgaria, an official endorsement by the Ministry of Education was printed on the inside front cover, and it was used in the official school curriculum for first and second graders.

One of the first Bibles released in India was in the Gujarati language. Another highlight was the launch of *Jesus and His Life*, a fully illustrated gospel of Luke, with Indian drawings and study notes. We first introduced this book in a school in Kottayam, Kerala, and that celebration included a marching band leading us into the school assembly in the open air. Little did we realize that this particular book would be used all over India in more than a million copies, prompting thousands of children to write to our office, seeking spiritual guidance.

One of the most touching distribution stories came from India. A 35-year-old man had been paralyzed, and was lying on the floor of his thatched-roof, mud-walled hut. It was dingy, and a foul smell emanated from every corner. The man, Saidulu, had been abandoned. His wife had run away, and his parents had deserted him. He was an invalid left to die.

He could not afford medical help but, even if had been able to, none was available. In his desperate state, Saidulu tried witchcraft, worship of evil spirits and prayers to his ancestors, but nothing helped. Depressed and dejected, he wanted to end his life, but he could not bring himself to do so.

In June 1995, *IBS* released the Gospel of Mark in Lambadi—the first-ever Scripture in the language. Copies were distributed among the nomadic Lambadi tribe where more than 10 million people move continually throughout central parts of India.

As evangelists went from village to village to distribute the gospel, one came to the smelly hut. He simply tossed the gospel into Saidulu's hut and left. It fell right on his face. He opened his weary eyes and picked it up with his left hand. The attractive book, *Message of Life,* was in his mother-tongue, Lambadi. Until that moment, he hadn't seen a book in his language since the textbooks in primary school.

He began reading the book. The second page caught his attention because it told of a man called Jesus who performed miracles! He read further. The beginning of the second chapter told of a paralytic person who was lowered from the roof and laid before Jesus where he was healed.

Saidulu was moved by the similarities between himself and the man in the book. He was in desperate need of healing. But Jesus was not available physically, and he had no one to help him know Jesus. Saidulu prayed aloud, weeping, "Jesus heal me as you healed this paralytic man. I need your touch. I am a sinner."

Instantly, power entered his right hand. It began to shake. Saidulu realized that Jesus was healing him, and his faith in Jesus began to increase. In a month, he was completely restored to health. The news created a sensation throughout the village as his relatives found out about the change in him. Saidulu told them about the book and Jesus. Soon, he was witnessing to the power of God in surrounding areas.

In six months, Saidulu memorized the entire Gospel and began to recite the verses to those who came to visit him. He literally spoke God's Word to them. He was invited to come to homes and pray for the sick. The Lord honored his faith and healed many from chronic sicknesses. People who had suffered from paralysis, breast cancer, tuberculosis, snakebite and even hemorrhages experienced complete healing.

Through Saidulu God was building the Church among the Lambadi tribe! Saidulu was thrilled. He became a modern-day Apostle Paul to his tribe. Today, wherever he goes, he helps win people for the kingdom through preaching, teaching and healing. A few years after his conversion, over 150 Lambadis turned to the Lord and many were baptized.

The projects in Russia kept growing. We had accomplished much during the *LBI* days, moving truckloads of New Testaments from Sweden. Now we could even print Scripture within the country. A letter from a lady in Eastern Russia reached my office. It simply stated, "For a long time I have known there is a book like the Bible, but I have never seen one. Now I own a Bible all to myself. I read it over and over and over again and I cannot see the end of what I will get out of it."

One edition of the New Testament was even printed on the Pravda press! Since Pravda means truth in Russian, someone commented, "That is the first time truth has been printed on these presses!"

In countries like Sri Lanka, translation and publication continued in languages such as Sinhala and Tamil. A special distribution project took New Testaments as gifts to as many as possible of the country's 30,000 Buddhist temples.

School projects continued in Brazil, where millions of high school students received the Portuguese New Testament and studied it during school hours. A similar project also worked well in Nigeria, where we provided the entire Bible to be used in religious education classes because the NIV was approved as a textbook.

I will never forget the arms of six-year-old Georgia around my neck. She was an orphan who had been thrown out on the street an hour before I turned up at the orphanage in Croatia, and she held me tightly. She read for me from her copy of *My First Bible* in Croatian, which I had just given her. I didn't understand what she said. But as I talked to the staff, I realized that the only hope for this little girl was a Heavenly Father, for she would never know any other parents.

There are so many great stories. I recall tears streaming down the cheeks of a Chinese pastor in a remote part of China after we had just given him three copies of the Chinese Bible. Through those tears he said, "Lars, next time you come, will you bring me a few more copies?"

And then there was the face of an incarcerated man in Florence, Colorado, who profusely thanked me for the Bible we had sent him. He beamed as he told me, "When I come out, I'm going to become a pastor."

In 1997 Doreen accompanied me on a trip to various *IBS* projects around the world, including a Youth Crusade in the city of Kottayam, India, in conjunction with the release of the Malayalam Bible. On the opening night of the crusade we picked a young man and a young woman from the audience and presented a Bible each to them on the stage in front of some 10,000 spectators. Imagine my astonishment when one of the first persons to come forward to receive Christ that night was the young lady who had received her Bible!

Forum of Bible Agencies

At the Lausanne Convocation in Manila 1989, one track focused on the use of Scripture in evangelism and church life. Ninety percent who attended were leaders for Bible organizations! We suddenly realized that while people were there because of the Bible, there was little interest in how to use it or further its importance in society. "How can we address all this?" exclaimed Fergus Macdonald from United Bible Societies. "What if we met somewhere and began talking to each other?" I suggested. The result of these conversations was the formation of the *Forum of Bible Agencies*, a group of some 14 to 15 organizations. The presidents or senior representatives for these organizations met for a few days every year. In the beginning everyone held their cards tight to their chest, but as the years went by, this became a great fraternity, a place where ideas could freely be exchanged, and where we addressed some serious issues (such as misleading statistics for Bible distribution).

We also were able to work together. We took on a project to provide Bibles for the church of Ethiopia, and because of our joint effort several million Bibles were made available. As long as I was involved in the Forum, I served as its treasurer and was part of the leadership group.

New Captain and an Old Ship

At *IBS*, I soon saw that major steps needed to be taken. We were handing out more grants than our donated income. To make things work, we needed to go from negative to positive cash flow. We were still adjusting after the merger, and with a growing program, this was not easy. My major concern was to generate revenue. When two organizations merge, it may be assumed that income will be the sum of that which both were receiving, but in fact it is much less. Donors are not sure about the new organization and become hesitant. During such a time, expenses need to be managed more carefully than ever. If income and expenditures move in the right direction, the result can be a strong ministry. In a Christian organization, the bottom line is not profit for shareholders, but the fulfillment of a mission, hopefully with an end-of-year surplus to provide reserves and stay solvent.

We needed a fundamental change in the way we carried out almost every process and ministry aspect. To implement a merger globally was as challenging as implementing it in the Colorado Springs office.

In one of the program areas, we had some major problems. The more I studied the situation, I realized I had to move swiftly. Overnight I collapsed the Ministry Division, moved programs needing ongoing funding under the president's office, and then established a translation division, which was badly needed to give oversight and guidance to over 100 translation projects around the world.

There were some technical problems, similar to what I had just dealt with at *LBI*. Many not-for-profit organizations were in what I called the "technology gap." The old mainframe computers we had bought for hundreds of thousands of dollars were not even worth the metal scrap anymore. When we left *LBI*, we walked away from a "mainframe mastodon" we had purchased for $ 150,000 seven years earlier. Now it was obsolete. When I came to *IBS*, they were ready for the change but had not yet made it. The organization had one mainframe and 130 monitors. When accounting ran their reports, all the computer screens in the entire building dimmed. I could not even run a simple Lotus spreadsheet in the entire building. Within two years we had dismantled this system into operating networks with desktop computers and laptop computers for those who traveled.

We needed to become the Bible society of choice for people. Often when our development staff or I visited churches or donors, they would respond to us, "We already give to Wycliffe." While Wycliffe Bible Translators does a superb job, and *IBS* provided no end of dollars to Wycliffe to publish almost half of all their New Testaments, I was quick to point out that Wycliffe worked in minor languages, while *IBS* worked in the major languages, where the masses were, and where enormous distribution was needed.

Time and time again I needed to communicate to the staff, using the most plain, simple, basic terms, driving conviction and action throughout *IBS*. I tried to be as direct as possible. That was often misunderstood. My job was to lift the horizon of everyone - donors, staff and board members - to the vision.

We attempted to organize around the mission, finding cross-functional teams that could make things happen. We tried to eliminate horrendously long processes. I encouraged the leadership team to read books like *The Fifth Discipline* by Peter Senge. People like John Cruz, heading publishing, Norm Whitney in operations/development and later Bob Dinolfo in finance were able lieutenants who did all they could to move us forward.

Early on I gathered all the senior vice-presidents, vice-presidents, senior directors, directors and managers in the conference room and showed them the rather complex organizational chart. Jokingly I said, "Why don't we get rid of this chart and all these titles and just call each other brothers and sisters?" Quickly a hand went up and one of them responded, without joking, "But, couldn't we have senior brothers and senior sisters?"

Over the years we lost some great leaders, but others took their places. John Cruz, who had built the entire publishing group, decided after my first four years to go back to New York and work for American Bible Society. This was a huge loss. Norman Whitney, whose home I had stayed in during a mission conference in Rochester, New York in 1986, left Xerox behind and followed me to *IBS*. After serving in a variety of positions, he also resigned in 1996, heading back to Chicago to be one of the vice presidents at *AWANA*. That was painful. But others took their places, like Dean Merrill, who had been a vice-president of publishing at *Focus on the Family*, and Bob Peters, who had ably served the personnel department of both *Compassion* and *Focus*. Bill Jefferson came in to work with programs, fresh from the *Billy Graham Evangelistic Association's* work in Russia. Paul-Gordon Chandler, who had been my assistant for a while when I joined *IBS*, came back after a short stint serving the Anglican church in Tunisia and the *SPCK* publishers in the UK.

Other Challenging Issues

We debated many of the philosophical differences and at times hammered them out. With little background on how *IBS* became so focused on the NIV, I tended to raise questions such as, "Are we the NIV Bible society or are we the *International Bible Society*, serving the world, where NIV is the flagship?"

While we had 130 staff in the building, we also worked with approximately 800 others, as well as reviewers of our translations around the world. It was hard for many to understand that I needed to spend the majority of my time with those projects and staff development, rather than being in Colorado Springs to "mind the store."

Mergers are not easy for any company, church or blended family. While the merger happened quickly on paper, it took years to make it a reality in operations. The two organizations continued somehow to exist side by side. A true merger was really difficult, however hard we worked on it, both on a board level and a staff level. Long after I left I heard staff continue to refer to the unmerged areas of the organization.

I also wanted to change the economic model from dependency on royalties of the NIV to income raised through development. Knowing that sales could level out or even drop at any time, I wanted to ensure we had a strong development department. However, it costs money to raise money and for some of the board members the progress was far too slow to warrant the expense. We tended to dig up the kernel to see if it was growing and ruined the harvest in the process. It was also hard to find good development people, who knew their area of expertise, and were willing to stay for a long time.

To be able to do this more effectively, my staff and I worked to develop a strategic initiative within which we could present all the aspects of *IBS*, and raise funds for it during a three-year development program campaign. We called it *Let There Be Light*, and every project around the world was incorporated into this plan, as well as all future projects. We launched it in 1997. The timing was catastrophic. We were unaware of the campaign that would be launched against *IBS* in the months to follow over the gender-specific translation work that the Committee of Bible Translation was involved in. While *Let There Be Light* took a major step forward, raised some major funds and set the stage for many projects to take a leap forward, we could never have estimated how this "attack" would color everything we did during my remaining time at *IBS*.

The NIV Crisis and Brouhaha

The Committee on Bible Translation, an independent Committee of evangelical scholars who originally had worked on the NIV, met every year to consider updates. Beginning in February 1992, the Committee started to meet for longer periods every summer to work on what we were calling the Simplified NIV. The aim was to make the Bible text easy even for a seventh-grader to understand. Later, this was published as *New International Reader's Version* (NIrV).

They continued working on what we were calling the "Gender Accurate Edition." For this edition, the committee attempted to ensure that the Greek and Hebrew manuscripts were rendered as accurately as possible as far as any gender issues were concerned.

The "Gender Accurate Edition" first appeared in Britain where the publishers subtitled it "Inclusive Edition." This was unfortunate because when, in 1996, the edition appeared in the United States, several conservative evangelical groups came together to attack *IBS*. They claimed we were giving in to feminist pressure and were about to present God as He or She.

Nothing could have been farther from the truth, but the onslaught was enormous. People who were not experts on Bible translation, whipped up emotions by making misguided public statements. Our building was the subject of bomb threats from Christians, and my life was threatened.

The accusations, which took all kinds of absurd forms such as, centerfold articles, editorials, news clips on CNN and other leading networks, endless interviews on Christian and secular radio, also included a caricature of me and others on the front of a well-known weekly publication, bailing out of a plane in parachutes with a church spire almost hitting me from below.

The crisis was really about differences in translation philosophy. Both sides were and are committed to faithfulness. The question is *how* to be most faithful to the original text. Translation issues are often created between formal equivalence and dynamic equivalence. NIV, in its translation methodology, employs both.

The question really was whether formal equivalence or functional equivalence produces the best translations for our day. As I mentioned before, formal equivalence (also called literal translation) believes that the original wording, grammar and syntax should be retained as long as the resulting translation is understandable. *King James Version, New American Standard Bible* and *Revised Standard Version* are good examples of this methodology. Functional equivalence (also called dynamic translation) believes that the text should have the same impact on the modern reader as the original had on the ancient reader.

According to this approach it is not the *original terms* but the *meaning of the whole* that is important, asking the question: How would Isaiah or Paul say this *today* to get his meaning across? *Good News Bible* and *New Living Translation* are good examples of this translation methodology, while the NIV and New RSV are sometimes literal and sometimes dynamic.

A purely literal translation is impossible. KJV and NASB do not keep every nuance of the original text intact, nor can they. Every translator has to decide the best way to translate the words of one translation into another, and that means changing not only the words but also idioms and grammatical structures. Translations cannot be accomplished by slide rule.

A basic thought of all translation theory is to express the ancient text in the thoughts and idioms of the receptor language. Both formal and functional techniques have the same goals: *accuracy, clarity and rhetorical power.* Literal translations prize word-for-word accuracy and dynamic translations seek both accuracy and clarity in communicating the meaning of the text.

Jokingly I have said that there are three things people should not know: 1. How taxes are determined by our government; 2. How sausages are made; and 3. How Bible translators arrive at the final rendering, because what is rejected at nine in the morning is often accepted at four in the afternoon!

Every translation represents great scholarship, but we must never forget that all Bible translators are human, including the scholars appointed by a king in the 17th century.

The word "inclusive" is a neutral word. It is not used from a feminine point of view but from a linguistic point of view. Other terms that have been used are also meant to give the word a neutral position, such as gender-neutral or gender-accurate. Inclusive language has never intended to change the godhead to God the "father-mother," or Christ to "the child of God."

Yet that is what the general Christian public believed *IBS* had done. To date, there is only one version in the world that has done just that. This version, which was not distributed by any Bible organization, was published by Oxford University Press. It had limited circulation and seems to be long since forgotten.

Inclusive language can have a tendency to go too far into the ridiculous. Even the NIV Committee on Bible Translation went too far in places, using awkward constructions to demonstrate inclusivity, when the text or the contexts were questionable.

What we were looking for in the revision process was a judicious use of inclusive language. Albert Mohler, president of Southern Seminary, Louisville, Kentucky has stated, "Every translation should seek to be as inclusive as the original text intends and no more inclusive than the original text intends."

It is important to use *gender-sensitive* language, wherever there is a neuter singular in the original manuscripts. However, the English language does not have a gender neuter singular. All through the crisis I maintained my view that the main issue was a linguistic problem and not a theological problem. The hero of Bible translation, Martin Luther, used the German term *Mensch*, which is neuter singular in German and includes both man and woman. The Dutch used a similar word *mens*. The Scandinavian languages followed suit with *människa* or *menske*.

Translation issues in those days had absolutely nothing to do with feminist influence, or a unisex attitude. Neither Luther nor Calvin were feminists. For 475 years these terms have functioned fine in Bibles for the

European Christians, from whom we have received most of our systematic theology.

Here are some of the debated renderings:

John 12:34 in KJV, *"When I am lifted up I will draw all men unto me."* The same passage renders it like this in NRSV, *"I will draw all people to myself."* In 2 Cor 5:17 we read, *"If any man is in Christ"* (KJV). NIV changed that to be rightfully inclusive, *"If anyone is in Christ."*

In John 1:4 the NIV reads, *"In him was life and that life was the light of men."* Today's NIV renders it, *"In him was life, and that life was the light of all people."*

Mark 8:36 in NIV reads, *"What good is it for a man to win the whole world..."* while the TNIV reads, *"What good is it for you to gain the whole world?"*

Some groups have formed a theology around the usage of the word "man" that is really not reflected in the original languages. The male overtones of "Adam" are not necessarily there in the originals.

The challenge is to be culturally relevant without being culture bound. Whenever a detail within a culture is not inimical to biblical Christianity, the church should adapt its proclamation to that practice. Replacing *man* with *people* or *he* with *they* in most cases does not contradict the meaning of the biblical text, while retaining them can be at worst offensive, and at best misleading to many modern people.

Some maintain that you must be more precise than that. However, it is not more precise to retain *he* when it refers to a group. In fact if we were being that precise, we should also call the Holy Spirit "she" in the OT, which uses the female form of the word *ruach*, or call the Holy Spirit "it" in the NT, where the Greek text uses the neuter form of the word *pneuma*.

Making the text inclusive is not a new issue. When Paul quotes the Old Testament, he at times goes from individual usage to inclusive usage. In Romans 4:7 he quotes Ps 32:1, which reads, *"Blessed is he whose transgression is forgiven."* Paul renders it as, *"Blessed are they whose transgressions are forgiven."*

Sometimes it has worked in reverse. In the King James Version we read, *"Blessed are the peacemakers because they shall be called the children of God."* This stood for 400 years until ASV, NKJV and NIV changed it to the gender-specific *"sons of God."*

The King James Version also translates *"sons of Israel"* as *"children of Israel"* 644 times when it refers to the tribes in the wilderness and only four times as *"sons of God"* when the phrase specifically refers to men.

Are there problems when going through the changes? Of course there are. Every time you move the text from singular to plural, plural can become a problem as the individuality is lost. Psalm 1:1-2 reads, *"Blessed is the man who does not walk in the counsel of the wicked or stand in the way of sinners or sit in the seat of mockers. But his delight is in the law of the LORD, and on his law he meditates day and night."*

To some the Hebraic overtones are lost in the TNIV translation, which reads, *"Blessed are those who do not walk in step with the wicked or stand in the way that sinners take or sit in the company of mockers, but who delight in the law of the LORD and meditate on his law day and night."*

During this crisis, I received over 1,500 letters from pastors, who often literally "wished me to hell!" Someone wrote, "This is a feminist effort to re-engineer society and abandon God's parameters for the home and for the church" or in a letter from a dean of a theological seminary, "We don't want people 'tampering' with the Word of God." But isn't all translation tampering?

The chief editor of a magazine accused *IBS* of "Misquoting God" and "Changing God's Word." A Christian leader wrote that we had created an "erosion of trust in our English Bibles." One of the most hurtful comments stated that we had created a "he/she" unisex Bible because of feminist influence in the translation committee. Yet the committee was made up of some of the most solid and pious evangelical scholars you could find in the world.

This was not an attempt to compromise the Word of God to make women feel included. It was a step to adhere to the most basic translation principles: fidelity to the originals in conveying the meaning of the text as accurately as possible using today's usage of the English language.

Imagine an exact translation into Chinese of "Let's cut class and hang out at the mall." That phrase would befuddle any recipient if translated literally. Translation is discerning the thought and intent of the author and putting it as clearly as possible into the reader's language.

In the King James Version the following phrase is used several times by Paul in the epistles, "*God forbid.*" However the Greek word for God *Theos* is nowhere to be found in the text. "*May it not be*" would be a more accurate translation. While the latter communicates nothing, the former contains the meaning. No one has complained about that tampering with the word of God for almost 400 years!

"You are just doing it for the money," someone wrote. When the issue hit the press, the Biblical Manhood camp accused us, "They are only doing this to increase sales!" When *IBS* decided not to continue the dialogue, the Egalitarian camp boldly stated, "Capitalism wins!"

A lot of misinformation was passed around and anger and fear prevailed. People voted to remove the *current* NIV from shelves in Christian bookstores, while others desecrated the NIV by drilling holes through them and then shipping them back to my office.

It did not matter what we said about the situation. It is like when someone is falsely accused by someone's father, yelling in your face, "You raped my daughter!" However false the accusation, your explanation that you merely embraced will never be enough for the father.

All translations have to be a work in progress. Not because God changes - God doesn't change His revelation one iota – but because language is like a kaleidoscope: it keeps changing. The day you stop evaluating your translation is the day you decide to let it die and go into history.

The enemy's most potent weapon is inciting dissension among God's people. This is, sadly, a lesson we had to accept and deal with. Keep in mind that two weeks before the crisis began the Board of *IBS* had voted to move forward in the largest worldwide Scripture program ever, *The Let There Be Light* undertaking. Staff around the world had worked and prayed diligently for almost two years to see it launched. At that point some of us said, "What will the enemy do to stop this one?" It was difficult to accept that we were side tracked by well-meaning, righteous, godly people.

We could have dallied on. A meeting at a well-known denominational headquarters was the decisive point for me. After a three hour meeting, the president of Zondervan Publishing House, the secretary of the Committee of Bible Translation and myself, stood on the street together and felt like we had been whipped in the principal's office.

One of the denominational leaders had ended our talks with a smarting statement. "Dunberg, if you can do this to the Biblical text now, next time you will take away the cross."

If denominational leaders did not understand the heart of the issue, but acted emotionally, how would we ever get "Joe churchgoer" to understand it? We had to let innate stubbornness and pride be side-stepped so we could make the tough decision. There and then we made the decision to go to the *IBS* Board and adopt a position that we did not necessarily share individually. The purpose of *International Bible Society* in those days began with, "To serve the Church...," and for the first time we were faced with a decision about how to serve a church divided. The important lesson for *IBS*, and for all believers, particularly those in authority, is that the issue brought about disunity, not disagreement within the context of godly unity.

People in a position of authority have a responsibility to model the greatest command that Christ gave. We have been told that the whole world will know we are His disciples if we love each other - not if we take the "right" stand on a political issue, or represent the cause of righteousness in the court of public opinion.

In those days I was reminded of Mahatma Gandhi's statement, "The problem with you Christians is that you're so unlike your Christ." Our first responsibility, beyond our walk with God, is how we treat each other. In short, issues and agendas can never supersede the biblical mandate to love each other.

During one interview with the Philadelphia Inquirer, the reporter concluded by saying, "Well, I guess that's religion for you." That was heartbreaking. The image he had of my God was based on the way he had seen Christians behave. The harsh reality is that we as Christians are often judged by the way the world perceives us. Today they see abortion protests, judgmental positions against sinners instead of sin, hypocrisy, and the list goes on. This is not how I want the world to see me, or Jesus in me. When I die, I don't want my tombstone to read, "He took the right stand on issues." Big deal! The issues belong to God and my responsibility is to win the world with a better way.

Over Memorial Weekend 1997, the *IBS* Board met in a historic phone meeting, where we made strong public statements on this issue, including the decision to withdraw from the project altogether.

While one camp was jubilant, the bombardment from the egalitarian camp got stronger. I counted over 2,000 letters in the next few days. In some of them I was presented as a person without any principle. Some of the letters compared me to William Tyndale, stating that he was willing to die and be burned at the stake for what he believed, but the president of *IBS* had no guts!

After I stepped down as International President, rumors began to fly. The Christian community didn't seem able to understand why someone would move from a comfortable leadership position into the unknown. There had to be a hidden reason!

The worst rumors were so laughable that they did not bother me. One was that I had an affair with two secretaries and was forced to leave. Another claimed that one of my overseas staff members had stolen more than a million dollars and I had covered up his crime!

The serious claims of financial mismanagement were even more difficult to take. The people spreading such claims had no idea of the struggles I had trying to move the entire organization from negative income to a better net asset position. If they would have checked the audit statements for the seven years I was there, they could have found that net assets in 1992 were $15.5 million and, when I left, they had risen to $18 million. The year I arrived, *IBS* had a negative gap of $1.3 million between income and expenses. When I left, we were $ 2.4 million in surplus. Hardly a position over which to be fired!

A few weeks after my resignation I was invited to the *IBS* building to address the staff in chapel, and I did so by talking about Peter stepping out of his boat. At the end I encouraged them:

> *"What is in my future? Walking on more water, trying to stay focused on Jesus. You have stepped out of your boats, and it feels like sinking. You have the brightest possible future, because Jesus is walking toward you. You're going to go through a new phase; it's going to be different. You're going to influence people around the world like never before.*
>
> *Let me give you a couple of admonitions:*
>
> (1)   *Never lose sight of the fact that there is a tremendous power in the Word of God.*

(2)   *Never lose sight of the fact that 85 percent of those that come to Christ do that before they are 15.*

(3)   *Never lose sight of the fact that there is not one problem in the world that can be solved through any other means than Jesus Christ stepping into people's lives.*

(4)   *Never lose sight of the fact that there are more people alive today that have never heard the gospel than in any other time of history. And God is as concerned for those people as He was when He sent Jesus to die on the cross 2000 years ago.*

(5)   *Never lose sight of the fact that He has called you to be here and do a job for Him.*

(6)   *Never lose sight of the fact that He is with you. Jesus said to go into the world and I will be with you.*

One of my heroes, the founder of the Salvation Army, General William Booth, penned this statement not too long before he died in August 1912. I will not give you the whole statement, but just a few pieces of it. He wrote this, after he had established the Salvation as a church in more than 100 countries:

'As long as women must suffer and cry, I will fight.
As long as children and young people are without home and shelter, I will fight.
As long as the prisons are full, I will fight.
As long as there is one soul living without God's light, I will fight.
I will fight right to the very end.'

Now let me change that statement a bit, and perhaps change the word fight to serve. And this is what I want to leave with you this morning:

As long as there are people in the world who have never heard the name of Jesus, I will serve.

As long as there are young people who have not been challenged to discipleship, I will serve.
As long as there are people who have never been impacted by the Word of God, I will serve.
As long as there are children in need of a Savior, I will serve.
As long as there are pastors and evangelists not having basic training, I will serve.
I will serve right to the very end."

There were some things I felt strongly about – and still do - but could not address after my resignation. Today I am not sure how many voices are being raised regarding one of the toughest things happening to society, but also to the church worldwide – the marginalization of the Word of God.

More and more people around the world and certainly in the U.S. have access to Bibles, but do not read them. We read less and less. That same trend is obvious in our church services. We evangelize without the Bible and worship without the Bible. This is true for those who both characterize their places of worship as traditional Protestant churches or staunch evangelical churches. In many churches you may hear one or two Scripture verses, often as part of an illustration of a sermon.

A recent survey in a progressive, seeker-sensitive, exploding Colorado church, where the median age among those surveyed was 34 years, revealed that more than 25% of regular attendees never read their Bibles, two thirds of regular attendees can recall less than 10 Bible verses from memory, over half the regular attendees pray less than 10 minutes per day, and approximately 70% of regular attendees acknowledge that they are not currently fulfilling God's will for their lives. In spite of this, approximately 80% are satisfied with their spiritual growth.

In another shocking survey conducted in Great Britain, it was revealed that 20% of regular churchgoers have not read anything from the Bible in the last year and 66% of regular churchgoers don't read the Bible from one week to the next. Only 25% had ever read through the entire Bible.

It is a worldwide problem. An African leader said, "The decline in Biblical literacy in our nation is the result of most preaching being testimonial."

Our over-emphasis on spiritual experience, worship and psychological counseling is taking the place of God's Word in worship and in the Christian's life. The shift to electronic media is leading people, especially young people, away from reading.

With less Bible awareness, what will happen to evangelization and church attendance? What will it do to the spiritual health of people? What more will it do for us not following God's will?

Biblical literacy is the process of becoming aware of the basic content of the Bible as the unfolding story of God's love for the world and beginning to know, understand, live and share it. Making a congregation biblically literate is a long-term process that requires the engagement and participation in every aspect of church life, using all available mediums, to encourage daily involvement with the Bible.

I pray that Bible agencies around the world will continue to address these issues. If not, our Church will fall away from its very foundation and lose its influence in society. May it not be so!

CHAPTER 14
Global Action: It's All About Risk

The first few weeks after we decided to launch *Global Action* were scary. Doreen and I went through our personal address book, making note of friends we used to send Christmas cards to. We penned a letter of introduction, made an audio cassette about the vision and mailed it out to a couple of hundred people. There was hardly any response. After three months we had raised $ 19,500!

Humble Beginnings

A few weeks earlier I had gone down to the post office to learn how to rent a mailbox, so we would have a business address. Standing in line, the enemy was very active! I heard him whisper, "Dunberg, what are you doing here? A few weeks ago you led a huge organization. Do you think anything ever will come of this? You are finished, Dunberg!" I was ready to get out of line and rush home.

Every day I asked myself, "Did we hear right from God? Did we start *Global Action* in some kind of 'walk-on-water' faith that was too simplistic?" I questioned God every day. I cried, prayed and struggled with a balance of fear and faith.

One month after launching *Global Action* Doreen and I flew to Sweden to meet some ministry leaders and talk about speaking and teaching opportunities. Some were interested, while most did not see where I could possibly fit into the Swedish scene after so many years away. The U.S. has often been viewed negatively by Sweden, and a Swede coming to minister from the U.S. had no major role to play in the future plans of the Swedish Church. On the flight home that early November day in 1998, I mentioned to Doreen, "We're not receiving any income, so we'd better close down before we really get going or we'll make it worse!"

When we arrived home, jetlagged and depressed, I found a letter in our private mailbox. It was from an old friend who also operated a foundation. In her letter she mentioned that her foundation could not yet give us any funds because the Internal Revenue letter of tax-exempt status had not yet been issued to *Global Action*. She did tell us, however, that she wanted to help us get the organization started, so enclosed was a personal check from her for $25,000! That gift helped us put *Global Action* on the map!

Anne Craft, who had been my assistant at *International Bible Society*, left her position there in September of 1998 and offered her services as a volunteer until I could pay her. For the next three months we met almost every day outside the post office. One of us would go in, stick a hand in the mailbox and feel around to see if there were any letters. Most days our meetings were brief after we realized that no checks had arrived. It was a challenging time.

Working out of our basement was not the best solution, so we asked Woodmen Valley Chapel, where Anne, Doreen and I attended, if they had any available office space. We rented a big room that we divided into two and we were ready to take occupancy January 1, 1999.

In the middle of December 1998, Anne and I visited the church offices to sign the lease. We brought the lease papers into the "mobile office" in my van. Sitting in the church parking lot I just stared at the documents.

"Sign the papers!" Anne urged.

I looked at the lease with its commitment of $34,000 for the next two years and I could not fathom where we would get these kind of funds.

"I have seen you sign contracts for millions of dollars at *IBS*," Anne sighed. "What are you waiting for?"

With tears welling up in my eyes I told her how hard it was for me to trust that God would provide, but as we talked, I was ready to step out in faith, and the first public office of *Global Action* became a reality.

During those first few months I spoke at meetings in Mexico, Britain and Sweden. I visited possible funding and prayer partners across the United States. When the board met by phone in January, several members stressed that it was important for *Global Action* not only to be an umbrella organization for my own speaking ministry, but also to begin launching out in other areas. Ray Schenk said in no uncertain terms, "Let's ask Lars to find a project or two that can help us, because it's impossible to raise funds for his travel schedule!"

How could we accomplish that, being so small? I saw the solution through partner organizations. Galo Vasquez was a friend of many years who had worked with me both at *LBI* and *IBS*. He and I had talked about doing some projects together in Latin America.

In 1985 I had been invited to Mexico to attend a conference where *VELA* (Vision for Evangelization in Latin America) launched their "10,000 by year 2000" project. Galo, the president of *VELA*, and his staff had researched Mexico City, the largest city in the world, and found that there were only approximately 1,500 churches and Bible study centers in the entire city.

Together with a steering committee of pastors, they imagined what it would be like if every citizen in the largest city of the world would be within walking distance of a Bible study group or even an evangelical church.

As I listened to their presentation, I shook my head. It had taken hundreds of years to establish 1,500 evangelical churches - and now they were going for the stars in 15 years! I cautioned Galo Vasquez not to lose his credibility, but he ensured me that they would map the city and work with all possible denominations to make this happen.

At the end of November 2000 Doreen and I were back in Mexico City where we celebrated the *completion* of this 15-year project. They had actually reached their goal by October and by November the number had grown to 11,200. More than 550 pastors gathered to celebrate. I had the opportunity to address them and challenge them for the next steps in reaching out with the gospel in Mexico.

It was a privilege for *Global Action* to provide the funding to print the final report on the growth of the evangelical church in Mexico City. A pastor told us that morning, "Everything you do at *Global Action* is needed here!"

Since the launch of *Global Action* we have worked with *VELA* in co-sponsoring pastors conferences and youth conferences in Ecuador, Guatemala and Mexico. At the same time we provided a platform for *VELA* leaders, including Galo Vasquez and David Ruiz, in other parts of the world.

Out of the blue, Jason Burden of *Pierced*, walked into our little office. This young Canadian evangelist had read about us in a short article in *Christianity Today*. He wanted to learn more and shared with us his big idea to reach out to Gen-Xers. We gave him a desk and office space and mentored him the best we could.

Through the events happening in Kosovo during the spring of 1999, Britain's *Eurovangelism* became a partner organization, and we worked together in many countries in Eastern Europe.

When I returned from India in February 1999, having been challenged to launch Global Module Studies (GLOMOS) to train pastors in Asia, I hired an Indian college principal to run the program. I knew I also needed help to create some of the written material. On a snowy day in March, I drove to the store to buy flowers for my wife, almost hitting a man in the store parking lot. When I looked carefully I noticed a man sprawled across the front of my van. It was a Chinese man, and when I looked closer I recognized him. "Alvin, what are you doing?" I yelled through the window. "Being killed by you," Alvin Low teased with his typical smile. We exchanged pleasantries and I asked him to come and meet with me. The next day we agreed that Dr. Alvin Low from *ACTS International* would be involved with writing our training program for South Asia.

I called a meeting in June 1999 for the leaders all of these partner organizations to come together for two days at our office. We had no funding for these kinds of gatherings, but we offered to provide room and board. Two weeks before the partner meeting I emailed a couple who had shown great interest in our work and said, "If you ever want to get in on the ground floor and grow with an organization, that time is now. We have a partnership meeting on June 6 and 7 and I would love to hear from you."

The leaders from *Eurovangelism*, *ACTS*, *VELA* and *Pierced* all attended our partnership meeting, along with Emily Voorhies and Anne Craft.

We prayed together, planned together, and brainstormed until the walls were covered with sheets of paper. The sheets were full of ideas, from reaching out to children to retirees, with corny slogans like, "Don't retire – re-fire!" As I looked at it all, fear gripped me.

"It would take at least $300,000 a year to do all this and we don't have this kind of money!" I exclaimed.

Galo Vasquez gently reminded me of the devotion that morning. I had spoken from 2 Kings 4 about the widow and the oil and pointed out that: "We need to know where to go when we don't know what to do and we need to look to God as our source." We prayed that God would provide the income.

A few days later I received an answer from the partner I had emailed a couple of weeks before. He briefly stated that he wanted to be part of what God was doing through us and he would send us 5,000 shares of stock in his company. When the shares finally sold, they sold at $ 65 per share providing money for all the programs we had outlined in faith!

This became the foundation for trusting God in moving us into the program areas I had dedicated to the Lord at the inception of *Global Action*. Stepping out in faith, the work exploded as we continued to trust God for income to meet the need. The income doubled the first year, then continued growing steadily 30 to 40% every year. When we launched *Global Action* we prayed that God would provide a budget of $500,000 for the first five years. We passed that milestone after 7 months in operation. Today our budgeted income is approximately 10 million dollars, with about 700 people providing 85% of those funds.

Most weeks we do not know where the funds will come from to finish in the black. But believing the principle that "if we do the possible, God will do the impossible," we have moved forward.

Fundraising is still our Achilles heel. We have tried many different approaches, some recommended by the best in the industry. Most have failed miserably. We have tried to hire people who could effectively present the ministry to others in order to raise funds, but have not always seen the expected results. If experts are formed from the making of many different mistakes, we are indeed experts in this area! We pray that the group of individuals now representing the ministry of *Global Action* will succeed beyond our wildest dreams.

After our initial partnership meeting, other partner organizations came along, such as The Salvation Army. We have worked with them in humanitarian projects in India, Dagestan, Ingushethia and Moldova, as well as pastoral training conferences and summer camps.

InterAct is a Swedish denomination created in 1996 by the merger of three "old" denominations: two Baptist denominations and the Holiness church. Over the years *Global Action* has assisted with mentoring and training leaders and pastors as well as motivating congregations to greater missions involvement. *Global Action* has also worked with some of their core missions projects around the world.

Many years later organizations such as *Mission Possible* in Bulgaria, *AWEMA (Arab World Evangelistic Ministers Association)* in the Middle East, *BEZA International* in Ethiopia, *The Salvation Army Humanitarian Aid* in Sweden and many others joined forces with us.

Philosophy and Organization

While long-term planning and business strategies are important, *Global Action* believes seeking God's will and listening for His prompting are far more important. As Henry Blackaby says in one of his books, "Find what God is doing and join Him!"

Over the years several core values have been crystallized. These include:

WE ARE BIBLICALLY BASED. We have a high view of God and His daily intervention. The Bible is God's Word and it guides God's people today as it has in the past. Prayer is a force to be reckoned with. Prayer keeps us close to God. Prayer keeps us close to one another. Prayer is not an extra activity we can do without!

Humankind is lost for now and eternally without Christ. Christ is the only and unique way to God. Faith without works is dead. The church is Christ's idea of His body here on earth.

We believe in servanthood. We believe in equality when it comes to national background (neither Jew nor Greek), when it comes to organizational structure (neither slave nor free) and when it comes to gender (neither male nor female) as well as when it comes to the universal priesthood (no titles.)

We believe in leadership that encourages rather than tears down. We value servant leaders who humble themselves and wait for God to help them up; who follow Jesus rather than seek a position; who give up their personal rights to find joy in serving others. Servant leaders take the initiative to serve others because they are confident that God has control over their lives. Servant leaders "pick up the towel" to serve the needs of other people. Servant leaders share the responsibility and authority with others to meet even greater needs.

WE ARE COMMITTED TO MEETING NEEDS WHEREVER THEY ARE FOUND. We are committed to a quick response to these perceived needs (within the limits of our ability and in doing so being driven by an entrepreneurial spirit.)

We are committed to meeting these needs on location – not just as we perceive them from the global coordination office.

WE ARE COMMITTED TO A MINIMUM OF BUREAUCRACY AT EVERY LEVEL. This means fewer policies at a board level, less structure at organizational level and fewer hindrances to effectively operate at any staff level. We desire to have a low organizational profile while fulfilling our mission. As such we are pilgrims doing a task and do not desire to become wrapped up in permanent structures, such as ownership of property except for rare cases when it is absolutely necessary.

WE ARE COMMITTED TO PARTNERSHIPS TO FULFILL OUR MISSION AND VISION.

WE ARE COMMITTED TO SEEK GOD'S WILL IN EVERYTHING WE UNDERTAKE. While long term planning and "business strategies" are important to us, far more important is seeking God's will and listening for His prompting.

WE ARE COMMITTED TO FILLING MINISTRY GAPS WHEREVER NEEDED.

WE ARE COMMITTED TO FLEXIBILITY IN PROGRAMS AND STRUCTURE.

WE ARE COMMITTED TO BE NON-TRADITIONAL VERSUS TRADITIONAL.

David Foster and I present Bibles to Prime
Minister Menachem Begin of Israel in April 1982

David Foster and I present a Bible to Teddy
Kollek, Mayor of Jerusalem, in 1982

Family picture taken 1984. Back Row: Carin
and Maria. Front Row: Me, Paul and Doreen

LBI's India director Noble Massey and I meet in September 1985 with Governor Shankar Dayal Sharma of Andhra Pradesh, India who later became the president of India

PLN Murthy and I meet with church leaders Ron Shaw and Rev. Roychowdery to lay plans for the *It's a Great Life* campaign in Kolkata in 1985

Conducting a Leadership Seminar in Kottayam, Kerala, India in November 1986

My philosophy, "Eat what is set before you." Dining on pig's ear in the Peoples Republic of China in 1985

Trying to blend in with the wall at the Galle Face Hotel in Colombo, Sri Lanka

Two crazy "Coconuts!" Me and Bill Jefferson drinking coconut milk fresh off the tree in Kerala, India in 1985

With Billy Graham at *Amsterdam 86* where
LBI provided a special Bible, including the
Amsterdam affirmations, for the 10,000
evangelists from around the world

Launching *It's a Great Life* at the
Assemblies of God church
in Kolkata in 1986

Victor Oliver, Donna Birkey and I listen
to Luis Palau at *LBI's* International
Council meeting in Nairobi in April 1987

Mother Teresa and I in October 1993

Sharing the need of the Word of God for a
nation with President Fidel Ramos of the
Philippines in October 1993

Presenting *IBS's* Golden Word award to
Joni Earickson Tada in September 1994

Anne Craft and I in *Global Action's* first office

Meeting with pastors from Bhutan at a pastors' conference in Katmandu, Nepal in January 2000

Speaking at *The Salvation Army* Roots conference in Jyväskylä, Finland in July 2002

Mentoring a young man at a *New Generation* conference in Lucknow, India in October 2002

Ministering to a capacity crowd in
Hyderabad, India in October 2002

Speaking at the GLOMOS graduation in
Kolkata, India in October 2004

Sometimes you have to go the extra mile! Alvin
Low, George Carr and I at a graduation in
Yangoon, Myanmar in 2004

Crowds beyond expectation in Bhubaneswar,
Orissa, India for the *New Generation* festival
in October 2007

A desk not used too often at the *Global
Action* office in Colorado Springs

The Dunberg clan September 2008
From left to right, back row: Me and Paul,
middle row: Maria, Andrew, Carin, Amanda, Doreen and Ron,
front row: Eleanor, Katelyn, Joshua and Ryan

WE ARE COMMITTED TO BEING ADMINISTRATIVELY SMALL AND BIG ON MINISTRY OUTREACH.

WE ARE COMITTED TO BEING RISK-TAKERS. As such we challenge other believers to become risk-takers who in turn impact the world for Jesus Christ.

WE ARE COMMITTED TO HAVING FUN DOING IT.

Often people ask me, "What did your first strategic plan look like and how did you come up with it?" As I look back over the past 10 years, I can see that we have tried to be strategic, but not through creating detailed plans apart from our connection to the Lord or the rest of the world. Instead, God came to us and opened opportunities in our direction. I call it God's imploding doors. It is as if He told us, "Here is an opportunity. Do you want to go through this door?"

When we *have* gone, it has been like stepping out in unchartered territory. Sometimes funding and staff have been available as needed. Other times we have followed only to find that we had the timing wrong. Our dream is to continue to stay close to His voice as we take the steps for the future.

During the first five years, we finalized the mission and the vision statements that lead us to work in the various areas of ministry around the world. As long as lives are transformed, we are ready to serve.

Our first mission statement was too long. I could not remember it! So it was re-crafted into this statement: *Declaring the Kingdom of God in word and deed to people around the world.*

It was followed by this vision statement: *To Challenge, Inspire, and Equip Believers to become Risk-takers for God, who Radically Impact the World for Jesus Christ.*

CHAPTER 15
Evangelism and Outreach

R ight after *Global Action* was founded, I received an invitation from the Baptist Association in Andhra Pradesh, India to conduct a pastors' conference and hold a crusade in the city of Kurnool, India. The invitation was for February 1999.

India Sets the Stage

I had never heard of Kurnool and had to bring out a map to find this city of close to 300,000 people, situated five hours by car south of Hyderabad, in the rice belt of India. I searched for information about the city and found this description, written by Dr. Edwin Orr, of the Christian history of Kurnool:

> *"In 1906 typhoid, smallpox, and cholera raged and a famine swept over the villages around Kurnool. Right when conditions were at their worst, "suddenly and unexpectedly like the rushing of a mighty wind" revival came. A common quarterly prayer meeting was turned into a revival, lasting two weeks. Without any person leading it, it began in a great force of prayer, getting more and more intense until all the people were praying aloud and crying to God for mercy.*
>
> *All day and far into the night this continued—'burning, cleansing, quickening and transforming lives by divine power.' It*

was the mightiest movement of the Holy Spirit that Kurnool had ever known.

The fruit of the revival was seen in the lives of people who professed the name of Christ. They began sharing Christ with the people in their neighborhoods. But the church at Kurnool had to wait six years before the great awakening among the non-Christians followed. In 1912, people began to turn to Christ, and more than a thousand were baptized after they professed their newly-found faith in Christ."

I was going to speak in the Baptist church that had been constructed after this mighty move of God. Driving into the city, I noticed extreme poverty on a level I had not seen in other places than Kolkata.

Outside one of the schools, I observed children sitting with their teacher around a huge blackboard. Everywhere I looked, there were people, beggars, animals and garbage. Kurnool is both a Muslim and Hindu city and the call to prayer sounded regularly from the Minaret outside my hotel window.

I shared my bed with an army of invisible but effective insects. By morning, big grape-like boils had risen all over my shoulders and back. To say the least, I itched all over.

The water in the rather primitive hotel was brown like tea and extremely cold and unpredictable, making showering an adventure.

Some 200 pastors and Christian workers turned up for the conference, and despite the heat (the only ventilation was open windows) we met for sessions all day long. Lunch and dinner were served from big pots heated by open fire in the church yard, then poured in buckets holding the curry and samba, and then scooped over rice on banana leaves and metal plates.

At night it was time for the crusade meeting. Around 20,000 people gathered each night on the grounds of the Christian college, ensuring that the meetings taking place were officially on church property. Just a month earlier, an Australian missionary, Graham Staines and his two sons had been martyred, burned to death in their car while they were asleep, in the nearby state of Orissa, so tension was high.

Because my face was plastered on 5,000 posters around town, the pastors warned me not to leave the hotel. A van, followed by a police vehicle, picked me up every night for the services and as we met in the school grounds, militant Hindu demonstrators gathered to do all they could to disturb the proceedings. At the same time, some very noble Hindu scholars attended the crusade meetings every night, sitting on the front row, and sending me notes with comments after each preached message.

For the first time I had to deal with an issue that I never before had thought of. "What is worse? To be burned to death or be beaten to death?" Both were a strong possibility and the odds for being accosted grew minute by minute as the invitation was given every night and people committed their lives to Christ.

It was at that point I realized that my better role in India would be to train the country's Christians to evangelize their own people, rather than standing in the limelight on the crusade stage, however glamorous that could seem, and however much it was in line with my personal calling. I knew then that the future of *Global Action's* ministry in India would be more about training than public evangelism.

Still, the opportunities to share Jesus did not go away. There were constant knocks on the hotel room door. One by one the hotel staff, from cleaning boys to security guards, wanted to see the Western visitor. But each one also turned to me, their smiles suddenly transformed to serious looks, and said in a whisper, "Pray for me!"

How many of those understood my simple prayers? Those hearts the Holy Spirit opened so that the seed could bear fruit will only be known in heaven. But there was sheer joy and exhilaration on their faces when we equipped them with Gospels of John and Telugu Bibles and sent them back to their duties.

Sharing the Gospel With Students

Students always provide both an opportunity and challenge for dialogue about Christ. While I always want to take every opportunity to speak to students, they intimidate me. Will I be able to communicate? Will they roast me alive with their cynical questions? Will I be able to "defend the faith" in an adequate way so Jesus can be seen and heard instead of Dunberg?

During the second year of *Global Action's* existence I was back in India again, this time in the northern city of Lucknow. I had been invited to address the students at the *Isabella Thoburn College*, a ladies college founded in 1886 by an American Methodist missionary. While some of the teachers, including the principal, are Methodists, many are Hindus, and the college is now a secular liberal arts college.

I was told that more than 2,000 students might gather in the assembly hall, and that probably no more than 10% of those would have any Christian background. The rest would be from leading Hindu, Muslim and Agnostic families. The principal ensured me that although she wanted me to speak for an hour, the students would get fidgety after 20 minutes and I would need to take a break every 15 minutes and have them stand and relax for a while!

When we entered the hall, it was packed to capacity, with people sitting in the aisles and many standing outside. The windows and doors were wide open for those outside to hear.

I spoke for one hour and five minutes! There was plenty of eye contact and such silence that you could hear a pin drop! Having considered how to capture their attention with thoughts about their future, I began by giving general leadership principles, but then focused the last 30 minutes on the five questions every young person, anywhere in the world, has to tackle:

Who am I?
Why am I here?
Who are the ones around me (my community)?
Will I leave any legacy behind?
Where am I going when I die?

The answer to each one of these questions led to a strong presentation of the gospel.

On the way out, the principal grabbed my arm and said, "When are you coming back? You can speak to my girls any time, for as long as you like, on whatever topic you want!"

There is no end of tension between Christians and Hindus in this part of the world and proselytizing is a sensitive issue. The average Hindu's view of Christianity is best portrayed in the film *Gandhi*, where one Hindu tells a British Anglican clergyman, "My wife is a Christian! She drinks blood! Blood of Christ - every Sunday!"

A year or two before my visit, several U.S.-based para-church groups had focused their fundraising letters on what it might cost to make a convert in India, explaining it would take 35 cents or some such amount. Somehow the India government got access to this information, which in turn gave the average Hindu the idea that he is not worth much! There are so many barriers to overcome.

As a matter of fact, the secret police had made inquiries to the Principal's office the day before my visit. We were informed we could not say in the auditorium, "We want to give you New Testaments after Dr. Dunberg's presentation." Instead we had to say, "We have New Testaments available for each one of you. If you want one, please come to the foyer and request one and we will give you a copy."

We did not have enough! We had to come back the following day with several hundred more because of the enthusiastic response.

After a quick cup of coffee we headed for *Lucknow Christian College*, which is the male counterpart to the *Isabella Thoburn College*. Founded by the Methodist church, it is now a secular college, with a few of the professors being Methodists, and some of the professors representing other faiths.

Here the voluntary session was held in the chapel that only seated some 1,000 students. It was jam packed, with more than 500 students listening outside through the open windows.

I gave the same presentation I had communicated at the ladies college. We offered *New Testaments* here as well, and they went like hotcakes!

At all these gatherings, the students were invited to the evangelistic rallies, held every night in the Lal Bagh Methodist Church. This was the church that was once pastored by the well-known missionary E. Stanley Jones. When I visited the church, the pastor was a young man from Chennai, Rev. Sundar Singh Moses, a man with a heart burning to see life transformation in the lives of these students. What will be the fruits of such labor? Only God knows, but the seed was sown with force, attempting to find fertile ground for the truth.

Secular TV Becomes a Window for the Gospel

One day I received a phone call from Gary Cox of *Eurovangelism* in Great Britain. Would we be interested in co-sponsoring a program on secular TV in Russia that would put Christ into millions of homes over Christmas? He told me of the programs depicting the *Life of Christ*, and another program about C. S. Lewis that would be placed on a powerful Moscow channel, as well as on other regional stations from St. Petersburg to Siberia!

Production costs were already covered, and only the technical bills, plus costs for the presenter remained. But even though these were comparatively modest, we had no funds designated to cover them. The minimum amount to ensure transmission was approximately $4,000. Soon a partner came forward and underwrote the programs.

The response was so dramatic that we have been running similar programs in Russia every Christmas and Easter since then.

Transmissions over the Christmas period included six different programs, two of which were especially for children, featuring the facts and meaning of Jesus' birth. Additionally, most of the stations ran the entire *Life of Christ* series that had been filmed in Israel in locations covering Jesus' birth (Bethlehem), life and ministry (Nazareth and Galilee) and death and resurrection (Jerusalem).

Programs were transmitted weekly, on Saturday and Sunday, at times ranging from early morning to late at night. They were so well-received that many TV stations requested permission to re-run them.

Four Moscow channels ran between four and six programs each, ranging from a major channel reaching 2 million viewers to a small cable outfit with just 30,000 subscribers. St Petersburg's Channel 49 took all five programs offered, plus the series. Other regional stations airing programs included TV stations in other parts of the former Soviet Union, including Belarus, Estonia and Ukraine.

There is no way of ascertaining actual viewing numbers, but the potential number of viewers submitted by each station was between 9 and 10 million each time. Bearing in mind that only one station ran a single program, and most aired from four to six programs, the total (same viewers watching different programs) could be ten times that number! Can you imagine a greater impact? Spending $4,000 to reach 10 million people! It is these dollar-stretching programs that makes *Global Action's* ministry so unique.

The programs were introduced by Tatiana Tcherniava, who is a believer. Before she became a Christian, Tatiana presented the longest-running and most popular TV program during the Communist era, a children's presentation, entitled *ABC*, which was both educational and entertaining. It was Russia's equivalent to *Sesame Street*. The program has since been revived, and its renewed popularity gives Tatiana a high profile which adds to her recognition with viewers when presenting Christian programs.

Here are just a few excerpts of the thousands of letters from viewers addressed to Tatiana:

> *"I am a teacher telling children about God. Your programs are very helpful. During Sunday School we watch them, and it is so exciting for me to see children coming to know God. Thank you very much for your work."*

> *"Dear Tatiana: I watched your TV program ABC when I was a small child. Now I am 30 years old. When I was 22, I became a believer. I am so happy to find that you are now a believer as well, and that you help people to find God through your TV programs. These help us to raise our children in the right way, and we thank you for this."*

> *"Peace to you and to all your family. Your Christian programs bring us so much joy. In our rural area, we don't have a church, so I travel to another place to worship. The nearest church is 38 kilometers away, and the bus runs only twice a week. So when I saw your TV programs about Jesus, I wept because I was so happy. I like these programs so much."*

> *"Hello! It is so good that you are showing these TV programs about God. All the soap-operas teach our children how to be cruel and angry. Your programs are so necessary for children who, without God, will not respect anyone. We grew up without God, and it was very harmful. May our children come to know Him."*

Textbooks Evangelize Africa

Thousands of school children in Malawi and Tanzania are now able to read and study the Bible during school hours thanks to a project where *Global Action* provided English Bibles for the students.

A teenager named Thelma wrote to us at *Global Action* sharing that she was a believer, had to study the Bible in school but could not afford one, and needed it both for her studies as well as sharing Christ with her friends!

Many school children longed for a Bible of their own, but there simply were no major supplies available in the country. And those that were available were too expensive. I remembered the school Bible we produced at *International Bible Society*. By buying them in bulk, we could afford to make them available to Thelma and students in similar situations. As Bibles are made available, these young students can study the Word of God as part of the school curriculum. In the evenings they take their Bibles home and share it with the extended family, often consisting of more than ten people, and many of them simply cannot read. As the children read to their families the impact of the gospel spreads like ripples on the water.

If enough funding were available *Global Action* could provide 1,000,000 Bibles in Africa annually without even scratching the surface!

The Pierced Generation

When Jason Burden contacted *Global Action* with his idea to reach out to the pierced Generation X, I became very interested. For a year and a half, *Global Action* assisted Jason and his organization in planning and executing a program to Gen-Xers that took place in October 2000.

Some 2,500 young people gathered in a downtown auditorium in Colorado Springs to listen to the band *POD*, well-known from *MTV*. The band does not play Christian music, but the men in the band are all Christians.

For three hours the band played and the crowd jumped, rocked, head-banged and crowd-surfed. Toward the end of the performance the guitarist shared his testimony. Jason followed, and for ten minutes talked about the pierced generation and the pain they are experiencing. While Jason was speaking, Jesus was literally, dramatically crucified on the stage beside Jason. As he concluded, Jason turned to Christ on the cross, stating "…and this man was pierced for you!"

We will never know the impact this gospel presentation had on thousands of these un-churched kids that night, but one of the results from this evening was a weekly service for the pierced generation that is still meeting, many years later.

Responding to 9/11

While America regrouped and reestablished emotionally and financially following September 11, 2001, *Global Action* created a 32-page, full-color booklet called, *Worried? Who Isn't...But There Is Hope,* for anyone anxious about the future and seeking answers during days of uncertainty.

Developed for churches and individuals to share with family members, friends and neighbors, the booklet addressed a variety of issues Americans are confronting today. It also featured vivid photography from New York City's Ground Zero, heart-felt impressions of the worries people across the nation ponder, notable quotes from contemporary and historic leaders as well as suitable Bible verses.

Many churches ordered major quantities of the book. Some churches handed them out as gifts during Easter services in 2002. We selected 10,000 random addresses in Manhattan and mailed the book to them with a nice letter. Some people called and were angry. Some thanked us. A few wrote and said they had accepted Christ as their Savior. Another example of a situation where we will never know about the seed that fell in the good soil.

Gospel Festival in Sri Lanka

The day I arrived in Sri Lanka in November 2003, the country's president declared a state of emergency and called out soldiers to keep order on the streets. All public meetings became greatly suspect.

Global Action's national coordinator, Lal Whitanage, had planned an unusual way to present the gospel to non-Christians, and it was in the open air. Now this was in jeopardy! He appealed to the police who turned him down, but asked him to come back the next day. At the same time, the monsoon rain had begun – later than usual – and it was raining like the heavens were opened.

A team prayed through the night – that the rains would stop and that the police would say yes. In the morning the rain stopped. Though the police had finally given a go-ahead to Lal, I was advised not to speak. Lal still felt it was all too risky and that agitators and religious fanatics might turn up and create no end of disturbance and even bodily harm.

That night the concert-cum-rally started with the theme "Thank you for the music." Secular pop stars who are also believers and enormously popular on the island shared in songs of love, using secular songs with a double meaning of the Christian message. Crowds gathered, literally thousands of young people who had no idea who the Christian God was and had never heard the name of Jesus. Lal invited the chief of police as the guest of honor. In the middle of the concert Lal turned to me, "Lars, if you want to risk it, you are on!" I had no choice but to speak, as I wrote a book on risk-taking!

So I got up and spoke, thinking the crowd of Buddhist young people would disperse. For 20 minutes they stood absolutely still and quiet, listening to the message.

The following night was equally successful, with almost twice as many people. I was not used to speaking on a huge open-air stage with smoke machines, strobe lights, spotlights and pop stars. There were even people dancing in front of the stage before I spoke. Some people were drunk. One man climbed the stage before I had finished preaching and asked how he could be saved! He was counseled there and then on the side of the stage. Jesus was present that night!

Both nights people stayed behind, and although no public appeal was given, many found the Lord. It became clear to the participants more than ever what it means that Jesus went out to the parties and to where the sinners were. As the evening came to its conclusion, a Hindu parade came by with thousands of people carrying their gods, followed by a Buddhist parade, at least a mile long, with statues, costumes, flags and 11 live elephants dressed up in fancy coverings! We did not carry our God that night, but He surely carried us!

A Message for Indian Students

As I spoke at several Indian colleges I wished I had a booklet I could leave behind with these well-educated Hindu, Muslim and agnostic young people.

To be able to tackle the message from their point of view, we conducted almost 3,000 questionnaire interviews at secular colleges. We learned what college students worry about, think about and are planning for the future. Based on that information, the team that put together the *Worried* booklet, went to work on a new one. Some Indian staff helped with the project and the result was *Our Whole World Is Changing; Are You?* This booklet, 32 pages in full-color, brings a student from their fears and worries into a clear presentation of the gospel. It even uses a Hindu Diwali prayer to present the gospel! The first 25,000 copies were printed and used all across the country with university students. The response has been so positive that we will go ahead and publish the booklet in several Indian languages for high school students as well.

In Delhi, 1500 copies were distributed to young people. In Kolkata, 300 students in school and colleges received copies. In the Lucknow area, several thousand were distributed in 15 colleges, and the response was overwhelming. In Bhubaneswar, copies were distributed widely, including 500 at a book fair. After reading the booklet, some 30 young people called our coordinator, Rev. Songram Singh, with questions. He was able to answer them and provide the enquirers with copies of the New Testament.

Himalayan regional coordinator, Rev. Kiran Kumar Sharma, reported from Kalimpong about the impact the booklet had on the lives of young people who received it. He said that older people also appreciate it. As a result of the booklet's distribution, many people requested and received copies of the New Testament. He added, "After reading through the New Testament, more than 50 young people asked for copies of the complete Bible."

CHAPTER 16
Training and Motivation

Worldwide, 65 million people join the church annually. Approximately 44,000 new churches are started during the same time period to meet this need. At the same time nearly 10,000 students outside of the USA are finishing seminary studies each year to serve the church. After five years, almost half of these graduates end up teaching or as full-time theologians. There is an ever- widening gap between the number of new churches and new pastors, a gap that becomes even wider as people leave the ministry, retire, or die.

Another problem facing the leadership crisis in the church is the fact that of all pastors in the world, approximately 62% have no biblical training. Providing basic Biblical, theological and practical training for would-be evangelists, pastors and lay leaders who live and minister in developing countries has long been a challenge of the Church. Pastors also need continuous and practical training to be more effective in their ministries. They need to be aware of and utilize effective strategies to help them evangelize in rural and urban settings. These leaders also need to know how to disciple and mentor new believers to become fully devoted followers of Christ.

What happens when pastors, lay leaders and evangelists do not fully understand the Bible and its message of sin, repentance and forgiveness? They cannot communicate the complete, life-changing message of the Gospel. As a result, often new converts become syncretistic and incorporate their limited knowledge and understanding of God's love with their old religious beliefs, such as spiritism, animism or ancestor worship. These syncretistic practices also prevent the new converts from growing into fully devoted followers of Christ.

In India, more than 35 million people call themselves Christian, and there are approximately 170,000 pastors and clergymen to serve those Christians. With the exploding population of this country, that means there are almost a billion people who have not yet responded to the gospel. Without training great numbers of evangelists and pastors to meet this challenge, many may never have the opportunity to respond to Christ's message of love.

If pastors do not have an adequate knowledge of core subjects for ministry, they struggle to lead and disciple their congregations. They are ill-equipped to help believers apply the Bible to the problems they face in everyday lives.

My translator at the crusade held in Kurnool, India in February, 1999 was a Bible college principal. As we talked and I met some of his colleagues, I exclaimed, "What are you going to do about this leadership problem in India? There are not enough seminaries to take those who need to be trained, and four years in seminary doesn't seem to be the only solution." They looked at me and then responded, "We know the problem...but what are you going to do to help us solve the problem?"

GLOMOS Is Born

These thoughts haunted me as the plane returned me to the United States. There must be a way to train more people effectively, people who could be given the necessary theological training to pastor village churches. A short-term training program began to take shape in my mind. Would it be possible to give them in-depth training a few days a month?

As I mused about the organizational possibilities of such a program I also sighed in frustration and thought, "I must not repeat the obvious mistakes so visible around the world." I was thinking about the programs where well-meaning Westerners have taken their best evangelical theology materials, translated it and sent it around the world as new textbooks. The problem with this is that while Westerners often use linear thought patterns, Easterners use circular thought patterns. Linear material, while comprehensible, often would not penetrate the circular world of thought.

"I am no theologian," I sighed to myself, "where do I find someone who can help me? And how do I pay someone if I find him?"

Alvin Low came to brainstorm some of these issues further. My friend P.L.N. Murthy, who I had brainstormed this idea with before I left India, had already come up with a name, *Global Module Studies*, GLOMOS for short. The principal in India was asked to develop some courses and Alvin flew to India to meet him.

After some ups and downs, GLOMOS began to take shape, and we launched it in Lucknow, India with some 60 students in 2001.

GLOMOS is a training program without walls, without a campus and without permanent faculty. Highly qualified adjunct faculty who are experienced in ministry, have theological training and work effectively in cross-cultural settings travel to key cities and areas where the students live. The first year, apart from Lucknow, we also tested the program in Kolkata, and Colombo, Sri Lanka. It was an immediate success.

Over the years we added Kalimpong, Delhi and Bhubaneswar in India, Kathmandu in Nepal, Crimea in Ukraine and Honduras and El Salvador in Latin America. Some 25 locations are asking us to start the program as soon as we can.

GLOMOS has cut through denominational lines, fostering unity and harmony among churches. Lal Whitanage remarked that for people from 26 denominations and 12 Christian organizations to come and study the Word together without any quarrel is a miracle!

Dr. C. S. Thevabalasingham, one of Sri Lanka's most respected Christian leaders says about GLOMOS, "This revolutionized concept of theological education is proving to be of great blessing and encouragement to all. I thank you for offering this program to our people."

Attending GLOMOS is not without cost. On the day of the first graduation from GLOMOS in Colombo, Chamila Ranasinghe received a call from her home informing her that her family boutique in the predominantly Buddhist village had been destroyed by Buddhists. She shared, "We were Buddhists first. Then we believed in Christ. There are about 200 families in our village (Polonnaruwa). Only three of them are Christian families. We have many problems with the Buddhist people. We have been warned by them several times. But we were not afraid and we prayed to God. My father is a farmer. He has a small boutique in the village. This boutique was destroyed by them last night. As Polonnaruwa is famous for Buddhism, they do not allow other religions there. That's why they have done this. They had warned us that they would burn our boutique. Not only this, they did many things to stop our worshiping Jesus. All the villagers are angry with us."

Faculty

Over the years we have developed a strong global faculty. The professors do not just hold degrees - most of them are also practitioners in their profession. At the moment the faculty is represented by professors from India, Sri Lanka, Ukraine, Honduras, El Salvador, Costa Rica, Britain, Sweden, USA, Canada and Norway.

Multiplication

We realized that the GLOMOS program would work best if each student trained others. If you learn something you often retain approximately 7 % after a month, while if you train someone else with the same material you tend to retain up to 93% after a month.

In the current GLOMOS program, each student has to be willing to train five others, using the same material, while going through the course. Then we graduate all the students together. So if we train 60 in class, we will graduate at least 360.

Sister Urmila from Delhi is teaching the same GLOMOS modules she is learning to eight new believers in her area. All of them are from a Hindu background. As she is teaching and helping the new believers to grow in the Lord she is finding that the modules have made it easier for her to reach this new area with the message of Jesus Christ.

Pastor Manuel, who is being taught in GLOMOS, has established a ministry of church planting. As many as 96% of his congregations come from a Hindu religious background, but they're growing in the Lord just because of the teaching he is giving from GLOMOS books.

Another student, Arun Pratap, has told us that he studies the whole study book and meditates on the Word of God throughout the night (till 3 or 4 a.m.) on the 1st and 2nd days of GLOMOS so that he will be able to teach his eight students after the third day of GLOMOS!

Mrs. Tabitha Chand took the instructions to teach another five people using the material *Global Action* had provided and was so moved by what God was doing in her own life that she is teaching the same GLOMOS courses to 25 participants!

Jonathan Thapa, who is a student of GLOMOS in Kalimpong, pastors a Tibetan believers' assembly in Kalimpong. He started worship services at an abandoned house supposedly belonging to a Buddhist monk. The congregation has grown in number and he is looking for a larger place.

Students attending GLOMOS in Kalimpong from two villages called Nimbong and Pemling start walking at 3 a.m. and walk for more than three hours to reach the place where they board a jeep to Kalimpong, which is another four hour trip. This is an example of these students' commitment. They are so eager to attend GLOMOS classes every month. They are active evangelists in their respective churches and help their pastors in every possible way.

Pranati Vengraj travels over 300 miles a month to attend GLOMOS in Bhubaneswar. While she studies, her five students of the Monda tribe wait eagerly for her return to teach them new lessons. They expressed their gratitude for GLOMOS, facilitating their studies even at such a remote corner.

Holding a day for all Global Module Studies (GLOMOS) graduates in Delhi in the fall of 2006, I noticed two turban-clad Sikhs as I looked out over the 400 people. At first I thought they were from the Indian police, and I felt somewhat uncomfortable to see them sitting in the middle of the audience. Then I asked a discreet question of our coordinator, who smiled, and introduced me to one of them, Mr. Singh, who told me the most fascinating story:

"Two years ago I was living a miserable life in our extended family of 35. We would beat each other up with shoes, slippers and with wooden sticks and even with knives. There was no hope for us. Then one day a lady came and shared the gospel with me, and Jesus came into my life and gave me hope, life and purpose. Later I found out that the lady was a student at something called GLOMOS where they encouraged people to share their faith with others.

My life was suddenly turned around and I shared Jesus with the other 34 people in my family, who also came to faith in Christ. We live in a big house and we wanted to open it up to worship Jesus. So we began visiting houses around us, and went also to people who were the worst of the worst. In the last two years we have visited over 20,000 homes. From those homes people came to our new house church and eventually we ended up with more than 300 people who have turned to Jesus and are now part of our church. In the past few months we have baptized over 100 people.

With the church going well, my colleague and I realized that we needed training to continue to pastor the church. We wanted to join *Global Action*'s GLOMOS program earlier, but we simply did not have time. Now we need the training desperately and are glad to be part of this program."

A few months later I met the gentleman again, and he shared about their visits to the family villages over the Christmas holidays. "We went to present Jesus to our relatives, and they did not like it," explained Mr. Singh. "They told us to return to our gurus, holy books and the temple. I told them, 'when the gurus, the holy books and the temple can give us what Jesus has given me I will,' knowing full well that Jesus is more than all of it put together."

In 2003 Ashok Das, along with his wife, Sheela and son, Rajesh moved to Delhi to find a job. Soon he found employment as a taxi driver job with a travel company. Ashok was a Brahmin (high caste Hindu) and a strong believer of Krishna, a Hindu god. As part of his religious duties, Ashok used to visit temples and take a dip in the river, and only eat vegetarian food. He also wanted his wife Sheela to follow the Hindu rites as well, but she was not interested.

Sheela had come into contact with a Christian woman in their neighborhood who shared the gospel with her and Sheela began to believe in Christ. She attended Bible studies and prayer meetings with the Christian family. It disturbed Ashok very much, and he asked Sheela not to associate with the Christians. Sheela decided to continue to worship Jesus without Ashok's knowledge, in order to keep peace in the home.

One day Ashok went to work for the night shift. Sheela took advantage of it and went to the prayer meeting. But there was a change in Ashok's schedule and he returned home early. When he did not find Sheela at home, he knew that she had gone to the prayer meeting and waited for her return. When Sheela returned, Ashok asked her, "Where did you go?" She told the truth. "Now I'm a believer in Jesus Christ and I went to attend a prayer meeting." It was shocking news for Ashok.

He took his belt and started beating her. He demanded her to deny Jesus and she refused. Ashok kept beating her. Finally she became unconscious and fell to the floor. It took a moment for him to realize that he had beaten his wife to the point of unconsciousness. Something happened to him and he began to cry over his brutal behavior. Meanwhile she returned to consciousness and found Ashok crying over his cruelty. He kneeled down before her and asked for forgiveness. She told him, "I can't forgive you, only Jesus can." This was a perfect gospel message for her sinner husband. Without delay Ashok confessed his sin and accepted the Lord Jesus Christ as his personal Savior. Sheela accepted him back. He went to the local church and was baptized.

A year ago Ashok came in contact with GLOMOS in Delhi and joined the course. Currently Ashok holds a key role of evangelism in the local church. He says GLOMOS is an answer to his prayer. He proudly says, "I am a trained evangelist now." The training has given arms and legs for him to minister to the local church as well as to the people of other faith he comes in contact with every day. He has reached out with the gospel to hundreds of Hindus and Muslims. He is effectively teaching GLOMOS to another five people, including Sheela as a part of the multiplication program!

New Direction

In January 2006 Alvin Low decided to launch out on his own with a training program for pastors, which meant we needed to develop new material to keep GLOMOS going. Within a year, 22 new training manuals were developed by 17 different authors from 11 countries. In 2008 GLOMOS II was launched. While GLOMOS I is more of a basic theological course, GLOMOS II is a practical ministry course.

Rev. Pervez Sethna, a newly introduced faculty member from North India, commented on the new GLOMOS program, "I was blessed indeed as I interacted with a very wonderful group of godly and committed men and women who took time off from their families, work responsibilities and travelled long distances to study God's precious word and be in turn a witness for the Lord.

"The group that I taught comprised mostly of men and women who came to the Lord from other faiths: Sikhs, Brahmins and other Hindu groups. I am amazed as I witness what the Lord is doing in my great land of India in and through GLOMOS."

Risk-Taker for God

Greater Ministry

Being a pastor is not easy. Being a pastor where there is little help to stimulate you and encourage you is even tougher. That is why *Global Action's* original vision was and is to encourage pastors in ministry around the world. The first year I conducted conferences on my own, addressing topics such as: *Jesus, the role model for pastors*; *The pastor's vision*; *Leadership lessons I learned along the way*; *Yesterday's, today's and tomorrow's leader*, as well as *Sharing your faith in the 21st century*.

The first pastors' conferences were held in May 1999 in Minsk, Belarus, Prague, Czech Republic and Bratislava, Slovakia. Pastors from many different denominations attended. For 70 years the church behind the iron curtain was an isolated church. People met secretly. Open evangelism was unthinkable. Even inviting your neighbor to church could have meant imprisonment and concentration camp. But with the fall of the wall in 1989, a new world opened up for the church.

In the spring of 2000 *Global Action* conducted a set of pastors' conferences, with topics encouraged by the leadership of the church in Eastern Europe. During the month of May 2000, Alvin Low and I visited key cities in Central and Eastern Europe, addressing the need for the church to reach outside of its walls.

In Prague pastors from Baptist, Czech Brethren, Pentecostal, Adventist and Lutheran churches gathered for the lectures. The Czech audience was rather formal, but good discussions were held over meal times, breaks and question and answer times. Since the "velvet revolution," the country has turned very Western, and in doing so, also has become extremely secular. Someone made the statement that Christians would rather go to the shops on Sunday than to church and that pastors were struggling to keep the attention of their church members. We left knowing that this conference had inspired the pastors and given them direction for the future.

In Bratislava, Slovakia, we had the smallest conference, but probably one of the most fruitful ones. The pastors were like sponges, taking everything to heart. There was good interaction, especially when it came to questions of reaching out in their cities and cooperating together. One pastor said, "I have never talked to other pastors in my area! Just think if we could get together and brainstorm how to influence our city for Jesus Christ."

We arrived in Novi Sad, a city of approximately 300,000 people. The war had ended less than a year earlier and destructive results from the NATO bombing could be seen everywhere. All the bridges across the river that divides the city were gone, bombed to pieces just some 14 months earlier.

The conference was held in a crowded and hot church building in one of the back streets in the city and attended by Baptist, Pentecostal and Lutheran pastors. The church also runs a small Bible school for 10 students and they were all in attendance. There was great response to the presentations and the conference finished with prayer for the city and for the country.

One of the senior pastors, Rev. Aleksander Mitrovic, a former Foreign Legion soldier, took us aside and said, "We have never been able to talk about such things in our churches. You told the truths but you were also sensitive to the different denominational backgrounds and were not eager to sell 'your brand.' This nation needs fathers in more ways than one, this is a fatherless nation: Fathers have died in the last 10 years of wars and left families fatherless. The political system has gone through various forms of changes and is bankrupt - leaderless and fatherless. The economy has lost its leaders and we are fatherless. The church is fatherless, without direction, and in you come like two fathers, guiding, steering, encouraging us…while telling us truths we find difficult to normally talk about."

I will never forget the following sentences. "Once in 1000 years the Lord seems to have opened the door to this country and we believe there is another such door opening right now, created by suffering. Through the last ten years of war people have gone from being angry to confusion to hopelessness. Now they are empty of anger and ready to listen to answers that could be 'the real thing' in their lives.

"We have seen a flood of New Age, Yoga, Transcendental Meditation and other movements. Now the floodwater levels have come down and everyone is emptier than before…and now the people are ready to listen. At the same time the church is stuck in an archaic form. Normally none of the elder leaders would have listened to the points you made, but they listened to you.

"The church has never dared to speak out either what they are for or against. Abortion is rampant in our country, and while we see it as a sin, the church would never whisper a word. We need fathers, we need direction. In the war times we have seen many people come from the West with what we call 'fashionable theology'. One minute it is the faith movement, next time Kingdom theology, or fundamental reformation theology. People are shallow and accept the 'fashionable theology.' 'Let's do this, let's try that,' they say. It is all bent on our self-centeredness. But you came to show that the old message has not changed...but the methods it is presented in need to change to communicate the message."

To enter Minsk, Belarus was like going back to the Soviet days in 1970s. The government was tightening the situation for the church. Church leaders had just protested to the second largest newspaper in Minsk because of an article that charged Christians with carrying out fanatical rituals, including the use of human sacrifice and blood. The report in the newspaper *Narodnaya* claimed that members of a church in Yakutia tortured their children, beating them with metal wire and scalding them with water to persuade them to become Christians.

Bishop Sergei Khomich, head of the Union of Christians of the Evangelical Faith in Belarus, commented that he believed the unfounded report incited religious hatred - a criminal offense. "We have written a refutation...but are by no means certain that it will be published," he said. The controversial article accused the Protestants of trying to undermine the authority of the Orthodox Church.

With 443 congregations, Pentecostals make up the largest of the country's Protestant communities. Many evangelical churches face harassment. One unregistered Baptist church has been denied electricity for almost three years. Another church that has existed over twelve years in a secular building was told to cease. No non-church buildings can now be used for church services...and services in homes are also forbidden!

On the Sunday of our visit, we preached to two packed Baptist churches with lots of young people in attendance. For the pastors' conference we had 176 pastors from 58 different congregations representing every possible denomination. Some had never met together like this and some were not quite sure about the other. The greatest challenge they faced was the concept that they could actually work across denominational lines. One young pastor hugged me as we had finished the day and said, "Lars, you have given us hope for the future!" What a blessing.

In 2001 Alvin and I returned to Novi Sad, this time together with Galo Vasquez. We met in an evangelical church under the leadership of Daniel Kuranji and his wife Vera. They had lived in Canada for many years but sensed God's calling to return to Novi Sad, where they serve in meeting social as well as spiritual needs.

In the opening session of the pastors' conference I noticed a couple right in front of me crying as I spoke, and I was not sure if I had blessed them or offended them. I spoke about Jesus being satisfied with spending three years only teaching twelve, who in turn would go out and train others to turn the world upside down. The more I spoke, the more they cried.

Afterward they told me their story. A few years ago they had come to this church as Muslim refugees from Bosnia. After finding Jesus Christ and being trained for the ministry, they had returned to their own village in Bosnia after the war to plant an evangelical church.

Now they had been there for three years. It had been hard and they were ready to give up. Without growth their work did not seem to have any impact. After all, during the three years they had been there, they had only been able to train twelve!

Nepal

Another pastors' conference was held in freezing cold Katmandu, Nepal in January 2000. This conference gathered close to 200 pastors from far-flung places, such as the countries of Sikkim and Bhutan, as well as the host country. The pastors were all eager for the training, for more materials and for helps of any kind. We provided them with the quarterly newsletter for pastors called ACTION, which features leadership ideas, sermon outlines, illustration helps, practical tips for pastoring and updates on the church around the world. One young leader from Bhutan stated, "I feel I am pregnant with all I have learned and I cannot wait to get home to give birth to it, to teach and equip the Christians of my country!"

"I don't have any helps regularly and need encouragement," commented one pastor. "These conferences and the ACTION newsletter will help me better train my own people, as well as staying on track personally."

Several young leaders, pastors-to-be, attended as well, and it was fascinating to see their interest and hear their comments. More than once, they said things like, "This kind of teaching, which is so direct, dealing with issues in our personal lives and in the church, is new for us! This helps us sense God's call to the ministry."

India

In Lucknow, India, my interpreter, Dr. S.W. Prasad, a Haggai Institute graduate and a professor of English at the Lucknow Christian College, underwent a transformation throughout the week while interpreting in the pastors' conference as well as in all the evangelistic services. Formal and somewhat reserved when we first met on Wednesday, he blossomed and as we came to the closing rally said, "Can't we go on for another week? This is just the beginning! The Lord is speaking to me personally as he speaks through you and me as a team! Sometimes I am so overwhelmed by the message I don't know if I can go on!"

At the evangelistic rallies held night after night in the large Lal Bagh Methodist church, people came forward to find salvation, dedicate their lives or commit themselves for Christian service.

In the "high tech" city of Hyderabad, in the state of Andhra Pradesh, the initial plans for a pastors' conference was for 300 people. There was such interest during pre-registration that more than 1,500 pastors, lay leaders and seminary students attended the one-day conference. About 1,200 found seats in the overcrowded Rock Church where the seminar was held. Ceiling fans attempted to cool the crowd inside, while more than 300 followed the teaching by closed-circuit television under a canopy in the courtyard.

In conversations with many of the pastors, it became obvious that this conference offered a new focus for many of them, especially the younger pastors. They were eager to talk about ways to apply the principles in their churches, so they could minister to young people more effectively while encouraging the more mature believers to be "disciple makers."

India is a nation where tremendous opposing forces are at work— some focusing on moving the country forward through development, especially in the areas of information technology and education of the masses. To do this, India needs to remain a "secular" nation where religions, different cultures and people groups can co-exist happily side by side. Other forces would rather see India become "Hindu-ized," and be a society where there is little room for Islam and no room for Christianity, which is still viewed as a "foreigner's religion."

Churachandpur is situated in one of the more remote areas of India between Bangladesh and Myanmar. These areas have been restricted because of political upheaval, and this was the first time in 30 years I had special permission to visit. The city of Churachandpur in the state of Manipur can only be reached after several hours by jeep on bumpy "holy" roads. Soldiers with ready machine guns walked along the roads and across the rice paddies, ready to curb any insurrection. It gave us all a very eerie feeling.

A total of 1,200 pastors and leaders attended the conference. Together with Rev. George Carr, one of our *Global Action* associates, we ministered with gusto! I know of no greater joy than to invest in brothers and sisters who in turn mobilize, train, equip and empower others.

Varanasi, sometimes also named Benares, is called the holy city and is a center for Muslim, Hindu and Buddhist training with universities representing all three major religions. At the river Ganges, thousands of people flock every day to go through Hindu rites in the water. This is a place of darkness and oppression and we need to shine the light of the gospel brighter than ever before. We provided training for many pastors and leaders to bring God's light into this darkened environment. In a hall seating 750 people, more than 900 people, with standing room only for many, listened intently for a whole day about ministering effectively in the 21st century.

"We have never had anything quite like this in Varanasi", exclaimed one of the pastors, "and this teaching is not theoretical but extremely practical and can be applied to our local situation."

Some 710 pastors and leaders gathered in the city of Kalimpong, in the foothills of the Himalayas, in northern India. In chilly weather, at 7,000 feet, a church seating no more than 550 became so overcrowded that some people had to sit outside in the freezing cold, listening by loudspeakers.

Participants came from the countries of Sikkim, Bhutan and Nepal, as well as from all the hill stations in India. They represented more than 40 denominations and agencies.

"A training conference like this has never happened in Kalimpong as long as anyone can remember," explained one of the leading pastors. "*Global Action* has accomplished the impossible," exclaimed another.

Risk-Taker for God

Sri Lanka

Sri Lanka is a small country with a close-knit evangelical community. Civil war has made evangelism extremely difficult and there is need for much encouragement. Apart from the actual pastors' conference, there was good interaction among the 150 delegates who attended. When I mentioned about the possibility of *Global Action* introducing GLOMOS in Sri Lanka the following year, there was a flood of young people wanting immediate information.

There are 31,000 villages in Sri Lanka and only a little more than 1,000 of those have any kind of church. There is a real need to see young people gain basic ministerial education and then move out and live in those villages to plant home churches.

In the late afternoon we traveled around central Colombo and our host, Rev. Lakshman Peiris, showed us where some of the recent suicide bombers had exploded their deadly load. We stopped for a moment on the busy road outside the parliament building. None of us could imagine at that time that within 24 hours another bomb would explode in exactly the same place, killing 28 people. Afterward, we thanked the Lord for his protecting angels.

Myanmar

The first time we took part in arranging a pastors' conference in Myanmar 200 pastors attended. The weather was extremely hot. We were meeting in the chapel of the ACTS Bible College, which has no air-conditioning, no windows that can be closed and a tin roof. It was at least 110 Fahrenheit inside by the time of the afternoon sessions.

Pastors came from different parts of Myanmar, and we returned year after year. The last year I was there we had hoped for 1,200 participants, but 1,700 registered, representing over 50 denominations and church agencies and some 200 local congregations. In almost 100 degree heat we met in a huge tent structure on the grounds.

Imagine walking for four days, taking a river boat for one day and a bus where people hang out the doors and sit up top for two days, to attend a pastors' conference. Many of them did. Some who came had rather interesting backgrounds. Pastor Maung Ko was a Buddhist priest for 16 years before coming to Christ in 1996. Evangelist San Thein was imprisoned for 7 years because he refused to stop preaching Christ. While in prison, he was tortured and sometimes he was refused food and water for 24 hours. Rev. Shalum La Awag, Pastor of Kachin Baptist Church, traveled for three days to come to the conference. He has a church of 800 members. Zaw Min Htun was a Buddhist monk until recently, when he was introduced to Christ.

The receptivity of the pastors was most remarkable. They wanted to learn and their singing was most joyful. There is a deep sense of unity among these pastors from so many denominations and organizations. One said, "A training program like this gives us encouragement to carry on the tough work. After this conference we cannot wait to go back and train people to be effective in their witness for Jesus Christ."

Mexico

When I addressed a pastors' breakfast in Mexico at the end of November 2000, a huge man came forward, hugged me in true Mexican style and exclaimed, "You must come to Villahermosa to do a pastors' training conference!" A year later, in November 2001, that became a reality.

Villahermosa is a city in southern Mexico with approximately 650,000 inhabitants. There are more evangelical churches in the city than Catholic churches. Many of the pastors, while on fire for God, lack basic training for ministry and therefore developing and nurturing leaders is one of the greatest needs in the church.

Approximately 650 pastors registered for the 3-day conference called "Leading with Jesus as an Example," where David Ruiz, Timoteo Ost (from Mexico City), Alvin Low and I dealt with subjects like "Jesus as a model for leadership," "Growing healthy churches with Jesus as focus," "How to communicate the gospel so people understand it," and so on.

Ministries and relationships were restored, pastors who were ready to quit dealt with their issues and recommitted their vows to ministry. Marriages were even healed!

Here are some comments from the delegates:

> *"I want to tell you that I feel happy to have been part of these days where God has, through you, showed Himself in a new way in my life. I want to be a real disciple of God. I want to serve Him in truth and be a great leader and speaker, if that is what He wants me to be."*

"Brother Lars. I give thanks to God for your life. Two days ago Thursday, when you spoke about purpose, I asked that God would confirm what I should do in the work. And believe me He did it, one more time. You were used by God to speak into my life."

"God has been here in these two days of this blessed encounter. The Spirit has spoken in a powerful way in my life. Since my baptism I have just lived with good intentions. Today I make a pledge and declare that I will be a follower and disciple others."

"My name is Gabriel Arias. I grew up in idolatry. On July 8, 199 Christ called me to serve Him in the Church of God in Mexico On Oct. 21 I became the youth director of the district and the invited me to this congress. I want to tell you that God is blessing me because I am learning how to develop a youth ministry. I ask for your prayers, that we might raise up youth for Christ."

Every night approximately 900 young people gathered for the youth rallies. Night after night we dealt with the subject, "The person God is looking for." Many young people committed their lives to Christ while others found their life purpose.

Sunday morning I spoke in a huge Baptist church. Approximately 20 people in each service came to the Lord for salvation. One couple was in a church for the first time, sitting on the front row in shorts, and this couple gave their hearts to Jesus. That in itself makes it worth it all.

"Forty Under Forty"

While it is a great challenge and blessing to address large crowds, I realized that there was little opportunity for feedback or personal interaction. How could we find a forum that was more interactive, and focused more on the younger pastors and leaders?

For a prototype held in Kolkata, we invited forty leaders who had to be in full-time ministry and had to be less than 40 years of age. This program proved to be a great success. No one could attend without filling in a questionnaire in advance, which then set the stage for that day's agenda. In this way, issues were raised and dealt with which normally are never brought up in church settings.

Similar conferences have now been held in five areas in India and in Ukraine and will continue to be a great way of influencing younger church leaders for the future.

Encouraging Pastors in South Asia

Global Action launched ACTION in 1999, a quarterly newsletter for pastors in South Asia. Right now the circulation is almost 30,000 in five different languages: Hindi, Bengali, Telugu, Nepali and English.

Mr. Vijay David Navire wrote and told us, "I read your Action Journal and find it to be very useful for Christian Ministry. I am a Christian leader and serve the Lord in a Christian organization." Mr Pankaj Kumar commented, "praise the Lord to all the brothers and sisters working with Action Ministries. We are thankful to you for sending us Action Magazine continuously. With the help of it we are able to know new things!"

CHAPTER 17
A Compassionate Response

It was March 1999 and tension was increasing in the Balkans. Everyone was waiting for NATO to fulfill its threats to attack the region and potentially add even more confusion to a civil war that from the outside made little sense. In the middle of these warring factions, thousands of innocent civilians were fleeing their homes with their children and the few possessions they could carry or push in wheelbarrows or baby strollers.

On March 31st of that year the war became a reality as NATO forces attacked, adding trauma to innocent victims already terrorized by hatred and ethnic cleansing. Children, parents and grandparents were brutally ripped from each other and everything they knew and loved, then forced to march in the freezing rain to an unknown land and uncertain futures. Within a few days Macedonia had received 115,000 refugees. One newscast described the latest arrivals "huddled in a muddy stinking field at the border for another chilly night, waiting for the start of an airlift that was promised Sunday but did not materialize."

If you are like me, you had to blink - it was hard to believe this was not some old film footage from a long ago holocaust, but something that was unfolding *now* - live before our eyes.

I had not paid much attention to the human suffering, trying to numb myself to the obvious needs. I always thought, "That is why we have the Red Cross, World Vision and others." I was the Bible man and while humanitarian aid in the name of Christ was probably a good thing, it certainly wasn't my responsibility. My role was to concentrate on people's spiritual needs. Surely others could take care of the humanitarian problems.

For years I had observed my friend David Foster's excitement about assisting people in Eastern Europe. Since he had come on the board of *Global Action*, he began to talk even more animatedly about this as the crises in the Balkans exploded.

On the day the war broke out I was sitting, sipping coffee in my sister's kitchen in Stockholm, Sweden. The phone rang. Somehow David had located me and in rapid sentences he began to tell me what was happening:

"Eurovangelism has brought in five trucks of clothes, medicine, staple food items, but they will be gone tomorrow. Other international humanitarian organizations are here assessing the situation, but it could take weeks before they are operational. We are working with the Christians of the Evangelical Church in Skopje, (Macedonia), but much more is needed. We need to equip them with food and clothing as well as blankets, meeting the need just where it is. We also need Scripture booklets. Dunberg, you and *Global Action* have to help us!" We have always used our last names when addressing each other. Strange to some, but just natural for us!

"But, Foster, you know, we just began six months ago! There's only Doreen and I and Anne and a couple of folding tables. We cannot do anything!"

"Your name is Global isn't it?"

"Aha…."

"And it's Action, isn't it?"

"Mmmm…"

"Well, Dunberg, act then for goodness sake…" and the phone slammed down in my ear! I sat with my empty coffee cup and stared at the wall for at least five minutes. We could not do much, but surely we could do something!

I have always been bothered by people who take the approach that helping a few people doesn't make a dent in the larger world need. "It doesn't matter one iota that you help a few," they say, and my response always is, "It matters to those whose lives are impacted!"

So I lifted the phone and called Anne. "Are you awake?" I asked and she retorted, "I am now! It is 4 a.m. in the morning!" I told her to get dressed and hurry to the storefront office we rented from our church. "There's an email waiting. Turn it into a personal letter and don't go to bed again until at least 1,000 copies are sent out. Get my daughters to help you fold them. Do whatever it takes!"

Overnight, *Global Action* was into compassion ministries, and during the following few days almost $100,000 was raised to provide help in Kosovo.

Gary Cox, the director of *Eurovangelism* also called me. "Lars, we do not need to send any material from Britain or the U.S. because national partners in areas of need are able to purchase bulk supplies much nearer. This cuts transportation costs and enables the entire operation to be much more cost effective." That was music to my ears!

Having seen a lot of "compassion" type ministry around the world, one thing concerned me. While aid agencies often do a superb job of feeding and clothing those in need, few tend to their emotional and spiritual needs. If relief supplies were all they needed, that's all we'd send. I applaud the excellent humanitarian work of secular agencies, but that's all they can provide. Our partnership with Christian nationals in areas of need could allow us to ensure spiritual input for traumatized, innocent victims.

A flashback brought visions of the Rwanda-Burundi massacres, where hungry refugees welcomed spiritual input and help. I thought back to the days of *IBS* when, after the earthquake in Los Angeles, I was involved in developing a Scripture-based booklet for innocent victims of disasters. Knowing that this "disaster" booklet, published by *International Bible Society*, already had been translated into Serbian and Croatian for use in other trouble-spots of former Yugoslavia, I discovered that an Albanian edition of 20,000 had already been distributed to refugees and tens of thousands more were needed.

Working with Hans-Lennart Raask of *IBS*-Europe we were able to make some of these available. But I also needed Scriptures. It seemed impossible to find anyone who had Albanian Scriptures. As a last resort I called Frank Arthur in Sweden. Frank, who is British and married to Finnish Leena, had served with OM for many years before he and Leena joined the staff of *Living Bibles International* in the 70s and worked with us for some 16 years, overseeing production and developing various Scripture editions all around the world.

Frank was happy to talk to me and to my astonishment explained that his wife Leena had just produced a gospel of John in Albanian, which she was making available to various agencies. I managed to purchase 20,000 copies that could be used in conjunction with the deliveries of humanitarian aid.

A few days later David Foster called again. "You won't believe this, Dunberg! The UK customs have contacted us at Eurovangelism because they just confiscated a shipment of fake designer clothing! It's mainly jeans, shirts and underwear, all useful stuff in this situation. Customs usually destroy what they confiscate but in this case they didn't, because the quality is superb. A Trading Standards officer called the manufacturers who were being copied and, without exception, they all said, 'Don't destroy the stuff if you can get it to the Kosovo refugees.'"

"Lars, *Global Action* needs to help us with the freight! The value Customs gave us for the consignment is £250,000...what's that in dollars? About $400,000? And all we need for the freight is $10,000." A few days later, I watched CNN and other newscasts covering the Kosovo situation and realized that many of the refugees were wearing designer shirts - and I knew how they got there!

Dagestan and Ingushethia

For years there had been unrest in the tiny republic of Chechnya, situated in southern Russia between the Black and the Caspian Sea, not far from the country of Georgia, and surrounded by other areas like Dagestan and Ingushethia.

Aspirations for independence from Moscow prompted Russia to act in this troubled region bordering Chechnya. In the fall of 1999 the conflict became even more intense. According to the Russian Defense Ministry, 275 Russian troops and police were killed. News agency reports claimed at least 2,000 rebels died in the fighting. Over one weekend alone, the Russian military carried out approximately 100 raids. No figures were given about the number of innocent civilians who died in the crossfire, but an estimated 30,000 refugees fled the war zone.

A few months earlier Doreen and I attended a Salvation Army conference in Sweden where the main speakers were Captains Geoff and

Sandra Ryan, a Canadian couple based in Rostov-on-Don, Russia. They were pioneer workers for The Salvation Army church and social work in southern Russia. We struck up a friendship and he shared some of the most urgent needs with us. Although we had no resources available at the time, we promised to pray and see if there ever was anything *Global Action* could do.

We did explain, though, that we were the gnat while The Salvation Army was the elephant. How could we provide help that would be of any significant value to such a huge organization? A few months later we found out.

On September 12, 1999 I received an urgent email from Geoff, "I am writing you this note from the road using a friend's email..." In vivid terms he described the fighting in the Caucasus Mountains, in particular Dagestan, the neighboring republic to Chechnya. "Islamic fundamentalist fighters have been capturing villages and causing havoc there, the Russian military are fighting them off and it looks like Chechnya all over again."

His email mentioned 29,000 refugees, basically women and children, grandmothers, mothers and their babies. The men were either dead, fighting or in hiding.

Geoff continued, "This conflict is likely not going to get much notice in the world press - unless it escalates to the level of the Chechnya war (which it might). At any rate, very little humanitarian assistance will be forthcoming. There is no evidence of any relief activity among the refugees."

He described the need to show credibility for the cause of Christ: "If a Christian organization can be proactive in assisting Muslims who have been displaced by Muslims, then we need to act. Can *Global Action* come up with anything by way of either supplies or money? The Russians have started bombing there again and the refugee problem is starting up all over. They are looking for medicine and food help. I wish I could do more. I need an answer quick and, if we can do something, to move fast on this. I'll go there myself to oversee things. Thanks in advance for any help possible."

I immediately emailed him back, suggesting he work through the Army hierarchy, but he let me know that it would take too long to be heard, as he was nothing but a "young captain in an obscure part of

Russia." Anyway, he was not sure that Dagestan would even register on his bosses' radar screens.

Jeff mentioned he needed $25,000 and we had barely $26,000 in the bank. I agreed to send the money we could come up with, $10,000 now and the rest a few days later. Having attended the "James Bond school of Evangelism" I had some idea from my old days in Eastern Europe on how to make the funds available, and within a few days, Geoff confirmed that they were in his hands.

Our quick response seed gift of $25,000 yielded other results. Other organizations picked up the slack and The Salvation Army itself saw the potential to do something and major funds became available through other organizations to meet the long-term need. *Global Action* did what it does best: offered a quick, catalyst response to meet an immediate need, making it possible for others to follow.

After the second gift was sent I received this report from Geoff:

"Last week I went on a trip to Ingushethia and Chechnya with regard to refugees. The Dagestan situation has cooled down somewhat and the refugee situation has moved more into the neighboring republic of Ingushethia. Ingushethia is a Muslim republic bordering on Chechnya and the only republic that has opened its borders to the Chechen refugees from the latest conflict with Russia. In a republic with a population of 300,000 in the last few weeks they have allowed to enter up to 150,000 Chechen refugees -needless to say the situation is a lot worse than the one in Dagestan."

"I looked at three refugee camps and decided to use the money at a small camp of 1,000 people just inside the border with Asetia. The refugees there include mostly elderly, women and children. They are living in tents provided by local authorities with no heat, light or running water. Winter is already upon us here, even in the South, and it looks like they will be there for the whole winter. We have purchased clothing in Stavropol and Rostov and are shipping it down ourselves to distribute to the camp in order to provide them with winter apparel to get through the coming cold months."

Global Action responded with as much emergency humanitarian aid as its supporters made possible. Working with responsible and reliable partners, like Geoff Ryan, it is possible to meet immediate and desperate needs of civilians suffering through no fault of their own. According to Christians in these predominantly Muslim republics, such compassionate action provides a unique opportunity to build credibility for future ministry there.

To give you an idea of how much can be accomplished with comparatively little, it cost only 50 cents per day to provide two nourishing meals for each refugee.

Women's Micro-enterprise Training Program, Addis Ababa, Ethiopia

In June of 2000, Emily Voorhies and I were invited to visit an exploding church in Addis Ababa. We were overwhelmed by their passion to ensure that people were not just transformed inwardly by the gospel, but that people who had been saved "from the street" were also equipped and trained to re-enter society.

The initiative for women was conducted by an Ethiopian lady, named Alem, who presently resides in the U.S., but was committed to be in Ethiopia until this program was well off the ground.

Alem was training approximately 100 ladies at a time in a six-month-long training program. Of these 100 ladies only five had ever had a job. Some had been prostitutes, others had never believed enough in themselves even to apply for a job. The country has an unemployment rate of 50-60% while the outlying villages have an unemployment rate of 90-95%.

First she taught them to believe in themselves, in personal hygiene, how to dress neatly (with whatever they had) and how to present themselves. She impressed each person's value, so they would have faith that the Lord can work through them. It takes very little to create hope.

These ladies were trained in crafts like sewing, weaving, hairdressing, becoming "nannies" and being cooks. They also received a "loan" of 150 *birr* (approximately $20) to begin a little business. For example, they might buy yarn and embroider a cloth that they then could sell, repaying part of the loan with the profit. One of them shared her story:

"I came to know the Lord during my senior year in high school. Because of my new faith I was evicted from home and suffered severe persecution. No one supported me. I used to wander the streets and had nowhere to go. For two years I only had scraps to eat and hardly any clothing nor any shoes on my feet. Every night, I took turns sleeping on a mattress in a broken-down, infested toilet facility, while eight others were awake, waiting their turn.

"Then I heard of the *Global Action* program and came to meet the people. I was given food, a place to stay and clothes. I was placed in the pre-school teacher training program and after a year I graduated as one of the top three in the program. The Lord is blessing my life every day now. I have my own house, I can choose what to buy, whether to cook or even go out to eat. The Lord has made me increase in every aspect of my life. Even my own family, who threw me out, is now understanding that the Lord is with me. They have asked me for forgiveness and want to be together with me again."

Global Action worked with this program for several years, took a break, and is now back working in a similar project in Addis Ababa.

Hope for Afghanistan

During the Afghan crisis we worked with an organization out of Sweden to help hurting families during the Christmas season. One day I received this note. What a blessing to see a dollar stretch so far in this report:

"We have helped 1,500 of the neediest families in this desolate corner of North Afghanistan ravaged by 22 years of war and three years of devastating drought.

We will provide emergency wheat food aid to another 6,700 families and then another distribution of beans, oil and sugar to the total 8,200 neediest families in Chah Ab district. We also distributed clothes and blankets to 5,205 families as well as shoes to 4,126 children.

When we visited the district of Chah Ab, our staff had to walk for hours through the snow to get to these villages, cut off from any roads. We found that in most of the villages they had already run out of all food for their families, or this month was their last ration of food from the last harvest. In many villages, the people had sold all they could sell and were taking the wooden beams from their houses to sell in the town to buy food."

Risk-Taker for God

Food for Body and Soul in Moldova

In one area of the tiny country Moldova, situated between Romania and the Ukraine, people have suffered terrible starvation and unemployment during the past winters.

Together with The Salvation Army in Moldova, *Global Action* has provided soup kitchens, food for several years and personnel who can serve the food and share the Gospel. For those families who cannot get to the soup kitchen, teams of workers visit homes and distribute staple food items and the Gospel.

Many children in Moldova have no shoes and, therefore, cannot attend school. This bothered me a great deal, but I realized it would be too expensive to send shoes from the USA. One day, while I was driving through Sweden, I was praying for these children and their shoes. Suddenly the Lord impressed a person's name upon me, and I called him immediately.

"This is a silly question, but do you know anything about shoes for Moldova?"

"I cannot believe this! How did you know?" he told me. "We have a truck full of shoes for Moldova but no funds to get the truck there!" That very afternoon I paid out the $ 2,800 needed to get almost 30,000 pairs of shoes to Moldova.

From Moldova we received this note, "We want to say THANK YOU to all those who sponsor *Global Action* Soup Kitchens project. Without your contribution many would never experience Christian brotherhood, love, a hot lunch and their HOPE would have not been brought back to life. Many elderly will be able to eat because of your kindness...many children will have food to eat because of your care. You have made a difference in the lives of many from this great land."

We received this note from a retired lady, named Olga. "My pension is only $30 a month. One day my friend told me about the free soup kitchen. I did not believe her. There is nothing in this world that can be free, especially nothing good. I went and the food was great. I do not remember when I ate hot food before. I was invited to the church where I have found many friends and God. Now, every day, I pray for sponsors who are helping Moldova and all people in the world."

Partnering with several Rotary clubs in Sweden, who provide 80% of the funding, we have been able to provide over $500,000 for this project over the past eight years.

Food and Education for Gypsy Kids in Bulgaria

For many years Gypsies lived in Bulgaria's capital Sofia, but in the last 20 years the government moved them all to run-down villages outside the city limits. In these villages there is 90% unemployment, no schools for most of the children and not enough food.

Global Action has sponsored a daily feeding program for several years, between October and April (the cold months), for the children in four villages. A total of 200 children are fed each day.

I visited one of the villages and about 80 children came in three shifts to this extremely tiny room, where a big pot of goulash soup was boiling on the woodburning stove. A similar pot with water was being heated at the side. The ladies never know how many children will turn up, but they will never refuse a child a meal, so if the children keep coming, more water is poured in the soup to ensure each child gets soup and bread.

None of these children go to school. Our partner *Mission Possible* has provided a teacher who comes from the city every day to teach them through a literacy program. And then we provide the children with a children's Bible to read.

When I saw these children, with dirty faces and hands, dirty torn clothes, plates with the enamel worn off, their ruffled hair and big eyes, I realized how so little can go such a long way. It looked like a film scene from Oliver Twist. Then my coworker said, "Lars, if we don't feed them, no one else will! These kids may not have made it through the winter! If we don't teach them, no one else will. And how will they hear the Gospel if their stomachs are empty?"

Earthquake Relief in El Salvador

The earthquakes were only a few weeks apart in the winter of 2001, one in Gujarat, India and one in El Salvador. Through *Global Action's* people on the ground, led by fearless business leader Mercedes Dalton, we were able to help with blankets, food, medicine, trauma counseling and Scriptures.

Since then, more long-term assistance has been established in both locations. For example, in El Salvador, through a lot of local donations and from the Hispanic community in the U.S., we provided 60 temporary shelters and constructed 60 permanent homes. Two churches have also been built.

Risk-Taker for God

Blanket and Sweater Distribution in North India

Northern India gets cold in the winter, temperatures often dropping below freezing, and many people - especially infants and elderly - die because they have no warm clothing to shield themselves against the bitter cold. Some of the little children have no clothes at all.

In the most rural villages in the interior of northern India, as well as in Delhi, *Action Ministries*, a ministry of *Global Action*, has distributed blankets to many of the poorest people. These people do not have enough money to buy blankets.

One of our staff members, Sheeba Subhan, described for me how she first got involved in the blanket project:

"Four days during the Christmas season I visited a very poor village, named Motipur. I saw real poverty, where children, some not older than two years were fighting the chilling weather of the Indian winter without sweaters or any other warm clothes.

"It was Christmas time and the kids at home in my city had toffees in their hands handed out by Santa Claus. But what did these little girls from the village have in their hands at Christmas? Some pieces of wood in their sweet little hands for their mothers, so they can heat the food for them to eat that night.

" 'Oh, it's really very cold,' I had said to my father that morning. He replied, 'Just come out of your room and see what a beautiful, sunny day we have, but don't forget to wear your warm clothes and warm scarf, otherwise you will get sick.' I obeyed my father's command. Though it was a sunny bright day, it was still very cold. As I came out of my room, I saw a group of little children shivering while they looked at me with so much excitement. Their body language made that absolutely clear!

"I signaled to them with my hands to come closer but they were just smiling and acting shy! Slowly I began to sing, and they came close and wanted to be my very good friends. I taught them several Christian songs with actions, played with them, laughed with them, walked with them in the forest area and we had so much fun together.

"They looked at me in a very curious way and so I asked them, 'Why are you looking at me like that?' And they replied, 'Because you look so good!' I responded immediately, 'So do you!' Then I heard a sweet, soft spoken, fearful voice, 'We are so dirty and ugly.'

"Then the father of this little dark girl came, turned to me and said, 'Madam, I feel so ashamed of my daughter because she is dark in color. We are Muslims where most of the family members are fair and good looking.'

"The moment he said these words, the little girl's eyes filled with tears. I took her in my arms, held her and said to her and her father, 'I am just as dark as you! But God has created her and everything He creates is good and beautiful.'

"Sometimes, it becomes very hard to control your own emotions when you see these needs. That is exactly what happened when I returned back from the village. A girl named Rani was standing there with tears in her eyes. The name Rani means a queen, but she certainly did not look like a queen. She was tiny and very dirty. So I asked her, 'What do you want me to bring from the city next time I come?' She responded immediately, 'I need a sweater!'

"At that point I could not control myself and tear drops flowed down my cheeks. I realized the Lord stirring me to action and I told Him, 'I want to do something.' Suddenly I remembered a few great words from Mother Teresa, 'I cannot do everything, but I can do something which will give some hope and joy to the poorest of the poor!' These poor children are literally dying from the cold weather, because they simply do not have warm clothes.

"The first house we visited to present a blanket was a house full of joy, because a baby boy had just been born in the house. As one of our volunteers handed over the blanket to the father, he was filled with joy. They were in desperate need of some warm covering for their newborn baby. It was God's plan to use *Global Action* to send the blanket to this needy family.

"The second house we went to give a blanket to, was a house of sorrow. The food had not been cooked because of lack of money. There was a small child with no warm clothes. As we covered him with the blanket, the mother was extremely happy and tear drops fell from her eyes. One of our volunteers also gave her some money to get some food.

"We distributed 115 blankets to 60 families, who did not have any warm coverings. After receiving the blankets the people were very happy and thankful because it was like a blessing in disguise for them. One of the old men exclaimed, 'God is here and He is watching us. We were in deep need of some warm quilts and God has sent them to us through you people. Thank you so much!' His joy in this time of pain was visible in his teary eyes.

"In one of the houses, where there was not even a candle to be lit, one of the poor women, receiving her blanket explained, 'It is not the blanket that touched me, but the love which was shown in giving the blankets to us. We did not have a single blanket but you people gave us two...' and then she started crying.

"Some people who received the blankets came and told us, 'Nobody ever came and looked at the situation in which we live, how our children are fighting the cold.'

"Another lady shared her story, 'I lost my son a few years ago, because we were not having any proper warm coverings for him. He got sick and died. But God has sent you people to us so that we may not lose our other children. Thank you for your help.'"

During 2006 James Dobson's assistant Sherry Hoover and her husband Bruce was part of the team handing out blankets in India. After she'd returned home she shared her burden for this project with her superior. The following year Sherry and I, as well as another couple, were part of two *Focus on the Family* radio broadcasts with Dr. Dobson. Many people responded.

The following winter was the coldest that most people could remember in North India. The cold especially affected the poor, those who have no shelter, and those who live in slums and huts.

That year the distribution began in Delhi. There are areas in Delhi inhabited by the poorest of the poor, those with no means of a livelihood. The team visited several areas of the slums in Delhi where many of the untouchables, the *dalits*, live. The slum dwellers always long to see and meet someone who can love them, who can care for them and express concerns for their daily needs. In such a season and weather the need has been warm clothing and blankets.

The team distributed blankets to elderly men, women and newborn babies. Many of them were just skin and bone, so weak and frail. In Motipur the blankets were distributed to the very, very old. They were weak and could not utter "Thank You" but began to shed tears. It was obvious that these tears were an expression of gratefulness. Here was the Gospel of Jesus Christ in action.

Near Motipur there are always people who are victims of floods; year after year the river takes away their belongings. They call it the "curse of the river" and the "curse of the floods." This thinking is related to their background of animism. When these affected people - both men and women - received the blankets, they also shed their tears.

Sheeba Subhan, leading this program for *Global Action*, told me, "Taking care of the hungry and thirsty and the naked must not remain a one-time event. My personal plea is that such action and demonstration must be a continued and on-going program. This must not be treated as alms-giving, but a gesture of our Lord Jesus Christ, uplifting the human beings who need us most. Christ was crucified and died for them as well. They need us and we love them."

Ministering with Medical Equipment

Many parts of the world are devastated by poverty. Their health care systems may have some of the best trained and dedicated staff, but the systems are often crumbling, due to little or no funding available for new equipment, medicines, or the most basic medical tools.

For example, until recently the maternity hospital in the city of Kerch, Ukraine, a city of approximately 175,000 inhabitants, had no hospital beds, no incubators and no gynecology chairs.

One day I received an email from a staff member who was upset after his visit to the maternity hospital in Kerch. He found nothing, except willing physicians and nurses. That same day we had one of these God-moments, when a friend from my youth in The Salvation Army contacted me, telling me that he was working with used medical equipment, receiving it from Swedish hospitals and the military, renovating it and sending it out to needy countries. And by the way, would we need an incubator, some hospital beds and a gynecology chair?

Thus began a partnership that over the past years has seen close to a hundred containers and trucks leave Sweden with medical equipment for around the world, valued at over twenty million dollars. They donate the medical equipment to us, and we pay the freight. For every dollar we raise for shipment, $20 dollars of equipment is released! Quite a return on your investment.

Most people have never seen a "walker" and wheelchairs are in great demand for both adults and children. In the city of Sumy in Eastern

Ukraine many people died one year because of lack of dialysis machines. There is no short-term solution to this problem, and in the meantime the common person suffers enormously for the lack of some of the most basic equipment and care taken for granted in the Western world.

Africa, and now India, are reeling from the devastation of HIV/AIDS. The epidemic has created a major health and socio-economic challenge for entire continents, with more than 28 million infected in Africa alone, where some 8,000 people die every day of AIDS. In some countries, an entire generation of adults has been wiped out and there are now more than 10 million orphaned children because of this disease.

Inadequate facilities and lack of equipment to provide the most basic hospice care make it impossible to help even half of the victims.

Through this organization in Sweden, *FA Bistånd*, *Global Action* has been able to receive children's and adult's wheelchairs, walkers, hospital beds, X-ray tables, dialysis machines, incubators and gynecology chairs. These are sometimes in brand new condition, or are slightly used, refurbished and in full working order .

Through networks with various government agencies and hospital associations, *Global Action* has been able to secure equipment for setting up complete AIDS hospices to meet this need in Africa and India.

During the time of the tsunami, the leader of *FA Bistånd*, Arne Nordberg called me. "Lars, do you want to have a field hospital?" he inquired. "Of course," I responded quickly, "but what is a field hospital?" Arne explained that this was a gift from the Swedish military. It consisted of twelve 40-foot containers and included three complete hospital set-ups with all needed equipment - completely brand new. These hospitals found their ways to various parts of the world where they are now being used to transform people's lives.

A Pair of Crutches

The rumors spread across Kerch in Crimea. At the *Global Action* Hope Center there were new crutches, other devices called "walkers," and even some wheelchairs available for those who needed them.

People with a variety of problems as well as those who were physically challenged turned up at the Hope Center. One was Alexander. He is a handsome, educated economist, approximately 35 years of age. After an accident he lost his leg and the scars from the accident can still be seen in his face. He could not keep his job as an economist because of his accident. The only solution the government could provide for him was simple crutches and then he was on his own.

Alexander received new crutches at the Hope Center and in his thank you speech he mentioned that his greatest dream was to get an artificial leg, although that would be a financial impossibility for him. Yet he was so grateful for the second best: his new crutches!

One of the people at the Hope Center that day was Ingegerd, a frequent visitor to the camp in Kerch. Ingegerd is married to Jörgen Edelgård from Sweden, who then looked after the development of the Hope Center. Ingegerd grabbed a nearby measuring tape and helped Alexander measure from the stump of the amputated leg down to the ground. She also took notes of the shoe size on the remaining foot.

A few weeks later, when Ingegerd returned to Sweden, she called a few people in the health department. She prayed before every phone call until she reached an orthopedist at the local orthopedic clinic. He promised to help immediately. "We have spare parts in the basement," he chuckled, "and I'll be happy to help. Come and pick up the artificial leg in a week. As this is for a good cause I will not charge anything!" It is remarkable what medical professionals keep in their basements.

Ingegerd picked up the leg and packed it in a suitcase together with her clothes and some toys for the children at the orphanages in Kerch, and took off on her next trip to Ukraine.

Because of Ingegerd's medical condition, having had blood clots in her lungs as well as suffering from severe asthma, Ingegerd travels in a wheelchair. She was concerned about what the customs officials would say when the suitcase passed the X-ray machine on arrival in Kiev, and no doubt would identify the extra leg. But because she was in a wheelchair, everyone was polite and did not want to ask any questions.

The next problem was even greater. How would Ingegerd find Alexander in the city of Kerch? No one had thought of writing down his address or phone number. It did not take many days before Ingegerd bumped into Alexander on the street, where he came limping along on his crutches, one pant leg pinned up with a safety pin.

The same night Alexander came to the Hope Center to pick up his leg. Ingegerd suggested to him that he practice, using it at home first, so he took the leg with him in the suit case and wobbled home.

A week later he returned to the Hope Center, proudly showing his new pair of shoes on both legs and told us that the artificial leg fit perfectly. Alexander was so pleased that his tears began to flow when he thanked the people at the Hope Center, thanked God, the Swedish people and its government!

Aid to an AIDS Center

In January 2004, I visited an AIDS center operated by Freedom Foundation outside Hyderabad, India. The conditions were among some of the worst I have ever seen. Patients slept in beds not fit for humans. There was no other furniture.

Twenty-five HIV-positive kids, staring death in the face, stood and sang for us. "We shall overcome some day," echoed through the eerie corridors. We had just walked through the dormitories, where people die every day in beds pieced together from metal scrap, looked into the bare laboratory and visited the clinic with hardly any medical supplies.

While we cannot stop the disease, we can do what is possible for these hurting adults and children to ensure their last weeks and days are spent in a better environment.

In September of 2004, *Global Action* was able to provide 30 beds, 30 mattresses, 1 examination table, 1 stethoscope, 1 blood pressure meter, 2 bed lifts, 1 portable bath, 2 walkers, 3 wheelchairs, 20 crutches, 2 handicap chairs, 10 portable toilets, in addition to office equipment, computers and a full set of laboratory equipment, including microscopes and centrifuges.

The medical director exclaimed, "It is like night and day. Before it took four people to lift a patient. Now we press a button on the mechanical bed. Thank you *Global Action* for making life better for these AIDS patients."

Relief for Tsunami Victims

Doreen and I were attending a wedding reception when the news became known about the tsunami. Hurrying home, I decided to call our national director in India, Pranay Mookerji, and our national director in Sri Lanka, Lal Withanage, so they could give me an assessment. They pleaded for help and promised to get teams ready to go as soon as it was feasible. At that point none of us knew how far-reaching the devastation was.

Apart from almost 200,000 dead, the waves also left thousands injured and hundreds of thousands homeless in Indonesia, India, Sri Lanka and Thailand. More than 50,000 people were reported dead in Sri Lanka. Thousands were missing and more than a half million displaced. The Sri Lankan government declared a state of emergency, and, along with the government of the Maldives, requested international assistance. While many organizations responded with immediate help, it was not enough to meet the enormous need. Many organizations withdrew after the initial emergency need was met with blankets, medicine and temporary tent shelters.

"This may be the worst natural disaster in recent history because it is affecting so many heavily populated coastal areas ... so many vulnerable communities," the U.N.'s Emergency Relief Coordinator Jan Egeland explained. U.N.'s former Secretary-General, Kofi Annan, noted that "...it will take 12 to 15 years to bring these areas back to a somewhat normal condition again."

Lal gathered as many graduates from our Global Module Studies program as he could find. Through them and others, he was able to mobilize over 8,000 volunteers in *Global Action* T-shirts, to assist in numerous tasks, from cooking and serving food to locating members of separated, displaced families.

For months these volunteers joined full-time staff to provide food, clothing and medicine, and to assist in establishing refugee camps, helping displaced persons, providing trauma counseling, running children's programs and feeding centers and other needed initiatives.

Five months after the tragedy I headed to Sri Lanka to see what had been done so far. Nothing could have prepared me for the devastation. I felt as if I was on a movie set in Berlin in 1945 for a World War II movie. But this was real. People were living in the rubble, kids playing in the debris.

While a small percentage of the victims lived in well-designed refugee camps, and others in tents, the majority still had nowhere to live, except in demolished houses and shacks cobbled together from left-over wood and boards. In the heat of the day, life in these shelters was unbearable. But housing was not the only problem. *Global Action* worked to ensure that these peoples' lives could return to some kind of normalcy.

Risk-Taker for God

Many young women and men lost their work because of the tsunami and needed basic training to begin a new kind of employment. *Global Action* trained many young women in the city of Moratuwa in a variety of trades, including training some as beauticians. The city was so impressed by the work of *Global Action* that the mayor donated a building for this purpose.

Many schools in the area were severely damaged when the waters rushed through the buildings. Our workers spent days clearing the rubble, refurbishing desks and repainting the classrooms and the assembly halls in several schools. To be able to start the educational programs afresh, new school uniforms and new textbooks were provided. A new computer lab was also provided.

We also realized the need to provide daycare centers for children of pre-school age. Initially, one daycare center for the little ones was established. The younger orphans were often pushed away from normal feeding stations. In this daycare center, they received food several times a day and had their basic clothing and hygiene needs met. A physician came regularly to provide medical check-ups for them. *Global Action* also furnished coloring books and crayons. Because of the the enormous need, we eventually established ten of these daycare centers, with an average of 50 students in each and qualified teachers administering the program.

In many affected areas, people lived in the rubble. During my visit, foundation stones were laid for several single family homes, an event welcomed by local government leaders, Buddhist monks, and with great expectation from local residents who celebrated with drums and firecrackers! Working with *Children in Need* from Sweden, almost 40 homes were completed.

Many people lost their livelihood on December 26, 2004 fishermen, grocery store owners, carpenters, plumbers, electricians and others. Most tools and supplies vanished. We quickly developed a micro-enterprise project, providing tools and a small loan to help these people get going again.

At the southern tip, around the city of Galle, most hospitals were damaged and some were totally demolished. Through our medical equipment partner in Sweden, *FA Bistånd*, *Global Action* was able to provide hospital equipment valued at over $700,000. All of this equipment was taken into the country with no government fees and made available to hospitals in Galle. Since then we have received several more shipments that are being used for the emergency hospital in Moratuwa built by *Global Action*. We will continue to provide basic medical equipment, as well as beds, bedside tables, mobile toilets, wheelchairs and walkers. Three ambulances have also been provided, two from Sweden and one from Norway.

Buckets Of Love

One day in October 2004, Rick Christian, the chairman of the Board of *Global Action* and I visited the garbage sorters village in Delhi. We were invited to the only Christian home among 1700, and found a man sick on the earth floor. As we knelt down to pray in the home made of cardboard boxes with a plastic tarp over a pole for a roof, I saw a big hole in the roof. "A little duct tape would help," I mused to Rick. One of the children came running in, bleeding from having scraped her knee caps and the mother took a dirty rag to wipe off the blood. "Band-Aids wouldn't hurt either," smiled Rick.

The following day Rick was sick and as he spent hours in bed he thought about what he had observed and an idea took shape. Meeting with me the following day he shared his conviction to do something for people living in slums worldwide, not just in India but everywhere.

"Imagine," he said, "if Christians everywhere could encourage the people in the slums with some of the most basic goods." He produced a list out of his pocket. Soon it became evident that he had a great idea and through trial and error we discovered that a bucket was the most needed item in any slum, and *Buckets of Love* was born.

As soon as we could, we field-tested it in the slums in India and learned what items were not needed and which needed to be replaced.

We were ready to launch, and then the tsunami hit south-east Asia. The program jumpstarted because of the need and then slowed down because every church was doing its own program. It was re-launched just a week before Hurricane Katrina, so the project was again diverted to deal with the needs there.

Many containers with filled *Buckets of Love* have been sent to Sri Lanka and Indonesia. As *Buckets of Love* could not be imported to India, cash donations were used to provide for local bucket purchases and distribution. Most of the distribution in India took place with tsunami surviving families. Here is an eyewitness report from *Global Action* staff member Supratim Dey:

"The villagers began arriving around 8.30 in the morning. With curiosity and astonishment they looked at the buckets. It was obvious they had never seen anything like this before. Though they had heard that *Buckets of Love* would be brought to them, it was beyond their imagination that all these items in the buckets were a gift for each one of their families.

"After a word of greeting and explanation the distribution began. The children present were taken to the side and given some of the toys and balls and jump ropes to play with as their parents were collecting their *Buckets of Love.*

"It was mostly the women who came to collect the *Buckets of Love*, as the men were out and about in search of daily livelihood. Some of the men had gone out to sea fishing, using nets provided by *Global Action*, while others traveled to nearby towns to work as laborers.

"While playing with the children, one of the *Global Action* workers noticed that two children were standing at the side and that nobody was playing with them. When they asked some questions they found out that Purnima and her brother Venket never were welcome in any children's group, as both of them are suffering from cerebral palsy.

"'They are not even allowed to attend any school,' their mother, who is a single parent and has raised them with a lot of hardship, told us. Her husband left her and married another woman because she gave birth to children with cerebral palsy. This is a normal practice in this part of the world

"When Venket and Purnima were given a jump-rope, ball and a small toy car, their eyes suddenly lit up with joy and happiness. The mother was so happy! 'Even if I don't get anything else, I am the happiest person,' she exclaimed, 'because for the first time I feel that my children are being treated like normal children.'

"The *Global Action* staff and volunteers talked to individuals as they were collecting their buckets and found that most of the families carried within them tragedies, sufffering and pain. However, in spite of all their heartaches they are again looking to life with renewed strength from the knowledge that they are not alone, that there are people around the world who care for them and love them. Many looked at the future with hope because of *Buckets of Love*.

"Velabani and Laskhmi Surrarra were very happy with the soaps, towels and comb. They expressed their gratitude by saying, 'You are the only people who came two times to help us, first with fishing nets and now with these wonderful gifts. These gifts are like luxury to us. For many days we have not seen such colorful things…and now we have them, given with love.' They added, 'We will never forget you people. May God bless you!'"

Nagappa owned a small shop, selling breakfast food near the beach. The shop was totally destroyed by the tsunami but he survived. "I will use the bucket to carry breakfast food to the village and sell it there," Nagappa said with a smile. Though he had managed to send his youngest son to the Government school, buying toys for his son or a razor for himself was beyond his capabilities. Nagappa explained, "You people are not doing mere relief but spreading joy and happiness…"

Another father was really happy that he could provide his daughter with her first notebook and pen this year. The tsunami limited his capabilities to provide and he felt so sad and helpless. He is now glad that somebody thought of all these needs and provided them.

Lal Withanage told us, "Here everyone needs a bucket! Without a bucket you have no water, no shower, no bath and nowhere to wash your clothes, vegetables or yourself! Without a bucket you cannot carry much - a bucket is life! And then to receive one filled with gifts is just an overwhelming experience for most people here!"

Hurricane Katrina

The leadership staff huddled in my office when the worst news of Katrina broke. "We must do something," I exclaimed, "we don't have much, but we can always turn on a dime!" "We don't even have a dime," muttered one of them. "But we have *Buckets of Love* full in the warehouse," I said. "Whether people have lost everything in India or in Louisiana doesn't matter. The need is the same. They have also lost everything!"

Later that day a Cessna pilot called and wondered if we had anything to take to the affected area. He was flying down to pick up a relative. We took cartons of buckets out to the airport and loaded his Cessna until there was barely any room for him. One of the local TV-stations was there filming the event. Later they came to the office and interviewed us and suddenly we were headline news.

We also managed to get a truckload of buckets to the area, with some staff members volunteering to go. A week later we received a phone call. "Are you the bucket people? This is the Red Cross, can we cooperate?" So the huge elephant invited the mosquito to work together. They provided food, beds and shelter and we provided buckets and hope!

We continued distributing buckets to Bulgaria, Rumania and Ukraine. Wrongly, we believed that churches would catch on to the project. The churches that completed it loved it. But it turned out to be extremely labor intensive. We could not raise enough volunteers or staff to make sure it continued to be a viable project. We shipped the last containers to Sri Lanka in 2008. Today, anyone can go on our website and donate enough funding for us to buy and fill a bucket on location – they are still needed as much as when we launched the project in 2004.

Providing Hope…in India

Imagine a set of villages of approximately 20,000 inhabitants, with temporary electricity, few phones, no functioning schools, and no well-functioning medical clinics nor medical professionals. The only available work is low-income jobs. Children beg or gather wood for their mothers to be able to cook a meager supply of food for their families. Young girls are taken into temple prostitution, while young boys deform other children to make them more effective beggars. Infanticide and child marriages are common practices.

This is Motipur, where *Action Ministries* is developing a project to provide hope, especially for the coming generation. I first heard about Motipur through the father of our two staff members Sheeba and Abhishek Subhan. I first met him at a pastors' conference in 2000, and we struck up a friendship. Soon he began sharing his burden for these villages and described what he was doing.

One day, he simply asked me, "Please come and take a look. I cannot finish this project on my own. I want to give *Global Action* the land I purchased and the buildings I have half-finished, if you complete the project!"

From 2006 until 2008, *Global Action* launched the first phases of the Orphan and Village Ministry project in Motipur, which we now call *India Hope Center.*

The Motipur village is situated 120 miles north of the city of Lucknow, the state capital of Uttar Pradesh and 27 miles south of the border to Nepal. The area is remote and extremely rural and many of the homes are made of nothing but grass and thatched roofs.

In the past, Motipur was "ruled" by 4 to 5 landowners who farmed the fields with the help of peasants who basically sold themselves to the landowner. When farm workers were sick, they received a loan to pay the medical bills. These loans were paid off by working many more weeks. The same scenario happened when a farm worker needed to pay the cost of a daughter's or son's wedding. The "dowry" or bridal gift could be as high as ten year's salary. Landowners practically owned their workers. If the worker died, the debt was transferred to the children in that family. To some degree the same procedure is followed today, as most of Motipur's inhabitants are poor and work as laborers for the landowners. The average daily earnings for a male farm worker today is approximately 50 rupees, or roughly $1.10, while female workers are paid only 30 rupees, or 70 cents per day.

Some men move to the cities to earn a more substantial income. At first, they come home with their pay to visit their wives and families. After a while, their visits are more sporadic and finally the facts become known: The worker has a new wife and family in the big city. This may eventually result in the spreading of AIDS and other sexually transmitted diseases.

There is tremendous poverty in Motipur. In the midst of high unemployment, social ills such as alcoholism, drug use and prostitution are rampant. While the government attempts to provide aid in the form of cash or food, middlemen find ways of marketing these for personal gain so that most assistance seldom reaches the people who need it most. That is why a project of this magnitude is so important.

Motipur is a predominantly, though nominally, Muslim village. There is no church within a 40 mile radius of the village. More than seventy years ago, a young man in North India, Jeetan (meaning victory) Subhan converted to Christianity from Islam, and took the name Victor Subhan. He was disowned by his father, leaving home in the only clothes he was wearing. Wanting to express his new-found faith, he trained for the ministry and became a pastor in the Methodist church. One of the first areas he was sent to was Motipur. He was not there long enough to see a church completely rooted, as he was soon transferred to pastor a city church. But he never forgot Motipur and, throughout his whole life, he talked about the need for Christ in this village.

My friend, his son Daniel, also felt God's call. After being trained in Korea and the Philippines, he began working in pastoral ministry. But he could not forget his father's burden for Motipur and, as time went by, his father's vision became his own. He often traveled to the village to meet with people and respond to opportunities for ministry.

Finally it was clear that he needed to establish a school and a church in the village. With meager funds saved from his own salary and the earnings of his wife as a nurse, plus small gifts from friends overseas, he managed to buy a piece of land and began to construct the school and church. Now, he asked me to come alongside him to work in this project.

Today, Daniel leads the *Hope Center* in Motipur. Daniel is not only fulfilling his father's dream but also giving "arms and legs" to the ministry *Global Action* wants to help him establish in this area.

The school building has been completed and it functions with four teachers. Current enrollment is approximately 100 children which includes our own children as well as other village children, going to school from kindergarten to third grade. Children are served breakfast and lunch during the school day. Instruction follows basic educational models of the India school system and includes daily chapel services and Christian education. A middle school with eight class rooms will open as soon as we can build it. Hopefully, a school with classes through 12th grade will be completed when we can purchase more land and raise enough funding.

We also want to meet the physical, emotional, educational, and spiritual needs of abused and neglected orphan children. The focus is on love and Christian care for children who have seen the worst that life has to offer, and deserve the best that we can provide. We are caring for the children in a Christian family home setting rather than in an institution. While the entire project will eventually comprise up to 14 such families, the first years began with just five. Rather than renting or building facilities for hundreds of children, the *India Hope Center* will group the homes together, each with residential foster parents who care for seven to eight children of different ages.

The church, which also functions as a community center and school auditorium, is already holding regular Sunday services. It will also be used as a training center and community library.

The training center will provide vocational training for children and adults. It will lay the foundation for future micro-enterprise projects. A mechanics' shop will teach basics of motorcycle engines, generators and car engines and, in practical ways, teach general mechanics. The welding and metal shop will teach basic welding, routing and metal skills and in practical ways ensure that students learn welding skills along with personal precautionary protection. The tailor shop, open to both men and women, will specialize in making clothes and embroidery. It will be equipped with at least ten sewing machines. A computer training lab will include basic training in operating computers and using software. It will also function as a business school for adults, teaching simple business principles and bookkeeping needed to conduct a micro-enterprise business project.

While the dairy farm, poultry farm and greenhouses are part of the vocational training, they are also planned to be self-sustaining and income-generating. The dairy farm will have a minimum of 20 buffalos to provide milk for the school and the orphan homes. It will also produce cheese and there will be enough to also produce milk products for sale in the village. There will also be 30 goats and 30 sheep for wool production. The poultry farm will initially contain 250 hens and a few cockerels. As the farm grows, produce and live chickens will be available for sale.

The greenhouses will train children and adults in planning and planting vegetable crops, irrigation and organic growth methods. This will produce fresh fruit and vegetables year round for the school, the orphan homes and the village.

Some adults trained in the vocational school will receive loans up to $150 each to begin small businesses. Others will need basic business training and equipment to get started.

There is no functioning medical clinic in the village and the nearest hospital is 40 miles away, which is four hours away when traveling by auto-rickshaw.

The clinic will function with nurses and a physician, assisting with minor injuries and children's ailments, dispensing over-the-counter medicine, and providing preventive routine check-ups. Visiting physicians and dentists will be able to provide more in-depth medical and dental care. An optician will visit occasionally to equip people with donated glasses.

The maternity hospital will provide pre- and post-natal care, and handle delivery of babies. Babies will be cared for in a clean and hygienic environment, which in turn will save many lives as mothers will not have to travel long distances for deliveries.

The foremost focus of the *India Hope Center* is children. These are children who have been denied education and most of them have been deprived of their families. During the time they attend school and live in a foster family, they will be educated through a well-designed curriculum, be taught hygiene, moral values, family relationships and good habits, be taught skills so their theoretical education is linked with practical training to help them find employment after school, or prepare them for university or other further education They will also have parental oversight, love and constant care in a family home.

Various projects at the *Hope Center* will equip village families with valuable skills. At the same time, they will be given opportunities to support themselves financially. They will learn discipline, time management and good work habits. Projects will give them opportunity to work and study in a Christian atmosphere.

CHAPTER 18
Children and Youth

During the 90s, the Europe director of *IBS* and I decided that it would be a good thing to run summer camps for orphanage children in Russia and the Ukraine. We had already blanketed major parts of the former Soviet Union with *My First Bible* and coloring books in many languages.

Two staff members, Mike Halleen and Tom Benz, took a special interest in this project and they visited the Ukraine over several summers, recruiting people from various churches to come and help them.

When I resigned from *IBS*, the new leadership looked upon the camps as activities outside of *IBS*' mission, and the program was terminated. Both Mike and Tom had also left *IBS* and came to me, encouraging me to continue the camps under the umbrella of *Global Action*, which I really wanted to do.

After the first years of Ukraine camps under *Global Action's* leadership I wasn't sure if we could afford to keep the program going, but a letter from one of our partners, Harry Hosmer in California, convinced me, "My son adopted twins from one of the orphanages. When they picked up the children, they could not keep anything, not even their underwear. But each of the girls was clutching *My First Bible* in Russian that they had received at the orphan camp. At that camp they had also asked Jesus to come into their hearts. Today I have believing granddaughters because you conducted the camps, told them about Jesus and showed them that you cared. Don't give up these camps! They provide hope for the future!"

Stories of transformed kids also reached us.

Nine-year-old Luda attended a *Global Action* camp in Ukraine. At first, she refused to get out of bed and play with the other children. Workers gradually coaxed from her a tragic story that made them understand why she was sure that even Jesus couldn't help her. One of 13 children, Luda saw her father die of cancer. Soon after, her mother sold their home for vodka and now "lives with some men" who supply her with hard liquor. The abandoned children joined thousands of others living on the street, surviving as best they can.

One of her brothers murdered her sister. Another died in an accident. Yet another sister died from "a strange illness." Luda now lives with an older sister who has her own baby.

After sharing all this to our workers, she was silent, sad and dejected. Our volunteer Nadia hugged her and said, "This is why we came here for you, because Jesus can help you and we want you to know Him."

No words can adequately convey our workers' emotions when, two evenings later, prayers were being said and kids were being tucked in bed. Suddenly Luda began to pray for all her siblings, bringing each one of them by name to Jesus. There was a new sparkle in her eyes. Next day, she was playing and having fun. She's just one of many children with similar stories to tell.

I am always amazed how the power of the Word of God works in people's lives. As I began using *My First Bible* to help needy children some 10 years ago, I wondered if it really would make a difference. Now I know it does! Some time ago I heard about a girl, Tanya, that confirms how those Bibles acted as great evangelists! During an orphan summer camp in the Ukraine, one of the girls was asked to tell about her life. "My life hasn't started yet," answered Tanya with glittering eyes. And then she told her story:

> "My mother never looked after me when I was small, so I and my younger brother always had to look after ourselves. Mom drinks a lot of vodka and has been in prison several times. No one ever thought of sending me and my brother to school as we grew up.

> "When I was 13 some Christian people came to my village. There they started a Sunday school. When one of the teachers realized

that I could neither read nor write, she bought me a school bag and took me to school.

"I started in the same grade as the 7-year olds. It was humiliating, but my Sunday school teacher encouraged me and helped me with the homework every Sunday after Sunday school.

"The only book I had to practice my reading on at home was *My First Bible*. I read it until I knew the stories by heart. When I read about Jesus and when we sang about Him I suddenly realized that He is not a fantasy figure...He is real! Jesus became my Savior and friend.

"I learned to write letters. Some of my pen pals now work at *Global Action*. I am so proud to have been selected as one of the first to be able to go through *Global Action's* vocational school here at the Hope Center in Crimea.

"That's why I want to say, 'My life has not started yet!'"

Hope Center in Ukraine

Hundreds of thousands of children live in institutions in the former Soviet Union. Literally thousands of children roam the streets of every major city. Others are living in horrible circumstances at home. Often these children do not receive even minimal care and provisions. Most of them may never hear the Gospel.

Children have ended up in these circumstances because of one or several reasons: Their parents are dead, one or both of their parents are in jail, their parents are alcoholics or drug abusers, there has been physical abuse at home or their family is so poor that they can't feed one extra mouth.

Though the children's most basic needs are usually met, the conditions in which these children live are tragic. Orphanages are typically understaffed and terribly underfunded. Rows and rows of babies may only have one or two caregivers. The older children can typically store all of their earthly possessions in a one-foot by one-foot wooden cabinet. This would include clothing, books, toys, shoes - everything.

Food is meager. The director of an orphanage for children with heart problems recently told us that the government is giving him the equivalent of less than one third of a cent per child per day! It is simply inadequate to provide nourishing meals.

Basic medical supplies like aspirin, ibuprofen, and Tylenol are usually nonexistent. Though the orphans may be abused while in the orphanage system itself, they face terrifying challenges when they graduate. Without parents, advocates, or marketable skills, and living in not a crumbling, but a crumbled economy, many of these children end up on the street, taking part in thievery, prostitution, drugs, organized crime - whatever they can find to numb the pain of their lives.

The camp program we began for these children is like a Vacation Bible school, with crafts and sports activities. The kids live in the camp, so there is time for campfires as well as that special time each night when the children are tucked into bed and each one is taught how to pray.

Hope Center Becomes a Reality

Barry Fluth and I met at a dinner in the spring of 2001. He was a successful Christian businessman, and listened with entrepreneurial enthusiasm to what I had to tell him. He had already decided to go to Ukraine on a *Global Action* mission trip. When Barry returned, his heart had been touched by the overwhelming needs of the children, but also appalled by the conditions in the state run facilities we were using for our orphan camps.

"The food is crummy, and the restrooms are nothing but a hole in the floor," Barry exclaimed, somewhat irritated when he returned. "Why doesn't *Global Action* have its own camp facilities in the Ukraine?" After I explained that we were not a "bricks and mortar organization," Barry turned to me rather exasperated, and asked, "But if I can raise enough money to buy one, will you run it?" Knowing it would not be possible for an American to buy land or property in Ukraine, I hastily said, "Of course I will run it!"

Barry worked relentlessly with many friends to raise enough money to purchase a large camp facility, a former communist Pioneer youth camp able to sleep 200 children, just outside Kerch on the eastern Crimean peninsula. He shared his enthusiasm for ministry to orphans with others, and today over 40 people from his congregation have been involved in outreach to orphans there.

The pastor of his church told me recently, "We were operating the typical church mission program, and excitement was not exactly high. Then Barry caught the vision for the Ukraine and communicated how it changed his life. Suddenly, people came out of nowhere to join in. People who had never traveled outside of the country caught a vision for being involved hands-on in mission. This partnership with *Global Action* has revitalized our church!"

In a world where Christians are being targeted, attacked, kidnapped, and even killed, we sometimes wonder if we dare to move out of our comfort zone. Perhaps we will be easy targets. It is easy to "stay put" and not ruffle any feathers. But the God of Israel, who was with David when he faced Goliath, is also our God. The God who gave power to the early Church is still alive. He is not taken by surprise. He is not wringing His hands in despair, wondering what to do. But He is looking for risk-takers who are willing to blaze a trail toward the victory that is ultimately assured when *"every knee will bow and every tongue confesses that Jesus is Lord."*

Barry is just one of many Christians in North America and Europe who have been motivated to take risks for God through *Global Action's* programs.

In 2002 this former Pioneer Youth Camp was donated to *Global Action*, complete with a larger-than-life-size statue of Lenin. I contemplated selling him on E-bay, but finally he was just torn down and a cross was put in its place. The property sits on 12 1/2 acres by the Black Sea. This property will exponentially increase the number of children who can be assisted and evangelized through camps, education and vocational training. The Hope Center now provides training for pastors and youth ministers, and serves as a ministry outreach center for local staff and Christians.

Five camps every summer are filled with activities like crafts, swimming, games and personal interaction. The highlight for the leaders is when they notice how open these children and young people are to the gospel.

Marsha was a 16-year old girl who attended the camp in Ukraine in July 2005. At the beginning of the camp she was shy and didn't want to talk to any of the international team members. During one of the Bible lessons we talked about salvation and Marsha accepted Christ into her heart. After that she was much more open to all of us and you could just see the love of Christ shining through her.

She said, "Here I started praying seriously and I feel that God helps me and gets me decisions or options I would never get by without His help. Earlier I would think it is weird, but not now! So if you pray for me in America my life will be much more easier!"

Another young person wrote to us:

"Thank you for letting me come to the Hope Center. It is my paradise! I live on the streets in Evpatoria and I am 14 years old. One of my buddies told me he had been invited to a Christian camp and would I come along? I thought, boring...but I was so hungry and thought, I'll be there for a few days and eat well, and then take off.

"I have been able to stay through two camps. Everyone is so kind! I have been respected although I am a wild one! I have learned about Jesus and found out what He thinks about me. Last Thursday, in the morning session I asked Jesus to come into my life. Now I am another person. I am not leaving here alone. The Lord is with me, I will continue to read the Bible you gave me every morning. The Hope Center must be Paradise... please promise me that I can return next summer!"

Impacting Kids in Moldova

Moldova is one of the poorest countries in Europe and most camps *Global Action* has operated there have been below basic! But eight camps and more than 1,000 kids later, it is clear that it was worth it all to introduce Jesus Christ to them.

One team returned with many "God stories," and the following typifies what God has done:

"During the week, the most-read bedtime story was 'Three Wishes.' At the end of each reading, the children were asked, 'If you had three wishes, what would you wish for?' The answers were usually the expected collection of, a computer, a car or a bicycle. However, on the next-to-last night, the answer from the dorm of girls was completely different. In unison they replied, 'a Bible!'

"The next evening was the last session with the children and Simon told the story of how one group of girls had unanimously wished for Bibles. While recounting the story he noted that each of the girls in the group were on the edge of their seats in eager anticipation.

"When he told them that every child at the camp would be receiving a new Bible, the cheering, applause, jumping up and down and general whooping and hollering was louder and more heartfelt than anything that had been heard all week...louder than any team's cheer when they won a competition and a sound and passion that no one will forget for a long time.

"When the adults handed out the Bibles, they noted that every child received it with both hands, many clutched them to their chests in gratitude. The children were told not to thank the team for their Bibles but to thank God. Many did just that, with tearful eyes of thankfulness raised to their newfound Savior."

Children's Camps in India

For several years *Global Action* has been working with street children in the ghettos of Delhi, India. Most of them have never been outside the ghetto.

What an experience to be taken 180 miles by bus up into the mountains to a Bible camp for the very first time. Some were Muslims, other Hindus and some had no religion at all. But here they met love and compassion and most of all, their new best friend Jesus Christ.

Here are some of the quotes from the kids and the leaders, "I like the games because I have never done anything like that before." "I want the international team to be with me all the time, wherever you go take me." "I have never imagined that I would be able to come to such a camp, it is a gift from God." "The morning bible lessons are great! Every one of them has meaning in it." "I have learned so many good things. When I go back to my family I will explain all the things I have learned to them." "The camp tells us how to pray to God, how to obey parents and how to obey elders." "I've met a new friend – Jesus!"

One of the leaders explained, "Here the children can learn the love of God, how we can share our love to others as our teachers and leaders share the love of Jesus to them.

Children's Camps in Kenya

One of the worst slums in the world is the Kibera slum in Nairobi, Kenya. The word Kibera means jungle, and it is a *people* jungle. Kibera has residents from many major ethnic backgrounds. Many come from rural areas due to the problems of rural underdevelopment. This multi-ethnic nature coupled with the tribalism of Kenyan politics has made Kibera the site of many ethnic conflicts throughout its near 100-year history, the most recent having occured during and after the latest presidential elections.

More than 1 million people live in this slum that is no bigger than 75% of Central Park in New York City. The ground in much of Kibera is literally composed of refuse and rubbish. Dwellings are constructed atop this unstable ground and therefore many collapse whenever the slum experiences flooding, which it does regularly. Well-constructed buildings are often damaged by the collapse of nearby poorly constructed ones.

Global Action has conducted several day camps here, aimed at AIDS-orphans. John and Diane Crews, our ever-tireless team recruiters and leaders shared this story from the camp in 2007:

"Another great day! The sun actually came out some today and took the chill off. Yes, I said chill! It's been very cool here. It's early spring here, but the winter has seemed to be extended longer than usual. We have been able to see our breath most mornings...how's that for mid-August! Everyone has been scrambling for blankets; quite a switch from what we're used to.

"These kids continue to amaze us! Bright, articulate, gifted, so creative....in spite of limited education and training, these young people persevere. Our afternoon sessions for the guys and gals remain the highlight of our day. Today, one of the girls gave two recitations, one on abstinence and the other on the African woman. Both were so powerful and eloquently presented!

"Tonight was the 'cultural show' where the kids share dances and songs from their various tribes. It's interesting to see how central one's tribe is to most everything in this culture. It's really fascinating to learn about the diversity and history of these groups.

"We have all been impacted so greatly. The local partners are thrilled with what has taken place. The kids seem to be soaking everything in and sharing more of their thoughts and questions. We have had some very deep questions during the sessions that let us know they are truly seeking to know and understand.

"Our hope and prayer is that this will not be just a 'camp experience' for them. We want them to have fun, and they have, but most of all, we hope that they realize how much Jesus loves them and wants them to know Him. The solutions to the overwhelming challenges here are in endless debate, but the core issue is still a heart issue; they, like everyone, need the Lord.

"Each day has been so full, and we see God at work! Today's session with the girls was another impacting time as we focused on how God sees them and what He thinks about them. Then they were lead into a time of reflection on their hurts, past experiences, which for many, include rape and sexual abuse, and given the opportunity to lay it all at Jesus' feet and receive the healing that only He can give. They then had the opportunity to make a commitment to remaining pure until marriage, or for those who have already been involved sexually, to begin anew and commit to abstinence until marriage. This has been such a powerful week with these girls, and we have seen how the Lord has been working in their hearts, freeing them from guilt and shame that they were not meant to carry, and to see themselves at His beautiful creation, created in His image, and the delight of His heart."

Children Praise Jesus in Delhi

In the slums of Delhi, *Global Action* works with Vanitha and Allen, a young couple who run a ministry to children on the streets. With only a few volunteers, they minister weekly to 3,000-4,000 children living in abject poverty.

Both Allen and Vanitha come from the south in India but experienced God's calling to move to Delhi and work among the slum children, most of whom have working parents, but spend all day on the streets. As they prayed for guidance, asking the Lord where He wanted them to go, they felt strongly that He was directing them to go north to Delhi. They knew little about Delhi, had few connections there, and realized that it was a much different city, language, and culture from their southern state. Though fearful about venturing into the unknown, they felt confident that God had called them to this place. So they packed a few belongings and traveled to the capitol.

They began by meeting under a tree, gathering a few children around them, sharing stories of Jesus, singing songs, and just loving them.

As the crowd grew, homes were opened up to them to have their "children's church." As soon as they began meeting in these desperate neighborhoods, they were instantly persecuted. Almost daily they were scorned and often stoned. Despite beatings, lack of money and food, and horrible conditions, they felt strongly that this was what they were meant to do.

They finally were able to secure a small, dingy apartment with a few tiny rooms. Since they had so few belongings and could not afford to buy furnishings, a blanket on the floor served as their bed and "sofa" for guests. The heat was intolerable, but the cold was equally harsh, so different from the temperate climate of their home. The dirt and filth were bad enough, but during the monsoon season, the only way to enter their home was through a sea of mud, which would then be tracked in on their "sofa." After the children left, Allen and Vanitha would scrape off the mud as best they could and wrap themselves with the same blanket to try to fend off the cold. Their health suffered, they had little to eat, had no source of heat, but they were committed to these children and determined to persevere. Things continued to be difficult.

The threats and beatings continued. They suffered numerous illnesses, and after prolonged trials, they began to question God. Had they heard Him correctly? Was this really where they were to be? They committed themselves to fasting and prayer, asking the Lord to make it abundantly clear if this was His place for them. If not, they would return home. They reasoned that there were plenty of needy children in their own city, and they could easily minister there, have much greater comfort and be near their families.

And yet they persevered. The children continued to come, even though many of them received beatings by their Hindu and Muslim parents for attending. When the group grew too large, they started another group in another section of the slum, and in a short time they had eight children's church locations. They now have close to 4,000 in these eight centers.

Though stretched beyond belief to provide what they can in food, medicine, teaching, and love, not only to the children, but to their families as well, they have a HUGE vision! They have a vision of 10,000 children, the largest children's church in India (or anywhere!), whom they intend to raise up as disciples of Jesus, prepared to go out into all parts of India and the world, even to the U.S., as ambassadors for Christ! If what they have accomplished already is any indication, they will greatly exceed that goal. Allen and Vanitha are living examples of total commitment to one another as well as to their Lord. Despite hardships, they exhibit such joy! The minute the children see them, they come running, anxious to hear more about the One who loves them and will never abandon them.

We launched and introduced an adult literacy program in the slums of Sangam Vihar in Delhi and the parents of the kids are attending this program. This initiative has encouraged many slum dwellers to spend the evening at our center and as a result they have become literate.

More than 1,000 kids attend the Vacation Bible School annually in the month of June. Many teachers and volunteers help to make this a successful event, ministering to children between 9 and 15 years of age. Many children, who were addicted to bad habits, like smoking, chewing tobacco and using liquor, have forsaken these bad habits. Vanitha and Allen shared the impact and the development taking place:

"One day I was teaching the kids from the Word of God, giving them examples of how it changes the person completely. I was sharing about Billy Graham, how the Bible changed Billy and made him the best preacher in the world. As I was explaining Billy's story and concluded it by saying that the word of God changes you completely, there were 7 to 8 boys raising their hands and telling me, 'We want to change like Billy!' I asked them why they wanted to change like Billy. Then the children began listing all the things they were addicted to. '*Didi* (Sister), we want to get rid of all this, kindly pray for us!'"

Hope Center in Kolkata

A few years ago one of our GLOMOS graduates from Kolkata, Pradip Chawdhury, asked us if his work in the slums of Kolkata could be incorporated in the work of *Global Action*. After studying his work, there was no doubt that this did fit us well!

Over 50 children from the slums are attending regular school classes from Monday to Friday at the center. At present three teachers are taking care of the classes and children.

At five other centers approximately 450 children meet once a week to sing action songs, listen to Bible stories, take part in Bible quizzes, learn such things as character development and health hygiene consciousness, enjoy drawing and painting, games and sports and spend time in prayer and sharing testimonies.

A two-year beautician training course is held each Thursday, led by two trained and experienced teachers. After training, both 1st year and 2nd year students take a final test. Once a week a Spoken English Class, a Drawing Class, and a Soft Toy Making Class are conducted by trained teachers. Un-used non-expired medicines are distributed free among the poor and needy, while a physician and a nurse volunteer weekly to provide free health checkups for children and adults.

Adults are being ministered to as well. For example, Anima Mondal, who is 37 years old, used to be beaten by her husband every day. She came to the *Hope Center* and talked about her problems. The staff prayed for her and talked with her husband. Now he has changed and is attending church regularly.

Equipping Young People

Young people are the capital we must invest in for tomorrow. They have the best chance to influence their own generation for Christ, but unless they themselves are a changed, radical generation, it will not happen.

After I started *Global Action*, I looked back to my time in *Youth For Christ* in the 60's, and wondered, "Who is impacting Christian young people today, influencing them with the core values of the gospel and training them to share their faith?"

In 1990 Galo Vasquez invited me to come to Mexico City as one of the speakers for a youth happening, which was inspired by the well-known URBANA conference held in the USA every three years. Approximately 3,000 Mexican young people met between Christmas and the New Year to listen to Christian music led by popular Marcos Witt as well as many Mexican speakers and one Swede. They were challenged to share their faith. One afternoon, they were sent out two by two with New Testaments in hand to do exactly that. The conference was an enormous success and today many young people from that congress serve as pastors and missionaries in Latin America.

As soon as *Global Action* was founded, Galo encouraged me, "Lars, we have to do something for the young people like we did in Mexico!" Thinking back to my time in *Youth For Christ*, I wholeheartedly agreed.

The Launch of New Generation

In cooperation with our partner *VELA*, we planned two conferences in Latin America in 1999 called "Youth Encounter: Young Leaders for a New Millennium." Speakers at the conference included Galo, David Ruiz (then Mexico director for *VELA*) and me.

A smaller conference was first held in Ambato, Ecuador in August 1999, followed immediately by a breakthrough youth congress in Guayaquil. This is a harbor city with over 3 million inhabitants. Along with the problems that usually come with a harbor city, high unemployment and an unstable economy have created an explosive crime rate.

Approximately 1,000 young people attended from many different denominations. The conference sessions were packed with Bible studies focusing on what we have in Jesus and how to follow Him. There were training sessions in personal evangelism, how to be a contagious Christian and of course music - glorious Ecuadorian youth music!

After two days of training, the kids teamed up in groups of two and three and went out in the streets to schools, parks and local hospitals to share their faith in Christ.

"I have only been a Christian for two months, and I was dead scared to go out on the streets to share my faith," said 17-year old Enrique, "but what I learned worked! Two out of the five people I talked to committed their lives to Christ!"

Many more stories like Enrique's were shared during the evening testimony time after the young people returned from the streets. Over 250 young people stood in line to share what Christ had done for them. One young man simply explained, "I went out for the first time to share my faith. The two persons I talked to came to the Lord, and here they are!" He pointed to two young men who immediately came to the microphone and shared their testimony.

The conference ended with a moving time of dedication and many of the young people came forward to dedicate their lives to service for Jesus Christ. With youthful enthusiasm and zeal, they pledged to live daily for Him and find ways to share their faith in Him.

As I watched Galo Vasquez ask the young people to come forward, tears began streaming down my face. Finally, the Lord had allowed me to return investing in other people in a tangible way, knowing that 10 or 20 years from now, the result of this conference would still be seen in the lives of these young people.

So many times I have heard the testimony, "I did not know much, but I attended a conference where people pointed me in the right direction. It was at a time like that, I realized what it really meant to follow Christ, and my life has never been the same." Here I saw it affect 1,000 young people in one moment, and I thanked God that *Global Action* and I could have even a small part in it.

The following year we were ready for Guatemala City. There was a lot of enthusiasm as hundreds of kids gathered for three days. Angelina, an 18-year old who attended the conference told us, "I have attended my church for years, but it was yesterday, when the messages were on evangelism, I realized I did not really know Christ myself! This conference has changed my life."

On the final afternoon, the young people took the gospel to the streets, returned to the conference (some with their harvest), reported and then dedicated their lives to be used in spreading the light of God in the cities where they live.

In May 2001 *Global Action's* first youth conference in India was held in the renamed city of Kolkata under the theme, *The New Generation.*

New Generation focused on training young Christian leaders to impact their generation for Christ. As many as 550 young people from across the state of West Bengal dedicated themselves to sharing their faith with at least five other people each after receiving training on what it means to be empowered, motivated and mobilized followers of Christ. Each delegate left the conference with six New Testaments, one to keep, five to share.

In some parts of the world, people are persecuted for their Christian faith. With *New Generation*, we talked about how to prepare for persecution and how to pray for a nation. Many of the Indian attendees came from as far away as 500 miles. Some were from nominal Christian or Hindu backgrounds. A lot of the teaching concentrated on how to grow from a nominal faith into an active, living expression of faith in Jesus Christ. Their reactions were astounding!

Weeks before the conference, the central government had suggested that Christians who have Christian last names, like *John* or *Matthew* etc, should change their last names to Hindu names. This was the government's attempt to move India from a secular nation to one with Hindu status only.

It was a very powerful moment when Rev. Ashok Andrews, who then pastored Carey Baptist Church in Kolkata, spoke on the subject of persecution. Taking the example of the life of Daniel, who also suffered persecution, he burned the following points into everyone's mind and heart:

They changed their names - but not their nature
They changed their food - but not their faith
They changed their language - but not their loyalty

One of the delegates said, "This conference has instilled in me a burning desire to proclaim Jesus to my neighborhood without shame!" Another one explained, "I come from a Hindu family. This conference has helped me to know and accept the Lord Jesus Christ."

Moses Sardar summed it up for many of the delegates, saying, "Before coming to this conference, I believed in God but I was afraid and ashamed to admit it publicly. After attending the conference and listening to the Word of God, all my fears and hesitations are gone."

The next year it was time to impact the lives of young people in the city of Lucknow. "I came here without any direction in my life," said Ranjit, "and I am leaving knowing that God has a perfect plan for my life! Now I have meaning and purpose!"

Sheeba Subhan, a 17-year old GLOMOS graduate from Lucknow and one of the conveners for the youth conference exclaimed, "The youth conference has been marvelous...excellent...I do not have enough words to describe it. This is the first time for me, and it has been wonderful to see 650 young people meeting in one heart and in unity. My life has been changed and God's message to us has been revealed. My friends have been filled up; they got a lot of answers to their questions."

As the youth conference came to a close with a time of personal dedication to the Lord, young people solemnly walked forward to receive six copies of the New Testament, five to give to their five non-Christian friends who they had been praying for during the entire conference and one for them to keep.

As they left to go back by buses and trains, they prayed they would be faithful and bold during the persecution that could await each one of them as they shared the gospel with their friends.

Risk-Taker for God

It took two years before we were ready for another *New Generation*. This time it was in Hyderabad, Andhra Pradesh. Despite possible persecution, 1,175 young people dedicated their lives to share the gospel with five each of their friends.

One of the participants, Pavithra, who was introduced to Jesus when she was 15, came from a strong Hindu family. She commented, "My family has rejected my witness. I have felt fearful of sharing the gospel for fear of losing relationships. But I was so touched during this conference and I must share the gospel and take the risk, even if they reject me."

Another one of the participants explained, "I didn't exactly know why I came, but God provided the finances for me to go. Now I know that God has something special for me. I am thankful for the unity I have felt in this conference. I have been convicted to opening up fully to the Lord. I have been challenged to give my best to the Lord."

A young man was very clear, "When my younger brother accepted Christ, I really didn't understand it and wasn't interested," he said. "I hated Jesus, didn't want to hear about Him and it caused conflict at home. But the Lord has touched my heart and I have accepted Christ. Now I want to be a strong witness for the Lord, and would like to go from village to village to share with people and pray."

Amrita is a student in university and had gone through hard situations with her family. Her abusive father abandoned them when she was quite young, and she and her mother had to go live with her maternal grandmother. "I am struggling with the pain of his abandonment," she shared, "and hatred for what he has done to our family. The Lord spoke to me through the conference about forgiveness, and I am praying for the Lord to enable me to forgive my father."

Some of the young people came from nominal Christian homes. During the first night, I spoke on transformation, pointing the young people to Christ as a basis for their salvation. Over 260 young people indicated that night that they had received Jesus Christ for the very first time in their lives. Galo Vasquez taught on holy living and vision, while Sundar Singh Moses shared about prayer, persecution and compassion. I also taught on the Word of God in a young person's life, sharing your faith and becoming risk-takers for God.

In 2005, 850 young people, age 14 to 30, gathered in Kalimpong in the foothills of the Himalayas. As they came from northeast India, Nepal,

Sikkim and Bhutan, they were challenged to become people of God's Word and prayer, live holy lives, and share their faith with others despite expected personal persecution and hardships. In the very first session over 100 committed their lives to Christ for the first time and close to 300 rededicated their lives to serve the Master.

"This conference has been a turning point in my life," explained Ringshan Shaiza from Darjeeling. "God has confirmed to me that I should be trained to be a youth pastor." Other quotes from the delegates were similar. "I've heard teaching on holy living before, but only today, here at the conference, has the teaching spoken to my heart." "There is now revival in my life because of this gathering." "I was confused but now things are clearer in my life." "The conference has helped me see the path for my life."

The state of Orissa is one of the Hindu strongholds in India. It is the center of many of the militant Hindu groups and is known for its persecution of Christians. At the end of the past century, an Australian missionary, Graham Staines, was burned alive along with his teenage sons while sleeping in their vehicle.

Here *Global Action* decided to call young Christian people together to yet another *New Generation* event in October 2007. We had planned for 1,000 delegates, and were told by the Christian leaders that we would be successful if 300 showed up. People kept on registering in advance until 2,300 people had done so. Quickly we had to adjust our plans—moving from a hall that could seat 1,200 to a hastily built tent structure that could hold over 2,000 people.

They came to the capitol Bhubaneswar from every possible district in Orissa, traveling by bus, train, rickshaws and even on foot. They represented every possible denomination. Some came from churches where the gospel is proclaimed. Others came from nominal churches where Christian principles are taught, but where members of the congregation may not know Jesus Christ as their personal Savior.

It had rained heavily the few days before, but people all over India were praying for sunshine. As the first evening came and we were ready to begin, the sun came out and turned the temperature to the upper 90's! The *New Generation* event was declared the largest Christian youth gathering ever in Orissa.

Risk-Taker for God

The first night over 450 young people made first time commitments to the Lord. During the next few days Dr. Rick Thompson, from Council Road Baptist Church in Oklahoma City, myself and Rev. Sundar Moses taught on subjects such as, "How to be a Christian in an unchristian world," "How to be people of prayer," "How to have a vision for the world," "How to share the gospel without being a Jesus freak" and "How to minister with the compassion of Jesus."

The young people were challenged to represent Jesus to the communities around them and, as we'd done in other events, to share the gospel with at least five non-Christian friends over the next few days.

Pulkit is a 19 year old college student. He was not hard to miss because of his intense enthusiasm and excitement. During the worship we found him jumping, laughing and singing. When asked what this *Global Action New Generation* Youth Event meant to him he said, "I was a Hindu and filled with pain. Since coming to know Jesus, I'm filled with joy and want to share this joy with everyone! This event has shown me that I'm not alone. I have met many friends who love Jesus just like me. I have learned how to tell others how wonderful our God really is. Thank you for letting me come to this event!"

Her smile was infectious and sincere. When she helped the worship team, there was an angelic glow about her. It belonged to a young girl named Esther. She wanted to come to *Global Action's New Generation* Youth Event in Bhubaneswar – but her parents didn't. It was too far. It was not safe. Esther was struggling with sinful habits she just couldn't break. She prayed again, "Lord, I need You to change me from the inside. I need to learn from You how to be the woman you want me to be. Please let me come to the *New Generation* Youth Event." Amazingly, her parents finally said yes. With tears in her eyes, she told us that God had given her a renewed strength to never, never quit and she knows that no matter how many times she falls away from Christ, He still loves her and gently draws her back. Knowing this kind of compassion from her loving heavenly Father is critical. Esther is planning on spending the rest of her life caring for victims of HIV/AIDS.

On the final night the young people provided an offering for *Global Action's* blanket distribution in north India that winter. It was a record offering providing over 200 people with warm blankets to survive the cold.

International Vocational Academy

In Ukraine and Russia, there are over 650,000 boys and girls living in state-run orphanages. While these children have a roof over their head, adequate meals and a relatively safe environment, all that changes when they turn 17. On that birthday or soon thereafter they are walked to the gate of the orphanage and sent on their way

A government study shows that within a year 33% are living on the streets, 20% have committed a crime and 10% have committed suicide.

Global Action launched *The International Vocational Academy* (IVA), just after the New Year 2005, with a small group of orphans and underprivileged youth, 16 of them, at the Hope Center.

The IVA is a full-time training program for young women and young men. Each one who is enrolled has employable skills. The training is taught in English with interpretation in Russian. It is equally focused on developing a transformed, positive, Christian mind-set as well as an occupational skill. A diploma is presented after completion. IVA is not a school that fits under any educational institution, a program to just fill in activities or a school that will train people only in an occupational skill.

While the test group was created so that we would be able to learn about and handle unforeseen problems, we still faced enormous challenges.

After one week, one of the students was in court and would have been sentenced to five years in jail. Due to the fact that he was at the *Hope Center* his jail sentence was reduced to community service.

Many of the boys tested HIV-positive and the young ladies had to be treated for a variety of venereal diseases. There was a lot of teen "ugliness" at the beginning of the program. However, the Lord intervened and the worst problem student in the beginning, Vitaly, came to Jesus Christ and is now part of the worship team in a nearby church.

The test resulted in 16 people graduating with a new life ahead of them. And *Global Action* was able to refine the process and start the next group at the *International Vocational Academy* with an even greater focus. With two years of history, the IVA is now well established.

Dima Tkachenko grew up in a small village in a working family. When Dima was nine, his mother died. His father started having casual relationships, and did not concern himself with Dima's upbringing. Dima had to start working when he was fourteen. He used to fish, as well as gather and purchase scrap metal. His father went to Russia and did not write or call for three years. Dima signed up for the army and when he returned he had neither money nor a profession to make money. His friends got addicted to alcohol or drugs. Many times Dima was arrested for assault and battery. Dima realized that one should not live a life like this, but he did not see a way out of the situation.

God brought him to the IVA project where he decided to become a qualified driver. It was at the *Hope Center* he heard about Jesus Christ and accepted Him as his personal Savior. Due to his diligence he graduated with a driver's license. Dima found new friends and new interests. Now Dima works at the *Hope Center*, is developing in Christ and actively participates in *Global Action* projects.

Oksana has never seen her father but she knows a lot about him from her mother's tales. He would often drink and beat his wife for everything or for nothing. When her mother became pregnant, nothing changed and the abuse continued. The mother gave birth to twin girls but one died of complications within the first month. Oksana survived but her life was not to be easy. Her mother left home with the children, driven away by her father. She let her sons, 7 and 10 years old, take care of the baby while she tried to earn money to buy food.

When the brothers became older, they left for Russia to seek a better life. Oksana stayed with her mother. When she finished school she had to start working. Life continued to be a struggle. Oksana went to stay at her friend's place while her mother stayed in a shack only big enough for one person. When Oksana found out about IVA, she jumped at the opportunity to make her cherished dream come true. She wants to become an economist and change the direction of her life for the better.

Alla is a pretty 18-year old girl. When she joined IVA, the staff asked her to share her story, but she avoided telling them about her family and changed the topic each time. After being at IVA for a while, she decided to share her pain.

Alla has six brothers and sisters who live in government-run facilities for children. Alla has never seen her father, and her mother does not bother herself with bringing up her own children - she drinks all the time and is not concerned with morality. Alla could not forgive her mother for having abandoned her when she was three.

When Alla was 10, her mother said, "I am still young and I am not going to bother myself with you." After spending four years in an orphanage and nine more years in a government-run facility, she often thought back on the reason their mother had abandoned them – it was simply to "have fun."

One day, when she was 16, Alla was grabbed and thrown into a car in the middle of the day and taken to Russia. Alla begged the border-guard officers for help, but they only grinned as they were bribed by the criminals who had kidnapped her. It turned into a nightmare. Alla was brought to a small flat in a Siberian city where eight girls already lived. They were prostitutes. The 16-year-old girl realized that they would not release her alive. During the first month she resisted, and as a result was severely beaten, starved and raped. She decided to do anything just to stay alive.

Six months passed. Finally, the day she was looking forward to came. The prostitutes and their security guards had gotten drunk and sent her to get some beer. In a shop she saw a man wearing a police uniform and she begged him for help. This man turned out to be an investigator. He invited her to stay at his place.

Alla was deported to Ukraine. Having returned to her Motherland, the girl was ready to kiss the native soil, remembering all the terrible trials she had undergone in a foreign land. She ran to her mother's place. Her mother did not even bother to ask her where she had been all this time.

Now Alla has gone through IVA. She has made a lot of new friends and is getting to know a new life, free of humiliation and pain. She is dreaming of a happy family without grief and tears. Alla desperately needs God to pour forgiveness into her life and to heal her wounded soul.

CHAPTER 19
Women of Global Action

At the end of January 2000, I received a call from Emily Voorhies. "Lars, you know that the A.D. 2000 movement is closing at the end of the year. But did you know they had a Women's Track and that these women around the world want to continue?"

I was very well aware of the A.D. 2000 movement, but I only had a vague awareness of the Women's Track, and did not know much more. Emily passed along their inquiry about whether *Global Action* would be a suitable umbrella for them. I asked her to give me some more background, which she did.

Lorry Lutz had been a missionary with her husband Al in South Africa for many years and was working in communications at Partners International when Luis Bush, director of A.D. 2000, asked her to take on the challenge of creating a Women's Track for the program.

Lorry established a strategic network of international women who were leaders on their respective continents. These women had been involved in training other women to evangelize their unreached neighbors, focusing on the 10/40 Window, and had a quarterly newsletter in six languages. They had participated in training programs and consultations around the world. They had a growing advocacy program that matched women who wanted to pray for others in the 10/40 Window. The initiative also included a strong and growing prayer movement.

As a result there were hundreds of new converts – more than 300 in Europe and 250 in West Africa. Thousands of women involved in the prayer movement used Evelyn Christenson's *Study Guide for Evangelism Praying,* which had been translated into 45 languages. Missionary women were going out to unreached groups in Philippines, West Africa, Cambodia, Burma and India. Churches were being planted and the network had participated in nearly 40 training programs and conferences. One of the highlights was the participation in several training conferences for Arabic women in Arab countries. They also provided training materials in many languages.

With the closing of A.D. 2000, the Executive Committee for the Women's Track, which was established with representatives from each continent, expressed their desire to have the women's network continue. For the past eighteen months, Lorry had been looking at various options on how this might happen.

It did not take me long to see the benefits of incorporating this network into *Global Action*'s program. The two groups shared a common mission and vision of evangelism and training. After taking this to the *Global Action* Board, they agreed and *Women of Global Action,* as they were re-named, was established and Emily Voorhies took over the leadership. I was overwhelmed by the scope – suddenly we had a network of 150,000 women around the world. They are not *Global Action* staff, but a network of partnering groups, many of whom are professional women in key political and government positions, as well as physicians, lawyers, Christian ministry leaders and other professions – a formidable power.

Since then many training conferences have taken place all over the world, where either Emily or other leaders have given leadership to literally thousands of women. The network continues to grow as younger leaders are being mentored and joining what God is doing through Christian women. As awareness of key issues impacting women and adolescent girls around the world has increased, the network has become involved in training to address the issues, which include human trafficking and forced early marriage, HIV/AIDS, female circumcision, poverty, lack of access to education and abuse.

Africa

More than 300 women from 20 countries convened in Gabarone, Botswana for the Fourth Assembly of Pan African Christian Women's Alliance

(PACWA), *Women of Global Action's* African partner, in 2001. *Women of Global Action* was one of the conference sponsors. Mrs. Judy Mbugua, who served as the chair of the executive committee of *Women of Global Action*, worked with the local Botswana committee to organize the conference around the theme "Pressing on in the New Millennium."

Emily Voorhies addressed the women on issues of leadership. Her topics included "the biblical mandate for leadership," "Jesus' model of leadership" and "the challenges and blessings of leadership."

Mrs. Mbugua challenged each participant to "love your neighbor" by responding in the name of Jesus to those whose lives have been devastated by HIV/AIDS. Of the world's 36 million infected, 25 million are in Africa. In Africa there are 12 million AIDS orphans. In Kenya alone, 700 are dying each day from AIDS and 2000 are being infected. Sharing Christ's love with your neighbor provides hope for this dying world.

In Zambia, more than 3 million have died of AIDS. Mrs. Leah Mutala, a participant from Zambia, shared how women are taking care of 400 AIDS orphans in that country. And the need is growing. Leah explained, "At each meeting, we would ask the women to share their needs. Over and over again, women shared the needs brought about by the devastating AIDS pandemic. We realized that we couldn't just pray for them and say 'Now, go and be blessed.' We had to do something."

Thus, the project to help AIDS widows and orphans began.

A panel of prominent Christian women lawyers in Botswana addressed the assembly on "The Abuse of Women and Girl Children and the Rights of Inheritance in Africa." They reminded those present that legal changes on these issues is not enough – passing laws will not bring about change. Christian women must be advocates for change as spiritual leaders as well. The panel presented specific ways in which Christian women should respond to abusive situations.

Botswana's President, His Excellency Festus Mogae, addressed the Assembly. He challenged those present to work alongside their governments to address the devastation of AIDS across the continent. A children's choir, comprised mostly of AIDS orphans, presented songs and dances. Dr. Tokunboh Adeyemo, Executive Director of The Association of Evangelicals in Africa, spoke to the group on the need for staying power in the new millennium.

One woman noted, "This conference has changed my life. When I go back to my country, I know I can make a difference for the Lord. I know that I am not alone in my struggles, but have sisters all across Africa who are standing with me."

Two years later more than 350 women leaders, representing eight countries, gathered for a five-day training conference in Kenya around the theme "Whatever It Takes: Making the Most of Every Opportunity," based on Ephesians 5:16, *"making the most of every opportunity, because the days are evil."*

Several sessions related to health issues plaguing women in Africa, including HIV/AIDS. Kenya's Minister of Health spent one morning with the conference participants discussing the partnership between Christian women and the government agencies to address those health issues.

Emily also taught sessions on "Jesus' View of Women" and "Being a Risk-taker for God." Esme Bowers led sessions on prayer and ministry. Representatives of the Billy Graham Association were also present and conducted sessions on evangelism.

Each evening, there were reports from each country represented, along with a time of prayer and celebration of what God is doing in East Africa. There were many testimonies about the impact and significance of the training.

Working with PACWA, *Women of Global Action* has been very active with AIDS patients over the past few years. Dianah, a young woman in Kenya, had little hope of employment or a future. *Global Action's* partners in Kenya helped provide training for Dianah and 67 other young women in working with and counseling HIV/AIDS patients and their families. This two-month intensive course trains young women in caring for the sick, providing nutritious meals, counseling the patient and family and sharing the Gospel. Since she completed her training, Dianah has trained 50 others to care for the sick and their families

Wangeni and her five-year old son John, who live in Kenya, are both suffering from AIDS. Her husband died four years ago from the disease. Left on their own, Wangeni is not able to afford medicine or food. *Global Action* is working with our partners in Kenya to assist victims like Wangeni and John, and to educate and inform women of the behavior change needed to prevent its spread.

Every 14 seconds, a child is orphaned by AIDS. In Kenya, thousands of young people are left helpless and hopeless as their parents die from this disease. *Global Action*, through *Women of Global Action* are

309

helping provide beehives and goats for one hard-hit village. The honey from the beehives is sold to pay school fees for the year for an orphan. The goats help Christian families, who are taking in the orphans, provide cheese and milk and are used for breeding more goats. Each beehive costs $50 and each goat costs $250.

Through our partners, *Women of Global Action* supports training for desperately poor young women from the Kibera slums. Recently, those being trained were even more destitute than usual, as a fire swept through their area of the slum, destroying the few possessions they had. The 16 young women were being trained in a professional tailoring course, sponsored by Pan African Christian Women's Association (PACWA).

This is the third group of students trained in the program. Those who have received the training previously have all been able to generate income, either through employment or through their own micro-enterprise business. *Global Action* also was able to provide Bibles for the students and the teacher. Their ongoing needs include fabric, lunch food for the students, two more sewing machines and general tailoring supplies.

In the village of Chuka, about a four-hour drive from Nairobi, *Women of Global Action*, partnering with PACWA, has attempted to help with some of the most basic needs. This is one of the poorer areas of the country and has also been affected by the drought. The local Presbyterian church and its pastor have been very supportive of the work being done by the women – which is not always the case.

As Emily Voorhies visited the area, the AIDS orphans sang a song for her. The words were, "Our parents have both died, but it is not our fault. What about us? Does our life end now too? Who will care for us? The women came and they cared about us. They are caring for us. We are so grateful for the women who came." It was a very moving experience as it was obvious that several of the orphans were also HIV infected and ill.

One of the AIDS hospice workers who received training shared that since she received the training, the YMCA has employed her to train others. She had already trained 50 other hospice workers in the past 18 months. All four of those present had made significant contributions to those in the community who are HIV-infected and affected.

When Emily visited the local district hospital with the pastor and a small group of women, she and her group were received and treated as dignitaries. It was humbling to see how inadequate the facilities are.

There was one doctor to care for 350 patients. The hospital has beds for 88 people so the sick they often must share a single bed. Sometimes they have as many as three patients per bed. The AIDS pandemic has completely overburdened the very basic healthcare system that is in place in most countries in Africa.

Women of Global Action is helping AIDS widows to purchase the ARV (anti-retro viral) drugs that are currently available to prolong their lives in order for them to take care of their children as long as possible. These cost about $25 per person. Emily met a mother and her five-year-old son who are benefiting from this program; both are HIV positive. She is like thousands of women who have been infected by unfaithful husbands, but have no right to refuse their husbands' demands.

Another crucial ministry in which our partners are involved provides support to women and children who are battered, or who have been expelled from their families because of being HIV positive.

One of the most desperately poor and needy groups in Kenya is the Masaai women. Our partners are training these women to read and write, about basic nutrition and health and other topics. The Masaai men have many wives and the spread of AIDS among the population is rampant. Often the girls are only 13 to 14 years old when they marry and they are expected to produce children right away. The cycle of children raising children in such conditions results in numerous problems and a high infant mortality rate. We are actively working to reach these young adolescent girls, share the Gospel message and let them know that God has a plan for their lives, before they make these devastating choices. They need assistance of every kind and a great deal of encouragement and prayer. It is hard not to be discouraged by the magnitude of poverty, disease, crime and corruption Yet, God reminds us that He has called us, and we must not give up – but do what we can!

During February 2006, hospital equipment was delivered to a rural hospital in Mawanga, Uganda through a gift from our partners in Sweden. Sarah Timarwa, East African coordinator, conducted a week-long training seminar in the rural area of Hoima. The training focused on poor, rural women. They were challenged to serve God fully despite their circumstances. An HIV/AIDS Day Care Center was also launched. Some of the hospice equipment was donated to the center.

In 2006, a 5-day training conference was held in Monrovia, Liberia for 52 women leaders from 10 of the 15 countries in West Africa. Many of these women walked for more than three hours before they could catch public transport to the conference. Three women walked for six hours; two had to sleep overnight in the forest and it took them two days to travel 200 kilometers. Despite the travel difficulties, these women were determined to come.

"They arrived with only a small bottle of water and a change of clothes," reported Esme Bowers. "We spent a week together, and I listened to the most gruesome war experiences told by women who thought the world had forgotten about them. They had lost all hope, but God met these women during our time together. During the session on 'Reflecting on Our Past,' women shared things they experienced, but had placed in the back of their minds because it was too painful to deal with them. When they began hearing other women's trials during the war, they began to recall their pain and felt safe to share and listen to the painful history of this country and the effect it had on the women and children. 75% of the women participants had been raped during the war and are now raising children from unknown fathers!

"We spent two days listening and praying for each other. God met us in a very powerful way and as women left the conference changed, I know that God had brought us here to begin a process. My experience in reconciliation was also put into effective use. One of the most valuable aspects of the conference was that women came together, listened to each other, realized that we as Christian women leaders care, and they went back with hope and new skills to effect change in their homes and communities."

The "Africa Prayer Summit" held in Pretoria in February 2007 highlighted the need for both prayer and social action if we want to transform Africa through the Gospel. Women at this conference were eager to rise up and train transformational leaders for Africa.

USA

The women came. Airlines had heightened their security precautions and travel anxiety was evident among passengers. People around the world cancelled plans, vacations and business meetings. Nations sat on the edge while world leaders contemplated positions of alliance on a 21st Century battlefield. A major convocation for Christian women had been planned in Houston from September 19 to 21, 2001. *Women of Global Action* was one of the sponsors. The world's worst act of terrorism could not deter them from their appointed place in history.

The women came anyway—just as they did that first Easter morning—leaving behind their families, their comforts and their personal sense of security. They came from every corner of the world—the Philippines, Brazil, the United States, Cote D'Ivoire, Serbia, Egypt, Hong Kong, Great Britain, Honduras, Canada, Kenya and numerous other nations.

Despite the shadow of eminent war heralded across TVs and newspapers, more than 10,000 women worshiped and praised God each day, acknowledging common struggles of life in a post-modern world, and, more importantly, accepting the overriding challenge to share Jesus Christ to an international community desperate for hope and mercy.

True to its promise, the Global Celebration for Women, directed by a partnering coalition of 13 faith organizations, featured 40 workshops about living in a hostile world, leadership, cross-cultural learning, AIDS, spiritual warfare, micro-enterprise, prayer and reaching 21st Century women, to name a few.

Guest plenary speakers Anne Graham Lotz, Elizabeth Dole, May Feng Lee and Judy Mbugua commissioned Christian women to rely on God's strength, ministering wherever they are and using the gifts He gives.

On Friday, organizers extended an open invitation to Houston churches, swelling attendance to an estimated 15,000 for the conference's closing ceremony. Alicia Williamson, Kathy Troccoli and The Salvation Army Band provided a unique blend of praise and worship music, contemporary Christian favorites and traditional hymns.

Leading Bible study curriculum developer and author Beth Moore delivered a commanding final message loaded with Scriptural references about the times and how Christians can respond.

As women from more than 156 nations flowed into Houston the third week of September, they brought with them a calming demeanor of peace and solidarity. Restaurant and hotel staffs noticed and appreciated their friendly greetings, their positive outlook and even their gentle songs of praise while they waited on buses bound for the Reliant Astrodome.

Women of Global Action conducted its international leadership meetings for two days following the Global Celebration. Nearly 100 leaders from around the world were present to discuss how to implement what was learned at the Global Celebration. They established a plan of action, with a 6-month evaluation, for each of the regions. The impact of the Global Celebration will continue to be felt around the world in the months and years ahead.

Global Celebration for Women launched a movement that promised to live far beyond 2001. And the impact continues around the world.

Chapters of *Women of Global Action* continue to spring up in the United States. It began with a focused strategy to establish a chapter in Los Angeles and one in Charlotte. Many more are now being established where Christian women can meet, be trained and link up with *Women of Global Action* projects around the world by visiting them, praying for them and supporting them.

Asia

The *Women of Global Action* are active in Thailand, Philippines, Hong Kong, Vietnam, Malaysia, Korea and Myanmar and upon the close of the Global Celebration in Houston 2001, they all returned ready to set into action a mighty movement of prayer and action for God.

In January 2006, a planning meeting with WOGA leaders from Thailand, Myanmar and Vietnam was held in Thailand. The WOGA-Korea Global Conference in October 2007 drew nearly four thousand women to Seoul, Korea to train these emerging leaders for ministry in the 10/40 window.

In Hong Kong, the government has now granted tax-exempt status for all donations. All funds for the WOGA work in Hong Kong are raised locally and these funds help support work in China as well. The WOGA ministry in Hong Kong focuses on nurturing and building up women leaders through seminars, fellowship gatherings, mentoring and coaching.

Nearly 500 women from West Bengal gathered at the Calcutta Girl's School to participate in a Women's Conference hosted by *Action Ministries*. The conference theme was "Being a Godly Woman in the 21st Century." Delegates were also present from Lucknow and even from

Seoul, Korea. Organized by a local multi-denominational committee, the conference included representatives from 13 denominations.

Session topics included, "Jesus' View of Women," "Being a Godly Woman in the Home," "Being a Risk-taker for God," "Living a Life of Victory," "Being a Godly Woman in the Community" and "Being a Godly Woman of Prayer." Speakers included Juliet Thomas, Director of OM's Arpana Ministries, Emily Voorhies, and Mercedes Dalton, Director of *Global Action Latin America*.

There was also a question and answer session and many of the younger women had questions about their role. In a culture that limits the freedom of young women, they are struggling with their desire to serve the Lord.

Many women came forward for prayer as there are tremendous needs in the country, particularly among women. Divorce rates are soaring with one in five marriages ending in divorce. The abuse of women is another crucial issue.

The conference was closed with communion and a candlelight service. A number of local pastors joined in this closing celebration. *Action Ministries* gave them each a Bible in Bengali, or English, to encourage them in their spiritual growth.

A similar conference was also held in Hyderabad, India and gathered almost 1,000 ladies.

Latin America

In 2003 a Brazilian conference for the *Women of Global Action (WOGA)* network was held in the city of Belo Horizonte. More than 200 women from throughout the country of Brazil registered to attend the event. The theme of the conference was, "Woman, Rise and Shine! Praying and working for a church for every people, the Bible translated for every language, the Gospel accessible to every person in Brazil and in the World."

Ana Maria Costa, Brazil's National Director for WOGA, shared how she, as a young mother of four children, had asked God how He could use her for His purposes. She also shared her deep passion for reaching Unreached People Groups, inviting those women who had not already done so to adopt an Unreached People Group. Nearly 100 women agreed to make this commitment.

Emily Voorhies challenged the women to get involved globally. As Emily shared stories of courageous women of faith throughout Africa, Asia and the Americas, she told them how women are adopting AIDS orphans in Africa, starting a school for children in India, ministering to gang members and prostitutes in Latin America and quilting for Moldovan orphans in the United States. The leaders were so inspired by the creative ways women are ministering throughout the world that they scheduled a special session after the conference to brainstorm new visions for ministry for the coming year.

Emily Voorhies and Cheryl Lovejoy, our WOGA Training Associate, also held several sessions on "Training Women for Ministry." They outlined the following practical steps in their session: 1) Maintain a close and dynamic walk with the Lord; 2) Find your spiritual gifts and your passion for ministry; 3) Find a mentor/discipler who has more experience using your spiritual gift than you do and learn from her; 4) Equip yourself with manuals, books and magazines in your ministry area; 5) Gain experience in your area of ministry by jumping in and doing it, 6) Practice the action-reflection-action model as you minister (take time to reflect with your mentor as you minister); and 7) Find other women to mentor/train as you minister.

Several women shared wonderful testimonies about how God is working in their lives. One woman shared how God had turned her heart from the pursuit of material blessings toward the pursuit of heavenly ones. Another shared how God taught her to instill a passion for the Lord in the hearts of her children. The final testimony of the morning encouraged the women to shine for God at every age. The speaker shared with humor on how "Autumn Flowers" are often the most trained, most experienced women with the greatest opportunities to serve the Lord.

Many times throughout the conference, women were heard to say that the Lord was blessing them "to overflowing." Based on feedback, women were healed from past hurts and freed for ministry; women repented of misplaced priorities; women had their vision for ministry confirmed; women were deeply touched by testimonies of what others are doing around the world in the Lord's service and women were challenged to put new talents to use in ministry.

Women of Global Action is also reaching out in Ecuador, Colombia, El Salvador, Honduras, Mexico and Guatemala. Many exciting projects are underway under the able leadership of Mercedes Dalton, who heads up *Global Action's* work for the entire continent.

Yet another conference was held in Brazil in 2007, where almost 300 women from all over Brazil gathered in the country's capitol, Brasilia, for a 3-day training conference around the theme "Praying for a Genuine Revival." Prior to the larger conference, the Regional Leaders from each part of the country held a one-day meeting to report on and plan for the *Women of Global Action* work in the nation.

Plenary sessions included, "Revival and Women Leaders," "Women as Risk-takers for God in 2007," "Prayer and Revival," "Revival and Social Action," "Revival, God's Word and Unity" and "Revival and Missions."

During the conference, intercessors prayed 24/7 for the Lord's presence and guiding through the Holy Spirit. The conference concluded with a time of worship and holy communion. Many commented on how much the training had helped them renew the vision of what God can do through women in their churches and regions.

Nancy, a recent widow, shared how devastating her husband's sudden death from a heart attack two months earlier had been. Yet, she felt God was using the training and meeting with other WOGA leaders to encourage her and better prepare her for the task He had for her.

Arab World

Different teams of women from *Global Action* have ministered in several Middle East countries, networking with Christian women there. A leadership conference held in one of those countries was the first Christian conference in that area in 800 years! Today, through partnerships and national workers, *Women of Global Action* has a strong influence in most of the Arab world.

CHAPTER 20
The Multiplication Factor

G*lobal Action* expects every program undertaken to include a multiplication component. Thus we work with church planters, churches that show growth potential and training programs that can multiply.

Addis Ababa, Ethiopia

For some time I had heard stories about the tremendous church growth in Ethiopia, and when *Global Action* was invited to come explore various ways of cooperation with one of these growing churches for the future, I was not slow to say yes.

Some years ago a few Ethiopian Christian refugee couples returned to Addis Ababa from Nairobi and began a home fellowship. Soon they rented a property and the church began to grow. After five years the church had grown to more than 12,000 members. When we were there they met four times on a Sunday in a government arena called the Dome. On Sunday morning I preached in two of the four services in the church. The arena was packed to capacity both times – more than 3,000 people in each service. The services lasted over two hours each and included a lot of Ethiopian worship singing. Many people came to the Lord for salvation or to be renewed in their walk with the Lord.

Around that time approximately 500 people were coming to know the Lord every month. To ensure that the church created "fruit that lasts," these new converts were invited to a discipleship class every Monday night. This discipleship class lasted for six months, after which the people could be baptized. Fifty new churches in Ethiopia had also been established out of this "mother church" in Addis Ababa.

What is happening in Ethiopia reminds me of the book of Acts: Orthodox people, Muslims and people with a secular background are being impacted in a miraculous way. One Muslim priest had a dream about Jesus, and because of this traveled to the church, where he had a powerful conversion. With the Koran in hand he returned to his village and preached Jesus from the Koran and the Bible. After a while the entire village came to the Lord and they replaced the crescent on the mosque with the cross!

An orthodox priest, alone on a sacred island in the middle of a lake, had a vision, with Jesus appearing before him. He was led to travel to Addis and visit the church and he too had a powerful conversion experience. Dressed in his "holy garb" he began preaching Christ with conviction. This man, fully dressed in his priestly robes, took part in the service where I spoke.

Sweden

Today Sweden is a mission field. While 32% of Europeans believe in a God "of some kind," the corresponding percentage for Sweden is 9%. The only thing that will turn Christianity around in Sweden is a show of vibrant, transformational Christianity.

That is why *Global Action* has linked hands with two denominations representing such a transformation, namely The Salvation Army (Frälsningsarmén) and *InterAct* (Evangeliska Frikyrkan).

With *InterAct* as our major partner, *Global Action* has supported church planting and church development both financially and with training. *InterAct's* goal is to plant 75 vibrant new congregations by year 2010.

Johanneskyrkan, in the city of Linköping, is a brand new church reaching out to university students. Meeting at 4 p.m. in a school cafeteria, the service started with coffee and sandwiches around circular tables. I was not sure when the service started and the coffee ended. The pastor, wearing shorts, sat on the edge of one of the tables and shared from Scripture. The audience average age was 24. Most of the 300 to 400 people attending had no church background and the new converts knew no barriers in introducing their friends to Jesus Christ.

Elimkyrkan in Stockholm is a fascinating project. A few years ago, this small, declining Baptist church of 30 people meeting in an old building decided it was time for a change. They invited a friend of mine to be the new pastor and he offered to take it on, if the small church was willing to work toward change.

And change took place! The first time I preached in this church in March 1999, half of the ground floor was filled. When I was back in September 2000, the entire ground floor was packed. In March 2001, the gallery surrounding the ground floor on three sides was full, people sat everywhere and almost all of them were young people!

The building is the most impractical church building I have ever seen in the Western world. You have to walk up two flights of stairs to come to the ground floor. The church is shaped like a shoebox standing on its side - narrow, high - and not very conducive to young people's activities. But there is a spirit of expectation, a transformational message, where professionals as well as young people have attended over the past years and found the meaning of life.

Hope for the Balkans

Imagine growing up in a world where God is nonexistent. What would it be like to face each day without the hope of eternal life? Can you see yourself there? Though political turmoil and ethnic strife have plagued parts of Eastern Europe for the last decade, Bulgaria has remained peaceful. Yet today's Bulgarians face an even bigger battle: the spiritual vacuum left by communism's godless society. Many have lost hope for a better life.

Since the end of World War II Bulgaria was under strong atheistic, communistic leadership. Bulgaria was often described as a nation that had gone farther than the Soviet Union. Persecution of the church was intense. During the Communist years many pastors spent time in prison, some became martyrs and the church struggled.

When the wall came down in 1989 the evangelical church was small. One denomination had only 900 believers 19 years ago. Today they have grown to 30,000.

At the same time the secular press and the government communicated to the Bulgarians that evangelical Christianity was a sect, with its members sitting at home on Sundays, "eating their children and drinking blood." Comments like that did not provide avenues for easy, friendly evangelism!

Since 2002 *Global Action* has invested time, staff and resources in *Hope For The Balkans*, an evangelistic outreach of historic proportions, serving to put Christ's love into action in cities and villages across Bulgaria.

How can we best describe *Hope for the Balkans?* The vision and intent was to create a set of initiatives that, in turn, would empower the church to turn the country upside down. How could doors be opened so the average Bulgarian would understand that believers are caring people, wanting to share the love of Christ through word and deed? How could the church people be re-shaped, given a new paradigm shifting from hiding in their churches to wanting to share Christ with boldness to the people around them? This was the challenge. Working hand in glove with the Evangelical Alliance of Bulgaria we learned to take new risks to make this a reality.

To be able to accomplish this, *Hope for the Balkans* concentrated on two major tracks, one internal and one external. The internal track brought together more than 800 Christian women, 65% of all the pastors in the country and approximately 1,000 youth. The team of speakers had the opportunity to challenge them to be salt and light in their own country.

The other track concentrated on public interaction with the people of Bulgaria through outreach teams in towns, villages, prisons, orphanages, universities, schools and restaurants. A marathon run across Bulgaria drew thousands of people to hear the gospel and opened the doors, for the very first time, for the evangelical church to "sit at the same table" as the mayors, police chiefs and political leaders of the cities visited, and be treated as equals.

Garbage clean-up programs, tree planting programs, as well as a set of lectures at the university about the roots and early influence of the evangelical church, preceded these days of major thrust.

While only 600 ladies were registered, more than 800 showed up and listened intently to talks about being risk-takers for God, understanding their culture, being women of prayer as well as sharing Christ in their neighborhoods.

One group of Turkish women had traveled by bus for many hours from a Bulgarian border town to attend the conference. Most had been persecuted and many were from abusive family relationships. They desperately needed prayer. As we rallied around them to pray, one woman said, "My seven-year-old daughter is very sick. I brought her blouse, please lay your hands on it and pray for her." Another woman told us, "My husband is not saved. I brought his shirt. Please pray for him." They were blessed by the prayers and we were overwhelmed by their needs!

There was also prayer for those suffering from abuse. When one of the pastors weepingly confessed how the church had been silent on this issue and asked the women for forgiveness, an indescribable groan went through the entire congregation, eventually turning into praise. One of the women leaders said, "Until now there has been no hope for Bulgaria, but now we are willing to work on, knowing there is hope!"

There were also surprises. On the opening night, the event organizers opened up the side doors to the auditorium and volunteers swept through the audience, handing out to each woman, a giant, beautiful flower decorated with a bow. It happened in such a way that this simple gesture just energized the crowd, and you could feel the joy.

More than 65% of the evangelical pastors in the country listened intently for three days as key Bulgarian communicators joined hands with Dr. Alvin Low, Galo Vasquez and me. "This conference has been the transformational watershed for the church in Bulgaria," exclaimed Rev. Teddy Opranov, the General Secretary of the Baptist Union in Bulgaria.

Some of the pastors came from extremely difficult situations. Dimitar Michev, his wife and two children (16 and 12) share one room together in a run-down house. There is no running water, and the kitchen and the toilet are outside. Ninety percent of the church's congregation are unemployed.

Rev. Pavel Ignatov, at that time superintendent for the Church of God, commented, "*Global Action* has been able to communicate in three days what it would have taken us 20 years to put on the table. During these 20 years we would have disagreed about it and fought about it, but you presented these truths in such a positive way that our pastors are ready to rally around them. This will bring unity, give us the incentive to go forward and to impact our nation with the life-changing power of the gospel. These days have been historic for the church in Bulgaria."

One of the younger pastors expressed his gratitude, "God showed me, in a personal way, the plan for spiritual growth for my church."

Some 130 social workers from various churches met for a day to listen to Gary Cox, the director of Eurovangelism, one of *Global Action's* partner organizations. Telling about his experience with compassionate church programs making an impact in Kosovo, former Yugoslavia, Chechnya and Russia, he encouraged every church in Bulgaria to do something to reach out to their neighborhoods.

When one of the Gypsy churches in Bulgaria heard about the need to minister to a poverty-stricken church on the Turkish border, this church—which itself is poor—sent its members home to gather anything of value that they could share. They came back with "the widow's mite" in the form of clothing and household items. What a lesson for us to learn! "I now have a stronger desire to help people in need without asking for a payback," commented one of the delegates, while another said, "I have now learned how evangelism goes hand- in-hand with caring for people."

For three days, approximately 1,000 Christian young people packed the hall, singing exuberantly along with Christian youth bands from Bulgaria, as well as the group *Cede* from Colorado Springs. I received the best introduction I have ever had! "Now speaks a teenager in an old man's body!" exclaimed the emcee, Nasko Lazarov when I came to the stage. During these days the young people were challenged to take the gospel to their own generation and to be people of the Word and of prayer, living holy lives and sharing their faith with boldness. Every speaker encouraged the young people to identify and pray for five of their non-Christian friends and to think about what sort of bridges were needed so the gospel could reach them.

At the dedication ceremony each delegate received six copies each of a special Scripture portion created for *Hope for the Balkans*, consisting of the books of Luke, Acts, Ephesians and Philippians with *Life Application* notes. Once again, each delegate was expected to keep one copy and share the other five with their friends.

One 17-year-old told me, "This conference has totally changed my life. I will never be the same again!" Another teenager commented, "Now I really believe there is *hope* for the Balkans. God can use us when we share the gospel with our friends."

Seven different teams ministered throughout Bulgaria during these weeks. The music team *Cede*, together with Jason Burden from *Pierced*, went to the local university one day to speak with local students. The forum had to be billed as "Life in the United States" in order to attract anyone. *Cede* started playing outside, and more and more people stopped to listen. We used a question and answer format and while the questions started off simple, they eventually moved into deeper topics of spirituality. One person asked, "We don't have much hope here in Bulgaria. Where do you get your hope?" The local interpreter was so impressed, recognizing that this was a new form of evangelization that the Bulgarian churches had not been familiar with.

In a church service in the town of Veliko Tarnovo, *Cede* led the music and Jason spoke. The team reported they felt the Holy Spirit moving powerfully in that place. As evidence, people in the audience were moved to tears. Moreover, as the team began to pray for people—asking for God's mercy on broken families, broken relationships, alcoholism, and unsaved family members—the weeping grew louder. These hurting people were moved by the grace and promises of God shared during this special time.

Later in the day, the team presented a concert at the church for about 70 youth from the area. Jason preached and gave a gospel invitation. When he asked for a public show of hands as to who was putting their faith in Christ, 18 raised their hands. Praise God for showing such mercy!

A local pastor asked a radio station to promote one of *Cede*'s concerts. The manager refused on the basis that Jason and the band were members of some evangelical "cult." But Jason and the band went down to the station, met with the manager, and prayed that God would change this cold, unrelenting man. By the end of their conversation, the man apologized, and the team heard the ads playing over a radio in a public marketplace the next day. Some 60 kids came, and many stayed afterward to talk about the Christian faith.

A women's team from Canada sensed how God had led them to the right places at the right time to minister to hurting people. How did the crowds react? At times there was laughter, as jokes brought welcome relief to what is often a dreary atmosphere of economic and social struggle in Bulgaria. At other times, there was open weeping, especially during times of prayer and intercession. As selected attendees shared stories of broken homes, unsaved family members, racial oppression, addictions and sick or handicapped children, the group prayers became a powerful time of drawing closer to God.

One afternoon the Canadian team visited the women's prison in the city of Sliven. It was a powerful experience, and the team was able to identify with their many pains. When one of the girls sang, which was followed by a translation, you could have heard a pin drop! It was difficult to say how many were saved, however, everyone stood for prayer, and there were many tears. The team prayed for the women's children. They also prayed that the prison would become a house of prayer for all nations, praying for women all over the world. Many came and embraced the team afterward.

Then one day a secular TV station in Kazanlak called and invited the 10 Canadian women for a 25-minute interview, enough time so that each woman on the team could share her story and why she was in Bulgaria. This was totally unscheduled. The host, a non-Christian lady known for her abrupt and edgy manner, was so touched by the experience that she stayed long after the interview to talk and eat with the women. The station was flooded with calls from viewers asking for more information about what they saw on TV, which opened still other doors for future ministry through the local church hosting the team.

One particular church determined that they would add a ministry to hurting women in their new facility. The decision was, in large measure, the result of their interaction with the team.

Another team met with a Gypsy pastor who called his small body of believers together in an old building without heat. When it got too cold, they moved across the street to a restaurant run by a Mafia boss who had never set foot in a church in his life! This "boss" listened in on a gospel message talking about doing right and trusting in God's provision instead of doing wrong and trusting in yourself. The pastor said that if the "boss" ever repented, the whole Mafia organization in that area might be transformed.

The wildest part of *Hope for the Balkans* was seeing what God did with the planned cross-country run. The Bulgarian people who followed this event were interested in learning more about the deeper meaning behind the run. It was billed as a Friendship Run, and it naturally led to discussions about the *Greatest Friend*.

The then 59-year old ultra-marathon runner Stan Cottrell ran 300 miles across the country in 11 days—basically a marathon a day—seeing the secular media come alive to his presence in the country. On April 12, at a pre-run press conference in Sofia, the entire group of assembled journalists, save one, got up and walked out midway through the conference when they heard the run was associated with the evangelical church. There is an unwritten rule that the press will not publish anything about the evangelical church. Several days later, however, it was clear God had other plans. With the run half over, and Stan telling people in every town and village along the way about true hope in Christ, event organizers had to rent a hall to hold up to 150 press people who were now scrambling to cover the event.

Pastors along the route could not believe what was happening, and some said this had moved Christianity forward decades in a single week. People who would otherwise never enter a church or pause long enough to even speak with a Christian stopped to listen.

In North America, we tend to address evangelism "head on," that is, we try to get a direct conversation going about the gospel in the shortest possible period of time. In Bulgaria, where evangelical Christianity is viewed as a cult, this is not effective. Here, it is absolutely critical that Christians establish a relationship of trust, first, before presenting the gospel. Otherwise, people are conditioned simply to walk away or tune Christians out.

It is remarkable that Stan's run and the work of the teams served to build relationships quickly, opening doors for presentations of the gospel – sometimes right away, but, just as often, later.

For example, as Stan was meeting with the Mayor of Kazanlak, he mentioned that he had a friend in Washington D.C. who was a general in the U.S. Army. Stan quoted the general as saying, "One of the roles of a real leader is to keep hope alive." The Mayor turned to Stan and said, "Tell your friend in Washington that a former Bulgarian general agrees with him." An important connection was made with a high-ranking official, one that church leaders can use later to open doors for various ministry opportunities. At the end of the run, Stan was front page news in most national newspapers and was the first evangelical Christian to be featured on the national TV program "Good Morning, Bulgaria."

On the final Sunday, the Orthodox Palm Sunday, a capacity crowd filled the Palace of Culture Grand Hall in the center of the city. This was the first time in more than 10 years Christians had filled this hall. Church members in the city had invited their non-Christian neighbors and the gospel was clearly presented in music and word, all by Bulgarian musicians and speakers.

Stan Cottrell ran in to finish his marathon and shared his personal testimony with gusto! "I was giving all I had for business and running, until one day I simply ran out of myself...but I ran into Jesus and he transformed my life!"

As the grand finale drew to a close and everyone stood up to sing the hymn *God Bless Bulgaria*, there were few dry eyes in the audience. When people left they were presented with two items: A Scripture portion and an invitation to a church service on Easter, listing the churches in each city.

Two days later one of the Baptist pastors commented, "This is unbelievable. It has never happened. In the last two days I have had 18 phone calls from people I do not know asking me what time our services are held!"

Never in 40 years of ministry have I been part of anything that so totally has impacted a nation so quickly and where you can sense a real spirit of transformation, no matter whom you turn to talk to. *Hope for the Balkans* began as an idea, blossomed into a dream and a vision and became a reality far greater than I could ever have prayed or hoped for.

Bulgaria Revisited

It did not stop with *Hope for the Balkans 2002*. It continued with *Hope for Bulgaria*. Year after year, teams and I returned to minister in Bulgaria. In the streets, in institutions, in orphanages, on college campuses as well as in prison, *Hope for Bulgaria* team members shared the Good News through music and testimony.

The power of God's Word became very evident as Scriptures, such as the specially prepared *Hope Book* (Gospel of Luke, Acts, Ephesians and Philippians with Life Application notes), *My First Bible* in Bulgarian for the smaller children, and other material were strategically distributed.

One small team ministered among Bulgarian Muslims, Turkish Muslims, and Gypsy groups in the southern part of Bulgaria's mountains. Together with local pastors and a Bulgarian interpreter, they visited small churches, home churches and orphanages where they shared the gospel in a variety of ways.

Risk-Taker for God

Dan Simmons, the team leader reported, "After we shared the message, we were asked to pray for their needs. While sharing the message only took 15 minutes, people had so many needs that praying for them took almost three hours!"

In 2003 Stan Cottrell did it again! Running a marathon a day, for 11 straight days, he covered the 330 mile distance from Burgas by the Black Sea to Sofia. The weather changed every day: Heavy rains, fog, sleet, snow, blizzard and gorgeous sunshine. The churches saw this as a tremendous opportunity to witness to people who would never set foot inside a church.

Thousands of people came out to run with Stan along the route. Each was given a specially prepared booklet, sharing Stan's life and testimony. In it, the people could read:

> There was a time when I ran only for myself and, hopefully, to have my name written in the sports record books. I ran because I thought running would bring me meaning, significance and fulfillment. I thought running would make me complete and whole. But I learned, as so many millions before me, I am not here for Stan's glory but for God's glory! I learned a person cannot run to God until they have first run out of his- or herself.
>
> I had run out of myself, and in my own strength I could not solve life ahead. But I found that there is a God, greater than the Universe, who cares for me personally. He loved me so much that He sent his Son Jesus Christ to communicate it to me.
>
> Earlier I had heard and read about him, that he came to Earth as a baby, lived, did miracles, was crucified by the Romans, died and rose again. It was just a story to me.
>
> But now I ran into His loving embrace!
>
> Empty handed and out of breath I understood that because He is alive He forgave me my past, filled my emptiness and made me a new person. I can have daily fellowship with Him. He is my best friend.
>
> Today He gives me more than physical strength to run. He gives me spiritual strength to live, and I know of no greater joy than to share that fact with you.

Did they respond? Overwhelmingly! In every city Stan ran through, crowds gathered to listen to his testimony and to receive the booklet about his encounter with Jesus Christ.

In 2002, in the city of Kritchim, Elisabeth, a young pregnant lady ran with Stan. She was delivering eggs from house to house, but she put her egg cart aside and as she ran she panted, "This is good for me, this is good for the baby, this is good for Bulgaria!"

The following year Stan shared this story and found out that she was a pastor's daughter. Her determination became a symbol for the Church and the people of Bulgaria. One person can make a difference! During his visit in 2003, Stan met with the mayor in Kritchim, with Elisabeth and her baby beside him, sharing how we all can make a difference. As Stan ran out of Kritchim, he ran with the baby on his arm, and Elisabeth next to him.

The wife of a pastor who was attending the pastor's conference the first year came along to sing a solo. Before she began singing she turned to me on the platform and exclaimed, "Why aren't the wives invited? After all, we do 75% of the work!"

The following year we answered her prayer. Two hundred pastors and their spouses each attended three-day training programs in Bulgaria's former ancient capital Veliko Tarnovo and also in the city of Burgas. During those events, we took the opportunity to pray for the pastoral couples, which was an extremely moving experience for them and for us.

"This has been the most helpful and practical training session I have ever been to," said one pastor. "I can apply what I have learned in my church. The only question I have: When will you people from *Global Action* come back and do this again? We need you."

With tears streaming down their faces, a pastoral couple confided in me about their loneliness and pain in ministry. "We have been ready to quit, but your sessions have encouraged us to stay on working where we are, serving the Lord."

"In our youth group we have some sexual problems. In our culture we cannot talk about these things. You helped me see how I can deal with it. Thank you for listening to our problems and giving us solutions."

"If you want to be blessed...go to Bulgaria!" That sums up the visit of the two youth teams from the Denver area who spent two weeks ministering to young people. Through concerts, outreach to orphanages, Gypsy villages, youth groups, and even a denominational soccer tournament, the message of Jesus Christ reached children and young people. Not surprisingly, the team members themselves had a fresh encounter with the Lord. This is what some of them said after their outreach:

"Visiting the Gypsy villages was the most eye-opening experience I have ever had." "I have resolved to go back to Denver and serve those around me with all that I am." "It has changed my life. I am excited to see what God has in store for me next." "I have learned that I need to let go and let God do the work and not get so caught up with trying to think everything through." "This trip has changed everything: how I look at priorities and people." "The biggest thing I learned was servanthood. I never met so many people who just want to serve others." "Forty minutes in the Gypsy village church changed my life forever!"

A team from Canada traveled across Bulgaria in nine days, visiting prisons, schools, orphanages, institutions and holding women's meetings and church services. The team leader, Gwen McVicker from Vancouver, Canada, wrote a *Prayer Journal for Suffering Women*, which was published in Bulgarian.

Kathy Smorodin from the team told us, "I have found on this trip that God meets me at the most unexpected moments. When we were in Pazardjyk we had a whirlwind sharing our presentation on God's heart for suffering women. After the service we stood in a long line outside the church to greet everyone. It was freezing cold and windy. There was only one lady left straggling behind.

"One lady came up to me with tears streaming down her face. She spoke softly as she related the story of the violated and abused woman. 'I *am* that woman!' she said. We held each other and prayed. After praying, she lifted her head and made eye contact for the first time. I could see some hope there. It was a short encounter. She kept looking over her shoulder – I suspect to see if she was being watched. God broke my heart for all those who are 'that woman.' May they find freedom in Christ. May they learn of His gentle love."

While the men were meeting for a three-day conference in Sofia, a Prayer Day for women was held in two locations - one in Sofia and one in a nearby Gypsy village. This was the first time that women from different denominations had come together to pray for men in Bulgaria, their families and the issues they face.

Emily Voorhies shared from the Sofia location, "More than 100 women came together in a church in Sofia for a day of prayer. Throughout the day, the women were introduced to specific prayer topics, which led into a time of corporate and small-group prayer. Praise and worship times were interspersed throughout."

One participant shared, "We have never done anything like this. I believe this is the beginning of bringing women together from different churches to pray. We will see God transforming our husbands, children, fathers and brothers because we prayed for them."

One of the biggest challenges of the church is the absence of men. At best, no church has more than 25% men, and often they are not very active. Until now, there had not been any direct men's ministry and a conference just for men was unheard of.

We tried ministering to men and it worked! Six hundred men, packed into the Palace of Culture, finished three days of fellowship, music and teaching, standing up with their hands over their hearts, making a 10-point commitment to become men of faith and honor. There was hardly a dry eye in the audience!

The conference began with Stan Cottrell running in for the final "leg" of his run across Bulgaria. The message of salvation was proclaimed as the foundation for any man's life and 40 men committed their lives to Jesus Christ on the opening night.

During the sessions, men from all over Bulgaria were challenged to become better family men, faithful husbands, people of character and integrity and to learn to serve through their churches.

Stan challenged the audience to do the impossible. As he went out in the audience and picked out a tiny friend who is severally physically-challenged (and works with a program in the church for the physically-challenged), everyone was moved. Stan sat on the floor and shared how he was so small himself as a child and was told he would not amount to anything. Stan finished by illustrating that this man was the tallest man in the audience!

Both in the introduction and the closing address the men were reminded of what it means to be men of faith and honor. A booklet called *Ten Principles for a Godly Man* was distributed to all participants, and its principles were referred to in session after session.

Rev. George Carr from Baltimore spoke in a soul-searching way about unity between brothers, pastors and denominations. At the end of his message, he invited all pastors and denominational leaders to come forward, form a circle and place their arms on each other's shoulders. Then he invited all the participants to stand around these pastors and pray for new unity and love among them.

One of the pastors said, "I have never had any contact with some of the pastors. Even if I knew of them, it was odd to be in the same room as them. Now the walls are broken down, and we want to see how we can work together to bring the Kingdom forward in our part of Bulgaria."

Wherever I have traveled during my many visits to Bulgaria, I encountered stories of changed lives:

"One church in Sliven, by no means a wealthy church, has planted 25 daughter churches in Gypsy villages around the region. The gypsies are at the lowest economic level in Bulgaria. The church in Sliven has foregone a nicer home church building in deference to providing physical, emotional and spiritual nourishment in the name of Jesus to the poorest of the poor."

"Although my group only spent a little time in the Gypsy village today, my heart was filled with thanksgiving for a ministry that reaches out to the group that is the target of so much prejudice in Europe.

"Every time I have been to Eastern Europe and Russia, I have noticed that Gypsies are ostracized and treated like animals by a large portion of the population. Yet Jesus desires their salvation and a relationship with them. I think that Jesus has a special place for them in His heart, as they are treated as He was treated on earth."

My friend and supporting partner Art Cyphers told me, "In Veliko Tarnovo, we went up to *Czaravets*, the fortress high above the city, where the ancient palace of the Kings of Bulgaria was located. For centuries, proclamations and commands were sent out across Bulgaria from there.

"We were there to pray for the city and to proclaim a new King over Bulgaria – Christ Jesus – and to call upon the Lord to encourage and strengthen His church throughout Bulgaria. We prayed for unity and boldness among the factions of the church. We prayed for the Church to carry Jesus, the hope of Bulgaria, to every group and every person in Bulgaria.

"It was a proclamation to begin the harvest because the fields of Bulgaria are ripe. We prayed that the Lord of the harvest would send workers from inside and outside Bulgaria to complete the task together."

Michelle Swanson from Colorado Springs made this observation, "The Bulgarian Christians stated they *must* pray to God for *everything*, because they have nothing...they must depend on Him. As American Christians, I wonder if we have too much, if we do not depend on ourselves first and then on God, if it does not work out. My prayer is that I can say as Paul that I can live in every circumstance (Phil 4:12), but if not, God will place me in the circumstances where I can and will fully depend on Him."

One Sunday morning in Sofia, I met with the former local communist leader, who had come to Christ through the Alpha outreach program in the church. As the training started she made clear to all that she was attending the course to protect her daughter who was a participant, but her own "heart door" was solidly closed to any gospel message. However, the Lord penetrated her hardened door, and she was baptized. In the same service where I met her, several people accepted Christ when they listened to the message of Christ riding into Jerusalem on Palm Sunday.

Bulgaria has many needs: training for lay people, women, leaders, pastors as well as spouses. Training programs impacted lay people in cities with such exotic names as Pleven, Levski, Veliko Tarnovo, Sliven, Kardjali and Kazanlak. An email from Sliven weeks after one of my visits, in broken English explains, "We still talking about your preach and, believe me, this is a truth." Marriages were healed, broken relationships restored, encouragement for future service given.

One evangelical church leader explained, "Without *Global Action's* participation in Bulgaria over the past years we, the evangelical churches, could never have moved forward as we have: working together, taking initiatives and impacting our country. Please continue what you are doing!"

Touch the World Outreach Teams

For 20 years I had attempted to form short-term outreach teams for ministry, but there were always leadership staff who were against the idea, whether at *LBI* or *IBS*, so I had given up. But when *Global Action* was launched we took on this idea.

I am well aware that any team going from one country to another will not be able to accomplish much in a two-week period. But I know the enormous way it can change the people who serve. Fifteen years after people have been on an outreach trip, they often end up as the leaders in their churches, the best mission givers, and in pastoral or missionar roles.

The first few years, teams went to Ukraine, Rumania an Honduras. The summer of 2001 we had more teams than ever before.

One of the teams went to Sweden to reach young people with th love of Christ during an annual Mardi Gras-type festival in the city c Kristianstad. The outreach featured a variety of activities, including a 30 foot climbing wall, darts, basketball, face painting, Christian concert and a "living room" setting where the team members spent hours simpl talking and praying with whomever was interested.

This outreach, collectively called *Frizon* (meaning the free zone took place daily from 2 p.m. until midnight. From midnight to 3 a.m the team served coffee and *bullar* (rolls/pastries) to help people sober u after an evening of drinking and partying. When the festivities were ove Kristianstad Festival organizers as well as police and security personne reported that *Frizon* had a calming effect on that area of the city durin the festival.

The team's presence gave young Swedes a reason to talk wit "the Americans," enabling them to see that Christians have fun too an that interacting with "them" isn't so bad! Without *Frizon*, this uniqu opportunity to learn about each other and Jesus Christ would never hav happened.

One of the first summers we existed, two teams went to Ukrain to run summer camps for kids from a variety of backgrounds. Followin his Bible lesson on perseverance, team member Barry Fluth invited kid who wanted to commit their lives to Christ to sign their names on hi *Global Action* polo shirt using a special marker. About 25 of the childre and young people there did so. Two 15-year old boys, Gayk and Nik, cam up to him and said they weren't ready to do that yet but wanted more tim to talk about this and consider it. On the last full day of camp, the boy appeared at Barry's door and said they were ready to sign.

The team also held discussion sessions each afternoon with th 25 teenagers at the camp, allowing them to ask whatever questions the wanted. In addition, at bedtime they met with children from each age grouy to tell Bible (or other) stories in a further effort to communicate God's lov to them. Some of their questions--and responses--were profound.

No one can go on a mission trip without being personally touche and motivated for the Kingdom of God. Many experience a deeper wall with the Lord. Here are some of the comments from *Touch the World* team members in the past:

"My perspective has exploded. I see things so differently. The experiences here in a different culture have opened my eyes to the great needs of others! My spoiled American viewpoint needed to be challenged. I bless the Lord for a new perspective."

"I feel humbled and grateful that God has used me. It adds another chapter of the amazing provision God has been in my life."

"It was an opportunity to be utterly dependant on the Lord, and rest in his provision – be that in speaking or traveling. Many times I was at a loss, without words or tangible things to offer. He blessed and provided in every instance."

"It has been a wonderful opportunity to 'join' God in the work he has started and to see how the historical culture of the country affects the church and religious freedom in general."

"I am a better person because of the experiences I have had in Bulgaria. I have seen the love of God displayed in many ways. I have been in the company of great saints. I believe that my faith has grown."

"It has been a deeply moving and eye-opening experience. I can't wait till the next trip."

"The worship in the different churches has had great effect. The oneness of the believers has been outstanding. I am reminded that there is much more that binds us together than that separates us – language and culture could not keep us apart."

The past few years teams have continually ministered in Kenya, Rwanda, Burundi, the Middle East, Sweden, Moldova, Ukraine, India, El Salvador, Honduras and Guatemala.

Teams are not just for teenagers. I believe every person in a church should go on a mission trip at least once in their lifetime. The teams that have been most effective are those that include both grandmothers/grandfathers and teenagers! A church is strengthened when its people go on teams. If you have never been on a team, the time is now!

Mentoring Moments

As *Global Action* conducts leadership seminars and conferences, there are always some people who come up to me, wanting more information, copies of notes or advice on various topics.

That is one of the reasons *Global Action* launched *Mentoring Moments* in January of 2000. *Mentoring Moments* is a personal letter from me sent to Christian leaders and pastors around the world. This letter is mailed or emailed every four weeks to approximately 500 leaders. We never dreamed that this letter would have such an impact.

One district superintendent from Africa wrote, "Every time your letter comes, the pastoral leadership team gathers to study it carefully. Last time you wrote about small groups. Our churches have never had cell groups, but after praying and fasting for three days, we decided to go ahead and implement your suggestion."

Another leader emailed me, "I was just ready to quit my ministry altogether, when your letter arrived. Its message was just for me that day, and I rededicated my life, my ministry and my family to the Lord. Thank you for being there for me."

CHAPTER 21
A Funny Thing Happened on the Way Around the World

I don't normally talk about the fun and challenges of international travel, but some stories are worth telling.

Early Days

My first travel incident started with a lie! On my first major international trip, moving to Britain, the entire trip was booked by train from Stockholm through Denmark, Germany and Holland for fellow student Gun and me. The booking continued by ferry from Hoek-van-Holland to Harwich in England, and then on by another train to London. As we arrived at Hoek-van-Holland, I was denied entry to the ferry, being told my ticket was for a day trip, not a night trip. I could not get on the ferry and had nowhere to go. I pleaded with the ticket master in very broken English, "…but my wife just went on…"

He probably had heard that lie before, so he just waved his hand. The idea of walking the streets of Hoek-van-Holland while waiting for the next day's ferry, trusting my bags were on the ferry, but not being too sure, created some real fear of international travel. I was told I could embark on the next ferry at six the following morning. Through the nights I walked the streets frightened and confused. "Who will meet me at the other end? Will anyone meet me now that I am delayed?" I learned the hard way to cope with the fact that things almost always go wrong when you travel internationally. Arriving at Liverpool Street Station in London the following evening, there was someone present from the Training College to take care of me after all.

While a student in Britain, I was sent out with other students to Doreen's home church and stayed with her parents, along with a fellow student, Tony Evans who was slightly taller than I. As we were shown the bedroom I gasped. We were both 6 foot 3 inches or taller, and the bed looked like it was 5 by 5. I did not sleep much that night, while Tony who was all arms and legs all night, did. I had not shared a bed with anyone but my father, and that was at least 10 years earlier.

Travel was a daily routine while working for Youth for Christ in Britain. When Doreen and I were first married, I had no driver's license, so most travel was by train. Even after I learned to drive on the "wrong" side of the road, train travel was somehow cheaper and less stressful. Almost every weekend I would be gone, speaking at a YFC rally on the Saturday and churches of all kinds on the Sunday. During those visits I always stayed with church members or friends.

There was the old widower in Sandy, where I stayed for a weekend. He was quite a miser, so I had to share a room with him because our joint body heat would improve the heating conditions in the freezing house. For breakfast, he toasted two dry slices of bread in front of the open coal fire in the kitchen, burning them beyond recognition. You preach with gusto after a Saturday night and a breakfast like that!

And then there was the visit to the very north of England in the middle of the winter. Nothing can be colder than inside an unheated house in the middle of the winter in Britain. It was very late when I arrived at the home of two elderly sisters. I had been on the train, lugging film projectors and my suitcase and I was absolutely exhausted. Having been shown where the bedroom and bathroom were, I went into the room and threw myself on the bed. Right then I heard it - the sound of the rather old and dried out rubber hot-water bottle bursting between the sheets as my weight hit the bed. That was a very wet and sleepless night, on one hand trying to dry out the bed with towels, and on the other hand attempting to sleep in the small dry portion!

A Funny Thing Happened on the Way Around the World

In Africa

As soon as I had been appointed the international leader for *Living Bibles International* I began my travels to Africa. Having never been there before, the African leader thought it would be good to give me a cultural experience, and, instead of putting me in a hotel, stuck me in a white hut with a thatched roof out in one of the game parks.

There was no glass in the windows, only wooden shutters, and within minutes the whitewashed walls and the cement floor, seemed to crawl with a rich variety of bugs. I have never been fond of spiders or lizards, and these spiders could run so fast that there was no way my shoe could kill them. I killed a few bugs, but they were immediately replaced by new ones. I thought I would never be able to sleep. I ate a quick dinner, downed two sleeping tablets, and fell asleep with bugs all around me!

On one of my long visits to Africa, Betta Mengistu and I first traveled to Brazil. Landing at Rio de Janeiro airport, the pilot suddenly pulled the plane up in a steep climb. After a few minutes, a rather shaken captain came on the intercom. "There was a small plane landing right under us and we were feet from colliding with each other!" We thanked God for His protection.

Having left Rio de Janeiro we arrived in Dakar, Senegal, and continued across the western countries of Liberia, Ivory Coast, Ghana and Nigeria. It was Betta's first visit to this part of Africa. It was in the middle of the night in Dakar and the airport was crowded with Muslims ready to fly to Mecca. We found a corner of the floor and tried to sleep, surrounded by the pilgrims. The noise was horrendous, the heat overbearing and we had nothing to eat or drink. Betta found a shop selling cokes and ordered one. But when he found the price was five dollars, he refused to drink it!

When we arrived in Ghana, we stayed at a Boy Scout camp outside Accra for a Bible translation conference. The food was meager and the water was not clean. Mosquitoes were everywhere at night, but we had mosquito nets. The first morning when I realized my net had a huge hole where my arm was, I counted over 60 bites on my arm. After traveling for many days we arrived in Nairobi, Kenya, staying in a small hotel at the foot of the Ngong Hills. That night my malaria broke out, and I wished I could have died. For many years after that, I would break out in new attacks every year, at regular intervals.

In the early 80's I was traveling in Ghana to meet our translation teams. There was a famine in the country, and no food was available at all. A chicken would sell for over $150 dollars. Betta Mengistu and I stayed in a run-down hotel in Accra where no food apart from one bottle of liquid a day was allotted each room. We had some canned foods and beef jerky with us to stay energized for the week.

As we traveled up to the city of Ho (which is not where Santa lives), the roads were so bad that the car battery jumped out of its socket and fell to the ground! Fortunately it did not break. When I met with the translation team in a small room at a church building, I exclaimed, "How can you be so calm? You have no food, you are starving and the heat is unbearable!" They looked at me and responded, "Our physical hunger is nothing compared to the spiritual hunger of our people! We have to carry on with our work!"

When we returned to the capital, one of the board members invited me for dinner in his home. That afternoon, he and his wife sold a piece of antique furniture from their home so they could afford to serve us some scrawny chickens that night.

Traveling in Nigeria is always a challenge, and during the 70's and 80's my visits there were particularly difficult. Sitting in the domestic terminal waiting for our flight to Enugu, where our national office was, I noticed an airline officer collecting the boarding passes from the passengers. Suddenly someone yelled, "Our plane is number three in that row!" and everyone rushed through the door out onto the tarmac toward the plane. As we approached the plane, the officer was there with the boarding passes, selling them back to us for a few dollars apiece!

On another journey, we made an unexpected landing at Port Harcourt. Suddenly a chief and his entourage of 15 people boarded, and the flight attendants hand-picked 15 passengers, asked them to leave the plane and gave the seats to the chief and his friends.

Leaving Nigeria was always a battle. Once, Dave Foster, Betta Mengistu and I stood in line at the check-in counter for hours. Nigerians came in, pushed ahead of the line and just went right to the clerk at the check-in counter. Finally Dave asked one of them how he managed to get in front of everybody. The answer was astounding, "This is easy. I have a brother behind the counter," explained the Nigerian, grinning from ear to ear. "For 20 dollars you can have a brother too!"

A Funny Thing Happened on the Way Around the World

As you entered Nigeria you had to fill in a currency form, with every foreign currency counted and noted. When you left, the form was collected and any money changed had to be noted, and receipts provided. However, the Nigerian customs officers enjoyed counting the money, then pocketing a good part of the dollars for themselves. "How can we keep our numbers straight on the form, when you take the money!" we complained.

On another visit, I came to the counter to check in. I had a confirmed ticket and the flight was on time. When it was my turn, the agent simply said, "You need to pay 100 dollars if you want your boarding pass." My first instinct was to say, "Never!" and I expressed it loud and clear. "OK," said the agent, "the next flight leaves in three days! Next!" I had just stayed in a horrible dump in Lagos, where the cost was $150 a night, the bed sheets were dirty and there was no room service. I realized I would not win the Nigeria money game however hard I tried, so I paid my 100 dollars and received my boarding card.

Driving on the country roads between the various cities in Nigeria was always an adventure. Every fifteen minutes there would be road blocks and police patrols. Our national director, Jeremiah Okorie, explained, "You have to be careful to determine if the roadblock is manned by police or bandits. At best the bandits shoot you!" "What do you mean? What can be the worst?" "They just steal the car and leave you on the road where you will be attacked by the wild animals and die slowly," he gently explained.

As we neared the next roadblock I wondered what would happen. We were properly stopped. The policeman had a machine gun in one hand and a half empty bottle of whiskey in the other. He leaned through the window on the passenger side where I was sitting, his whisky breath filling the front seats of the car. "Who are you and where are you going?" he asked with the machine gun solidly placed right at my temple. Things like this really increase your prayer life! Jerry's calm words in the Igbo language eased the pressure on my temple, and he waved us on.

Trucks and cars drove on both the left and right and in the middle of the street as well. Often there were religious slogans painted on the cars and trucks, like "Hallelujah" and "Praise the Lord." Even buildings had Christian connotations, but often not making much sense, like "Jesus saves beer bar" and "Bring down the strongholds Maternity home."

Being a Swede, I was eager that we should be on time for every service. As we traveled to one of the Nigerian cities to release the Igbo

Bible, I had seen the flyers listing the release ceremony times and locations in bold print. "The service is at 4 p.m.," I said nervously as Jerry drove us around showing us the town, and the watch-hands already pointed at 4:30. "Don't worry," Jerry smiled, "if you get there this early, you will only find a few chickens around in the hall!" "But how will you know when the meeting starts?" I responded exasperated. "Oh, that is easy," Jerry explained. "If it says 4 p.m. that means it starts at 6 p.m. If we want it to start at 5 p.m., we will say 5 p.m. Prompt. If it has to start at 4 p.m., it would say 4 p.m. Prompt. Prompt. All of us know that!"

In Eastern Europe

In November 1975 I was heading to Romania to find a Bible translator. I had the name of a Baptist church in Bucharest and the name and address of a lady there. In those days there were no maps, and you did not dare to have any paperwork on your body that could create problems for the people you had to visit - so you had to memorize everything.

That Sunday morning I sat in the Budapest airport with one of my colleagues, and waited for my propeller Russian-built, Romanian Airlines Tarom flight. Having not had breakfast and knowing we would miss lunch, we went to the restaurant to eat before the flight. We were handed a very fancy menu. I pointed at one item and was told, "We don't have that today." After five items and the same answer, I was exasperated. "So what do you have on this menu?" I retorted a bit angrily. "We have nothing on that menu," answered the waitress without a smile. "This is the only thing we serve," and she pointed to a sign on the wall in Hungarian!

Having eaten my fill of Hungarian goulash, we boarded the plane. There was a man with live chickens in a basket. There were not enough seats, so some were standing in the aisle. As the plane barely made it off the runway it started to snow. As soon as we passed the Romanian border the plane began circling. Finally the pilot announced, "There is a bad snowstorm in Bucharest and we cannot land, we will land in Arad instead." By this time I had come down with one of my typical migraines.

As soon as we landed we were shuffled into a room with armed guards standing at the door. I was desperate to vomit, as that is what usually happens when I have a bad migraine. I went to the guard and signaled for the toilet. Not a muscle moved in his face. However, when vomited on his boot, he let me go to the bathroom. Then they herded u to a hotel, where we slept for four hours before waking us at 3 a.m. to take us back to the airport. We sat there all day. That night buses took us to the railroad station. By Tuesday morning we rolled into Bucharest railroad station, and it was still snowing heavily.

We tried to get our bearings and set out to find the old lady. When we finally came to her door, she looked shocked to see two tall gentlemen. I was wearing my Russian fur hat, and that could have added to the confusion and fear. However, she went inside and came back with her daughter who spoke some English. We enjoyed soup and bread for lunch that was like manna from heaven!

Through their cryptic English we learned about another place to visit that night, and taking the old rickety trolley bus, we made it to an apartment in the outskirts of the city. When we walked in to the apartment there were almost thirty people gathered there for an English class!

The teacher asked us who we were and I mentioned we were pastors from northern Europe. Immediately they asked me to share about heaven. "These are tough days here," one of the men said, "and we want to know what the real future is going to be like."

After I had finished, the English teacher said to me, "Can I talk to you about Bibles?" I nodded, thinking he wanted us to supply them with Scriptures. Having worked with people like Brother Andrew's organization Open Doors and others, we always tried to meet the demand if we could get hold of enough Bibles in Eastern European languages.

He leaned toward me and whispered, "Some time ago someone brought me a *Living Bible* from the West. I have read it and it has blessed me immensely. I would love to see a translation like that in my country. You would not know anyone working with this translation, would you?"

I chuckled, and told him why we were there. That night we put the entire translation team together, as most of the people in the room were pastors or teachers from various denominations.

Suddenly the pastor from the church we had planned to visit Sunday night, had we been on time, spoke up. "I am so glad you came today and not last Sunday," he explained. "There were several people from the secret police in the service, and you would certainly have been questioned and some of us may have been arrested if you had approached us." There and then we thanked the Lord for His perfect timing and provision.

When we began working with this translation team, several of my volunteers traveled in with materials and brought manuscripts out, so I did not have to go myself every other month. However, now and then I did take the trip.

The team had requested that I bring a commentary on the book of Romans and so I found a heavy commentary called *Romans Verse by Verse*. My thought was that if I hid it in my suitcase, the customs officers would surely find it, so instead I stuck it right on top of my clothes and shut the lid.

Upon arrival to Bucharest airport I was summoned by the customs officer to open my case. My knees shook and my hands trembled, as I prayed the Bible smuggler's prayer, "You who can make blind eyes see please make seeing eyes blind." Eagerly the customs officer lifted the book out of the suit case and examined the title, while I became convinced I would be arrested, or at best be returning home on the next flight.

As he held the book close to his face, he exclaimed, "Romance... romance. I like love stories!" "So do I, sir, so do I," I quickly responded as he shoveled the book back in my suitcase, closed the lid and saluted!

Driving in Eastern Europe was always a challenge. Living just a ferry ride across the Baltic from Poland, I often would take a Board member or a friend, and drive to countries like Poland, Czechoslovakia, Ukraine and even Romania. The police loved to stop a car with foreign license plates, and although Sweden was neutral and on good terms with both East and West, we were always taken for American spies. My friend Dave Foster had taught me a good lesson. Whenever he was held up by border guards, he would quote Macbeth to them in the Queen's English like "Is that a dagger I see before me?"

I was not well versed with Shakespeare, but I knew all the old revival hymns in Swedish, and many a times when the police pulled us over for no other reason than to make it difficult for us, I would step out of the car, and in my loudest voice in Swedish and with a lot of gestures, quote all stanzas of several revival songs. After a few verses, they would wave us on in exasperation!

When the war was ending in the Balkan Peninsula in 1994, I headed for Croatia to visit our translation team and to meet with the Board. Every building I saw as I drove from Zagreb to Osijek had been damaged. As we came to a town where there was an orphanage where we had provided Children's Bibles, we drove down the main street. Every building was riddled with bullet holes. Windows were broken. Half of the roofs were missing. As we slowed, a tank, with the gun tower pointing directly at us, rolled out from one of the side streets. It was like watching a World War II movie, but I realized it was not on a set, it was real.

Arriving in Osijek, which is right on the border to Serbia, I was taken to a high-rise hotel. Stepping into my hotel room, I realized that the entire wall above the headboard was riddled with bullets. I slept fairly low down in the bed that night!

In May 2000 Alvin Low and I traveled through Eastern Europe together on trains, in cars, in buses and by plane. The day following the pastors' conference in Novi Sad, Serbia we had to travel to Osijek, Croatia. A few years ago, this was a complete war zone, and travel was still difficult. We took the public bus from Novi Sad to Vokuvar and this was one of the most memorable bus rides in my life! First we crossed a temporary bridge over the river, viewing the three bridges that had been blown to pieces by the NATO bombing, completely crippling this city, which is situated on both sides of the river.

We traveled on lonely roads through a completely devastated countryside - evidence of the NATO war, the Serbian-Bosnian war or the Croat-Serbian war. In one town of 12,000 people there was not one undamaged house standing. Windows, roofs or half of the house was missing, yet people had begun returning to live there.

At the border checkpoint - consisting of a lonely road, two guards and a beam across the road - Alvin was held for an hour. While he had an American passport, he is of Chinese origin and was born and raised in Penang, Malaysia. He was not allowed to stay in the country but neither was he allowed to leave. Prison suddenly did not seem too far from reality. I was called down from the bus to prove to the guards that we were not Jehovah's Witnesses! They are outlawed in Serbia. Finally they let us go to the relief of the 60 or so Serbians on the bus, who had waited for these two foreigners to be cleared across the border.

Five minutes later we came to the Croatian border and the Croatian passport police came on board and collected Alvin's passport again. The people on the bus began to hiss and we felt really awkward. After a few minutes it was returned but we were told to get off the bus, remove our suitcases and have them searched thoroughly on a table outside the bus, while all the people on the bus watched us through the windows. "Airing your dirty laundry in public" now has an absolutely new meaning for me, because that is exactly what the guards did, holding up every piece of clothing, including underwear, for everyone to see!

It was quite a job to convince the customs officials what my sleeping machine was all about, so finally I placed the mask over my face, while people on the bus looked like they had seen Darth Vader from Star Wars.

The bus stopped in Vokuvar, Croatia, a town completely destroyed in the Serb-Croat war. Rebuilding had started but it was still a devastating scene. We were met by the local pastor of the evangelical church, who fed us coffee and sandwiches, before we continued by car to Osijek.

A few days later we were ready to travel home from Riga, Latvia via Stockholm, Chicago and Denver. We were eager to get home for two reasons: Alvin's daughter was graduating two days later, and I was only going to be home for five days before returning to Europe again. Our flight into Chicago was delayed half an hour because of thunderstorms, which is nothing unusual this time of the year.

Initially, our continuing flight was listed as being "on time." After an hour, the board suddenly showed it was delayed and I went to stand in line to check what the problem was. I stood in line for nearly two hours to be told the plane had been diverted to Minneapolis, but there was no doubt it would come to Chicago and fly on to Denver.

After a further half an hour the flight simply disappeared from the board with no explanation, never to show up again. I went back in line, waited another two hours, and found it had been cancelled. Quickly I grabbed the phone and called United. I managed to get both of us rebooked on the direct flight to Colorado Springs leaving at 8 p.m. (8 hours after we had arrived at O'Hare) but half an hour later that flight showed as cancelled on the board as well.

I called United again and spoke for almost an hour with a rather irate customer service agent, who pointed out that she could not put me on a flight until Saturday at the earliest, but most likely not until Sunday. This was Thursday afternoon! After I pointed out that this was unacceptable, she came back with a possibility of flying me, but not Alvin, the following day to Fargo, North Dakota by United Express, then to Denver and on to Colorado Springs, making this a full 14 hour trip. I declined, knowing it snows in North Dakota this time of the year!

After talking to a supervisor I managed to force them to switch carriers. All carriers were full, but after a further half an hour on the hone, we were told there was a reservation for us at 6:40 a.m. the following morning from Midway Airport, flying Frontier Airlines. However we would have to have our tickets reissued at the 1K United desk.

The 1K desk was closed in our terminal so we took our heavy carry-on bags and moved to the next terminal. The line there was over an hour long, but finally our tickets were reissued. In the meantime I sent Alvin to book a hotel, knowing that everything would be fully booked. We were informed that all hotels from O'Hare to the Indiana border were already booked. Alvin somehow managed to get a reservation through his travel agent at a Comfort Inn, two miles from the airport and was given the street address. It was supposed to have a shuttle service.

We waited at the shuttle curb for ½ an hour. No bus. We then called the hotel, where someone told us that they had no shuttle service. After half an hour in the taxi line we gave the address to the taxi driver. He promptly drove us to Comfort Inn, dropped us off and took off in a hurry. Inside the hotel we were informed that this was not the Comfort Inn at the address we had given the taxi driver. The hotel address we had been given was 1 hour north of the airport and Midway is 45 minutes south of O'Hare!

This Comfort Inn was fully booked, but the lady kindly began to call hotels for us to find a room. She finally succeeded - in Tinley Park 60 miles south from the airport. It was now 10:45 p.m.

After an hour long cab drive, with the meter ending at $100 we were at the Sleep Inn in Tinley Park. I told the clerk that we needed a cab at 5 a.m. to make our flight and he agreed that there was no problem to arrange that. At 12:05 a.m. I went to sleep after being up some 32 hours.

At 2:30 a.m. my phone rang. It was the cab company. "Sir, you want a cab at 5 a.m. I just want to confirm that I cannot do it!" and he promptly hung up. Immediately I got dressed and went out to the front desk. For half an hour the clerk tried other companies, but no one could take us. Finally I had him call back the original company and offer double the meter if he could take us and he agreed and promised to be there at 5 a.m.

At 4:50 a.m. we checked out. At that point the phone rang and the cab driver again informed the clerk that he could not make it after all, despite the offer of a double fare!

Panic! If we missed this flight there would be no possibility to be home before Sunday and with only 5 days at home and with Alvin's daughter's high school graduation this was critical!

Finally I told the clerk, "Do you know of anyone that can be here in 10 minutes and wants to earn $100?" He grabbed the phone, called a girlfriend and in 15 minutes she turned up, chain smoking, in a very run down vehicle.

We turned up at the airport 50 minutes before the flight and rushed to the desk. When we presented our tickets to the clerk at the check in counter, she brusquely returned the tickets. "You are not booked on this flight! United may have said so, but sorry! I will put you on the standby list, but there are 30 people ahead of you!"

We sat down - because at this point I could feel my blood pressure reach dangerous levels - and we prayed. We were the last ones to get boarding passes and made it.

When we finally arrived in Colorado Springs, our suitcases somehow were on the same flight, but totally beaten up - mine was a complete write-off!

Middle East

Several times I had the opportunity to visit Beirut in Lebanon, where the translation team was working on the Arabic Bible. Most times there was either war or civil war in the city. Even going from the airport to the part of the city where the team was located, we passed many checkpoints. Several times I was told to lie down in the back seat of the taxi to avoid sniper fire hitting a "foreign white" individual.

Arriving one time in Beirut our coordinator met me and greeted me with a smile. "I am glad you came this week, Lars," he mused, "as the hotel we had you booked in blew up last week." It was with great apprehension I slept the nights I was there. A week after my visit, I received a note from the same coordinator. "Glad you were here last week. The hotel you stayed in blew up this week!"

In March of 1979, just seven months before the hostage crisis in Teheran, I visited Iran. The New Testament had just been published and we were trying to get as much distribution as possible. The coordinator was sharing horror stories with us about kidnappings of pastors, assassination of Christian leaders and how he and his family feared for their lives. The conflict between Iran and Iraq was close to breaking out as well.

I had one of the strangest experiences of my life in a restaurant in Teheran. Kenneth McVety, a Canadian missionary to Japan who was working with *LBI* in those days, was traveling with me. He wanted apple-pie and cheese for dessert. There was both apple pie and cheese on the menu, but not together. The waiter refused to serve us this combination. After arguing with the waiter for almost half an hour, we were told to leave the restaurant or the police would come!

A year later I was out in the parking lot at my office in Naperville, Illinois. And there was our Iranian coordinator, trying to find the door to our office. He explained to me, "We had no choice but to flee. The war is terrible. Both of our boys who are young teenagers will be called up to be gun fodder in the war. Now that we are here, we are not sure what the next step is." Settling in California, the family found the Christian Iranian communities and finished the entire Farsi Bible for us in a safer environment.

In India

I visited India for the first time in June 1974. Since then I have made approximately 3 to 4 visits per year, so many that I feel I have spent several years there. The India I knew in 1974 is not the India I know in 2008. In those days there was basically one car model, the Ambassador. Originally based on the Morris Oxford 1948 model, the car, while upgraded internally, still looks the same. Now every possible car model is manufactured in India, including the Mercedes. A middle-class has exploded. During my first visits, there were two TV channels, often displaying little more than Indian music and traditional dancing. Now there are satellite and cable TV, with hundreds of channels. A small group of industrious Indians have become very wealthy, while the majority still have become poorer. Some 600 million still live below the poverty line earning less than a dollar per day or nothing at all.

Traveling in India in the old days was strenuous. The old Avro propeller planes provided some of the bumpiest journeys I had ever known. Even when Indian airlines upgraded to 737s they were often rejects from Western airlines. It seemed they were often held together with rubber bands and Scotch tape.

Train journeys were equally exciting. I frequently traveled on overnight train trips, with my sermon notes and Bible as my pillow. Vendors would walk through the trains, along with pick-pocketers and

Hindu ladies begging, singing songs to the passengers to earn a few rupees.

P. L. N. Murthy and I had many strange hotel experiences. We most often shared a room to cut costs. Visiting Kottayam in Kerala, South India, our favorite hotel was fully booked, so we had to find a different hotel. The hotel room cost Rs 10 (about 25 cents today) but the luxury tax was Rs 14. (about 30 cents!). As we sat down at the table in the breakfast room, we realized that there were insects under every plate. We made the best of things and held cockroach races across the breakfast table!

During the crusade in Cuttack the hotel room was barely livable. The bathroom had a peculiar stench, and when I turned on the water for the shower, a few brown drips came out, sending cockroaches running in every direction.

Some things did not improve much with age. In 2003 Georg Carr and I were visiting Aizawl, in the state of Mizoram to conduct a pastors conference. While we had been booked in a nice government residence, officials turned up the same day so we were sent to Hotel Chief in one of the main streets. We climbed many stairs to padlocked rooms, where the toilets did not work and the beds were more than uncomfortable.

Because this was a restricted area, we were called to the equivalent of an FBI office in the other end of town to be registered. Entering a small cubicle where the police officer was seated with no end of paper files stacked on top of each other and tied together with string, we were told to sit down. Filling in a massive ledger by hand we had to give them all kinds of information, like my father's and mother's address. When I pointed out that my mother was deceased, they still needed her last address. I could see this massive book being tied with the other books and placed on a shelf. How would they ever be able to track down my mother and father, and for what reason?

In 2006 we were conducting a GLOMOS fellowship day in Bhubaneswar, Orissa followed by a Forty Under Forty conference. The following day, Friday, we were booked to fly to Hyderabad, where a men's conference with over 1,200 men would be held on Saturday. The main speakers were David Willson, my brother-in-law from England and I. We arrived at the airport early and after checking in were told that the flight had not yet arrived but would be on time. After waiting beyond the departure time we were told that the plane was delayed for a few hours.

We had watched all other flights leave Bhubaneswar, either for Kolkata or Delhi, and so there were no flights left except ours, which was duly cancelled.

Realizing there were no other flights until the following afternoon, we made a snap decision. We would drive. By now it was 5 p.m. I was told the journey would take fifteen hours. That would still get us into Hyderabad in the morning in time to speak.

Setting out, we realized the drivers had never driven this far, nor did they have maps. To stay awake through the night they played Indian music as loud as possible on their radios. We maneuvered around the usual cows and other animals, interspersed with people on the roads. There was nowhere to stop for food or even a drink. The much-needed humanitarian stops could not take more than five minutes. However, the journey did not take 15 hours, it took 21 hours. Just after 1 p.m. we drove into the church parking lot. Dr. Sujai Suneetha, who is one of my board members, had filled in for us in the morning. As we arrived, David Willson, who is diabetic, almost went into a coma because of lack of food for 24 hours. I grabbed the sermon notes for his sessions and ran into the church. Having only had a bottle of water and a few bites of a sandwich, I taught my 1-hour session, then had a sip of water and taught my brother-in-law's session using his notes. Thank God for interpreters, so I could read David's notes and formulate my own thoughts while the interpreter translated what I just said into Telugu. However, teaching using someone else's notes is like chewing on someone's chewing gum! I am glad this conference turned out well, although I am not ready to redo the same journey!

Meeting with Political Leaders

On my second visit to Sri Lanka in 1978, I was surprised when our national director Balakrishnan, asked me to dress in a suit and tie. It was over 100 degrees! After my protests he told me, "You have been invited to have tea with the president!" Driving through the gates of the palace, we were whisked into a nice reception room where high tea was prepared. Suddenly the tall and stately looking Junius Richard Jayewardene strolled into the room and firmly shook our hands.

Mr. Jayawardene served as the second president of the country from 1978 to 1989 creating stability in the restless nation. During the tea he told me how much he valued the Bible, having grown up in a Christian environment and attended Methodist schools. It was after his schooling that he turned to Buddhism. We asked for permission for wide distribution of the Sinhala and Tamil New Testament and Bibles, which he granted.

In 1982, I was with David Foster on one of his many visits to Jerusalem. He had many friends there, especially after our joint efforts in publishing the international co-edition, *People of the Book* on which he worked with Israeli artist Jossi Stern. One of the people he took me to meet was an American businessperson residing in the city. Her daughter had experienced some difficulty reading Hebrew in school, especially when it involved the Bible. Even trying to understand the King James Version in her mother tongue didn't help, so Dave suggested she try reading *The Living Bible*, a copy of which he gave her. This proved helpful not only for her daughter, but she herself found it useful when she attended a weekly Bible study group in the home of Prime Minister Menachem Begin and his wife Aliza. Discussion was in Hebrew, which the American could follow, but if she wished to contribute she would speak in English, which all the others understood. And if she wanted to read a Scripture, she did so from *The Living Bible*.

"What kind of Bible is that?" asked the Prime Minister.

"It's called '*The Living Bible*'," she replied.

"Do you mind if I borrow it?" he asked.

She was delighted to loan it to him but, when he failed to return it, she called one of his aides and asked if he knew what had happened to it.

"Oh, he is still reading it when he has a free moment," came the reply.

"In that case, tell him to keep it because I'm flying to Europe tomorrow and will be meeting the man who gave it to me. I'm sure he will be able to get me another copy."

She was right, and when Dave told me this story, we hatched a plan. I arranged for two special leather-bound editions of *The Living Bible* to be inscribed in gold with the names of Menachem Begin and Aliza Begin. When we presented these to him in his office, we were told that the visit could only be for a few minutes, but it lasted almost 45 minutes as the Prime Minister talked about world affairs, continually referring to the Bible and its timeless message for any nation.

The same week, a group from *Living Bibles International* hosted a dinner for Israeli guests at Jerusalem's King David Hotel. Dave arranged for the city's legendary mayor Teddy Kollek to address us, and I was able to present him with a copy of the Bible.

In 1993 I arrived at Manila airport, and as soon as I came off the plane I was met by secret service agents. We were told to follow them and then we were whisked through passport and customs and out to a waiting car, where Leo Alconga, the national director in the Philippines was waiting. "We have an appointment with President Fidel Ramos," he said with a smile. President Ramos was the 12th president of the Philippines and had succeeded Corazon Aquino in 1992. During the People Power revolution, Ramos defected from Marcos' government and had been one of the key figures in the civilian demonstrations that forced Marcos into exile. He was succeeded in 1998 by Joseph Eastrada. Fidel Ramos was the first Protestant president and was very close to many of the board members of the *LBI/IBS* Board in the Philippines. During our meeting he and I talked about the importance of the Word of God for the Philippines and what it could do to shape a nation, striving for righteousness and justice.

While I have never had an opportunity to meet any of the Swedish royalty or any of the United States presidents, I am grateful for a few letters addressed to me. The first came from President Bill Clinton, right after he took office. When he was elected I suggested we should send leather bound copies to the President and Mrs. Clinton, a gesture not appreciated by several of my leadership staff. But whether you are Republican or Democrat you need the Word of God! The president responded with a nice thank you note. I also received a personal letter from Governor George W. Bush, endorsing the *Let there Be Light* campaign and offering his help in any way possible.

In the U.S., one of our consultants, Thomas McCabe, and his associate Dale Hanson Bourke were close to many leaders in Washington. One day I received a letter from Senator Mark Hatfield. He sponsored a lunch in my honor for the entire senate at the Capitol, at which I had an opportunity to address the senate and hand them personally-engraved leather Bibles.

CHAPTER 22
Becoming a Risk-Taker and a Life-Changer

A mazement mingled with horror as I watched the sickening drama of September 11, 2001 unfold on television. Having trained as a firefighter in my youth, I knew the incredible challenges those in downtown Manhattan were facing. Entering buildings and running up stairs to rescue the injured and evacuate as many as possible, they willingly took enormous risks. They knew they were risking losing their own lives to save others, strangers they didn't even know.

At the same time, in another context, other people were investing heavily in a company that seemed to do no wrong. Employees entrusted it with their retirement savings. Others followed recommendations of stockbrokers and friends to invest in something that appeared to combine rock solidity and safety with sure-fire profitability. But with Enron's unexpected and surprising collapse in a mess of corporate sleaze, investors realized, too late, the dangerous risks they had been taking.

These are two totally different kinds of risk-takers, but I want to share with you what it means to be a risk-taker for God. When there's a Divine dimension to risk-taking, it can be the threshold of immense blessing.

354

Becoming a Risk-Taker and a Life-Changer

Past Pioneers Were Risk-Takers

History records countless pioneering risk-takers. In medical research, an English physician born in the 16th century risked his reputation on the true nature of blood circulation and the function of the heart as a pump. William Harvey was ridiculed for changing what had been "established knowledge" for centuries. But today we all benefit from his risk-taking.

A 19th century Frenchman named Louis Pasteur risked his health and reputation to prove the existence of germs. Most-known for originating the process of pasteurization, he also proved that micro-organisms caused fermentation and disease. He discovered a vaccine against anthrax and an antidote for rabies. His discoveries are protecting us against a variety of diseases today, and all because he was willing to leave the comfort zone of established medical practice.

German meteorologist and geophysicist Alfred Wegener was almost dismissed as a lecturer at the University of Hamburg for suggesting that the world's continents move about on great tectonic plates. Yet his risks ultimately opened the gateway to greater knowledge of earthquakes and other geophysical phenomena.

To escape persecution in England, a group of 16th century Christians convinced a London stock company to finance their voyage to America where they expected a better life and religious freedom. We remember them as the Pilgrim Fathers whose risky transatlantic journey and subsequent survival set an example of immense courage for us all.

Again history records that on July 2, 1776, the Continental Congress voted in favor of the resolution "that these United Colonies are, and of right ought to be, free and independent States." Two days later, the Declaration of Independence was adopted without dissent. On August 2, a parchment copy was presented to the Congress for signature, and most of the 56 men who put their names on it did so that day. They took great risks because signing such a document was to commit an act of treason punishable by death.

While some of those signatories went on to great political achievement, two becoming presidents of the United States, others suffered for having taken a risk for the new nation. Five were captured by the British, 18 had their homes looted and burned by the enemy, two were wounded in battle and some had their properties plundered. But what would have happened if they had not taken such a risk?

Risk-Taker for God

Bible Translators Were Risk-Takers

John Wycliffe is a good example of a Christian risk-taker. He lived almost 200 years before the Reformation, but his beliefs and teachings closely matched those of Luther, Calvin and other Reformers. This 14th century risk-taker challenged abuses and false teachings in the Church. What's more, he took a great risk by translating the New Testament into English.

The church expelled him from his teaching position at Oxford, and the Archbishop of Canterbury wrote, "This pestilent and most wicked John Wycliffe, a child of the old devil, has crowned his wickedness by translating the Scriptures into the mother tongue."

But Wycliffe was convinced that ordinary people could not know the basis of their faith unless they knew the Bible, and that could only be so if it was in the language they used every day.

Forty-four years after he died, the Pope ordered Wycliffe's bones to be exhumed and burned. Intense persecution stamped out his followers and teachings. But hundreds of years later, men like Martin Luther resurrected and expanded the reforms John Wycliffe had begun.

Similarly William Tyndale, born in Britain some 160 years later, broke with tradition by proclaiming that God's Word is the only measuring stick for the Christian life. He revolutionized the attitude of the Church toward Scripture. He proclaimed, "The Bible to all — even to the simplest ploughboy."

Tyndale had to flee the Church and the King of England. Hiding in Antwerp, Belgium, he continued translating until his first New Testament was published in 1526. It was smuggled into Britain in loaves of bread, baskets, barrels and even in ladies' underwear!

He was captured before completing the translation of the Old Testament. Betrayed by a friend, Tyndale was arrested in Brussels and found guilty of treason and heresy against the Church. He was executed through strangulation and his body burned. But Tyndale's translation became the model for many subsequent English Bible translations.

Because these men were willing to take enormous risks, the English-speaking world is blessed with access to the Bible today.

Missionaries Are Risk-Takers

A cobbler by trade, William Carey served as a lay pastor in Moulton, England, where he came to a clear understanding of the need for obedience to Jesus' Great Commission to go into all the world with the Gospel. But when he shared his vision with other ministers, one of them replied, "Young man, sit down; when God pleases to convert the heathen, He will do it without your aid or mine."

Carey was undeterred, and continued to read, study and encourage people for missions. His motto was, "Expect great things from God. Attempt great things for God."

He followed this when he sailed to Calcutta, India, in 1793, never to return to his homeland. He risked his family (his wife and several children died there), his reputation, his comfort and his future. But, as a result of that risk, he translated the complete Bible and parts of it into 35 different Indian languages. He also provided grammar textbooks in seven languages, dictionaries in six other languages, and founded the Agricultural Society of India, as well as Calcutta's first daily newspaper.

No wonder he is known as the "Father of Modern Missions," and has inspired thousands to follow him in risk-taking obedience to the Great Commission.

Amy Carmichael, born in Northern Ireland, became a missionary in southern India. There she adopted over 2,000 children who had been given to the temples at birth to become temple prostitutes. In some cases, the mother gave the baby girl to Amy rather than the Hindu priests. Other times she simply stole them from the temple.

The Hindu nationals repeatedly charged Amy with kidnapping and constantly threatened her with physical violence. Sometimes they kidnapped the babies back. But by far the most painful opposition came from the missionary community. They even questioned whether temple children were a "figment of Amy's imagination." When it was finally proven that the temple children were one of the best-kept secrets of the temple, the missionary community said Amy should not be so involved with "humanitarian efforts."

Risk-Taking Can Be Scary!

You may say, "But these people were great heroes, and I'm just an ordinary person. Surely, risk-taking is not for me!"

Fear of failure often hinders us from becoming risk-takers, even though we may suspect that life holds more excitement and satisfaction when we're willing to expand our comfort zones, try new things, and dare to achieve our dreams.

We may say we want to know God's will, but when we find out what that is, we cannot handle it. It sounds too scary, too difficult. So we look elsewhere.

People prone to focus on negatives in their lives, rather than on God, often offer a variety of excuses. These include:

"I'm too old."

"I'm not good enough."

"My health is too bad."

"It will never work out."

Problems may well come, but so will results – even if they look different than expected. It depends on one's perspective. Results that come from taking a God-directed risk can turn out to be far better than we dreamed.

God uses ordinary people. The Bible is full of characters like us, people of both sexes in a variety of professions, young as well as old, who were called to take risks for God. When they responded to the challenge, their lives were transformed and their impact is felt still today.

Bible Risk-Takers Look Like You and Me

One young man was ridiculed and gossiped about by his relatives. He was brutally separated from his family and later placed in a compromising situation with his boss's wife. He risked his life in order to be faithful to his God, and eventually he became the right-hand man to the ruler of Egypt. His name was **Joseph**.

Rahab was notorious as a woman who gave in to her sensuous feelings and engaged in promiscuous sex. But she risked hiding Israelite spies who came from Egypt to Jericho where she lived. Her action led to Joshua and the Israelites conquering Jericho and entering the promised land. Consequently, she and her family were rescued.

A young farmer's son named **Gideon** struggled with cynicism over what had happened because of the behavior of his father's generation.

Depressed because he was not popular among the young people, he didn't believe anything could change his circumstances. But, challenged to take a risk for God and trusting in His divine presence, he became an overnight hero and was placed in charge of his people for some 40 years.

At a time when women were constantly abused by their husbands and seen by many as sex-objects, **Deborah** risked becoming a prophetess to tell her people the truth from God. She was so effective that the military general Barak refused to go to battle without her.

Another woman was married to an immigrant but, after a short time of happy marriage, he died. It was a time of crisis in her country. They had no jobs, no money and eventually no food. **Ruth** risked becoming an immigrant in reverse, following her mother-in-law to her former husband's country. It took courage to change her country, culture and familiar surroundings. But her decision and action resulted in finding another husband who provided for her. Eventually, she became grandmother to one of Israel's most famous kings, David, the great psalmist.

David was the youngest of eight children. His older brothers thought he was so insignificant that he was never even invited home from his shepherding duties when anything important happened. In that solitude, David learned what it meant to rely on the Lord for strength and comfort. When the enemy threatened his nation, he was sent to the battlefield, not to fight, but deliver to his brothers, packed lunches of grain, bread and cheese. On arrival at the camp, he recognized that the greatest enemy threat was the enormous Goliath, who came out daily to ridicule Israel and their God. The young lad took an enormous risk facing Goliath, armed only with a slingshot and five stones. But his risk resulted in the enemies' defeat, and eventually David became sovereign over the entire kingdom.

Jeremiah was a young man when God called him to be His spokesman. Jeremiah's reaction was to say that he was too young to speak for God, and he shied away until he realized that the only thing worthwhile in life is obedient service to God, even if it involves risk-taking. He finally said, *"But if I say, 'I will not mention him or speak any more in his name,' his word is in my heart like a fire, a fire shut up in my bones. I am weary of holding it in; indeed, I cannot"* (Jeremiah 20:9 NIV).

Jeremiah took the risk of being a proclaimer, which led to persecution, imprisonment and eventual death. Yet thousands of years later, we still remember him as a great prophet.

Another Old Testament risk-taker was a farmer's son, a young plow-boy named **Elisha**. He was so insignificant that when plowing teams went out, he was put behind the rest. One day a prophet walked by the field and threw his cloak over Elisha. Elisha promptly sacrificed his team of oxen and the plow to the Lord, leaving everything to follow the prophet Elijah. As a result, he received a "double portion" of power, and took over the prophet's responsibility as the conscience of the nation.

Joseph of Arimathea was an aristocrat of great heritage, wealth, status, and learning. But when Jesus was crucified, this man took an enormous risk! He identified himself with the dead "criminal" by asking for his body so he could bury him. He and Nicodemus, another secret believer, openly confessed their faith in Jesus as the Son of God. We never hear of them again!

Three fishermen, whose physically demanding occupation was low on the social scale, responded to Jesus' call to be "fishers of men." It was a risky move to leave their nets and boats and even their families, and yet **Peter, James** and **John** left everything to follow Jesus. For three years, they were with Him and, after the day of Pentecost, they were natural leaders in the establishment of the early Church.

A despised government official, the tax collector **Matthew,** responded to Jesus' invitation to follow Him. By getting up and leaving his lucrative position, Matthew risked everything.

Joanna and Susanna were two wealthy women who left their families to follow Jesus. They took many risks. It was not fashionable, nor always safe, for women to travel with a group of men in those days. Joanna's husband managed King Herod's household. Both risked their wealth by using their financial resources to support Jesus and His disciples, helping make it possible for them to stay on the road.

Then there were the craftsmen **Aquila and Priscilla**, who were tent-makers and lay preachers. In Romans 16:3, Paul writes, *"Greet Priscilla and Aquila. They have been co-workers in my ministry for Christ Jesus. In fact, they risked their lives for me. I am not the only one who is thankful to them; so are all the Gentile churches."* (NLT)

Epaphroditus was one of the "unknowns" in the Early Church, one of many young men who were messengers between the churches and the apostles. In Philippians 2:25-30, Paul writes, *"I thought I should send*

Epaphroditus back to you. He is a true brother, a faithful worker, and a courageous soldier....he was very distressed that you heard he was ill. And he surely was ill; in fact he almost died....Welcome him with Christian love and with great joy, and be sure to honor people like him. For he risked his life for the work of Christ, and he was at the point of death while trying to do for me the things you couldn't do because you were far away." (NLT)

Timothy was a young man with an inferiority complex. Normally he would not have been noticed. But because he was willing to take risks in proclaiming the gospel, two books of the New Testament bear his name.

Paul persecuted Christians and cursed their cause before becoming an enormous risk-taker following his conversion. In one city, government officials shut all the escape routes to capture him. But he fled with the help of a basket and rope over the city wall, eased down by similarly risk-taking believers. Paul almost always had to take risks to proclaim Jesus.

The Early Church Was Made Up of Risk-Takers

At the beginning of the Book of Acts, Jesus and His followers had different ideas about the best way to proceed. *"They asked him, 'Lord, are you at this time going to restore the kingdom to Israel?'"* (Acts 1:6 NIV). But in their minds they were thinking, "Lord, this is really exciting. Everyone is going to see that you're the king any minute now, right?"

Their focus was on the present situation of their nation and on what they thought Jesus would do. But His reply indicated a different focus: *"You will be my witnesses in Jerusalem, and in all Judea and Samaria, and to the ends of the earth"* (Acts 1:8 NIV). The disciples were looking for comfort and resolution; Jesus was pushing for risk and ambiguity.

There is risk in leaving the comfort of a safe environment

The Church's evangelism began in Jerusalem, and for a time everything went well. Thousands were saved and the world's first mega-church was formed, first with 3,000 members, then with 5,000.

Then an unbelievable tragedy happened. Stephen, one of their brightest and best, was opposed in his preaching. Brought to trial, he preached an inflammatory sermon and was put to death. The effect of this was that everyone left the city, with the exception of the apostles. They stayed with the Church in Jerusalem.

While the disciples may have feared that this was the beginning of the end for the Church, the Spirit knew that it was only the end of the beginning, fulfilling the words of Jesus.

As the disciples scattered because of the persecution, it seems that the disciples "went everywhere and gossiped the gospel." Despite what had happened to Stephen, they were willing to take risks to bring the gospel outside the comfort zone of the very first church.

There is risk in reaching out to people who are different

If Jesus' first area of concern was Jerusalem, His second was Judea and Samaria. Rumor reached Jerusalem that Philip had gone and preached in Samaria, and that some Samaritans had become believers in Jesus without receiving the Holy Spirit.

Imagine the conversation at the church office in Jerusalem, "No Holy Spirit? What d'you mean, no Holy Spirit! They simply can't be real believers. Becoming a disciple means receiving the Spirit. To be honest, I'm not convinced that Samaritans can be disciples anyway. There always was something strange about them and their religion. Everyone knows that."

Peter and John were sent to check it out. Even after three years of being around Jesus, watching Him challenge one religious tradition after another, they were still nervous when it came to doing the same.

God seemed to be telling these church leaders about new risks: "Notice what's happening here," He seemed to be saying, "Never forget it. The Gospel is for everyone, even Samaritans!"

There is risk in the seemingly insignificant

Philip continued his fruitful evangelistic ministry in one Samaritan city. Hundreds came to faith. Dozens were healed. Demons fled in terror. A little scary - but so exciting.

One morning, the evangelist announced he had to leave. To go and preach to bigger crowds? No, just the opposite. God had called him to leave the crowds and the success of his ministry, to take a walk on a desert road in Gaza. Then he surprised Philip with a divine appointment.

Ethiopia's Finance Minister, who identified himself with the Jewish religion, was the only man traveling on that otherwise deserted road at that particular moment. He had just fulfilled a long-time ambition to worship and sacrifice at the temple in Jerusalem. Now returning home, he struggled with unanswered questions while reading a scroll of Isaiah's prophecy: "He was led like a sheep to the slaughter." Who could this be?

Suddenly the Ethiopian was aware of someone alongside his chariot.

"Do you understand what you're reading?" asked the stranger.

"How can I unless someone helps me make sense of it?" he replied, "If I give you a ride, will you tell me what it means?"

Philip needed no second invitation to jump aboard.

Sometimes encounters take place by divine appointment. As the Ethiopian unburdened himself to Philip, the evangelist's mind was probably, "What if I hadn't come? What if I'd pretended not to hear? Lord, thank you...thank you so much for the seemingly insignificant moment!"

The Ethiopian returned home, probably the only Christian in his country, for a short time at least. Philip, the risk-taker, had not simply led someone to Christ, but sown the seed of the Gospel into an entire nation.

There is always risk of physical danger

In Acts 9 we are introduced to another risk-taker named Ananias. He's a respectable, law-abiding citizen, still enjoying the honeymoon of his new relationship with God. The only blot on his horizon was an evil man named Saul. But he was still far away in Jerusalem and not an immediate threat.

Then God told Ananias to do the unthinkable and go looking for Saul, a man notorious for persecuting Christians. No Christian ever went looking for him! Ananias could have disobeyed. And even if he risked obeying, it might have been the last time he went where God was directing him.

He was baffled when God referred to Saul as "my chosen instrument" and may have even considered it a case of divine mistaken identity. As Ananias followed God's direction to walk down Straight Street toward Judas' house, he might have been thinking, "It seems impossible to me, but I sincerely hope you're right, Lord!"

Taking a deep breath, he knocked on the door and was admitted. There was his former enemy, who he had prayed for but always avoided.

He was able to say, "*Brother* Saul." And Saul, blind since his life-changing encounter on the Damascus road, was relieved to meet the man sent from God to restore his sight and baptize him.

Ananias' obedience that day planted seeds that blossomed into some of the greatest evangelistic activity across the ancient world as Saul became Paul the Apostle. But you know what? Ananias is never again mentioned in the New Testament! There are no churches dedicated to St Ananias, the risk-taker, but his obedience was crucial to the growth of the Church, the reason we are believers today, and the whole purpose of *Global Action*.

There is risk in evangelism

The kingdom of God doesn't progress until His people are prepared to take risks. This is true in everything concerning the kingdom, especially in the realm of evangelism. Jesus said to His disciples, "*...you will be my witnesses in Jerusalem, and in all Judea and Samaria, and to the ends of the earth*" Acts 1:8 (NIV).

Where is my Jerusalem? Where do I feel comfortable, useful and unthreatened? There's nothing wrong with Jerusalem, but Jesus is unlikely to be satisfied with us simply being "at ease in Zion." He sees a potential harvest in Judea and Samaria. Who are the people I feel are not quite "kosher?" They probably strike me as all right in some ways, but at other times, I just don't feel comfortable around them.

The first Jewish believers didn't feel comfortable with Gentiles. Who are my Gentiles? Who are those people with whom I feel nothing in common, even those who make me thoroughly uncomfortable? Their lifestyles are alien to mine. I can't ever imagine being friends with people like that, nor finding any common ground.

The Acts of the Apostles continues to be written today. The Acts of Jesus have not stopped. He continues to press us, gently but firmly, into new areas of discomfort, growth and influence for the kingdom. We might as well give in graciously, and become risk-takers for Him.

The Gamblers

The word "risky" is derived from the Greek "*paraboleuothai.*" It's a gambler's term meaning "*to stake everything on the turn of the dice.*"

In the days of the Early Church, there was a group of men and women called *"the parabolani,"* - the gamblers. They visited prisoners and the sick, especially those afflicted with dangerous and infectious diseases.

In AD 252, a plague broke out in Carthage, a city in North Africa, close to where the city of Tunis is today. The people of that city threw dead bodies outside the walls, later fleeing the city in terror, leaving the sick and dying to perish. Cyprian, the main pastor of that area, gathered his congregation together to bury the dead and nurse the sick back to health. The city was saved because they were willing to take a risk.

Today's church needs the *parabolani* - the gamblers, the risk-takers. While you may never have reason to visit someone with an infectious, and possibly fatal disease, or a political prisoner, you may face other risky situations.

Three Risky Things

It may be risky to speak

Some Christians tell me that one of their greatest fears is talking to someone about their faith in Jesus. What if they get offended? What if they make fun of me? What if they ask a question I cannot answer? What if it has a negative effect on our relationship?

Speaking can be risky. Risky, but worth it. If you think you're running a risk by speaking about Jesus, think of the other person. They're at greater risk if they don't hear the Good News.

Are you waiting for someone else to tell them? God places some people within our circle of influence who may never be reached by someone else. He's counting on us. Chances are that most of us who have accepted Jesus did so because someone took a risk to share the gospel with us.

One of the last things Jesus said was, "Run the risk, tell everyone about me." Alright, those may not have been His exact words, but He did say *"preach the good news to all"* (Matthew 16:15 NIV), and often that involves taking a risk.

It may be risky to serve

When you accept that God calls us to be servants, first to Him and then to others, you take an immense risk.

Servants are not always appreciated. Sometimes people take advantage of them. And many Christians don't want to get involved in ministry because they're afraid it will cut into their own needs.

> "I don't want to get involved in the children's ministry because I need to be in the service myself. How will I get fed otherwise?"

> "I don't want to get involved in the youth ministry because I need to relax after a hard day at the office."

> "I don't want to get involved in the Saturday food outreach to the homeless because that's my day off."

> "I don't want to get involved in being an usher or greeter because that means getting to church earlier, and I need to sleep in on the weekends."

It's risky to serve because sometimes your own needs may be put on hold. But something interesting happens when we run the risk of serving. We soon discover that our needs *are* being met. God never short-changes us.

Jesus said one of the greatest things you can hear from God when you stand before Him will be, *"Well done, good and faithful servant."*

It may be risky to stand

It's risky to stand for what's right, what's true, what's moral. Perhaps your boss wants you to lie, and you say you can't do that. That's risky. And what if you don't join your co-workers in laughing at an off-color joke? That's risky, too.

When you decide to stand against lying and cheating, to be a person of integrity who is faithful, trustworthy, and has high standards of morality, you run the risk of being rejected and ridiculed. Sometimes when you take the risk of standing for truth, you may find you're standing alone. But take courage! Share your faith! (Who knows, maybe someone will be drawn to Jesus.) Serve! (Who knows, maybe someone may be blessed.) Stand! (Who knows, maybe you'll be ridiculed.) But Jesus said, *"God blesses you when you are mocked and persecuted and lied about because you are my followers. Be happy about it! Be very glad! For a great reward awaits you in heaven...*" Matthew 5:11, 12 (NLT).

It may be risky to speak, but it's worth it. It may be risky to serve, but it's worth it. It may be risky to stand, but it's worth it.

When Peter saw Jesus walking on the water, he leaped out of the boat to walk toward Him. Where would Peter have been if he had not stepped out of the boat? Unlike the other disciples still in the boat, Peter experienced Jesus' power first-hand as He rescued him from sinking.

Maybe God is asking us to step out of the boat of our comfort zones, to prove Him in new and exciting ways.

We need to be like Epaphroditus, like the parabolani, like Ruth, Jeremiah and Paul. Who knows what adventures await us when we are willing to be risk-takers for God?

Remember, the greatest risk is not to risk at all. If you are not a risk-taker, you become a caretaker. If you are a caretaker for too long, you may eventually end up being the undertaker for the talents God gave you.

Risks We Can Take for God

Most people don't even know their neighbors. Befriend them by inviting them for a barbeque. Don't force the gospel on them. Just take the opportunity to get to know them.

But be sensitive to God's Spirit in case He opens the door to share your faith. You may say, "You don't know my neighbors; with them the door is firmly shut!" Maybe, but closed doors are not always locked. They may simply be waiting for someone to turn the handle.

Invite a friend to your church, a Bible study or an Alpha course. There is a 50 percent chance they'll accept!

Pray for someone you don't really think the Lord can touch! Pray for salvation, for restoration of their marriage relationship, or even for healing. Take a risk and trust God to step in!

Find needs in your neighborhood. Perhaps a neighbor is in the hospital and the rest of the family needs transportation or help with shopping...or maybe what they need most is to be invited to your home for a meal!

Invite neighbors for coffee. They may ask questions about the obviously well-used (and well-placed!) Bible on your coffee table. Perhaps you might even risk asking them to move it so you can put down the tray! It may be the first time they've held a Bible in a long time, if at all. You could even take the greater risk of commenting, "Oh, I haven't had time to read my daily reading yet. Would you like to hear it? And it happens to be one of my favorites, the third chapter of John!"

This may sound far-fetched to you. But I heard of American Christians living in a Middle Eastern country who invited non-Christian neighbors to a Christmas celebration "to see how we do it at home." At the appropriate point, they said, "And this is when we read the Christmas story...and, by the way, so you can follow as we read in English, we managed to find New Testaments in your language." Later, when their guests were leaving, they said, "Please, take the New Testaments with you because we can't read them."

Use your financial resources for the kingdom beyond what you thought possible. Plan for greater kingdom dividends by investing in Christian nationals. While there is still a need for traditional missionaries in some areas, nationals can be more effective in their own culture. They already know the language and the best way to approach their own people. What's more, they can usually be supported at a fraction of the cost of a missionary from another country.

Share your story of Jesus with someone. Tell them in three minutes who you were before you met Christ, how the meeting took place, and the difference it made after He came into your life. They cannot argue with this. It's your story, and it's worth the risk!

Go on a mission trip somewhere in the world. Latin America, Eastern Europe, Western Europe, India and Africa are waiting for you. If you're like others I know, your first trip will not be your last. Chances are you'll make it a regular experience.

Encourage friends in your church to consider taking on a mission project, either locally, nationally or internationally.

Become a catalyst to take a risk for God in your church. Look for opportunities to step out of your comfort zone. Encourage others to join you. Discover what it means for you personally to step out of your boat.

A New Measure for Effectiveness

Over the past years, I have been to more than 45 pastors' conferences, attended by some 48,000 pastors. As I hear them talk, it seems effectiveness is measured by such criteria as:

> *"A full range of activity programs for everyone."*
>
> *"A new building, or at least some kind of building program on the drawing board."*
>
> *"A growing number of members and attendees."*
>
> *"A budget that expands as attendance increases."*

Just imagine if effectiveness was not measured by people coming to Christ. What would happen if the health of the church was measured by the effectiveness of making disciples?

Jesus said, *"All authority in heaven and on earth has been given to me. Therefore go and make disciples of all nations, baptizing them in the name of the Father and of the Son and of the Holy Spirit, and teaching them to obey everything I have commanded you"* (Matthew 28: 18-20 NIV).

Our primary purpose in taking risks for God is to "make disciples." And the only measurement for success is the quality and functionality of those disciples who, in turn, make other disciples. Today, that measurement of success is severely lacking in many churches.

Jesus Calls Us to Risk

He asked His disciples who were called by Him then, just as you and I are called by Him today. Jesus' disciples became extremely passionate about serving Him, and that gave them a strong incentive to become risk-takers for God.

How many Christians do you know who have "making disciples" as their life purpose? How many believers wake up every morning, saying, "I can't wait to get out of bed to make some more disciples today!"

Discipleship is not about reading books and storing up knowledge. Disciples are learners in love with and having a passionate desire to please Jesus. He is the Master, and they are apprentices.

In the movie series *Star Wars,* one of the Jedi masters, Yoda, portrays this principle well. In his strange English he proclaims, "Two there always are...a master and an apprentice." The Jedi apprentice's sole desire is to become like his Jedi master.

That is the essence of our Christian walk: to become like our Master, Jesus Christ.

In his book, *Growing True Disciples*, George Barna writes, "... few churches have a church of disciples. Maybe that's because for many Christians today, including Christian leaders, discipleship is not terribly important. If we can get people to attend worship services, pay for the church's buildings and salaries, and muster positive, loving attitudes toward one another and toward the world, we often feel that's good enough."

But risk-takers are people completely sold out to Christ.

Barna continues, "To what are you absolutely, fanatically devoted? Jesus did not minister, die, and rise from the dead merely to enlist fans. He gave everything He had to create a community of uncompromising zealots – raving, unequivocal, undeterable no-holds-barred, spiritual revolutionaries. He has no room for lukewarm followers. He is not interested in those who have titles, prestige and self-sufficiency. He's searching for the broken, hopeless, helpless, spiritually dependent individuals, who readily acknowledge that they cannot make any headway without total and absolute dependence on Him.

"He is seeking the hearts of those who are willing to surrender everything for the blessed privilege of suffering for Him, just as He suffered for us. He wants people who are dedicated to getting beyond the offer of mere salvation to those who are willing to do what it takes to complete a personal transformation."

Discipleship is a lifelong calling that demands every resource we can muster, trusting God for the strength we need. It is about a passion to reach our full potential in Jesus Christ.

Jesus Sends Us

Jesus sent His disciples to various parts of their world, simultaneously to Judea, Samaria and the ends of the earth. Today He has placed us just where He needs us, in our "Jerusalem." Are we willing to risk being led further, to "Judea," "Samaria" or even the "ends of the earth?"

Some of us may be able to go for a short-term mission trip, but we can also enable others to go by our prayers and through our financial support.

Recently I worked with a small church in Europe, assisting them in formulating their mission statement. I was amazed and thrilled when they suggested, "We want to be a church with life and power that changes the world by influencing people to become followers of Jesus Christ."

They understood what it means to be risk-takers!

Jesus Promises To Be with Us

Jesus promised to be with His disciples as they went out, with power beyond their own human resources. This promise still holds good for us because Hebrews 13:8 assures us, *"Jesus Christ is the same yesterday and today and forever"* (NIV). His relationship with 21st century disciples is the same as with those of the 1st century.

The problem is that we tend to sit and simply be recipients. He will bless us even in that sedentary position, but not to the extent that we experience when we take risks for Him. That's when we discover His presence in the very power that raised Him from the dead!

Dutch holocaust survivor cum evangelist Corrie ten Boom once said, "When Jesus calls us to walk a rough road, He gives us strong shoes."

The Results of Becoming a Risk-Taker

People's lives change! Communities can be transformed. Society is shaken when a church is true to God's Word and His commands. In some parts of the world, I've seen that lead to persecution. But don't be deterred by that. I've never seen a persecuted believer who expressed regret at being a risk-taker for God. I've even met pastors in areas of intense pressure who smile and say, "They think the worst thing they can do is kill me, but that's not so. The worst thing they can possibly do is dilute my devotion to God."

We cannot help but have a positive impact on the world when we are being Christ-like, but we will not be loved and accepted by everyone.

God is calling us to become risk-takers for Him within our own spheres of influence...in our home, to our wider family, friends and neighbors, to those with whom we work, and perhaps to those who serve or work for us.

The major hindrance to the advancement of the gospel today is not money, resources, equipment or even properties from which to minister. As someone once said, "The heart of the problem is the problem of the heart"...my heart and your heart.

But when we allow God to touch our hearts, He creates a willingness within us to take risks for Him!

Life-Changers!

God doesn't just ask us to take risks. He expects us to affect people's lives, introducing them to Him who can change lives forever. The first Christians were risk-takers but through Christ they were also life-changers.

The message of Jesus was revolutionary. The sacrifical offerings and the worship in the temple was fulfilled through Him. The priesthood went from a few chosen ones, to everyone; there was neither Jew or Greek, man or woman, slave or free, and what characterized the early church was life.

Why did the early church grow so fast?

The first Christians had no buildings, no vehicles, no funds to speak of, no organization throughout the empire and still it managed to penetrate the then-known ancient world within a period of 100 years. There are several reasons why Christianity spread so rapidly apart from the benefit of one language, one culture and decent roads.

The first main cause of the rapid growth and ultimate triumph of Christianity is found in its own absolute value as the religion of salvation. In the center of its faith, we find God-who-became man, who proves Himself to every one who believes in Him to be their Savior. This was the burning conviction that drove the early believers. They had experienced His power of transformation. Now they wanted to share it with everyone in their path.

Second, Christianity adopted all classes, conditions, nationalities and races, all grades of culture, whether slave or slave-owner, whether Jew or Greek or Roman.

Third, Christianity gave a new sense of worth to women that previously had not been known across the empire.

Fourth, the moral and spiritual testimonies of the people themselves demonstrated the truth that they had been transformed from darkness to light. Testimonies of miracles, which, according to the statements of many of the church fathers, continued to accompany the preaching of the Word, helped the church convince everyone that Christianity represented a God who had power.

Fifth, Christianity offered hope to a hopeless pagan world. The young, fresh, dauntless Christian faith that was fearless of death, strong in faith and glowing with love, was contagious. Christians showed a powerful contrast to a morally corrupt world through their moral lives. Their burden to help the poor and oppressed was seen as a noble act that was unknown and foreign to society.

Tertullian tells us that the pagans remarked, "See how these Christians love one another." That love found expression in caring for the poor, the widows and the orphans, visiting people in prison and offering compassion during times of earthquakes, famine or war. One of the ways this love was demonstrated was by providing burial services for poverty-stricken brothers and sisters. If people were not properly buried, they would fall prey to wild beasts or vultures. This is how Christians became associated with the catacombs, the underground corridors in and around Rome, where Christians buried their dead.

Sixth, persecution helped publicize the Christian faith. Thousands of people saw Christians die in amphitheaters. Many of these Christians witnessed about their faith before their violent deaths. That is what the word martyr means: to be a witness!

Today, God is looking for people with the same characteristics as the early believers. He needs risk-takers who are willing to become life-changers!

We live in a needy and hurting world. More than a billion people are living in abject poverty with an income of less than $1 per day. More than 40 million people are infected by the HIV virus, with three million people dying each year from this terrible pandemic. Not only has this death toll resulted in tremendous economic, social, and psychological consequences, but it has also resulted in more than 14 million orphans. About 12 million of these orphans live in Africa and have little hope for their future. In the middle of this physical despair, there is also spiritual hopelessness. Billions of people do not know the love and hope of Jesus' message of new life, transformation and an eternal future.

Lack of education keeps millions of children in the vicious cycle of poverty. Without micro-enterprise training and loans, peasants struggle to survive and support their families. Pastors, and future pastors, without basic Biblical and theological training are not able to disciple new converts and ground them in their faith in nations where the church is exploding.

Who will share His hope? Life-changers making a difference. You have an opportunity to significantly impact lives for eternity. *"Whatever you did for the least of these... you did for me"*

Let me introduce you to a few life-changers. Rick and Debra Christian live in Colorado Springs, Colorado, where Rick is the president of Alive Communications. "My wife and I travel extensively with *Global Action* and see firsthand how far they stretch our investment. We've tripled our commitment because they ensure that over 80 cents of every dollar is spent on Kingdom-expanding ministry rather than overhead and salaries. It's our great privilege to partner with them in providing a future and a hope to the most needy people in over 70 countries."

Barry and Barb Fluth are owners of BBF properties in Big Lake, Minnesota. "We have been involved in missions for many years, praying and giving, but not going. When we obeyed God's call to "Go!" on a short-term mission trip with *Global Action*, God was able to show each of us how He is working in other parts of the world. We have a new perspective on the needs of hurting people outside the USA, both spiritual and physical. Our advice? Pray, Give and Go!"

Scott and Priscilla Dickson live in Milwaukee, Wisconsin, where Scott served as the Vice-President of Marketing for Midwest Airlines. "*Global Action* is all about transforming lives in Jesus' name. We live in a world where people desperately need to experience positive, Christ-centered change. As such, we are thrilled to be a part of *Global Action's LifeChangers*. To paraphrase Romans 10: 14-15, people cannot hear the Good News, and experience transformation, unless we commit to support those who go out to share the Gospel. *Global Action* is a very effective and creative catalyst for facilitating this change."

It has been a great journey. I invite you to continue that journey with me. Become a risk-taker for God. Step out of your comfort zone and see what God wants to do in your life. Look for opportunities to get out of the boat. I can guarantee that it is worth that step.

Become a *LifeChanger* with *Global Action*. You can see what God is doing around the world. You can pray for His intervention in nation after nation. You can invest your resources in God's Kingdom and be amazed at what will happen. Write to me and ask how you can become a *LifeChanger*!

I invite you to contact us. Let me know if you want to come with us on a trip. The adventure is just around the corner. I invite you to give freely of what God has given you. Get involved financially in some of the projects you have read about in this book. We need you - act today!

Write to me:

Lars Dunberg
Global Action
7660 Goddard Street, Suite 200
Colorado Springs, CO 80920

Tel (within the USA): 1-888-725-3707 or (719)-719 8728

Email: globalaction@global-act.org

Internet: www.global-act.org

For more copies of this book, or other materials, please order on our website or call the telephone numbers above.

Bibliography

Books

Barna, George. *Growing True Disciples.* Colorado Springs: Waterbrook Press, 2001

Barnard, Kevin. *Evangelical by Choice.* Colorado Springs, CO: *International Bible Society,* 1991

Bowen, John. *Evangelism for "Normal" People: Good News for Those Looking for a Fresh Approach.* Minneapolis: Augsburg Fortress Press, 2002

Bramwell-Booth, Catherine. *Catherine Booth.* London, Great Britain: Hodder & Stoughton, 1970

Clark, William. *Samuel Logan Brengle.* London, Great Britain: Hodder & Stoughton, 1980.

Dowley, Tim; Briggs, John H. Y.; Linder, Robert D.; and Wright, David F. (Eds). *Introduction to the History of Christianity.* Minneapolis, MN: Augsberg Fortress Press, 2002

Dunberg, Lars. *Handbook for Living Translations.* Wheaton, Il: Living Bibles International, 1982

Dunberg, Lars. *Light Inside.* Colorado Springs, CO: International Bible Society, 1998

Dunberg, Lars. *Becoming a Risk-taker for God.* Colorado Springs, CO: *Global Action,* 2003

Dunberg, Lars. *Mentoring Risk-takers.* Colorado Springs, CO: *Global Action,* 2004

Dunberg, Lars. *What Bible should I read?* Colorado Springs, CO: *Global Action*, 2007

Göransson, Sven. *Allmän Kyrkohistoria* (Private compendium 1970)

Hall, Clarence W. *Samuel Logan Brengle.* Stockholm, Sweden: Frälsningsarmén, 1941

Larsson, John. *Say yes to Life.* London, Great Britain: SPPS Publishing, 2007.

Malmström, Evald. *Femtio års fälttåg i Frälsningsarmén i Sverige 1882-1932.* Stockholm, Sweden: Frälsningsarméns högkvarter, 1932.

Orr, Edwin. *Evangelical Awakenings in Southern Asia.* Minneapolis, MN: Bethany Fellowship, 1975.

Paulsson, Berthil;Hedlund, John;Karlsson, Gösta. *Somliga till EVANGELISTER.* Stockholm: Missionsförbundets Förlag,1953

Pollock, John. *Billy Graham.* London, Great Britain: Hodder & Stoughton, 1966

Shelley, Bruce L. *Church History in Plain Language.* Nashville, TN: Thomas Nelson Publishers, 1982

Skoglund, Waldemar. *Billy Sunday.* Uppsala, Sweden: Lindblads förlag, 1917

Taylor, Kenneth. *My life: A Guided Tour.* Wheaton, Il: Tyndale House Publishers, 1991

Webb, Joy. *And this is Joy.* London, UK: Hodder & Stoughton, 1969.

Wiseman, Clarence. *A burning in my bones.* Toronto, Canada: McGraw-Hill Ryerson Ltd, 1979.

Risk-Taker for God

Articles

Jacobs, Dave. *Be a risk-taker.* Church Planters' Sermon Preparation
     Manual

MacInnis, Simon. *Are you a risk-taker?* Devotional. March 17, 2001